W9-BIZ-260

eBay®
For Canadians
FOR
DUMMIES®

Walter Harris
Memorial Library

eBay® For Canadians FOR DUMMIES®

by Marsha Collier and Bill Summers

WILEY

John Wiley & Sons Canada, Ltd.

eBay® For Canadians For Dummies®

Published by
John Wiley & Sons Canada, Ltd.
6045 Freemont Boulevard
Mississauga, ON L5R 4J3
www.wiley.ca

Copyright © 2008 by John Wiley & Sons Canada, Ltd. All rights reserved. No part of this book, including interior design, cover design, and icons, may be reproduced or transmitted in any form, by any means (electronic, photocopying, recording, or otherwise) without the prior written permission of the publisher.

Library and Archives Canada Cataloguing in Publication Data

Collier, Marsha

EBay for Canadians for dummies / Marsha Collier, Bill Summers.

Includes index.

ISBN 978-0-470-15348-2

1. eBay (Firm)   2. Internet auctions.   I. Summers, Bill (Bill P.)   II. Title

HF5478.C638 2007   381'.177   C2007-905872-8

Printed in Canada

1 2 3 4 5 TRI 11 10 09 08 07

Distributed in Canada by John Wiley & Sons Canada, Ltd.

For general information on John Wiley & Sons Canada, Ltd., including all books published by Wiley Publishing, Inc., please call our warehouse, Tel 1-800-567-4797. For reseller information, including discounts and premium sales, please call our sales department, Tel 416-646-7992. For press review copies, author interviews, or other publicity information, please contact our marketing department, Tel 416-646-4584, Fax 416-236-4448.

For authorization to photocopy items for corporate, personal, or educational use, please contact in writing The Canadian Copyright Licensing Agency (Access Copyright). For an Access Copyright license, visit www.accesscopyright.ca or call toll-free, 1-800-893-5777.

LIMIT OF LIABILITY/DISCLAIMER OF WARRANTY: THE CONTENTS OF THIS WORK ARE INTENDED TO FURTHER GENERAL SCIENTIFIC RESEARCH, UNDERSTANDING, AND DISCUSSION ONLY AND ARE NOT INTENDED AND SHOULD NOT BE RELIED UPON AS RECOMMENDING OR PROMOTING A SPECIFIC METHOD, DIAGNOSIS, OR TREATMENT BY PHYSICIANS FOR ANY PARTICULAR PATIENT. THE PUBLISHER AND THE AUTHOR MAKE NO REPRESENTATIONS OR WARRANTIES WITH RESPECT TO THE ACCURACY OR COMPLETENESS OF THE CONTENTS OF THIS WORK AND SPECIFICALLY DISCLAIM ALL WARRANTIES, INCLUDING WITHOUT LIMITATION ANY IMPLIED WARRANTIES OF FITNESS FOR A PARTICULAR PURPOSE. IN VIEW OF ONGOING RESEARCH, EQUIPMENT MODIFICATIONS, CHANGES IN GOVERNMENTAL REGULATIONS, AND THE CONSTANT FLOW OF INFORMATION RELATING TO THE USE OF MEDICINES, EQUIPMENT, AND DEVICES, THE READER IS URGED TO REVIEW AND EVALUATE THE INFORMATION PROVIDED IN THE PACKAGE INSERT OR INSTRUCTIONS FOR EACH MEDICINE, EQUIPMENT, OR DEVICE FOR, AMONG OTHER THINGS, ANY CHANGES IN THE INSTRUCTIONS OR INDICATION OF USAGE AND FOR ADDED WARNINGS AND PRECAUTIONS. READERS SHOULD CONSULT WITH A SPECIALIST WHERE APPROPRIATE. THE FACT THAT AN ORGANIZATION OR WEBSITE IS REFERRED TO IN THIS WORK AS A CITATION AND/OR A POTENTIAL SOURCE OF FURTHER INFORMATION DOES NOT MEAN THAT THE AUTHOR OR THE PUBLISHER ENDORSES THE INFORMATION THE ORGANIZATION OR WEBSITE MAY PROVIDE OR RECOMMENDATIONS IT MAY MAKE. FURTHER, READERS SHOULD BE AWARE THAT INTERNET WEBSITES LISTED IN THIS WORK MAY HAVE CHANGED OR DISAPPEARED BETWEEN WHEN THIS WORK WAS WRITTEN AND WHEN IT IS READ. NO WARRANTY MAY BE CREATED OR EXTENDED BY ANY PROMOTIONAL STATEMENTS FOR THIS WORK. NEITHER THE PUBLISHER NOR THE AUTHOR SHALL BE LIABLE FOR ANY DAMAGES ARISING HEREFROM.

Trademarks: Wiley, the Wiley Publishing logo, For Dummies, the Dummies Man logo, A Reference for the Rest of Us!, The Dummies Way, Dummies Daily, The Fun and Easy Way, Dummies.com and related trade dress are trademarks or registered trademarks of John Wiley & Sons, Inc., in the United States, Canada and other countries, and may not be used without written permission. All other trademarks are the property of their respective owners. Wiley Publishing, Inc., is not associated with any product or vendor mentioned in this book.

WILEY

About the Authors

Marsha Collier spends a good deal of time on eBay. She loves buying and selling (she's a PowerSeller with her own eBay store) as well as meeting eBay users from around the world. As columnist, author of three best-selling books on eBay, and guest lecturer at eBay University, she shares her knowledge of eBay with millions of online sellers. Thousands of eBay fans also read her monthly newsletter, *Cool eBay Tools,* to keep up with the changes on the site. Currently, she has 15 books in print on her favorite subject — eBay.

Out of college, Marsha worked in Fashion Advertising for the *Miami Herald* and then as Special Projects Manager for the *Los Angeles Daily News.* In 1984, she founded a home-based advertising and marketing business. Her successful business, the Collier Company, Inc., was featured by *Entrepreneur* magazine in 1985 (today she's Entrepreneur.com's eBay columnist). Marsha's company later received the Small Business of the Year award from her California State Assemblyman and the Northridge Chamber of Commerce.

Most of all, Marsha loves a great deal — that's what drew her to eBay in 1996, and that's partially what keeps her busy on the site now. She buys everything from replacement toothbrush heads to parts for pool equipment to designer dresses. Marsha knows how to *work* and profit from eBay, and in this book, she shares that knowledge with you.

Bill Summers has been wrapped up in all things eBay for more than seven years on a full-time basis. He currently maintains several eBay IDs, holds PowerSeller status, and is recognized as Canada's leading Education Specialist trained by eBay. He ardently shares his knowledge of eBay and his passion for smart buying and selling on the site through private training and in his classes held at community centres and community colleges.

In his more than 25 years of diverse experience in the sanitation supplies industry, Bill was exposed to all aspects of business buying and selling operations. Over those years he also developed and ran many corporate and industrial training programs across Canada. After a prolonged period of traveling up to 35 weeks a year, and with a young family at home, Bill decided to leave the nine-to-five business world in favour of his own home-run business on eBay.

Bill is the first to admit that eBay has dramatically changed his life — for the better. eBay has afforded him the opportunity to use his accumulated business savvy in his own small business, and he is the first to admit that selling on eBay allows him the freedom and independence to live life at a much more relaxed pace.

Bill and his supportive wife, Susan, have been married for more than 30 years and live with their daughter Johanna in Kitchener, Ontario.

Dedication

Marsha: To all the future eBay buyers and sellers who have purchased this book to get a taste of how much fun online buying and selling can be. I look forward to seeing your auctions and hearing your stories.

I also dedicate this book to all the employees at eBay, who work very hard and don't always get noticed or appreciated by the community. I want to thank all of you for your endeavors; you make eBay a fun and profitable site to visit for millions of people. Keep on doing what you're doing.

Bill: I dedicate this book to all of my eBay students, past and future, who consistently inspire me with their entrepreneurial spirit.

Authors' Acknowledgements

Marsha: This book couldn't have been written without the input from thousands of eBay sellers and buyers whom I've spoken to from all over the country. You inspire me to work harder and do my best to help all of you.

I've made so many friends along my eBay travels. My original coauthor on the first book, Roland Woerner: If it wasn't for you, this book wouldn't be here. There's also my close friend and eBay buddy, Jillian Cline: Thanks for trying out all my wacky eBay ideas; I'm glad they've helped both of us! Thanks to the rest of my eBay buddies — who always seem to have a moment when I call.

I particularly want to thank my editors at Wiley Publishing, Inc.: my really fun and smart project editor Nicole Haims (who was also project editor for the 1st and 3rd editions of the U.S. edition of this book; my super tech editor Louise (aunt*patti) Ruby (who, by the way, was one of the very first eBay employees); Barry Childs-Helton (the best copy editor ever); Steven Hayes, who is always there for support and ideas; and Andy Cummings, my publisher, who really should be running Wiley by now but, — lucky for me — still takes my calls! Thank you all!

Bill: Canadianizing and updating any book about eBay presents a unique challenge. While adapting this book, the Canadian site was undergoing a significant face-lift, making it very difficult to be current on all of the changes. I'd like to express a sincere thank-you to Isabel Tremblay at eBay Canada for her assistance in answering specific questions about developments on the Canadian site.

I'd also like to express a big thanks to John Snyder and his daughter Lisa Kennedy — two eBay buyers and sellers in Chapter 5 who gave freely of their time and advice so that others may benefit from their experience.

Finally, a major thanks also goes out to the team at Wiley: Robert Hickey, who still amazes me with his inordinate amount of patience and the editor for this first Canadian edition of Marsha's original book, Pamela Vokey, the Project Coordinator, who worked exceedingly hard to keep my mistakes to a minimum, and Laura Miller, for her careful copy edit.

Publisher's Acknowledgements

We're proud of this book; please send us your comments at canadapt@wiley.com.

Some of the people who helped bring this book to market include the following:

Acquisitions, Editorial, and Media Development

Editor: Robert Hickey

Copy Editor: Laura Miller

Cover Photos: © iStockphoto.com/Tyler Olson

Cartoons: Rich Tennant
(www.the5thwave.com)

Composition Services

Project Coordinators: Lynsey Osborn, Pamela Vokey

Layout and Graphics: Carl Byers, Reuben W. Davis, Stephanie D. Jumper, Barbara Moore

Proofreaders: Laura L. Bowman, Susan Moritz

Indexer: Belle Wong

Wiley Bicentennial Logo: Richard J. Pacifico

John Wiley & Sons Canada, Ltd.

Bill Zerter, Chief Operating Officer

Robert Harris, General Manager, Professional and Trade Division

Publishing and Editorial for Consumer Dummies

Diane Graves Steele, Vice President and Publisher, Consumer Dummies

Joyce Pepple, Acquisitions Director, Consumer Dummies

Kristin A. Cocks, Product Development Director, Consumer Dummies

Michael Spring, Vice President and Publisher, Travel

Kelly Regan, Editorial Director, Travel

Publishing for Technology Dummies

Andy Cummings, Vice President and Publisher, Dummies Technology/General User

Composition Services

Gerry Fahey, Vice President of Production Services

Debbie Stailey, Director of Composition Services

Contents at a Glance

Table of Contents

Introduction

*T*hanks for opening up this book. This is the newly updated and revised Canadian version of the original eBay how-to guide, first published in 1999. You may soon be joining the hundreds of thousands of people interested in finding out the no-nonsense facts about eBay from two active users. Both of us are long-time eBay shoppers and PowerSellers. Marsha's original career was in retail marketing, but now it's full-time eBay — teaching and writing. Bill started out in industrial sales and marketing, but he's been selling full time on eBay for seven years and teaching eBay through the Education Specialist program for almost three years. Both of us work from our homes and apply our backgrounds successfully to all facets of the site.

Welcome to *eBay For Canadians For Dummies!* We can't begin to tell you how excited we are that our enthusiasm and excitement for shopping and selling on eBay has led to the need for an exclusively Canadian Edition. eBay users now total more than 230 million globally — that's quite a community. It's a community of buyers who don't feel the need to scour the cities for items to buy, and of sellers who forage out wholesale items to sell online and make a few dollars. eBay's the new international marketplace, and the best part is that eBay is available to anyone who wants to take the time to figure out how it works.

eBay is a constantly evolving Web site. It isn't too hard to master, but just as with any tool, when you know the ins and outs, you're ahead of the game. You can get the deals when you shop, and when you sell, you can make the most money. You've come to the right place to find out all about eBay. This book is (and has been from the start) designed to help you understand the basics about buying and selling at eBay, the most successful person-to-person trading community. Without the basics, you can't be successful in any endeavour. You get all the tools you need to get moving at eBay, whether you're new to the Internet or a Webaholic. You see how to turn your everyday household clutter into cold, hard cash — and how to look for items that you can sell at eBay. If you're an online shopper (or you want to be), we show you how to figure out how much you should spend, how to make smart bids, and how to win the auctions. How much money you earn (or spend) depends entirely on how often and how smartly you conduct your eBay transactions. *You* decide how often you want to run auctions and place bids; we're here to help with the smart part by sharing tips we've learned through our combined 17 years on eBay.

A Web site as complex as eBay has many nooks and crannies that may confuse users. Think of this book as a detailed road map that can help you navigate eBay, getting just as much or as little as you want from it. Unlike an actual road map, you won't get frustrated folding it back into its original shape. Just close the book and come back anytime you need a question answered.

After you figure out the nuts and bolts of eBay, you can start buying and selling stuff. We've included a ton of terrific buying and selling strategies that can help you get the most out of your auctions. With this book and a little elbow grease, you can join the ranks of the millions of people who use their home computers to make friends, find great deals, have a lot of fun, and make a profit. When you've got the hang of eBay and feel that it's time to graduate from this book, look for our other book, *Starting an eBay Business For Canadians For Dummies* (Wiley Publishing, Inc.) — it'll take you to the next plateau.

About This Book

Remember those open-book tests that teachers sprang on you in high school? Well, sometimes you may feel like eBay pop-quizzes you while you're online. Think of *eBay For Canadians For Dummies* as your open-book-test cheat sheet with all the answers. You don't have to memorize anything; just keep this book handy to help you get through the confusing parts of eBay. Over the years, some of the top eBay sellers and buyers in the United States have visited with Marsha when she's at a book signing or teaching an eBay University class just to show her their dog-eared, highlighted, marred copy of an earlier edition of *eBay For Dummies* that got them started. We hope that this book will do the same for you.

With all that in mind, we've divided this book into pertinent sections to help you find your answers fast. We show you how to

- Get online and register at eBay.
- Navigate eBay to do just about anything you can think of — search for items for sale, set up auctions, monitor your transactions, and join the community circuit.
- Bid on and *win* eBay auctions.
- Choose an item to sell, pick the right time for your listing, market it so that a ton of bidders see it, and make a nice profit.
- Communicate well and close deals without problems, whether you're a buyer or a seller.

✔ Handle problems with finesse, should they crop up.

✔ Become a part of a really unique community of people who like to collect, buy, and sell items of just about every type!

Don't adjust your eyes. To protect the privacy of eBay users, screen images (commonly called *screen shots*) in this book blur User IDs to protect the innocent (or not so . . .).

Conventions Used in This Book

In most cases, prices for goods and services shown in this book are in Canadian funds. But, from time to time, we may quote a price in U.S. greenbacks (for example, US$40). Because currencies can fluctuate so rapidly, we chose not to convert those prices and suggest you visit an online currency conversion site such as www.xe.com for accurate, up to the moment rates.

Foolish Assumptions

You may have picked up this book because you heard that people are making huge money trading at eBay, and you want to find out what's going on. Or you heard about the bargains and wacky stuff you can find in the world's largest shopping emporium. If either of these assumptions is true, this is the right book for you.

Here are some other foolish assumptions we've made about you:

✔ You have, or plan to have, access to a computer, a modem, and the Internet so that you can do business at eBay.

✔ You have an interest in collecting stuff, selling stuff, and buying stuff, and you want to find out more about doing that stuff online.

✔ You want tips and strategies that can save you money when you bid and make you money when you sell. (You too? We can relate. Talk about all things to all people!)

✔ You're concerned about maintaining your privacy and staying away from people who try to ruin everyone's good time with negligent (and sometimes illegal) activity.

How This Book Is Organized

This book has five parts. The parts stand on their own, which means that you can read Chapter 5 after you read Chapter 10, or skip Chapter 3 altogether. It's all up to you. We do think that you should at least dip into Chapter 1 and Chapter 2 to get an overview of what eBay is all about and find out how to become a registered user.

If you're already conducting transactions at eBay, you certainly can jump ahead to get good tips on advanced strategies to enhance your sales. Don't wait for our permission — just go for it. We won't argue with you that jazzy auctions equal higher profits!

Part I: Forget the Bricks and Mortar: Getting a Feel for eBay

In this part, we tell you what eBay is and how you use it. We take you through the registration process, help you organize your eBay transactions and interactions using the My eBay page, and get you comfortable navigating the site from the home page.

Part II: Are You Buying What They're Selling?

If you're pretty sure you want to start making bids on items, this part gives you the lowdown on searching, grading a collectible item's value, researching, bidding, and winning auctions.

That old cliché, "Let the buyer beware" (*caveat emptor* for the literati in the audience), became a cliché because even today (maybe especially today) it's sound advice. Use our friendly, sugar-free tips to help you decide when to bid and when to take a pass.

Part III: Are You Selling What They're Buying?

This part gets you up to speed on how to sell your items at eBay. Think of it as an eBay course in marketing. In this part, you can find important information on how to conduct your auctions, what to do after you sell an item, how to ship the item, and how to keep track of all the money you make. Even the Canadian taxman gets to chime in on his favourite topic: taxes. Know the rules so your friendly local tax office doesn't invite you over for a snack and a little audit.

We also show you how to snazzy up your auctions by adding pictures, and we show you how to use basic HTML to link your auctions to your own home page. (If you don't have a home page, don't freak out: Links are optional.) You can make your digital images look like high art with our tips, hints, and strategies.

Part IV: Oy Vey, More eBay! Special Features

Check out this part to discover how to handle privacy issues relating to eBay and how you can resolve buying and selling issues with the help of Trust & Safety, eBay's problem-solving clearinghouse. Also included are ways of having fun with the eBay community and using charity auctions to bid on great items for a great cause.

Part V: The Part of Tens

In keeping with a long *For Dummies* tradition, this part is a compendium of short chapters that give you ready references and useful facts. We share more terrific tips for buying and selling items, as well as descriptions of our favourite software programs that can help lighten your auction load.

In addition to all these parts, you also get an appendix. The appendix gives some insider information on how to spot a trend before the rest of the world catches on and how to acquire items cheaply that others may spend a bundle on. When you're ready to go to the next level, take a look at our other book, *Starting an eBay Business For Canadians For Dummies* (Wiley). It takes off where this book ends.

Icons Used in This Book

These are facts that you just *have* to know! Time is money at eBay. When you see this shortcut or timesaver come your way, read the information and think about all the moolah you just saved.

Think of this icon as a sticky note for your brain. If you forget one of the pearls of wisdom revealed to you, you can go back and reread it. If you *still* can't remember something here, go ahead, dog-ear the page — we won't tell. Even better: Use a highlighter.

Don't feel our pain. We've done plenty of things wrong on eBay and want to save you from our mistakes. We put these warnings out there, bright and bold, so you don't have the same bad experiences. Don't skip these warnings unless you're enthusiastic about masochism.

When you see this icon, you know you're in for the real deal. We've created this icon especially for this book to give you war stories (and success stories) from eBay veterans (*learn from their experiences* is our motto) to help you strategize, make money, and spare you from the perils of a poorly written auction item description. You can skip over these icons if you want to, but you may get burned if you do.

Although the word *technical* sounds way too high-tech for us, this Technical Stuff icon appears to the left of a few paragraphs in this book. Although these paragraphs may have been deemed *technical* by our editors, it's just part and parcel of the information you're going to need to know if you want to succeed on eBay.

What Now?

Like everything else in the world, eBay constantly evolves. Some of the eBay screens in this book may look slightly different than the ones you see on your home computer display. That's just eBay tweaking and changing things on the site. Our job is to arm you with everything you need to know to join the eBay community and begin conducting transactions. If you hit rough waters, just look up the problem in the Table of Contents or Index in this book. We either help you solve it or let you know where to go at eBay for some expert advice.

Although eBay makes its complex Web site as easy to navigate as possible, you may still need to refer back to this book for help. Don't get frustrated if you have to keep reviewing topics before you feel completely comfortable trading at eBay.

After all, Albert Einstein once said, "Don't commit to memory something you can look up." (Although we forget when he said that. . . .)

Feedback, Please

Communication makes the world go round, and we'd love to hear from you. Contact Marsha at talk2marsha@coolebaytools.com. You can e-mail Bill at bill@learningebayiseasy.com. Please know that we can't answer each and every question you send. There isn't enough time in the day — between selling, writing, teaching, and, oh yes, our personal lives! Do know that we'll read each e-mail. We can answer the most common questions in our respective newsletters.

Marsha's free newsletter comes out almost every month, full of new facts to ease your way on eBay. You can sign up for it at her Web site at www.coolebaytools.com. Bill's newsletter comes out every second month, and it's a great read, too — full of eBay news and ideas from a Canadian perspective. Sign up at www.learningebayiseasy.com.

eBay is always working to make the site even more new and exciting — that means switching things around to see if you notice. You may click a link on the home page that's there today and gone tomorrow, replaced with something else. When in doubt, use the main navigation bar as your own personal breadcrumb trail.

Part I

Forget the Bricks and Mortar: Getting a Feel for eBay

The 5th Wave   By Rich Tennant

"Oh, that there's just something I picked up as a grab bag special from the 'Everything Else' category."

In this part . . .

New technology can be intimidating for anyone. You've wanted to visit eBay, maybe make a few dollars selling or get in on some of the great deals, but eBay feels kind of big and scary. What you need is someone to point out the most useful tools you need to get around, help you find out how eBay works, and start showing you how to do your own transactions. That's what we do in Part I.

In this part, we give you the information you want to know about how eBay works and what it offers its members. Find out how to become a registered user, manoeuvre the eBay Home page, and customize your very own private My eBay page. You can also find out about the all-hyimportant feedback profile that follows every eBay user around like a shadow.

Chapter 1

Why eBay Is a Terrific Place to Buy and Sell

*e*Bay has emerged as *the* marketplace of the 21st century. In July 2003, *Wired* magazine predicted that eBay's promise is that "retailing will become the national pastime." The founder of eBay had a pretty great idea back in 1995 (read about some eBay history in the "eBay's humble beginnings" sidebar, later in this chapter), and the world has taken to shopping and selling online. eBay is a safe and fun place to shop for everything from collectibles to brand-new clothing, without having to move from your computer.

eBay is now also a marketplace for new merchandise. It's no longer just the destination for collectibles and old china patterns. These days, you can purchase all kinds of new and useful items, such as alarm systems, fancy electronic toothbrushes, light bulbs, clothing, cars, homes — just about anything you can think of.

Take a look around your house. Nice shoes. Great-looking clock. Spiffy microwave. Not to mention all the other cool stuff you own. All these great fashions, household appliances, and collectibles are fabulous to own, but when was the last time your clock turned a profit? When you connect to eBay, your computer can magically turn into a money machine. Just visit eBay and marvel at all the items that are just a few mouse clicks away from being bought and sold.

In this chapter, we tell you what eBay is and how it works. eBay is the perfect alternative to spending hours wandering through boutiques, antiques shops, or outlet malls looking for the perfect doohickey. It can also be your personal shopper for gifts and day-to-day items.

Not only can you buy and sell stuff in the privacy of your home, you can also meet people who share your interests. People who use the eBay site are a friendly bunch, and soon you can be buying, selling, swapping stories, and trading advice with the best of them.

To get to eBay, you need to access the Internet. To access the Internet, you need access to a computer — either a personal computer (PC) or Macintosh (Mac) — with an Internet connection. You can get an inexpensive, used laptop for as little as $350. If you're not ready to take the high-tech plunge, this book shows you how to start operating at eBay (and earning money) without owning a single cyber thing.

What Is eBay, and How Does It Work?

The Internet is spawning all kinds of new businesses (known as *e-commerce* to Wall Street types), and eBay is the superstar. The reason is simple: It's the place where buyers and sellers can meet, do business, share stories and tips, and have fun. It's like one giant online potluck party — but you sell the dish you bring!

eBay *doesn't* sell a thing. Instead, the site does what all good hosts do: It creates a comfy environment that brings people with common interests together. eBay is sort of like the person who set you up on your last blind date — except eBay often gives you much better results. Your matchmaking friend doesn't perform a marriage ceremony, but he or she does get you in the same room with your potential soulmate. eBay puts buyers and sellers in a virtual store and lets them conduct their business safely within the rules that eBay has established.

All you need to do to join eBay is fill out a few forms online and click. Congratulations — you're a member, and you don't have to worry about big fees or secret handshakes. After you register, you can buy and sell anything that falls within the eBay rules and regulations. (Chapter 2 eases you through the registration process.)

Start at the eBay home page (www.ebay.ca), shown in Figure 1-1, in your quest to find all the cool stuff you can see and do at eBay. You can conduct searches; find out what's happening; and get an instant link to the My eBay page, which helps you keep track of every item you have up for sale or have a bid on. You can get the lowdown on the eBay home page in Chapter 3, and Chapter 4 tells all about My eBay.

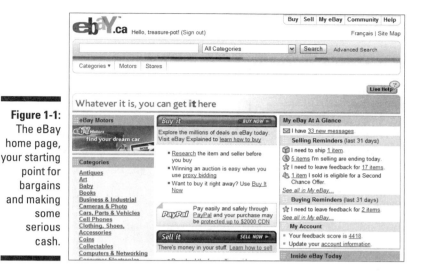

Figure 1-1:
The eBay home page, your starting point for bargains and making some serious cash.

Yikes! What happened? The eBay home page on your computer looks nothing like the one in Figure 1-1. Don't rub your eyes — even squinting hard won't help. eBay has a different version of the home page for those who have never registered on eBay. But even if you've never registered, someone else who uses the computer may already have. Take a look at Figure 1-2 and see if it's a closer match.

Figure 1-2:
The eBay Lite home page that appears for new users.

---

eBay's humble beginnings

The long-standing urban legend says that eBay started with a Pez dispenser. But as romantic as the story is (about the young man who designed the site to allow his fiancée to trade Pez dispensers), it is, sadly, a public relations spin. The founder, Pierre Omidyar, had the right vision at the right time, and the first item he sold on the site was a broken laser pointer. Day by day, new people were drawn to the site by Internet chatter. The site eventually grew to the point at which it began to strain Pierre's ISP. The ISP began charging him more, so he started charging a small listing fee for sellers — just so he could break even. Legend has it that the day $10,000 in fees arrived in Pierre's mailbox, he quit his day job. (We hope that's not just a Pez story!)

eBay was born on Labour Day, 1995. The name eBay is taken from Echo Bay, the name Pierre originally wanted for his company. Upon checking with the State of California, he found that the name was taken by another company, so he shortened the name to eBay — and the rest, as they say, is history.

All About Auctions

The value of an item is determined by how much someone is willing to spend to buy it. That's what makes auctions exciting. eBay offers several kinds of auctions, but for the most part, they all work the same way. An *auction* is a unique sales event in which the exact value of the item for sale isn't set. As a result, an auction has an element of surprise involved — not only for the bidder (who may end up with a great deal), but also for the seller (who may end up making a killing). Here's how an auction works — from both a seller's perspective and a bidder's perspective:

- ✔ **Seller:** A seller pays a fee; fills out an electronic form; and sets up the auction, listing a *minimum bid* he or she is willing to accept for the item. Think of an auctioneer at Sotheby's saying, "The bidding for this diamond necklace begins at $5,000." You might want to bid $4,000, but the bid won't be accepted. Sellers can also set a *reserve price* — sort of a financial safety net that protects them from losing money on the deal. We explain how this stuff works in the following sections.

- ✔ **Bidder:** Bidders in auctions duke it out over a period of time (the minimum is one day, but most auctions last a week or even longer) until one comes out victorious. Usually, the highest bidder wins. The tricky thing about participating in an auction (and the most exciting aspect) is that no one knows the final price an item goes for until the last second of the auction.

eBay auctions

Unlike traditional live auctions that end with the familiar phrase, "Going once, going twice, sold!" eBay auctions are controlled by the clock. The seller pays a fee and lists the item on the site for a predetermined period of time; the highest bidder when the clock runs out takes home the prize.

Reserve-price auctions

Unlike a minimum bid, which is required in any eBay auction, a *reserve price* protects sellers from having to sell an item for less than the minimum amount they want for it. You may be surprised to see a 1968 Jaguar XKE sports car up for auction at eBay with a minimum bid of only a dollar. It's a fair bet that the seller has put a reserve price on this car to protect him- or herself from losing money. The reserve price allows sellers to set lower minimum bids, and lower minimum bids attract bidders. Unfortunately, if a seller makes the reserve price too high and it isn't met by the end of the auction, no one wins.

eBay charges a fee for sellers to run reserve-price auctions. Nobody knows (except the seller and the eBay computer system) what the reserve price is until the auction is over (assuming that the reserve price is met and someone wins the auction), but you can tell from the auction page whether you're dealing with a reserve-price auction. Reserve-price auctions appear in the general listings alongside all other items, so you have to click and view an auction to find out whether it has a reserve. If bids have been made on an item, a message appears on the auction's page telling you if the reserve price hasn't been met. You can find out more about bidding on reserve-price auctions in Chapter 6 and about setting up a reserve-price auction in Chapter 9.

Live Auctions

If you yearn for that traditional, going-going-gone (highest bidder wins) sort of auction, you can participate in auctions that are running live at a gallery in real time. In *eBay Live Auctions,* you can bid via eBay's Internet hook-up just as if you were sitting in a chair at the auction house. These auctions are usually for unique and interesting items that you're not likely to find in your locality. For more on these sales, see Chapter 6. Figure 1-3 shows the Live Auctions home page, located at www.ebayliveauctions.com.

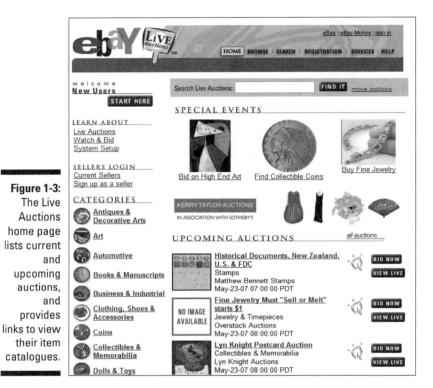

Figure 1-3:
The Live Auctions home page lists current and upcoming auctions, and provides links to view their item catalogues.

Restricted-access auctions

If you're over 18 years of age and interested in bidding on items of an adult nature, eBay has an adults only *(Mature Audiences)* category, which has restricted access. Although you can peruse the other eBay categories without having to submit credit card information, you must have a credit card number on file at eBay to view and bid on items in this category. Restricted-access auctions are run like the typical timed auctions. To bid on adult items, you need to agree to a Terms of Use page after entering your User ID and password. This Terms of Use page pops up automatically when you attempt to access this category.

If you aren't interested in seeing or bidding on items of an adult nature, or if you're worried that your children may be able to gain access to graphic adult material, eBay has solved that problem by excluding adult-content items from easily accessible areas, such as the Featured Items page. Children under the age of 18 aren't allowed to register at eBay and should be under an adult's supervision if they do wander onto the site.

Charity auctions: All for a good cause

A *charity auction* is a high-profile fundraising auction where the proceeds go to a selected charity. Most people don't wake up in the morning wanting to own the shoes that Ron Howard wore when he put his footprints in cement at Mann's Chinese Theater in Hollywood, but one-of-a-kind items such as that often are auctioned off in charity auctions. (In fact, someone did want those shoes badly enough to buy them for a lot of money at eBay.) Charity auctions became popular after the NBC *Today Show* sold an autographed jacket at eBay for over $11,000 with the proceeds going to Toys for Tots. Charity auctions are run like most other auctions at eBay — but because they're immensely popular, bidding can be fierce, and the dollar amounts can go sky high. Many famous celebrities use eBay to help out their favourite charities. Billionaire Warren Buffett auctions a private lunch each year to support one of his favourite charities — in 2006, that lunch went for over $600,000. We suggest that you visit these auctions often and bid whenever you can. Charity auctions are a win-win situation for everyone. You can read more about celebrity auctions in Chapter 18.

Private (shhh-it's-a-secret) auctions

Some sellers choose to hold *private auctions* because they know that some bidders may be embarrassed to be seen bidding on a box of racy neckties in front of the rest of the eBay community. Others may go the private route because they're selling big-ticket items and don't want to disclose their bidders' financial status.

Private auctions are run like the typical timed auctions except that each bidder's identity is kept secret. At the end of the auction, eBay provides contact info to the seller and to the high bidder, and that's it.

You can send e-mail questions to the seller in a private auction, but you can't check out your competition because the auction item page shows the current bid price but not the high bidder's User ID.

Multiple Item (Dutch) auctions

Multiple Item — Dutch — auctions have nothing to do with windmills, wooden shoes, or sharing the check on a date. A *Multiple Item auction* allows a seller to put multiple, identical items up for sale. Instead of holding 100 separate auctions for 100 pairs of wooden shoes, for example, a seller can sell them all in one listing. As a buyer, you can elect to bid for 1, 3, or all 100 pairs. Unless you're running an alternative boutique (or know a giant centipede who needs all those clogs), you probably want to bid on just one pair. For more on Multiple Item auctions, see Chapter 6.

A Multiple Item auction can't be conducted as a private auction.

Buying It Now at eBay

You don't have to participate in an auction at eBay to buy something. If you want to make a purchase — if it's something you *must* have — you can usually find the item and buy it immediately. Of course, using Buy It Now (*BIN* in eBay speak) doesn't come with the thrill of an auction, but purchasing an item at a fraction of the retail price without leaving your chair or waiting for an auction to end has its own warm and fuzzy kind of excitement. If you seek this kind of instant gratification on eBay, visit the eBay Stores. Or you can isolate these items by clicking the Buy It Now tab when browsing categories or performing searches.

eBay Stores

Visiting eBay Stores is as easy as clicking the eBay Stores link on the home page. Thousands of eBay sellers have set up stores with merchandise meant for you to Buy It Now. eBay Stores are categorized just like regular listings on eBay, and you can buy anything — from socks to jewellery to appliances.

Sellers who open an eBay Store have to meet a certain level of experience on eBay, and when you buy from eBay Stores, you're protected by the same fraud protection policy that you're covered with in eBay auctions.

Buy It Now and fixed-price sales

More and more sellers are selling items with a Buy It Now option or at a fixed price. This feature enables you to buy an item as soon as you see one at a price that suits you. For more on how these sales work, check out Chapter 6.

Best Offer

A new feature on eBay allows sellers to choose to accept offers for their merchandise in either fixed-price or classified ad listings. Buyers can make a price-based offer, which the seller has the sole discretion to accept. As with normal fixed-price listings, if the seller accepts the buyer's offer, the listing immediately ends. Read more about how Best Offer listings work in Chapter 6.

So You Wanna Sell Stuff

If you're a seller, creating an auction page at eBay is as simple as filling out an online form. Type in the name of your item and a short description, add a crisp digital picture, set your price, and voilà — it's auction time. (Okay, it's a tad more involved than that — but not much.) eBay charges a small fee ($0.23–$5.60) for the privilege. When you list your item, millions of people (eBay has over 230 million registered users) from all over the world can take a gander at it and place bids. With a little luck, a bidding war may break out and drive the bids up high enough for you to turn a nice profit. After the auction, you deal directly with the buyer, who sends you the payment either through a payment service or through the mail. Then you ship the item. Abracadabra — you just turned your item (everyday clutter, perhaps) into cash.

You can run as many auctions as you want, all at the same time. To get info on deciding what to sell, leaf through Chapter 9; to find out how to set up an auction, jump to Chapter 10; and to get the scoop on advanced selling techniques, visit Chapter 14. When you're ready to go pro, check out the appendixes in the back of this book.

So You Wanna Buy Stuff

If you're a collector, or you just like to shop for bargains, you can browse 24 hours a day through the items up for auction in eBay's tens of thousands of categories, which range from Antiques to Writing Instruments. Find the item you want, do a little research on what you're buying and who's selling it, place your bid, and keep an eye on it until the auction closes. When she wrote *Santa Shops on eBay* (Wiley Publishing, Inc.), Marsha had a great time visiting the different categories and buying a little something here and there — it's amazing just how varied the selection is. She even bought some parts for her pool cleaner!

Take a look at Chapter 5 for info on searching for items to bid on. When you see an item you like, you can set up a bidding strategy and let the games begin. Chapter 7 gives you bidding strategies that can make you the winner. After you win your first auction, look for expert advice about completing the transaction in Chapter 8.

You can bid as many times as you want on an item, and you can bid on as many auctions as you want. Just keep in mind that each bid is a binding contract, and you're required to pay for the item you bid on if you win.

Researching for Fun and Profit

eBay's awesome search engine allows you to browse through countless categories of items up for sale. As a buyer, you can do a lot of comparison shopping on that special something you just can't live without, or just browse around until something catches your eye. If you're a seller, the search engine allows you to keep your eye on the competition and get an idea of how hot your item is. With a little eBay research, you can set a competitive price for your item. To find out more about using search options and categories, check out Chapters 3 and 5.

The search engine also lets you find out what other people are bidding on, although, for privacy reasons, not all items may be displayed. From there, you can read up on buyers' *feedback ratings* (eBay's ingenious honour system) to get a sense of how good their reputations are — *before* you deal with them.

eBay's Role in the Action

Throughout the auction process, eBay's computers keep tabs on what's going on. When the auction or sale is over, eBay takes a small percentage of the final selling price and instructs the seller and buyer to contact each other through e-mail. At this point, eBay's job is pretty much over, and eBay steps aside.

Most of the time, everything works great, everybody's happy, and eBay never has to step back into the picture. But if you happen to run into trouble in paradise, eBay can help you settle the problem, whether you're the buyer or the seller.

eBay regulates members with a detailed system of checks and balances known as *feedback,* which is described in Chapter 4. The grand plan is that the community polices itself. Don't get us wrong — eBay does jump in when shady activity comes to light. But the people who keep eBay most safe are the community members, the buyers and sellers who have a common stake in conducting business honestly and fairly. Every time you sell something or win an auction, eBay members have a chance to leave a comment about you. You should do the same for them. If they're happy with your eBay transaction, the feedback is positive; otherwise, the feedback is either neutral or negative. Always keep in mind that your feedback sticks to you like glue, no matter where you go on the site.

Building a great reputation with positive feedback ensures a long and profitable eBay career. Negative feedback, like multiple convictions for auto theft, is a real turnoff to most folks and can make it hard to do future business at eBay.

Features and Fun Stuff

So eBay is all about making money, right? Not exactly. The folks at eBay aren't kidding when they call it a community — a place where people with similar interests can compare notes, argue, buy and sell, and meet each other. Yes, people have gotten married after meeting at eBay. (Take a guess how friends bought them wedding gifts!)

Chatting it up

eBay has dozens of specific chat rooms and discussion boards on both the Canadian and U.S. sites (even a Canada Town Square — for those who want to meet and chat with only fellow Canadians) with topics that range from advertising to trading cards. So, if you have no idea what that old Texaco gas station sign you found in your grandfather's barn is worth, just post a message on the Collectors chat board. Somewhere out there is an expert with an answer for you. If you don't get the help you need on the Canadian site, try visiting the U.S. site where you may find help on the Antiques, Collectibles, or Vintage chat boards. Your biggest problem may be deciding whether to keep the sign or put it up for auction. That's a good problem to have! For more about posting messages and participating in chat rooms, visit Chapters 5 and 17.

Trust & Safety

Trust & Safety is the catchall resource for information about making deals at eBay safer — and for information on what to do if deals go sour. We don't like to think about it, but occasionally — despite your best efforts to be a good eBay user — buyers or sellers don't keep their word. In a small percentage of cases, unscrupulous louts sometimes do invade the site and try to pull scams. You may buy an item that isn't as it was described, or the winner of your auction may not send the payment. Sometimes, even honest members get into disputes. Trust & Safety is an excellent resource when you want answers to your questions or you need a professional to come in and handle an out-of-hand situation. Chapter 16 tells you all about Trust & Safety.

Extra Gizmos You're Gonna Want

At some point in your eBay career, you'll become comfortable with all the computer-related hoops you have to jump through to make the eBay magic happen. At that time, you may be ready to invest in a few extra devices that can make your eBay experiences even better. Digital cameras and scanners can help make your time at eBay a more lucrative and fun adventure. You can find out how to use digital technology in your auctions in Chapter 14.

Chapter 2

The Bucks Start Here: Signing Up at eBay

In This Chapter

▶ Registering with eBay's easy forms (the shape of things to come)

▶ Identifying yourself with User IDs and passwords

▶ Stepping into eBay as a newbie

*Y*ou've probably figured out that you sign on to eBay electronically, which means you don't really *sign* on the proverbial dotted line the way folks did in days of old before computers ran the world. Nowadays, the art of scribbling your signature has become as outdated as vinyl records (although you can still get vinyl records at eBay if you're feeling nostalgic).

Compared to finding a prime parking space at the mall during the holidays, signing up at eBay is a breeze. About the toughest thing you have to do is type in your e-mail address correctly.

In this chapter, you can find out everything you need to know about registering at eBay. You get tips on what information you have to disclose and what you should keep to yourself. Don't worry — this is an open-book test. You don't need to memorize the names of all the Prime Ministers since Confederation, Morse code, or even the multiplication tables.

Registering at eBay

You don't have to wear one of those tacky "Hello, My Name Is" stickers on your shirt after you sign in, but eBay needs to know some things about you before it grants you membership. You and several million other folks will be roaming around eBay's online treasure trove; eBay needs to know who's who. So, keeping that in mind, sign in, please!

You don't have to be a rocket scientist to register at eBay, but you *can* buy a model rocket after you do. The only hard-and-fast rule at eBay is that you have to be 18 years of age or older. Don't worry, the Age Police won't come to your house to card you; they have other ways to discreetly ensure that you're at least 18 years old. (***Hint:*** Credit cards do more than satisfy account charges.) If you're having a momentary brain cramp and you've forgotten your age, just think back to the premiere of *The Cosby Show.* If you can remember watching the original episodes of that favourite show of the '80s, you're in. Head to the eBay home page and register. The entire process takes only a few minutes.

Registering Is Free and Fun (And Fast)

Before you can sign up at eBay, you have to be connected to the Web. So fire up your computer and connect to the Internet. After you open your Internet browser, you're ready to sign up.

Just type www.ebay.ca in the address box of your browser and press Enter. The eBay home page appears. Right there, where you can't miss it, is the Join Free button (as you can see in Figure 2-1). Click the Join Free button and let the sign-up process begin. See Chapter 3 for details.

The eBay home page frequently undergoes changes. If you don't see a Join Free button, look around the page — there's always a registration button or link somewhere.

Here's an overview of how to register with eBay:

1. **Enter the basic required info.**

2. **Read and accept the User Agreement.**

3. **Confirm your e-mail address.**

4. **Breeze through (or past) the optional information.**

The following sections fill you in on all the details.

The registration pages on eBay are through a secure SSL connection. *SSL* (Secure Sockets Layer) enables you to have an encrypted connection to eBay because a bunch of really smart techie types made it that way. You can tell because the normal http at the beginning of the Web address (also called the URL) is now https. Also, you see a small closed lock at the bottom-left (or bottom-right) corner of your screen. We could tell you how SSL works, but then things would get way too scary and technical. Instead, we just give you the bottom line: It *does* work, so trust us on this one and use it. The more precautions eBay (and you) take, the harder it is for some hyper-caffeinated high-school kid to get into your files.

When you're at the Registration form, you go through a four-step process, which we discuss in the following sections.

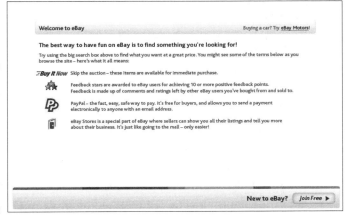

Figure 2-1:
Click the
Join Free
link to
register, and
soon you'll
be trading
online like a
pro!

So, what's your sign? Filling in your required information

After you click the Join Free button, you're taken to the heart of the eBay registration pages. You can register as a business or as an individual; Marsha chose to register as an individual, and Bill chose to register under his company's name. If you don't quite have a business up and running, it's perfectly fine to register simply as an individual. To get started, follow these steps:

1. **At the top of the first registration page, fill in some required information.**

   Here's what eBay wants to know about you:

   - Your full name, address, and primary telephone number. eBay keeps this information on file in case the company (or a member who's a transaction partner) needs to contact you.

   - Your e-mail address (`yourname@myISP.com`).

   After you input your personal information, you're ready to create your eBay persona.

2. **Scroll down the page and select your new eBay User ID.**

   See the section "A Not-So-Quick Word about Choosing a User ID," later in this chapter, for some tips on selecting your User ID.

Because many of the "good" User IDs are taken, eBay supplies a link to check on the availability of your preferred ID. Finding an awesome User ID can be as difficult as finding a four-leaf clover.

3. **Enter the password you want to use in the Create Password box, and then type it a second time in the Re-enter Password box to confirm it.**

    For more information on choosing a password, see the section "A Quick Word about Passwords," later in this chapter.

4. **Select your unique secret question and input the answer.**

    eBay uses the secret question you select here to identify you if you ever have problems signing in.

5. **Type your date of birth in the spaces provided.**

6. **Make sure all the info you entered is correct.**

    Think back to your second-grade teacher, who kept saying, "Class, check your work." Remember that? She's still right! Review your answers.

7. **Make sure to indicate in the check box that you have read and agree to eBay's terms and policies.**

    You can get more information on the User Agreement in the following section.

8. **Click the Continue button to move on to the review screen.**

If eBay finds a glitch in your registration, such as an incorrect area or postal code, you see a warning message rather than the review screen. This is part of eBay's security system to ward off fraudulent registrations. eBay won't allow you to move from the registration page until you correct any errors that eBay finds. Be certain to carefully review your information to ensure that it's correct. If you put in a wrong e-mail address, for example, eBay has no way of contacting you. So you don't hear a peep from eBay regarding your registration until all information is correct and you've carefully reviewed the information supplied.

If you make a mistake, eBay gives you the opportunity on the final review page to correct the information by using the Edit Information button.

Do you solemnly swear to . . . ?

During the registration, eBay asks you to check the box that says you agree to the eBay User Agreement and Privacy Policy. At this point, you take an oath to keep eBay safe for democracy and commerce. You promise to play well with others, not to cheat, and to follow the Golden Rule. No, you're not auditioning for a superhero club, but don't ever forget that eBay takes this stuff very seriously. You can be kicked off eBay, or worse. (Can you say "police investigation"?)

Be sure to read the User Agreement thoroughly when you register. So you don't have to put down this riveting book to read the legalese right this minute, we provide the nuts and bolts here:

- ✔ You understand that every transaction is a legally binding contract. (Click the User Agreement link at the bottom of any eBay page for the current eBay rules and regulations.)

- ✔ You agree that you can pay for the items you buy and can pay the eBay fees you incur. (Chapter 8 fills you in on how eBay takes its cut of the auction action.)

- ✔ You understand that you're responsible for paying any taxes.

- ✔ You're aware that if you sell prohibited items, eBay can forward your personal information to law enforcement for further investigation. (Chapter 9 explains what you can and can't sell at eBay — and what eBay does to sellers of prohibited items.)

- ✔ eBay makes clear that it is just a *venue,* which means it's a place where people with similar interests can meet, greet, and do business.

When everything goes well, the eBay Web site is like a school gym that opens for Saturday swap meets. At the gym, if you don't play by the rules, you can get tossed out. But if you don't play by the rules at eBay, the venue gets un-gym-like in a hurry. eBay has the right to get law enforcement officials to track you down and prosecute you. But fair's fair; if you click the appropriate box on this page, eBay keeps you posted by e-mail of any updates in the User Agreement.

If you're a stickler for fine print, click the links provided on the registration page for all the Ps and Qs of the latest policies. The User Agreement is vital to your success on eBay.

Before you can proceed, you must click the two check boxes, indicating that you really, *really* understand what it means to be an eBay user. Because we know that you, as a law-abiding eBay member, will have no problem following the rules, go ahead and click the Continue button at the bottom of the page. You're transported to a screen stating that eBay is sending you an e-mail. You're almost done!

The next step is confirming your e-mail address, which we cover in the following section.

It must be true if you have it in writing

After you accept the User Agreement and Privacy Policy, eBay takes less than a minute to e-mail you an activation notice. When you receive the eBay registration activation e-mail, be sure to print it, and don't delete the e-mail — save it somewhere special.

With your confirmation number in hand, head to the eBay Registration Confirmation page by clicking the link supplied in your e-mail. If your e-mail doesn't support links, go to this address:

```
cgi4.ebay.ca/ws/eBayISAPI.dll?RegisterConfirmCode
```

After you reconnect with eBay and it knows your e-mail address is active, you'll be heartily congratulated with an eBay e-mail, and it's time to start shopping!

If you don't receive your eBay registration confirmation e-mail within 24 hours, the e-mail address you entered probably contained an error. At this point, the customer-support folks can help you complete the registration process. Try visiting the Live Help link on the eBay home page. They're always happy to help.

If, for some reason (brain cramp is a perfectly acceptable excuse), you type in the wrong e-mail address, you have to start the registration process all over again with a different User ID (eBay holds the previous ID for 30 days). If you run into a snag, you can click the Live Help button. See Figure 2-2 for an example of a Live Help discussion.

Figure 2-2: When you click Live Help, you can be online with a real person who wants to help within a couple of minutes.

Getting to know you: Optional information

When you're a full-fledged, officially registered member of the eBay community, an eBay pop-up window may appear, giving you the option to provide more information about yourself. These optional questions allow you to fill in your self-portrait for your new pals at eBay.

Although eBay doesn't share member information with anyone, you don't have to answer the optional questions if you don't want to.

The following list shows you the optional questions eBay asks. You decide what you feel comfortable divulging and what you want to keep personal. eBay asks for this information because the company wants a better picture of who's using its Web site. In marketing mumbo-jumbo, this stuff is called *demographics* — statistics that characterize a group of people who make up a community. In this case, it's the eBay community. Here's a list of the optional information you can provide:

- ✔ **Gender:** This first choice gets right down to the basics; some people find it a good test of whether the requests for information seem too personal.

- ✔ **Annual household income:** Fill this in if you want to (eBay states that this info is kept anonymous), but we think this information is too personal. If you're not comfortable with it, skip it.

- ✔ **Your highest completed education level:** Again, if this information is too personal, leave this area blank.

After selecting your responses from the drop-down boxes, you can click Submit. If you're not in the mood right now, you can click the Answer Later link. (This pop-up window reappears for your response later in your eBay dealings.) If you don't want to answer any of the demographic queries ever, click the Please Don't Ask Me Again link at the bottom of the pop-up window.

When somebody you're in a transaction with requests your contact info, you get an e-mail from eBay also giving you the name, phone number, and location of the person making the request. Keep your information up to date. If you don't, you risk being banished from the site. See Chapter 15 for details.

A Quick Word about Passwords

Picking a good password is not as easy (but is twice as important) as it may seem. Whoever has your password can, in effect, be you at eBay — running auctions, bidding on auctions, and leaving possibly litigious feedback for others. Basically, such an impostor can ruin your eBay career — and possibly cause you serious financial grief.

As with any online password, you should follow these common-sense rules to protect your privacy:

- ✔ Don't pick anything too obvious, such as your birthday, your first name, or (especially!) your Social Insurance number. (*Hint:* If it's too easy to remember, it's probably too easy to crack.)

✔ Make things tough on the bad guys — combine numbers and letters (use upper- *and* lowercase) or create nonsensical words.

✔ Don't give out your password to anyone — it's like giving away the keys to the front door of your house.

✔ If you ever suspect that someone has your password, immediately change it by clicking the Personal Information link on your My eBay page. On the following page click Edit to change your password to something new.

✔ Change your password every few months, just to be on the safe side.

✔ Don't use the same password for both eBay and PayPal.

A Not-So-Quick Word about Choosing a User ID

eBay gives you the option of picking your User ID. Making up a User ID is our favourite part. If you've never liked your real name (or never had a nickname), here's your chance to correct that situation. Have fun. Consider choosing an ID that tells a little about you. Of course, if your interests change, you may regret too narrow a User ID.

You can call yourself just about anything; you can be silly or creative or boring. But remember, this ID is how other eBay users will know you. So here are some common-sense rules:

✔ Don't use a name that would embarrass your mother.

✔ Don't use a name with a negative connotation, such as `scam-guy`.

✔ Don't use a name that's too weird. If people don't trust you, they won't buy from you.

✔ eBay doesn't allow spaces in User IDs, so make sure that the ID makes sense when putting two or more words together.

If you're dying to have several short words as your User ID, you can use underscores or hyphens to separate them, as in *super-shop-a-holic*. If you sign in to eBay permanently on your computer, you won't have to worry about being slowed down by having to type underscores or dashes.

The craze that began with AW

Back in 1994, when eBay founder Pierre Omidyar had the idea to start a Web auction, he named his first venture Auction Web. The following figure shows a vintage Auction Web, eBay Internet auction from February 1997. There were some great deals even in those days!

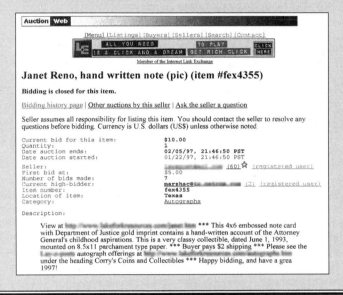

 You can change your User ID once every 30 days if you want to, but we don't recommend it. People come to know you by your User ID. If you change your ID, your past *does* play tagalong and attaches itself to the new ID. And if you change your User ID too many times, people may think you're trying to hide something.

Nevertheless, to change your User ID, click the My eBay link in the top-right corner of most eBay pages. From your My eBay login page, click the Preferences/Set-Up tab and scroll to the Change My User ID link, fill in the boxes, and click the Change User ID button. You now have a new eBay identity.

eBay has some User ID rules to live by:

- ✔ No offensive names (such as `&*#@@guy`).
- ✔ No names with *eBay* in them. (It makes you look like you work for eBay, and eBay takes a dim view of that.)

✔ No names with & (even if you *do* have both looks&brains).

✔ No names with @ (such as @Aboy).

✔ No symbols such as the greater-than or less-than symbols (> <) or consecutive underscores _ _.

✔ No IDs that begin with an e followed by numbers, an underscore, a dash, a period, or a dot.

✔ No names of just one letter (such as Q).

When you pick your User ID, make sure that it isn't a good clue for your password. For example, if you use Natasha as your User ID, don't pick Boris as your password. Even Bullwinkle could figure that one out.

Hey, AOL users, this one's for you: Make sure that your Mail Controls are set to receive e-mails from eBay. If you have Internet e-mail blocked, you need to update your AOL Mail Controls. To do so, enter the AOL keyword Mail Controls.

Your Licence to Deal (Almost)

You're now officially a *newbie,* or eBay rookie. The only problem is that you're still at the window-shopping level. If you're ready to go from window shopper to item seller, just zip through a few more forms, and before you know it, you can start running your own auctions at eBay.

Until you've been a member of eBay for at least 30 days, a picture of a beaming golden cartoon-like icon shows up to the right of your User ID wherever it appears on the site. This icon doesn't mean that you've been converted into a golden robot; the icon merely indicates to other eBay users that you're new to eBay.

Chapter 3

There's No Place Like the Home Page

. . . .

In This Chapter

▶ Getting the lay of the land

▶ Using the eBay home page's links and icons

▶ Getting the word on searches

▶ Looking the world over for that perfect eBay item

▶ Checking out featured auctions, charity auctions, and other fun stuff

. . . .

*T*he writer Thomas Wolfe was wrong: You *can* go home again — and again. At least, at eBay you can! We visit the eBay home page on a regular basis; it's a place where we can keep up with eBay's newest offerings. Month after month, millions of people (just like us) land at eBay's home page without wearing out the welcome mat. The eBay home page is the front door to the most popular auction site on the Internet.

Everything you need to know about navigating eBay begins right here. In this chapter, we give you the grand tour of the areas you can reach right from the home page with the help of links.

What's the Home Page?

The eBay home page (shown in Figure 3-1) includes the following key areas:

✔ A navigation bar at the top of the page with five eBay links that can zip you straight to one of the main eBay areas. Hover your mouse over any of these links and more links to important pages within those areas will be revealed. Also found at the top right of the page are links to the French Canadian version of eBay Canada as well as a link to the all-important site map. Found immediately below the search boxes near the top of the page are quick links to eBay Categories, eBay Motors, and eBay Stores. The little downward pointing arrow next to Categories indicates that many more links can be found by hovering your mouse over this link.

✔ A search box that helps you find items by title keywords, as well as a link to eBay's Advanced Search page.

✔ A list of links to auction categories.

✔ Links to eBay's specialty sites, featured auctions, fun stuff such as charity auctions, and information about what else is happening at eBay.

Don't adjust your computer monitor. You're not going crazy. Today, you may notice that a link that was on the eBay home page yesterday is gone. That's normal. The links on the eBay home page change often to reflect what's going on — not just on the site, but in the world, as well.

Figure 3-1:
The home page, your jumping-off point for fun and values.

Sign In, Please

Sign In is possibly the most powerful of all the links on the eBay pages, and it should be your first stop if you plan on doing any business at eBay (see Figure 3-3).

If you click the Sign In link to go to the Sign In page and then sign in, you don't have to continually enter your User ID throughout the site. You can set your preferences to take you directly to your My eBay page after Sign In. The My eBay page is an essential reference for every eBay user, and you should visit it on every trip to the site. (See Chapter 4 for info on My eBay.)

You can search for items on eBay without signing in, but what fun is that? eBay has a Guest sign-in option. Signing in as a guest is simple; check out Figure 3-2. If you haven't already registered with eBay, you have access to a special *My eBay for Guests* version of the site where you can keep track of items you want to keep an eye on (in your Watch List) — and you can also subscribe to e-mail reminders about your watched items. Just click the My eBay link on the navigation bar, and you're there. When you eventually register on eBay (which we know you will), you can transfer the watched items to your brand-spanking-new-member's My eBay page.

Figure 3-2:
The very special Sign In page for eBay guests.

If you're the only one who uses your computer, be sure to check the box that says *Keep me signed in on this computer unless I sign out.* With this box checked, you're always signed in to eBay every time you go to the site. The sign-in process places a *cookie* (a techno-related thingy — see Chapter 15 for details) on your computer that remains a part of your computer for the rest of the day. If you don't check the box, you're signed in only while your browser is open. After you close your browser, the cookie expires, and you have to sign in again.

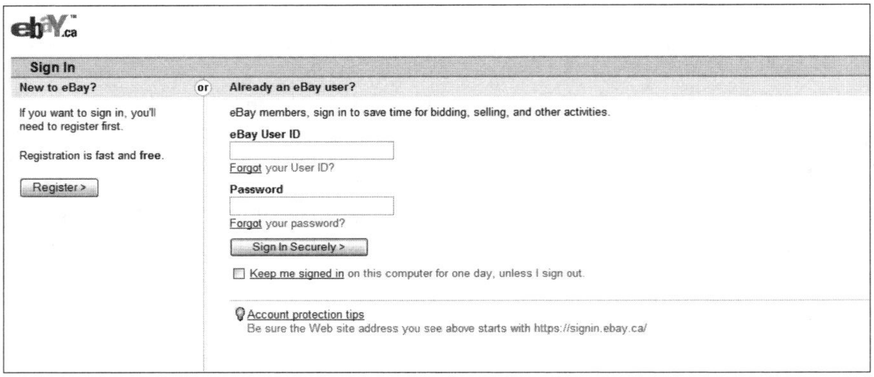

Figure 3-3:
The eBay
Sign In
page.

To get to the eBay Sign In page and sign in, follow these steps:

1. **Click the Sign In link below the navigation bar on any eBay page.**

   The new page that appears is a Secure Sign In page.

   The small, closed padlock at the bottom of your browser window (now moved to the top of the window in the most recent version of Internet Explorer) and the `https:` URL address indicate that your personal information is even more secure than usual. (See Chapter 2 for details about SSL.)

2. **Type your User ID and password into the appropriate boxes.**

3. **Click the Sign In Securely button.**

You're now signed in to eBay, and you can travel the site with ease. Enter your My eBay page by clicking the My eBay link that appears in the navigation bar. (See Chapter 4 for more on My eBay.)

This Bar Never Closes

The *navigation bar* is at the top of the eBay home page and lists five eBay links that take you directly to any of the different eBay areas. Using the navigation bar is kind of like doing one-stop clicking. You can find this bar at the top of almost every page you visit at eBay. When you click one of these five links, you're easily transported, regardless of where you are on the site, straight to the hub page for each of these topics.

Below the navigation bar is the Sign In/Sign Out link. This link, which toggles between Sign In and Sign Out, depending on your sign-in status, is important, and we remind you about it throughout this book.

Think of links as expressways to specific destinations. Click a link just once, and the next thing you know, you're right where you want to be. You don't even have to answer that proverbial annoying question, "When are we gonna get there?" from the kids in the backseat.

Here, without further ado, are the seven navigation-bar buttons and where they take you:

✔ **Buy:** Takes you to the page that lists Featured Items (see Chapter 6), all the main eBay categories, as well as links to popular stores and eBay promotions that vary from time to time. If you're signed in, this page also includes a link to your favourite searches and sellers. From this page, you can link to any one of the millions of items up for auction at eBay.

Under the Buy tab, you find links to browse by categories, keywords, or stores. If you scroll to the very bottom of the page, you find the Artist Pages. Below the Artist Pages link, you can click the Music, Movies, or Books link to search for your favourite artists' items quickly (see Figure 3-4). If you want to find your favourite artists' pages even more quickly, go to `artist-index.ebay.ca`. On this page, artists are ranked by their standing in eBay's Top Sellers.

When you click a link to browse a category (for example, Books: Antiquarian & Collectable), some tabs appear above the listings. These tabs offer you ways to search, and each tab gives you a different viewing option to browse:

• **All Items:** The default setting for the page. This option delivers on its promise — you see all items, including both auction and Buy It Now items.

• **Auctions:** This tab takes you to eBay's version of an auction catalogue.

• **Buy It Now:** Click this tab to see all items in the category that you can buy immediately if you don't want to wait for an auction to end.

Best selling Artists

Welcome to eBay's Best Selling Artists page. This page contains a list of the top-selling musicians, actors and authors based on their sales in eBay's music, movies and books categories. Click on an artist name to see a list of their works in each of these categories.

MUSIC	MOVIES	BOOKS
TOP 50 LIST	TOP 50 LIST	TOP 50 LIST
1. 1966 Lincoln Center Cast	1. Bruce Willis	1. J. K. Rowling

MUSIC	MOVIES	BOOKS
CD: Wicked (1966 Lincoln Center Cast, 2003) *No matching items found*	DVD: The Astronaut Farmer (2007) *No matching items found*	Book: Harry Potter and the Deathly Hallows (J. K. Rowling, Hardcover) *646 matching items found*

MUSIC	MOVIES	BOOKS
2. Beatles (The)	2. Johnny Depp	2. Mary Grandpre
3. Prince	3. Robert De Niro	3. James Patterson
4. Jay-Z	4. Rupert Grint	4. Nora Roberts
5. Elvis Presley	5. Nicolas Cage	5. Jim Dale
6. Eric Clapton	6. Daniel Radcliffe	6. Janet Evanovich
7. Babyface	7. Emma Watson	7. Stephen King
8. Michael Brecker	8. Clint Eastwood	8. Dean Koontz
9. Pink Floyd	9. Tom Cruise	9. Danielle Steel
10. Paulinho Da Costa	10. Walt Disney	10. Michael Ledwidge
11. Snoop Dogg	11. Tom Hanks	11. Tim Lahaye
12. Bob Dylan	12. James Gandolfini	12. Debbie Macomber

Figure 3-4:
The eBay
Best Selling
Artists page.

Not all sellers list their items in the Auctions area, so by not browsing All Items, you may be missing out on some special items or deals.

✔ **Sell:** Takes you to the start of the Sell Your Item form that you must fill out to start your sales. We explain how to navigate this form in Chapter 9. The links at the bottom of the page direct you to various seller guides.

✔ **My eBay:** Takes you to your personal My eBay page, where you keep track of all your buying and selling activities, account information, and favourite categories (you can find out more about My eBay in Chapter 4).

✔ **Community:** Takes you to a page in which you can find the latest news and announcements, chat with fellow traders in the eBay community, find charity auctions, and find out more about eBay. (Chapters 17 and 18 tell you how to use these resources.)

✔ **Help:** Takes you to one of the most valuable areas of the eBay site. The Help area can give you answers to many of your questions, as well as keep you apprised of eBay's rules and regulations regarding trading on the site. The eBay Help Centre overview page consists of a search box in which you can type your query, links for help topics, an A–Z Index, and a list of the top five questions on eBay. The page offers links to the answers to questions most frequently asked by eBay users — and to the Security & Resolution Centre.

✔ **Français:** Provides a quick link to the French Canadian version of eBay Canada. All eBay-created pages are replicated in French, but listings still appear in the language in which they were created.

✔ **Site Map:** Provides you with a bird's-eye view of the eBay world. Every *top-level* (that is, main) link available at eBay is listed here. If you're ever confused about finding a specific area, try the Site Map first. If a top-level link isn't listed here, it's not at eBay — yet.

Exploring Your Home Page Search Options

There's an old Chinese expression that says, "Every journey begins with the first eBay search." Okay, we updated the quote a bit. Very wise words, nonetheless. You can start a search from the home page in one of two ways:

✔ **Use the search box.** It's right there at the top of the home page, and it's a fast way of finding item listings.

✔ **Click the Advanced Search link to the right of the search box.** This link takes you to the Advanced Search page, where you can do all kinds of specialized searches.

Both options can give you the same results. The instructions we offer in the following sections about using these search methods are just the tip of the eBay iceberg. For the inside track on how to finesse the eBay search engine to root out just what you're looking for, check out Chapter 5.

Peering through the home page's search box

Every item offered for sale on eBay is required to have a "title," which is a collection of keywords that allows buyers to search for and find the item. To launch a listing title search from the home page, follow these steps:

1. **In the search box, type no more than a few keywords that describe the item you're looking for.**

   Refer to Figure 3-1 to see the search box.

2. **Click the Search button.**

   The results of your search appear on-screen in a matter of seconds.

You can type just about anything in this box and get some information. Say you're looking for *Star Trek* memorabilia. If so, you're not alone. The television show premiered on September 8, 1966, and even though it was cancelled in 1969 because of low ratings, *Star Trek* became one of the most successful science-fiction franchises in history. If you like *Star Trek* as much as many do, you can use the search box on the eBay home page to find all sorts of *Star Trek* stuff. We just ran a search and found 11,732 items — in hundreds of categories — with *Star Trek* in their titles (your results will probably vary).

Click the Advanced Search link to the right of the search box to narrow down your search. This link takes you to the Search: Find Items page, which the following section explains.

When you search for popular items at eBay (and a classic example is *Star Trek* memorabilia), you may get inundated with thousands of auctions that match your search criteria. Even if you're traveling at warp speed, you could spend hours checking each auction individually. ("Scotty, we need more power *now!*") If you're pressed for time like the rest of us, eBay has not-so-mysterious ways to narrow down your search so finding a specific item is much more manageable. Turn to Chapter 5 for insider techniques that can help you slim down those searches and beef up those results.

Going where the Advanced Search link takes you

One of the most important links on the eBay page is the Advanced Search link. When you click this link, you're whisked away to the Advanced Search page, which promptly presents you with three search options. Each option enables you to search for information in a different way. Here's how the search options on the left-hand menu can work for you:

- ✔ **Find items.** Search by keywords or item number. Type in the keywords that describe an item (for example, `Superman lunchbox` or `antique pocket watch`) and click Search, and you can see how many items with those keywords are available at eBay. The site gives you the option to search by one of the main categories — but to get the largest number of items, use All Categories and narrow your search from the results.

  Another handy way to search is by item number. Every item that's up for sale on eBay is assigned an item number, which is displayed to the right of the item name on the item's page. To find an item by number, just type the number in the box, click Search, and away you go. (To find out more about how individual sales pages work at eBay, spin through Chapter 6.)

  You can also find items by number if you type the item number into any of the small search boxes that appear on most eBay pages.

- ✔ **Sort your searches.** You can sort your searches in any of nine different ways. eBay makes it easy for you by allowing searches to be sorted according to when listings end, price, distance or country, best match, and category.

- ✔ **The Advanced Search link.** By clicking this link, you can define your search without using a bunch of code. It works pretty much the same as the Basic Search method, but you can exclude more features from your search. You can also take advantage of eBay's regional trading and find items for sale in your neighbourhood. Figure 3-5 shows the Advanced Search options. You can easily switch from the Basic Search to the Advanced Search by using the link near the bottom of the page.

The powers-that-be at eBay make an arbitrary search choice for you that you might want to change when using the Advanced Search engine. By default, the engine returns listings created on eBay's English and French sites (including eBay.com, eBay Canada, eBay UK, eBay France, eBay Australia, and more) that have been made available to Canada. To view the maximum number of returns for a search, you should select the Items Available To button, which increases the number of items to include all of those from eBay's worldwide sites that are available to Canada.

The Search By category filter is a snappy new search function that helps you figure out which subcategories have the item you want — or, if you want to sell, helps you decide where to list your item for sale. This filter produces a regular search in a selected category, but it also has a column on the left side of the page that lets you know which subcategories your item is listed in — and how many of that item are listed in each category.

Figure 3-5:
The Advanced Search page gives you many search options.

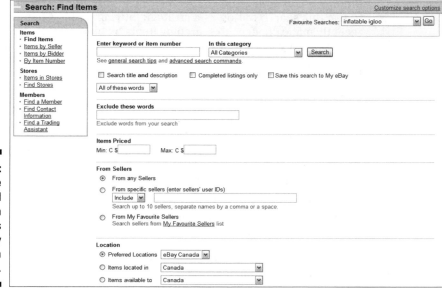

To find an item that sold at eBay in the past, indicate that you want to use the Completed Listings Only search. Type in the keywords of an item, and you get a list of items of this type that have been sold in the last 14 (or so) days, as well as at what price they sold. You can use this type of search to strategize your asking price before you put an item up for auction (or to determine how much you have to bid to win an item).

Although Chapter 5 tells you all you need to know about searching eBay, the following list explains some other searches that you can perform by clicking the appropriate link on the left side of the Advanced Search page. In a nutshell, here's what they do:

- **Items by Seller:** Every person at eBay has a personal User ID (the name you use to conduct transactions). Use an Items by Seller search if you like the merchandise from a seller's auctions and want to see everything the seller has for sale. Type the seller's User ID in the Enter Seller's User ID search box, and you get a list of every auction that person is running.

- **Items by Bidder:** For the sake of practicality and convenience, User IDs help eBay keep track of every move a user makes at eBay. If you want to see what a particular user (say, a fellow *Star Trek* fan) is bidding on, use the Items by Bidder search. Type a User ID in the Enter Bidder's User ID search box, and you get a list of almost everything that user is currently bidding on, as well as how much he or she is bidding. (We show you how to use this search option as a strategic buying tool in Chapter 6.) eBay recently made changes to searching items by bidder in an effort to protect bidder privacy. They now conceal some of the items that a person may have bought or is bidding on. We're not sure how concealing some of the items truly improves privacy, but, hey, it's their game.

- **Stores searches:** Here's something we bet you didn't know — when you use eBay's search engine, it searches eBay Stores for matching items, but only secondarily. (We think that's a bunch of malarkey — a search should report on available items from the entire site — but who are we?) If you search for your item by using the Items in Stores search, you see whether any matching items are available in eBay Stores (perhaps even at lower prices than the auctions).

  If you're looking for a particular eBay store, clicking the Find Stores link takes you to a search box that allows you to search for a store by name (or part of the name).

In addition to searching for items, you can also look for other eBay members or eBay Trading Assistants through the final three search links provided in the Members section. You can learn more about finding members in Chapter 5 and more about eBay's Trading Assistant program in Chapter 20.

Using eBay's Welcome Mat

eBay welcomes new users to its home page with a prominent welcome mat —
in the lower-right corner of the eBay Canada home page (www.ebay.ca), look
for the words New to eBay? Join Free. Clicking the Join Free button takes
you to eBay's registration page, one of the most important places on eBay.
(Of course, if you happen to be looking for a new welcome mat for you home,
you've come to the right Web site — generally, you can find around 130 of them
up for sale.) (We discuss how to register in Chapter 2.)

After you register as a member of the eBay site, you may not see the welcome
mat. It's not that eBay doesn't welcome you. It's just that eBay gives you new
information in the welcome mat's place when you're familiar with the site.

A Live Help button appears at the upper-right side of the home page. By
clicking this button, you can get into a direct conversation with an eBay
zcustomer-service representative who can answer any of your basic questions about the site. You can find out how Live Help works in Chapter 2.

Home Links, the Next Generation

If you look carefully, you can find several links on the home page that give
you express service to several key parts of the site. Here are the highlights:

- **Special Categories:** eBay provides a few links immediately below the
  regular Categories links that take you to specialized categories of items
  for sale. These categories include links to eBay Charity Auctions; eBay
  Pulse, where you can find out what's hot on eBay; and eBay Wholesale,
  where you can shop for bulk lots of products that are suitable for resale
  on the site.

- **Specialty Sites:** Clicking one of the links below this heading can get you
  to eBay's new specialty sites. Clicking the eBay Motors link brings you to
  cars.ebay.ca, an area dedicated to the sale of almost everything with
  a motor and wheels. The eBay Stores link (stores.ebay.ca) takes you
  to a separate area of eBay that's loaded with thousands of stores from
  eBay sellers — and eBay Stores are filled with items you can purchase
  without bidding. The PayPal link takes you to an overview of PayPal that
  includes links to register for eBay's favourite payment service. You can
  also find a link for Skype, eBay's great new way to communicate with
  buyers and sellers around the world. The most recently added new site is
  for StumbleUpon — eBay's newest acquisition that allows you to discover
  and share great Web sites from around the world. These links grow as
  eBay does and can take you to interesting places. Don't be afraid to click
  around and investigate.

✔ **Global Sites:** Select a country from the Shop Around the World drop-down menu and click the Go button to visit one of eBay's international auction sites. A quick and easy way to shop the world — just don't forget your translator.

You may notice that the graphic links on the home page change from day to day — even hour to hour. If you're interested in the featured areas of the site, visit this page several times a day to see the entire array of special happenings at eBay.

Manoeuvring through Categories

So how does eBay keep track of the millions of items that are up for sale at any given moment? The brilliant minds at eBay decided to group items into a nice, neat little storage system called *categories*. The home page lists most of the main categories, but currently eBay lists tens of thousands of subcategories — ranging from Antiques to Writing Instruments. And don't ask how many sub-subcategories (categories within categories within categories) eBay has — we can't count that high.

Well, okay, we *could* list all the categories, subcategories, and sub-subcategories currently available at eBay — if you wouldn't mind squinting at a dozen pages of really small, eye-burning text. But a category browse is an adventure that's unique for each individual, and we wouldn't think of depriving you of it. Suffice it to say that if you like to hunt around for that perfect something, you're in browsing heaven now.

To navigate around the categories, just follow these steps:

1. **Click the category that interests you, such as Books or DVDs & Movies.**

   You're transported to that category's hub page. The category's subcategories and sub-subcategories are listed on this page. Happy hunting!

   If you don't find a category that interests you among those on the home page, simply click the Buy button on the navigation bar, and you're off to the main categories page. Not only do you get a pretty impressive page of main categories and subcategories, but you also get a short list of featured auctions with links to them all.

   If you really and truly want to see a list of all the categories and subcategories, click the See All Categories link at the bottom of the main category page. Alternatively, you can go to `listings.ebay.ca/ListingCategoryList`.

2. **After the category page appears, find a subcategory that interests you. Click the subcategory link and keep digging through the sub-subcategories until you find what you want.**

   For example, if you're looking for items honouring your favourite television show, click the Entertainment Memorabilia category. The page that comes up includes the subcategories of that category. The Entertainment Memorabilia category has many links, including the Television Memorabilia subcategory. If you look under the TV Memorabilia subcategory head, you see links to various sub-subcategories that include Ads, Flyers, Clippings, Photos, Pins, Buttons, Posters, Press Kits, Props, Scripts, Wardrobe, and Other. At the bottom of that page, below the links, you can also find featured auctions that might currently be listed on the site. Click a link to see the listings for that sub-subcategory. Little *icons* (pictures) to the left of the listings tell you more about each item — whether it's pictured (pictured items have a gallery image or camera icon) and whether it's a new item (these items feature the sunrise icon). You can also click the tabs to isolate auctions only or Buy It Now items.

   By the way, we have a lot more to say about Featured Items in Chapter 10.

3. **When you find an item that interests you, click the item, and that item's full Auction page pops up on your screen.**

   Congratulations — you've just navigated through several million items to find that one TV collectible that caught your attention. (Forgive us while we both bid on that Lily Munster/Yvonne DeCarlo–signed picture.) You can instantly return to the home page by clicking its link at the top of the page (or return to the Listings page by repeatedly clicking the Back button at the top of your browser).

Near the bottom of every subcategory page, you can see a list of numbers. The numbers are page numbers, and you can use them to fast-forward through all the items in that subcategory. So, if you feel like browsing around Page 8, without going through eight pages individually, just click the number 8; you're presented with the items on that page (their listings, actually). Happy browsing!

If you're a bargain hunter by habit, you may find some pretty weird stuff while browsing the categories and subcategories of items at eBay — some of it supercheap and some of it (maybe) just cheap. (eBay even has a Weird Stuff category — no kidding!) Remember that (as with any marketplace) you're responsible for finding out as much as possible about an item before you buy — and definitely before you bid. So, if you're the type who sometimes can't resist a good deal, ask yourself what you plan to *do* with the pile of garbage you can get for 15 cents — and ask yourself *now,* before it arrives on your doorstep. Chapters 6 and 7 offer more information on savvy bidding.

Going Global

Back on the eBay Canada home page (www.ebay.ca), you can find links to eBay's international auction sites at the bottom of the page. You may enter eBay Argentina, Australia, Austria, Belgium, Brazil, China, France, Germany, Hong Kong, India, Ireland, Italy, Korea, Malaysia, Mexico, Netherlands, New Zealand, Philippines, Poland, Singapore, Spain, Sweden, Switzerland, Taiwan, United Kingdom, and (whew) United States. Click one of these links, and you jet off (virtually) to eBay sites in these countries. The international sites are in the countries' native languages. eBay France might be a good place to practice your third-year French — or maybe not! Remember that after you leave eBay Canada, you're subject to the contractual and privacy laws of the country you're visiting.

Using the Featured Items Links

Here at eBay, money talks pretty loudly. At the bottom of each category page, you see a list of the auctions eBay is featuring at the moment. eBay usually posts up to six Featured Items at any given time and rotates items throughout the day so that as many sellers as possible get a shot at being in the spotlight.

You can find everything — from Las Vegas vacations to Model-T Fords to diet products — as Featured Items. Featured Items aren't for mere mortals with small wallets. These items have been lifted to the exalted featured status because sellers shelled out some money to get them noticed. All you need to get your auction featured is $23.50, plus a second or two to click either Featured Plus! or Gallery Featured. Featured Plus! makes your listing stand out in the crowd when a buyer does a search by keyword or by category. Gallery Featured highlights your listing for all to see when bidders view the general picture Gallery. (See Chapter 10 if you have an item that all eyes must see.)

Bidding on Featured Items works the same way as bidding on regular items.

Featured Items are frequently some of the most expensive items sold on eBay. Sellers who put up high-priced items have been around the block a few times and often make it clear that they'll verify each bid on the item. That means if you place a bid on one of Jay Leno's autographed Harley-Davidsons (auctioned in 2005 to benefit tsunami relief and Hurricane Katrina relief), be prepared to get a phone call from the seller. The seller may ask you to prove that you can actually *pay* for the motorcycle. Nothing personal; it's strictly business.

Charities

Click the Charity Auctions link at the bottom of the Categories list, on the home page, and you're taken to a page with links to eBay Canada's approved list of charity fundraising auctions. Charity auctions are a great way for memorabilia collectors to find one-of-a-kind (and authentic) items. Winning bids contribute to programs that help charities. (Chapter 18 tells you more about what charity items you can bid on — and the good you can do with your chequebook.)

Promotion du Jour

The eBay community is constantly changing. To help you get into the swing of things right away, eBay provides a special box with links that take you right to the current word on the latest eBay special events. Frequently titled *Inside eBay Today,* it normally occupies a considerable space on the eBay home page and is where company promotions and special offers are to be found.

Even if the main promotion box doesn't appeal to you, usually you can find some interesting links dotted around the home page without a headline. You can find links to eBay's special promotions for the day (or is it the hour? — it can change as often as you can refresh the page).

You *can* get there from here — you can get a lot of places, in fact:

- A rotating list of special-interest links changes at least once a day. (Half the fun is getting a closer look at pages you haven't seen.)
- Special money-saving offers from third-party vendors can be a boon if you're on the lookout for a bargain.

Bottoming Out

At the very bottom of the home page is an unassuming group of links that provide more ways to get to some seriously handy pages. Here's a list of some important ones:

- **Feedback Forum:** This link takes you to one of the most important spots at eBay. The Feedback Forum is where you can find out whether you've forgotten to place feedback on a transaction. You can also place feedback and respond to feedback left for you — all in one friendly location.

✔ **Gift Certificates:** Send anyone an eBay gift certificate for any special occasion. You can print it out yourself, or eBay can send it to any e-mail address you provide. The gift certificate is good for any item on the site for the value you specify, ranging from US$5 to US$500, and you can pay for it immediately with PayPal. If the person you give the gift certificate to bids higher than the value of the gift certificate, he or she can make up the difference using another payment option.

✔ **PayPal:** This link takes you to the home page of PayPal, the eBay online payment service.

✔ **Affiliates:** If you have your own Web site and want to make a few bucks, click this link. If you sign up for the Affiliates Program and put a link to eBay on your Web page, eBay pays you between $10 and $35 (plus other bonuses) for any new user who signs up directly from your Web site.

✔ **Developers:** If you're a real techie and have a great idea for software or tools that can integrate with the eBay site, check out the Developers pages.

✔ **Currency Converter:** If you're wondering how far you can make your loonie stretch, visit this handy tool that converts the Canadian dollar into most worldwide currencies.

✔ **eBay Toolbar:** The eBay Toolbar is a great free tool that allows you instantaneous access from your computer desktop. The Toolbar allows you to quickly search the eBay site for items with a simple click. It also has an Account Guard feature that helps protect your eBay and PayPal passwords.

✔ **Kijiji Classifieds:** Kijiji (pronounced *key-gee-gee*) is a free, person-to-person local community classified site that's owned by eBay. You can use the site to post and find ads for electronics, furniture, jobs, cars, pets, services, housing, and much more. Best of all, it's free for both buyers and sellers. Currently, Kijiji is offered in 38 communities across Canada. In case you were wondering, Kijiji is the Swahili word for village.

✔ **About eBay:** Click this link to find out about eBay the company and to get its press releases, company overview, and stock information. You can also find out about eBay community activities and charities — and even apply for a job at eBay.

✔ **Announcements:** Visit the General Announcements board when you want to know about any late-breaking news.

✔ **Security Centre:** This link takes you to a page in which concerns about fraud and safety are addressed. It's such an important eBay tool that we dedicate an entire chapter to it. Before buying or selling, you may want to check out Chapter 16.

✓ **Policies:** Click this link to brush up on the site's policies and guidelines.

✓ **Site Map:** Another way to reach eBay's very handy road map of links.

✓ **Help:** A link to eBay's important question-resolving pages.

On eBay pages other than the home page, the links at the bottom of the page may frequently change. They often include fewer or more links so you can cruise the site quickly without necessarily having to use the navigation bar. The number of links is largely determined by eBay and is in relation to the nature of the particular page you're visiting.

Walter Harris
Memorial Library

Chapter 4

My Own Private eBay

*W*e know eBay is a sensitive, touchie-feelie kind of company because it gives all users plenty of personal space. Long preceding MySpace.com, eBay's My eBay page is your private listing of all your activities on eBay — sort of a "This Is Your eBay Life." We think it's the greatest organizational tool around, and we want to talk to somebody about getting one for organizing both of our lives outside of eBay.

In this chapter, you can find out how to use the My eBay page to keep tabs on what you're buying and selling, find out how much money you've spent, and add categories to your own personalized list so that you can get to any favourite eBay place with just a click of your mouse. You gain knowledge of the ins and outs of feedback — what it is; why it can give you that warm, fuzzy feeling; and how to manage it so all that cyber-positive reinforcement doesn't go to your head.

The My eBay page has become the hub for the zillions of features that eBay offers. As a beginner on the site, you'll be doing yourself a favour if you stick to the basics of the buying, selling, feedback, and account settings. eBay's offerings are fun, but they can do a heck of a job confusing you when you're just starting out. Ease into the extras slowly.

Walter Harris
Memorial Library

Getting to Your My eBay Page

Using your My eBay page makes keeping track of your eBay life a whole lot easier. And getting there is easy enough. After you enter eBay, sign in through the Sign In link (described in Chapter 3). After you sign in to eBay, you can access your My eBay page by clicking the My eBay link in the navigation bar (see Figure 4-1) at the top of almost every eBay page.

Figure 4-1: Click the My eBay link in the eBay navigation bar to access your My eBay page.

If you've forgotten your eBay User ID or password, click the Forgot Your User ID or Forgot Your Password link (each appears below the text box in which you enter the info). To get a reminder of your User ID, type your e-mail address in the Enter Email Address box (and the Re-enter Email Address box to confirm), click Continue, and eBay sends you an e-mail with your User ID. Your User ID appears in any search results, posts, or pages. To be given your password, you have to answer your secret question (the one you chose and supplied an answer to when you registered). If you don't remember the answer to your secret question, eBay will send you a password-reset e-mail after you input your correct contact information with telephone number.

After you click the My eBay link, you arrive at your My eBay Summary page. As you can see by Bill's absolutely busy Summary page in Figure 4-2, you can access just about anything you need right here. You can find some handy reminders on the center of this page. Useful buying and selling reminders also show up here. But when you're involved in a large number of eBay activities, these reminders may seem like the whining of a nagging spouse. Bottom line? These reminders help you keep your eBay life in control.

Look at the left side of the My eBay page. Under the My eBay Views heading, you can find many handy links. Actually, the links break the My eBay page into eight main link pages, in which you can view different areas of your eBay account: All Buying, All Selling (if you haven't sold anything as yet, this link reads Start Selling), Want It Now, My Messages, All Favourites, My Account, My Reviews & Guides, plus your Dispute Console. Table 4-1 gives you the scoop on these links.

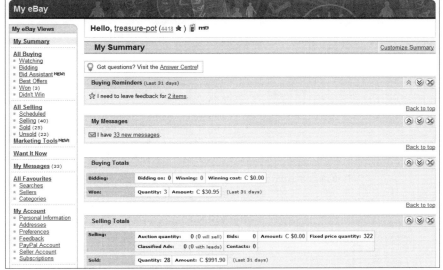

Figure 4-2:
Your My
eBay
summary
page is the
hub for your
eBay
activities.

Table 4-1	The Major My eBay Views Links
Click Here	**To See This on Your My eBay Page**
All Buying	Every listing that you're currently bidding on, have marked to watch, and made a Best Offer on, and the items you've won or didn't win.
All Selling	Every listing for items you're currently selling. Also, links to any listings you've scheduled to start at a later date, as well as links to your Picture Manager. Most importantly, you have links to lists of items you've sold (and not sold).
Want It Now	The status of items you've posted to the Want It Now area.
My Messages	Your My Messages area, eBay's private e-mail service for members. My Messages is the best and safest way to communicate with other eBay members.
All Favourites	Your collections of Favourite Searches, Favourite Sellers, and Favourite Categories.

(continued)

Table 4-1 *(continued)*

Click Here	To See This on Your My eBay Page
My Account	Your account settings. This area lets you select the activities for which you want eBay to remember your password so that you don't have to type it in every time (we like to have eBay remember our passwords when we're selling, bidding, managing items, and so on). It gives you the option to change your personal information on eBay. You can also see what you currently owe eBay, and it links to your PayPal account.
My Reviews & Guides	Reviews and guides you've written. After you get entrenched on eBay, you might want to review new media (such as books that you really like — hint, hint). You can write a review, à la Amazon's reviews. Also, if you're an expert, you can write an online guide to share your expertise with the world.
Dispute Console	If you're ever in a dispute with either a buyer or seller regarding a transaction, you can go to your Dispute Console and settle things.

At the bottom of each section, you can find important links to activities and information.

Don't confuse the My eBay page with the About Me page. The About Me page is a personal Web page that you can create to let the world know about you and your eBay dealings. (You don't have to have an About Me page if you don't want to — but they're free for the taking and fun to share.) We tell you how to get your own About Me page in Chapter 14.

Keeping Track of Your Personal Business

Your My eBay page has an area called My Account. (It's on the left side of the page with a lot of links below it.) If you click the link to My Account, you come to a summary page that has snippets of each topic covered in the My Account section. Alternatively, click the individual links below the My Account link on your My eBay page to go directly to the place you want to explore.

Houston, we don't have a problem

Here's an item we both wish we'd bought: a Neil Armstrong–signed official NASA portrait w/COA (Certificate of Authenticity). It was a very clean 8-x-10-inch color NASA portrait signed by Neil Armstrong, the first human on the moon. In recent years, Armstrong has been very reclusive, and his autographs are difficult to obtain in any form. Many forgeries and reproductions are being offered, so buyer beware. This portrait came with a lifetime COA. The starting price was $10, and the portrait sold on eBay in 1999 for $520!

Many believe that Neil Armstrong's autograph will be among the most important of the twentieth century. Just think about it. He was the first human to step onto another celestial body. This feat may never happen again. When Marsha updated the original *eBay For Dummies* (Wiley Publishing, Inc.) for the 3rd Edition, this same portrait was selling for $650. When she checked it out again while making revisions for the 4th Edition in 2004, the picture sold for $1,925. A quick scan on eBay today says that such a signed picture just closed at $2,025. Hindsight is a perfect 20/20, isn't it?

Checking your personal information

Two links relate to your personal information: Personal Information and Addresses. These links lead to places in which you keep your contact information updated. Initially, all this data comes from your registration. But it's policy on eBay that every user files his or her current contact information — so if you move or change phone numbers, e-mail addresses, or banks, you need to input that information here.

You can also change your User ID here (if you ever decide that *Charlie18907* doesn't really reflect your personality properly). Also, you can insert your instant messenger name here so that you can get IM alerts through Yahoo! Messenger, AIM, or whatever messenger program you use; add wireless numbers for auctions about which you want to be notified. You can also change your password and all your other registered information here.

On eBay, you can change your User ID at any time (every 30 days), and your feedback rating will follow.

Choosing your My eBay preferences

Because we live in a world where everyone has his or her own way of doing things, eBay allows you to set all kinds of preferences for your eBay account. One of the links you see under the My Account heading leads to the Preferences page. The Preferences settings are all very important to your eBay tasks. You have to decide which activities you want activated for your eBay account (you can always change these later). The most convenient thing to do is check all the options that make sense to you. The Notification Preferences you can set on the Preferences page are many:

- **Notification Delivery:** Let eBay know which method of notification works best for you. You can also indicate whether you want HTML or text-based e-mails.

- **Buying Notifications:** Be careful here. If you indicate that you want all this e-mail and you plan to be active on the site, prepare to be deluged. Select wisely! But remember, you can always make changes. You can get the following eBay notifications:

  - Watched items ending reminder
  - Watched item daily list
  - Watched items e-mails for relisted items
  - Bid confirmation
  - Outbid
  - Winning buyer
  - Non-winning bidder
  - Second Chance Offer
  - Personalized New Item Updates
  - Daily buying status
  - Want It Now reminder

  As you can see, you can get way too many notification e-mails, especially if you do a lot of buying and selling. For sanity's sake, narrow your selections to the minimum.

- **Selling Notifications:** If you're selling on the site, most of these notifications will be very useful to you. You can indicate you want to receive the following e-mails:

  - Notification that you've saved a draft on the Sell Your Item form
  - E-mail confirmation each time you list an item for sale
  - Yay! — the end-of-listing e-mail when your item has sold

- Boo — the e-mail you get when your item doesn't sell

- Notification when your buyer performs checkout

- Monthly e-mails with your eBay seller invoices

These notifications are all pretty important, especially when you're a new seller. When you become more active as a seller, you might want to whittle these down a bit — but not too much! Information is power!

✓ **Other Transactions and Notifications:** Again, up to you. These notifications can be overwhelming. eBay gives you the option to receive e-mails in the following areas:

- A daily status report of all your listings

- Reminders to leave feedback

- An alert when one of your feedbacks has been removed (you can find more on feedback in the section "Getting and Giving Feedback," later in this chapter)

Without going through everything else (we can see you're about to doze off), you can also opt into (or opt out of) eBay surveys, promotions, telephone updates, and direct postal mail (nowadays called snail mail) from eBay. Also (and this is very important), be sure you're signed up to receive any changes in eBay's legal arena. User Agreement changes and changes to the Privacy Policy are important when transacting business on the site.

Next on the Preferences hit parade are your *actual* selling preferences — how you want to conduct business on the site. These are settings for the more advanced seller. You can make most of these decisions on the Sell Your Item page. If you have time, though, click through each of the individual Show links to see the options and be sure the default settings work for you.

A recently added area is the Member to Member Communication Preferences that allows you to add a Skype link in your auctions. We talk more about the advantages of Skype in Chapter 18.

A setting you shouldn't ignore is in the General Preferences area. Indicate whether you want to stay continually signed in to eBay on your computer by checking or unchecking the box and clicking the Apply button. If you don't choose to stay signed in on your computer, you have to sign in every time you close your eBay window. Do *not* indicate that you want to remain signed in if your computer is shared by other people — you don't want others participating in your signed-in eBay activities!

When you finally get your My eBay page set up the way you like it, save yourself a lot of work and time by using your browser to bookmark your My eBay page as a favourite. Doing so saves you a lot of keystrokes later. If you want to send a shortcut to your desktop, in Internet Explorer, choose File➪Send➪ Shortcut to Desktop. With this shortcut in place, you can open your browser directly onto your My eBay page. Some eBay members make their My eBay page their browser home page so that their My eBay page appears the minute they open their browser. That's true dedication.

Your Feedback link

Below Preferences in the My Account link list is your Feedback link. In the Feedback area, you see all the items that need your feedback attention, and you can see the recent feedbacks that have been left for you. Save yourself a trip; you can more conveniently leave feedback from your All Selling or All Buying page.

Account links

Not surprisingly, the My Account link leads you to more links for your PayPal and eBay Seller accounts.

After you start selling, your Accounts pages become very powerful. Figure 4-3 shows you an example of the Seller Account section of a My eBay page. You can look up every detail of your account history, as well as make changes to your personal preferences (such as how and when you want to pay fees). Before you jump into the money game, you may want to review the links that eBay gives you to manage your money:

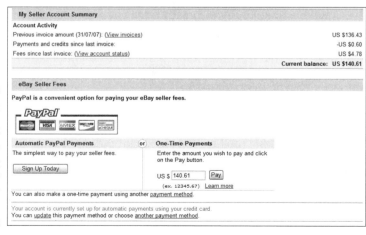

Figure 4-3: Manage your money in the Seller Account section of your My eBay page.

What's that thingy?

For the first 30 days after you register or change your User ID (which you can do anytime, as Chapter 2 explains), eBay gives you an icon that appears to the right of your User ID (it shows up when you bid, run an auction, or post a message on any of the chat boards).

So why the icon? eBay calls the graphic of a beaming robot-like critter the New ID icon. It's sort of a friendly heads-up to others that you're a new user. (If you've changed your User ID, the icon consists of two of the little guys with an arrow connecting them.) You still have all the privileges that everybody else has on eBay while you're breaking in your new identity. The icons are nothing personal, just business as usual.

✔ **View Account Status:** Click here to get a complete explanation of your eBay account — charges, credits, and your current balance (see Figure 4-4) since your last invoice.

✔ **View Invoice:** Click here to see your most recent invoice and details of the transactions.

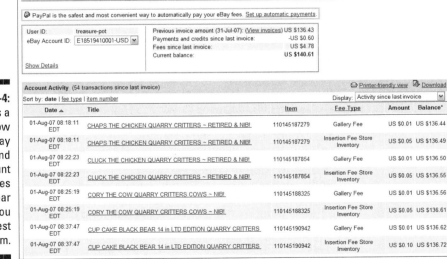

Figure 4-4: Here's a look at how eBay invoices and account statuses appear when you request them.

Account Status

PayPal is the safest and most convenient way to automatically pay your eBay fees. Set up automatic payments

User ID:	treasure-pot	Previous invoice amount (31-Jul-07): (View invoices)	US $136.43
eBay Account ID:	E18519410001-USD	Payments and credits since last invoice:	-US $0.60
		Fees since last invoice:	US $4.78
Show Details		Current balance:	US $140.61

Account Activity (54 transactions since last invoice) 🖨 Printer-friendly view Download

Sort by: **date** | fee type | item number Display: Activity since last invoice

Date ▲	Title	Item	Fee Type	Amount	Balance*
01-Aug-07 08:18:11 EDT	CHAPS THE CHICKEN QUARRY CRITTERS ~ RETIRED & NIB!	110145187279	Gallery Fee	US $0.01	US $136.44
01-Aug-07 08:18:11 EDT	CHAPS THE CHICKEN QUARRY CRITTERS ~ RETIRED & NIB!	110145187279	Insertion Fee Store Inventory	US $0.05	US $136.49
01-Aug-07 08:22:23 EDT	CLUCK THE CHICKEN QUARRY CRITTERS ~ RETIRED & NIB!	110145187854	Gallery Fee	US $0.01	US $136.50
01-Aug-07 08:22:23 EDT	CLUCK THE CHICKEN QUARRY CRITTERS ~ RETIRED & NIB!	110145187854	Insertion Fee Store Inventory	US $0.05	US $136.55
01-Aug-07 08:25:19 EDT	CORY THE COW QUARRY CRITTERS COWS ~ NIB!	110145188325	Gallery Fee	US $0.01	US $136.56
01-Aug-07 08:25:19 EDT	CORY THE COW QUARRY CRITTERS COWS ~ NIB!	110145188325	Insertion Fee Store Inventory	US $0.05	US $136.61
01-Aug-07 08:37:47 EDT	CUP CAKE BLACK BEAR 14 in LTD EDITION QUARRY CRITTERS	110145190942	Gallery Fee	US $0.01	US $136.62
01-Aug-07 08:37:47 EDT	CUP CAKE BLACK BEAR 14 in LTD EDITION QUARRY CRITTERS	110145190942	Insertion Fee Store Inventory	US $0.10	US $136.72

✔ **Make a One-Time Payment:** On a single-payment basis, you can pay with a cheque, money order, credit card, pre-authorized debit, or even from your PayPal account. Even though eBay welcomes Visa, you can also use American Express or MasterCard. You can also change credit cards here at any time. Every month, eBay charges your card for fees you incurred the previous month. You can see these charges on your credit card statement, as well as on your eBay account.

✔ **PayPal link:** A quick click here, and you're taken to the PayPal home page. Check out Chapter 6 for more on the PayPal payment service.

When you give eBay your credit card information, eBay attempts to authorize your card immediately. Your credit card company's response, either Declined or Approved, appears on your View Account Status page.

✔ **Payment Terms:** Although you need to post a credit card for ID purposes to sell at eBay, you can pay your eBay bill in one of four ways. You can change your method of payment at any time. See Table 4-2 to find out when the different payments are charged to your account. Here are your payment options:

• **Credit Card on File:** You can place your credit card on file with eBay so that, each month, eBay can place your selling charges on your credit card. We have both been using this option for years and we both find that it works out very well.

• **PayPal:** You can make single payments directly through your PayPal account. If you have a cash balance in your account, you can have it applied to your eBay bill; if you don't have a cash balance, you can pay the amount through the credit card you've registered on PayPal.

• **eBay Direct Pay:** This form of payment allows eBay to swoop into your personal checking account once a month and remove the money you owe. When you sign up for this option, your bank account is automatically debited on a predetermined day, based on your billing cycle. Neither of us are big fans of this payment type. We just don't like anyone removing funds from our bank accounts without personally authorizing the withdrawal each time.

• **Cheque or Money Order Payment:** This payment method can be a bit dodgy if you plan to do any volume of selling on eBay. Your payment must arrive at eBay on time. No kidding. eBay can charge you 1.5 percent interest a month on the unpaid balance or just suspend your account — not a pretty picture.

The downside of paying eBay fees by cheque or money order is that you're charged if you bounce a cheque or miss a payment. You might even be suspended if you fail to pay on time with any frequency. You're supposed to get an e-mail invoice at the end of the month, but even if you don't, eBay expects to be paid on time. A word to the wise: Keep close tabs on your account status if you choose to pay this way.

✔ **Make a One-Time Payment:** If you're about to hit your credit limit, or you don't want eBay making monthly charges on your credit card, you can make a one-time payment. Check out the eBay Seller Account area to make a one-time payment. To pay by cheque, you need an eBay payment coupon, which you can get by clicking the Mail in a Cheque or Money Order link, printing out the coupon page, and following the directions. If you want to make a one-time credit card payment, click the Pay with Your Credit Card link; or to write a virtual e-check from your bank account, click the Pre-Authorized Debit Payment link. In both scenarios you'll be taken to an SSL-secured area to type in your information. Click Submit, and the information is sent to eBay for processing. It's just that easy.

Table 4-2	eBay's Automatic Payments		
Billing Cycle	*Invoice*	*Deducted from Chequing Account*	*Credit Card Charged*
15th of month	Between 16th and 20th of month	5th of the following month	5–7 days after receipt of invoice
Last day of month	Between 1st and 5th of following month	20th of following month	5–7 days after receipt of invoice

Using the Dispute Console

If you sell an item and the buyer backs out (a rare but disheartening situation), you can at least get a refund on some of the fees that eBay charges you as a seller. These are the *Final Value Fees,* and they're based on the selling price of the item. In the Dispute Console, you can keep track of the disputes in progress and send or receive messages from the other party regarding payment.

Before you can collect a Final Value Fee refund, the following conditions must apply:

✔ After your listing is over, you have to allow buyers at least three business days to respond to you. If they don't respond, you can send them an e-mail politely reminding them of their commitment to buy.

✔ If at least seven days have elapsed since the end of the transaction and you have the feeling that you're not going to see your money, you *must* file an Unpaid Item Alert. After you file this notice, eBay sends the bidder an ominous e-mail (you are sent a copy) reminding him or her to complete the transaction.

You have up to 45 days from the end of the auction to file an Unpaid Item Alert — and you can't get a Final Value Fee credit without filing this alert.

✔ The following ten days after you file the Unpaid Item Alert are your "work out" period — the period in which you and the bidder hopefully complete your transaction. You can try to give the bidder a call or e-mail through the Dispute Console to resolve the situation during this time.

✔ After 10 days, but no more than 60 days, have elapsed since the end of the auction, you may file for a Final Value Fee credit.

If you've begun the process and filed for a Final Value Fee credit, but you manage to work things out with the buyer, eBay etiquette says you should have the Unpaid Item Alert removed from the buyer's account. Buyers with too many of these warnings can be suspended from using the eBay site. You can automatically file to have this alert removed through the Dispute Console.

Getting Your Favourites Area Together

Part of the fun of eBay is searching around for stuff that you'd never in a million years think of looking for. Wacky stuff aside, most eBay users spend their time hunting for specific items — say, Barbie dolls, designer dresses, plumbing supplies, or postcards. That's why eBay came up with the All Favourites area of your My eBay page. Whenever you view your My eBay All Favourites page, you see a list of your favourite searches, four of your favourite categories, and a list of your favourite sellers and eBay Stores. But because eBay isn't psychic, you have to tell it what you want listed.

Choosing your favourite categories

You can choose only four categories to be your favourites, and with more than 50,000 categories to choose from, you need to make your choices count. If you're having a hard time narrowing down your category picks, don't worry: Your choices aren't set in stone. You can change your Favourite Categories list whenever you want. (Chapter 3 offers details on eBay categories.)

To choose your favourite categories and list them on your My eBay Favourites page, follow these steps:

1. **Click the All Favourites: Categories link on your My eBay page.**

2. **Click the Add New Category link on the far right side of the screen.**

   A window appears that contains the major categories.

3. **In the window that appears, click the main category you want.**

   A new window will open to the right of your selection to automatically reflect more choices — or subcategories — based on the main category you select. Continue to refine your selection until you've selected the category, subcategory, sub-subcategory, and sub-sub-subcategory, as shown in Figure 4-5.

4. **After you make your choice, click Save This Category.**

   An acknowledgment that your changes have been made appears. Click the My eBay link at the top of the page to see your new favourite category.

5. **Repeat Step 2 through Step 4 for Favourites Category 2 through Category 4.**

   If you don't want to use all four choices, you don't have to.

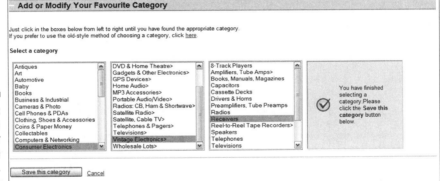

Figure 4-5: You can choose your favourite categories.

How specific you get when choosing your favourites depends on how many items you want to see. The narrower your focus, the fewer items you have to wade through. The more general your favourites, the broader the range of items you have to view. Just below each of your favourites are four options for screening your favourites. Which link you choose to view auctions depends on what kind of information you're looking for. Whether you're doing some preliminary searching on a category or monitoring the last few days (or minutes) of an auction, you can find a sorting link that best meets your needs.

Here's a list of the sorting options that will appear in each of your Favourite Categories areas and when to use them. You can also use these options to browse eBay categories when you're in a shopping mood:

- ✔ **All Active:** Shows you every item currently being auctioned in the category, with the newest items shown first. If you want to look at all the current auctions for a category, you end up with a gazillion pages of items awaiting sale for the following week in a particular category.

- ✔ **Starting Today:** Shows you every item that was put up for auction during the past 24 hours. The little rising sun icon to the right of the item tells you that the item was listed today.

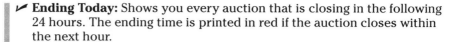

✔ **Ending Today:** Shows you every auction that is closing in the following 24 hours. The ending time is printed in red if the auction closes within the next hour.

If you're pressed for time, we suggest that you use the Starting Today link or the Ending Today link. Both links narrow down the number of listed auctions to a manageable number. For more information on narrowing down searches at eBay, see Chapter 5.

✔ **Ending Within Five Hours:** Shows you every auction that's ending in the following five hours, all the way down to the last few seconds. This link offers a great way to find items you can bid on down to the wire.

When you view auctions from the Ending Within Five Hours link, remember that eBay updates this page only every hour or so, so be sure to read the Auction End time. (Use the eBay time conversion chart on Bill's Web site, www.learningebayiseasy.com, to decipher time differences.) Because of this hourly update, sometimes the Ending Within Five Hours items actually *are* gone — the auctions have ended.

Your favourite searches and sellers

If you shop eBay anything like we do, you'll be looking for similar items and sellers over and over again. The My eBay Favourites area allows you to make note of your favourite searches and sellers. You can perform these searches and visit these stores with a click of your mouse.

Favourite searches

You have the opportunity to list a maximum of 100 searches on the page. When you want to repeat one of these searches, just click the Search name to search for the items. eBay will even e-mail you all 100 of your searches when new items are listed. (For more on that advanced function, check out Chapter 18.)

To add a search to your favourites, perform a search. (For details on how to perform a search, see Chapter 5.) When the search appears on your screen, click the Save This Search link that appears to the right of the number of items found, as shown in Figure 4-6.

The search is now transported to your My eBay Favourite Searches area for that particular search, as shown in Figure 4-7. If you want to be notified by e-mail when new items are listed, select the check box and choose from the drop-down menu the time frame in which you want to receive these e-mails. This is a great feature, particularly if the item you're searching for is hard to find and rarely appears on eBay. Instead of conducting frequent searches for that prized collectible, let eBay check on a daily basis and e-mail you if one is listed.

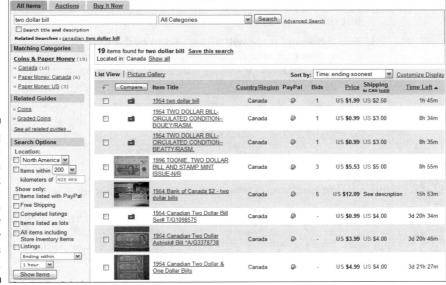

Figure 4-6:
Click the
Save This
Search link
to send a
search to
your My
eBay
Favourites
page.

Figure 4-7:
Adjust your
favourite
searches in
the Save as
Favourite
Search
page.

Favourite sellers

When you find a seller whose merchandise and prices are right up your alley, and you want to occasionally check out that seller's auctions, you can list the seller in the Favourite Sellers area. Just follow these steps:

1. **When you've shopped eBay and found a seller that you're happy with, make note of the seller's Store name or User ID.**

2. **Go to your My eBay Favourite Sellers area and click the Add New Seller or Store link.**

3. **Type in the seller's User ID or Store name, then click the Continue button.**

4. **The following page will allow you to add a note to yourself about this seller. You can also choose whether you want to receive e-mail notifications of new items listed by this seller from eBay or e-mail marketing campaigns that might be sent directly from the seller.**

The seller or store now appears in your My Favourite Sellers area. To view the seller's current auctions or visit his or her store, click the link to the right of the seller's name.

If you find a seller that you want to make a favourite while you're browsing or buying on the site, use the Add to Favourite Sellers link in the Seller Information box, which is shown on every eBay listing.

Got the time? eBay does. Click the eBay Official Time link, which is at the very bottom of virtually every eBay page (in small print). The eBay clock is so accurate that you can set your watch to it. And you may want to, especially if you want to place a last-second bid before an auction closes. After all, eBay's official time is, um, *official*.

All Sorts of Sorting: Keeping Track of Your Items

If you want to keep tabs on the items you're selling and bidding on (and why wouldn't you?), start thinking about how to sort them *before* you start looking for the first item you want to bid on. That's also pretty good advice for planning your first auction.

From the My eBay page, you can sort the items you're selling and bidding on several ways. That gives you a lot of options to think about, dwell on, and ponder. Each sorting method does pretty much the same thing, so pick the one that catches your eye and don't lose any sleep over your choice. After all, life's too short — and you can change how things are displayed on your My eBay page by clicking the option titles. (Wish the rest of life was like that?) Table 4-3 goes into more detail about sorting methods.

Table 4-3	Sorting Methods and What They Do
Sort By	*Does This*
Current Price	Lists items by their opening prices or by current high bid (only for items you're selling).

Sort By	Does This
High Bidder ID	Lists items by the User ID of your bidders; this sorting method lets you keep track of multiple-item buyers.
# of Watchers	Lists items according to how many eBay members have set your item to Watch in their My eBay Watching area.
Bids	Lists the popularity of items by the number of bids they've received.
# of Questions	Sorts the popularity of items by the number of questions eBay members have asked about them.
Time Left	Lists items by the time left in the sales period. You can choose to sort either by ascending or descending time remaining.
Format	Lists items based on the type of transaction (auctions, fixed-price items, and store items).

All auctions at eBay.ca are based on eastern daylight saving time or eastern standard time, depending on the time of year.

You can customize which details of transactions you want to show on your my eBay pages. Figure 4-8 shows the Options page that appears after clicking the Customize Display link at the top of the All Selling page. Select what you want to see on the page and then click the Save button, and you're set with your customized display!

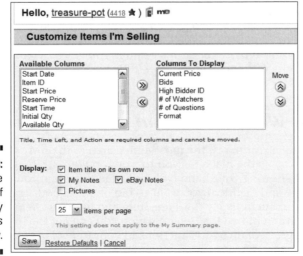

Figure 4-8:
Customize
the look of
your My
eBay pages
individually.

Following the Action on Your Bidding and Watching Pages

If you're like the two of us, you'll have the most fun at eBay when you're shopping. Shopping at eBay is exciting, and you can find a zillion great bargains. Fortunately, eBay gives us a place to keep all our shopping information together: the All Buying area.

Seeing the Items I'm Bidding On

When you bid on an item, eBay automatically lists the item in the Bidding area of your My eBay page. If you're winning the auction, the price appears in green; if you're losing, it appears in red. After the auction's over, the listing moves to Items I've Won (yay!) or Items I Didn't Win (boo!). You can watch the progress of the auction from here and see the number of bids on the item, the high bid, and how much time is left until the end of the auction. All this information can help you decide whether you want to jump back in and make a bid. eBay also keeps a total of all your active bids in the Bidding Totals area at the top of the Items I'm Bidding On page — which should hopefully help you stay within your spending limits.

Keeping track of Items I've Won

When you've won an auction or purchased an item in a store, it appears in the Items I've Won area. From here, you're supplied links to visit the auctions you have won to print out the auction page or double-check it. From the links in the Action column, you can also pay for your item through PayPal direct from here; if you've already paid, you can view the PayPal payment details. You can also click a Leave Feedback link — after you've received the item and are satisfied (or not) with your purchase — to leave feedback.

Sleuthing with Items I'm Watching

Items I'm Watching is, for many, the most active area of their My eBay page (see Figure 4-9). This is the place for you to work on your strategy for getting bargains without showing your hand by bidding. In this area, you can watch the auction evolve and decide if you want to bid on it. A good strategy might be to watch several auctions for the same item and monitor them as they develop. You can then bid on the one on which you can get the best deal. You can track the progress of up to 100 auctions in your Items I'm Watching area.

Moving auctions into this area is easy. When you find an item that you want to keep track of, look for the Watch This Item button, which is located just below the Item Location and bid history on the listing page. If you click this button, the item is transported to your Items I'm Watching area.

Figure 4-9:
Keep your eye on items by putting them in the Items I'm Watching area of your My eBay page.

Surveying Your Sales on Your My eBay Selling Page

Your My eBay page supplies you with the tools to keep track of items you're selling on eBay. The My eBay Selling page works very much the same as the Bidding page, but this time, you're making the money — not spending it! Your current auction sales are listed in the Items I'm Selling area. The items with bids on them appear in green, and the ones without bids (or where the reserve hasn't been met) are in red. At the bottom, you have a dollar total of the current bids on your auctions.

Items I'm Selling

Very much like the Items I'm Bidding On area of the All Buying section, the Items I'm Selling area keeps track of your ongoing auctions at eBay. You can observe the auction action in real time (or, at least, every time you refresh the page). You can see how many bids have been placed, when the auction closes, and the time left in the auction. If you want more information about what's going on, click the handy All Item Details link, which gives you a mini-version of each auction (without the description).

Items I've Sold

When the sale is final, the items go into the Items I've Sold area (shown in Figure 4-10). Here, you can keep track of the sale. You can check whether the buyer has paid with PayPal and what the transaction status is. If the buyer has completed checkout, you can get his or her information by clicking the Next Steps/Status link. If the buyer hasn't completed checkout, you can click the Send Invoice button to send the buyer an invoice. Very handy!

If you haven't heard from the buyer after three days (the prescribed eBay deadline for contact), you may need to resend your invoice or send another e-mail. See Chapter 12 for more information on post-sale correspondence.

After the transaction is complete (which means the item has arrived and the buyer is happy with his or her purchase), you can click the handy Leave Feedback link to leave feedback about the buyer.

You can also relist the item from a quick link or place a Second Chance Offer to an underbidder if you have more than one of the item. See the sidebar "Your secret seller tool — Second Chance!" in this chapter for more on the Second Chance feature.

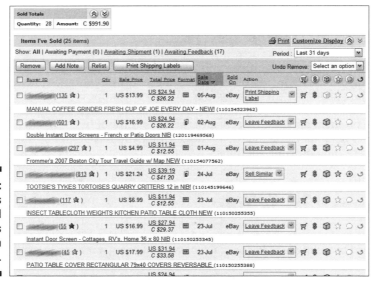

Figure 4-10: The Items I've Sold area gives you a bunch of options.

TIP

Your secret seller tool — Second Chance!

Those cagey great minds at eBay have come up with another great selling implement. Say that you have multiples of a single item (you *did* sell that set of Minton china one piece at a time, didn't you?) or the winning bidder backs out of the transaction without paying. Second Chance gives you the opportunity to offer the item to one of the underbidders (okay, the losers) at his or her high bid price. You can also create a Second Chance if you set a reserve that wasn't met before the auction ended. The Second Chance opportunity is available for up to 60 days after the sale ends.

You can offer the item to as many of the under-bidders as you have merchandise to cover, and you can make this personal offer good for one to seven days. The bidder receives an e-mail regarding the offer and can access it on the site through a special link. This listing is only visible to you and the bidder for the duration of the offer.

The best part of Second Chance is that eBay doesn't charge any additional listing fees for this feature, but you *are* charged the Final Value Fee if the bidder accepts your offer and makes the purchase.

eBay's Selling Manager/Selling Manager Pro

If you're at the point where you're selling bunches of items on eBay, you may want to subscribe to one of eBay's Selling Manager tools. These tools make your Selling area look completely different. The tools give you the opportunity to handle more sales in a compact and convenient design. See Chapter 20 for detailed information on Selling Manager.

Keeping Track of Your Transactions

Yes, we bug you about printing stuff out — not because we're in cahoots with the paper industry, but because we care. The eBay transaction process can be daunting, and beginners can easily lose track. The best way to protect yourself is to keep good records on your own. Don't depend on eBay to cover you — not that eBay doesn't care. This is your money, so keep a close eye on it.

Now, don't become a pack rat and overdo it. To help point you in the right direction, here's a list of important documents we think you should print and file, whether you're a buyer or a seller:

- ✔ Auction pages as they appear when they close
- ✔ Bank statements indicating any payment you receive that doesn't clear
- ✔ Insurance or escrow forms
- ✔ Refund and credit requests
- ✔ Receipts from purchases you make for items to sell on eBay

Always, always, *always* save every e-mail message you receive about a trans-action, whether you buy or sell. Also save your EOAs (End of Auction e-mails) that eBay sends you. For more information about EOAs and correspondence etiquette after the auction is over, see Chapter 8 and Chapter 12.

Why should you save all this stuff? Here are some reasons:

- ✔ Even if you're buying and selling just a couple of items a month on eBay, you need to keep track of who you owe and who owes you money.
- ✔ Good e-mail correspondence is an art, but if you reference item num-bers, your e-mail is an instant record. If you put your dates in writing — and follow up — you have a nice, neat paper trail.
- ✔ Documenting the transaction through e-mail can come in handy if you ever end up in a dispute over the terms of the sale.
- ✔ If you sell specialized items, you can keep track of trends and who your frequent buyers are.
- ✔ Someday, the taxman may come knocking on your door, especially if you buy stuff for the purpose of selling it on eBay. Scary, but true. For more on where you can get tax information, take a look at Chapter 9.

When it comes to keeping records and documents about transactions via e-mail, we say that after you've received your feedback (positive, of course), you can dump all those transaction materials. If you get negative feedback (how could you?), hang on to your paperwork for a little longer. Use your dis-cretion, but generally, you can toss the paperwork from a bad transaction after it has reached some sort of resolution. (You can find out more about feedback in the following section.)

Once a month, do a seller search on yourself and print out your latest eBay history. Chapter 5 tells you more about doing seller searches, organizing your searches, and starting files on items you want to track.

Getting and Giving Feedback

You know how they say you are what you eat? At eBay, you're only as good as your feedback says you are. Your feedback is made up of comments — good, neutral, or bad — that people leave about you (and you leave about others). In effect, people are commenting on your overall professionalism. (Even if you're an eBay hobbyist with no thought of using it professionally, a little businesslike courtesy can ease your transactions with everyone.) These comments are the basis for your eBay reputation.

At the time of writing, eBay is in the process of rolling out significant changes to the manner in which buyers can leave feedback for sellers. In addition to an overall rating of positive, neutral, or negative, Feedback v2.0 allows buyers to also rate sellers on the accuracy of the item description, communication, shipping time, and shipping and handling charges. These additional ratings are based on a one- to five-star rating, with five stars representing the highest rating. These ratings give buyers the opportunity to provide additional information about the transaction, but they don't count toward the seller's overall plus/minus scorecard. The transaction can be rated for these elements only after the buyer has left a general positive, neutral, or negative comment. Sellers can't view the detailed ratings left for them by buyers.

Because feedback is so important to your reputation on eBay, you don't want others leaving feedback or making bad transactions under your name. The only way to ensure this doesn't happen is to always keep your password a secret. If you suspect somebody may know your password, change it before that person has a chance to sign in as you and ruin your reputation. (For more on selecting and protecting your level of privacy, see Chapter 1 and Chapter 15.)

When you get your first feedback, the number that appears to the right of your User ID is your feedback rating, which follows you everywhere you go at eBay, even if you change your User ID or e-mail address. It sticks to you like glue. Click the number to the right of any User ID to get a complete look at that user's feedback profile. The thinking behind the feedback concept is that you wouldn't be caught dead in a store that has a lousy reputation, so why on Earth would you want to do business on the Internet with someone who has a lousy reputation?

You're not required to leave feedback, but because it's the benchmark by which all eBay users are judged (whether you're buying or selling), you should *always* leave feedback comments. Get in the frame of mind that every time you complete a transaction — the minute the package arrives safely at the buyer's address, if you're a seller, or an item you've bid on and won arrives, if you're a buyer — you should go to eBay and post your feedback.

Every time you get a positive comment from a user who hasn't commented on you before, you get a point. Every time you get a negative rating, this negative cancels out one of your positives. Neutral comments rate a zero — they have no impact either way. eBay even has what it calls the Star Chart, shown in Figure 4-11, which rewards those with good-and-getting-higher feedback ratings.

Figure 4-11:
The eBay feedback star ratings reward good eBay users.

Here's what the different stars mean:

Yellow Star (⭐) = 10 to 49 points

Blue Star (⭐) = 50 to 99 points

Turquoise Star (⭐) = 100 to 499 points

Purple Star (⭐) = 500 to 999 points

Red Star (⭐) = 1,000 to 4,999 points

Green Star (⭐) = 5,000 to 9,999 points

Yellow Shooting Star (🌠) = 10,000 to 24,999 points

Turquoise Shooting Star (🌠) = 25,000 to 49,999 points

Purple Shooting Star (🌠) = 50,000 to 99,999 points

Red Shooting Star (🌠) = 100,000 or higher

The flip side (or Dark Side to you *Star Wars* fans) of the star system is negative numbers. Negative comments deduct from your total of positive comments, thereby lowering the number beside your User ID. Here's an eBay riddle: When is more than one still one? Gotcha, huh? The answer is, when you get more than one feedback message from the same person. Confused? This should help: You can sell one person 100 different items, but even if the buyer gives you a glowing review 100 times, your feedback rating doesn't increase by 100. In this example, the other 99 feedback comments appear in your feedback profile, but your rating increases by only one. There's one other thing: Say you sell to the same eBay user twice. The user can give you positive feedback in one case and negative feedback in another case — neutralizing your feedback by netting you a 0 feedback rating from that person. eBay set up the system this way to keep things honest.

Just because a user may have a 750 feedback rating, it doesn't hurt to click the number after the user's name to double-check the person's eBay ID card. Even if someone has a total of 1,000 feedback messages, 250 of them *could* be negative. If you fail to check a seller's feedback, you could be the next one in four to have a bad experience.

You can get to your personal feedback profile page right from your My eBay page by clicking the number to the right of your User ID.

Feedback comes in three exciting flavours:

- ✔ **Positive feedback:** Someone once said, "All you have is your reputation." Reputation is what makes eBay function. If the transaction works well, you get positive feedback; whenever it's warranted, you should give that positive feedback right back.

- ✔ **Neutral feedback:** You can leave neutral feedback if you feel so-so about a specific transaction. It's the middle-of-the-road comment. You might want to leave neutral feedback if you bought an item that had a little more wear and tear on it than the seller indicated, but you still like it and want to keep it.

- ✔ **Negative feedback:** If there's a glitch (for instance, it takes six months to get your *Charlie's Angels* lunchbox, the seller substitutes a rusty thermos for the one you bid on, or you never get the item), you have the right — some would say *obligation* — to leave negative feedback.

How to get positive feedback

If you're selling, here's how to get a good reputation:

- ✔ Establish contact with the buyer (pronto!) after the auction ends (see Chapter 12).
- ✔ After you've received payment, send the item quickly (see Chapter 12).
- ✔ Make sure that your item is exactly the way you described it (see Chapter 10).
- ✔ Package the item well and ship it with care (see Chapter 12).
- ✔ React quickly and appropriately to problems — for example, if the item's lost or damaged in the mail, or the buyer is slow in paying (see Chapter 12).

If you're buying, try these good-rep tips:

- ✔ Send your payment fast (see Chapter 8).
- ✔ Keep in touch via e-mail with the seller (see Chapter 8).
- ✔ Work with the seller to resolve any problems in a courteous manner (see Chapters 8 and 12).

How to get negative feedback

If you're selling, here's what to do to tarnish your name, big time:

- ✔ Tell a major fib in the item description. (Defend truth, justice, and legitimate creative writing — see Chapter 10.)
- ✔ Take the money but "forget" to ship the item. (Who did you say you are? See Chapter 16.)
- ✔ Package the item poorly so that it ends up smashed, squashed, or vaporized during shipping. (To avoid this pathetic fate, see Chapter 12.)

If you're buying, here's how to make your status a serious mess:

- ✔ Bid on an item, win the auction, and never respond to the seller. (Remember your manners and see Chapter 6.)
- ✔ Send a personal check that bounces, and then never make good on the payment. (See Chapter 16 — and don't pass Go.)
- ✔ Ask the seller for a refund because you just don't like the item. (Remember how to play fair and see Chapter 8.)

The Feedback page

When you click the feedback number to the right of a member's User ID, you see all the tools you need to gauge the member. Think of your feedback profile as your eBay report card. Your goal is to get straight A's — in this case, all positive feedback. Unlike a real report card, you don't have to bring it home to be signed.

When someone clicks the feedback number to the right of your User ID, he or she sees the following information (see Figure 4-12):

- ✔ **Your User ID:** Your eBay nickname appears, followed by a number in parentheses — the net number of the positive feedback comments you've received, minus any negative feedback comments you may have gotten (but that wouldn't happen to you . . .). Here, anyone interested in looking can see the date you first signed up as a member of the eBay community. Beneath that is the country from which you're registered, your star rating (refer to Figure 4-11), and any icons leading to more areas related to you on eBay (such as your About Me page, which we talk about in Chapter 14). This area also notes whether you're a PowerSeller (see Chapter 20) and whether you have an eBay Store.

Extra, extra, read all about it!

Normally, we believe in the adage, "Keep your business private." But not when it comes to feedback. The default setting is for public viewing of your feedback. If you keep this default setting, everyone at eBay can read all about you.

If you want to make your feedback a private matter, you need to go to the Feedback Forum. Click the Feedback link under the My Account heading of the My eBay page, then click the Go to Feedback Forum link. On the Feedback Forum page, you need to click the Hide My Feedback link.

Hiding your feedback is a bad idea. You want people to know that you're trustworthy; being honest and upfront is the way to go. If you hide your feedback profile, people may suspect that you're covering up bad things. It's in your best interest to let the spotlight shine on your feedback history.

It's your reputation, your money, and your experience as an eBay member. Keep in mind that all three are always linked.

✔ **A Contact Member link:** eBay takes privacy seriously, so members should use this link only if they have serious eBay-related questions for you. All correspondence through this link is sent directly by eBay without revealing your e-mail address to the member trying to make contact.

✔ **A View Items for Sale link:** This link goes directly to a listing of all items you're offering for sale.

✔ **A View Seller's Store link:** Here's a quick link directly to your eBay Store (provided you have one, of course).

✔ **A More Options Link:** If a member hovers his or her mouse over this area, he or she is offered options to View ID History, Add to Favourite Sellers, View eBay My World, View Reviews and Guides, or View About Me Page.

✔ **Your Feedback Score:** This area sums up the positive, neutral, and negative feedback comments people have left for you.

✔ **Your Recent Feedback Ratings with a summary of the most recent comments:** This area is a scorecard of your feedback for the last 12 months. At the bottom of the feedback tote board is a summary of your bid retractions in the past six months — the times you've retracted bids during an auction.

✔ **Detailed Seller Ratings:** This section is devoted to information buyers have provided for sellers only. It's intended to help prospective bidders get a better picture of what transactions with the seller might be like.

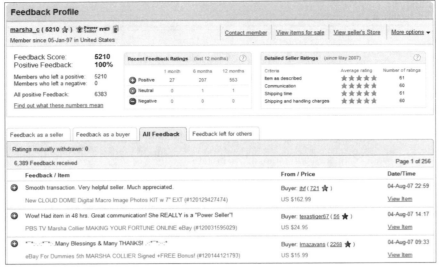

Figure 4-12:
Every eBay
member has
a Feedback
Profile.

Be careful when you retract a bid. All bids on eBay are binding, but under what eBay calls "exceptional circumstances," you may retract bids — very sparingly. Here are the circumstances in which it's okay to retract a bid:

- You've mistakenly put in the wrong bid amount — say, $100 rather than $10.

- The seller adds to his or her description after you've placed your bid, and the description considerably affects your opinion of the item.

- You can't contact the seller (your e-mail continuously bounces back and the phone number doesn't work).

You can't retract a bid just because you found the item cheaper elsewhere, you changed your mind, or you decided that you really can't afford the item. See Chapter 6 for more information on retracting bids.

Reading your feedback

Your eBay reputation is at the mercy of the one-liners that buyers and sellers leave for you in the form of feedback comments.

Each feedback box contains these reputation-building (or -trashing) ingredients:

✔ The feedback that the member left about you, followed by the item description. The description remains visible for approximately 90 days or while the item remains in the eBay system. With the introduction of Feedback v2.0, feedback comments older than five years are no longer visible.

✔ The User ID of the person who sent the feedback. The number in parentheses to the right of the person's name is his or her own feedback rating. The winning bid or purchase price also appears here.

✔ The date and time the feedback was posted and a direct link to the listing (if the listing is less that 90 days old).

Feedback bullets come in different colors: positive feedback is green with a plus mark, neutral feedback is grey with a white dot, and negative feedback is red with a minus mark.

You have the last word —
responding to feedback

After reading feedback you've received from others, you may feel compelled to respond. If the feedback is negative, you may want to defend yourself. If it's positive, you may want to say thank you.

To respond to feedback, follow these steps:

1. **Click the link to the Feedback section of your My eBay page, then click the Go to Feedback Forum link at the top of the Feedback page.**

   You're transported to the Feedback Forum, where you can follow up and reply to feedback comments left for you.

2. **Click the appropriate link, depending on whether you want to reply to feedback received or follow up on a reply to feedback left.**

3. **Find the feedback you want to respond to and click the Reply or Follow Up link.**

4. **Type your response into the space provided, then click Leave Reply or Leave Follow-up Comment.**

Don't confuse replying to feedback with leaving feedback. Replying to feedback doesn't change the feedback rating for you or the user who left the feedback; it merely adds a line below the feedback with your response to that feedback.

Leaving feedback with finesse

Writing feedback well takes some practice. It isn't a matter of saying things; it's a matter of saying *only the appropriate things.* Think carefully about what you want to say because after you submit feedback, it stays with the person for the duration of his or her eBay career. We think you should always leave feedback, especially at the end of a transaction, although doing so isn't mandatory. Think of leaving feedback as voting in an election: If you don't leave feedback, you can't complain about lousy service.

eBay says to make feedback "factual and emotionless." You won't go wrong if you comment on the details (either good or bad) of the transaction. If you have any questions about what eBay says about feedback, click the Feedback link on your My eBay page and then click the Go to Feedback Forum link.

In the Feedback Forum, you can perform six feedback-related tasks:

- ✔ **See feedback about an eBay user.**

- ✔ **Leave feedback for many auctions at the same time.** On your Leave Feedback page you see all pending feedback for all transactions within the past 90 days. You're presented with a page of all your transactions for which you haven't left feedback. Fill them in, one at a time, or with one click you can leave as many as 25 feedback comments at the same time.

- ✔ **View a Feedback Profile.** This provides a quick link to the Feedback Forum: Find Member page where you can enter a User ID and retrieve that user's feedback comments for review.

- ✔ **Review the feedback you've left for others.** You can also leave follow-up feedback after the initial feedback if situations change.

- ✔ **Make your feedback profile public or private.** Remember, if you make your feedback profile private, you may hinder your future business on eBay. See the sidebar "Extra, extra, read all about it!" in this chapter.

- ✔ **Review and respond to existing feedback about you.** If you feel that a trading partner hasn't accurately described your transaction, here is your chance to set the record straight.

In the real world (at least, in the modern North American version of it), anybody can sue anybody else for slander or libel; this fact holds true on the Internet, too. It's a good idea to be careful not to make any comments that could be libellous or slanderous. eBay isn't responsible for your actions, so if you're sued because of negative feedback (or anything else you've written), you're on your own. The best way to keep yourself safe is to stick to the facts and don't get personal.

Mincing words: The at-a-glance guide to keeping feedback short

eBay likes to keep things simple. If you want to compliment, complain, or take the middle road, you have to do it in 80 characters or less. That means your comment needs to be short and sweet (or short and sour if it's negative, or sweet and sour if you're mixing drinks or ordering Chinese food). If you have a lot to say but you're stumped about how to say it, here are a few examples for any occasion. String them together, or mix and match!

Positive feedback:

- ✓ Very professional
- ✓ Quick e-mail response
- ✓ Fast service
- ✓ A+++
- ✓ Good communication
- ✓ Exactly as described
- ✓ Highly recommended
- ✓ Smooth transaction

- ✓ Would deal with again
- ✓ An asset to eBay
- ✓ I'll be back!

Negative feedback:

- ✓ Never responded
- ✓ Never paid for item
- ✓ Check bounced, never made good
- ✓ Beware track record
- ✓ Not as described
- ✓ Watch out — you won't get paid

Neutral feedback:

- ✓ Slow to ship but item as described
- ✓ Item not as described but seller made good
- ✓ Paid w/MO (money order) after cheque bounced
- ✓ Poor communication but item came OK

If you're angry, take a breather *before* you type your complaints and click the Leave Comment button. If you're convinced that negative feedback is necessary, try a cooling-off period before you send comments. Wait an hour or a day, and then see whether you feel the same way. Nasty feedback based on emotion can make you look vindictive (even if what you're saying is true).

Safety tips for giving feedback

Study up on these safety features that you should know about feedback:

> ✓ **Feedback, whether good or bad, is *sticky*.** eBay won't remove your feedback comment if you change your mind later. Be sure of your facts and carefully consider what you want to say.

✔ **Before you leave feedback, see what other people had to say about that person.** See whether what you're thinking is in line with the comments others have left.

✔ **You can leave your feedback comment as long as the transaction remains visible.** Transactions usually are removed from general view 90 days after the end of the auction. After 90 days have passed, you must have the transaction number to leave feedback.

✔ **Your comment can be only a maximum of 80 letters long.** Eighty characters is really short when you have a lot to say. Before you start typing, organize your thoughts and use common abbreviations to save precious space.

✔ **Before posting negative feedback, try to resolve the problem by e-mail or telephone.** You may discover that your reaction to the transaction is based on a misunderstanding that can be easily resolved.

✔ **eBay users generally want to make each other happy, so use negative feedback only as a last resort.** See Chapter 8 and Chapter 10 for more details on how to avoid negative feedback.

If you do leave a negative comment that you later regret, you can't remove it. You can go back to follow up and leave an explanation or a more positive comment, but it won't change the initial feedback or rating, so think twice before you blast.

The ways to leave feedback

You can leave feedback comments in several ways:

✔ If you're on the user's Feedback page, click the Leave Feedback link; the Leave Feedback page appears.

✔ In the Items I've Won area of your My eBay page, click the Leave Feedback link to the right of the auction details.

✔ Go to the auction and click the Leave Feedback icon.

✔ In the Feedback Forum, click the Leave Feedback link to see a list of all your completed auctions from the last 90 days for which you haven't yet left feedback.

To leave feedback, follow these steps:

1. **Select a transaction for which you want to leave feedback by selecting the Positive, Neutral, or Negative radio button.** A box will appear where you can type your feedback comment. Choose your words carefully because eBay only allows you 80 characters.

2. **Continue to select transactions as in Step 1 above.** eBay allows you to submit up to 25 feedback comments at a time.

3. **Click the Leave Feedback button.** Remember, once submitted, eBay won't allow you to retract or edit your comments, so it's always a good idea to thoroughly review your comments before committing.

---

eBay will consider removing feedback if . . .

eBay generally takes a hands off approach to feedback comments left by members, but will consider removal for one of these very valid reasons:

✔ eBay is served with a court order stating that the feedback in question is slanderous, libellous, defamatory, or otherwise illegal. eBay will also accept a settlement agreement from a resolved lawsuit submitted by both attorneys and signed by both parties.

✔ Negative feedback can be expunged, when both parties agree that it was left in error, by filing for a Mutual Feedback Removal. Click the Feedback Disputes link on the Feedback Forum page.

✔ The feedback in question has no relation to eBay — such as comments about transactions outside of eBay or personal comments about users.

✔ The feedback contains a link to another page, picture, or JavaScript.

✔ The feedback is comprised of profane or vulgar language.

✔ The feedback contains any personal identifying information about a user.

✔ The feedback refers to any investigation, whether by eBay or a law-enforcement organization.

✔ The feedback is left by a user who supplied fraudulent information when registering at eBay.

✔ The feedback is left by a person who can be identified as a minor.

✔ The feedback is left by a user as a part of harassment.

✔ The feedback is intended for another user. eBay has to be informed of the situation, and the same feedback has to be left for the appropriate user.

Part II

Are You Buying What They're Selling?

The 5th Wave   By Rich Tennant

"Guess who found a Kiss merchandise blowout on eBay while you were gone?"

In this part . . .

After you have an idea how to get around the eBay site, you probably want to get started. You've come to the right place. In this part, you can find all the information you need to start bidding and winning auctions.

Although eBay is a lot more fun than school, you still have to do your homework. After you register to become an eBay member (which we explain in Part I), you can place a bid on any item you see. But first you have to find the item that's right for you . . . and then maybe find out what it's worth. And what happens when you win?!

In this part, we show you how to find the items you want without sifting through every single one of eBay's millions of auctions. We also give you an insider's look at determining the value of a collectible, determining how much you're willing to spend, and using the right strategy to win the item at just the right price. When the auction is over, follow our advice to make closing the deal go smooth as silk. Watch the positive feedback come pouring in!

Chapter 5

Seek and You Shall Find: Research

*P*icture all the stores you've ever seen in your life, located in one giant mall. You walk in and try to find the single item you're looking for. Yikes! Consider also walking into a store with thousands of aisles of shelves with tens of millions of items on them. Browsing the auction categories at eBay can be just as pleasantly boggling, without the prospect of sore feet. Start surfing around the site, and you instantly understand the size and scope of what's for sale there. You may feel overwhelmed at first, but the clever eBay folks have come up with a lot of ways to help you find exactly what you're looking for. As soon as you figure out how to find the items you want to bid on at eBay, you can protect your investment-to-be by making sure that what you find is actually what you seek.

Of course, you can search more easily if you have an idea of what you're looking for. In this chapter, for collectors, we offer first-time buyers some expert tips and tell you how to get expert advice from eBay and other sources. We also give you tips for using the eBay search engine from a buying perspective.

The best advice you can follow as you explore any free-market system is *caveat emptor* — let the buyer beware. Although nobody can guarantee that every one of your transactions will be perfect, you should research items thoroughly before you bid so that you don't lose too much of your hard-earned money — or too much sleep.

The ultimate family station wagon for sale

Need a lift? Drive in style in a 1977 Cadillac Fleetwood hearse. Only 91K miles! Fully loaded: V8, P/S, P/B, P/W. Gray & Black w/Black interior. Good engine, good brakes, five extra tires, and a stereo system. Buyer must pick up after check clears.

This hearse sold in 1999 at eBay for US$600. It seems the value of these old hearses just goes up. When updating this book for the third edition, Marsha found a 1971 Cadillac hearse, fully loaded, but with untold miles, selling for over US$2,500. For the fourth edition, in 2003, she found a gleaming 1972 Cadillac Superior Crown Sovereign hearse — with only 91,000 kilometres! Retired in 2002, this baby sold for US$7,400!

For the first Canadian edition, we found this amazing gem dating back to the '50s. Picture yourself rolling up to your favourite burger joint in a stunning 1957 Cadillac Landau hearse. Here are the listing details: Low Mileage (only 72K kilometres), Excellent Condition Inside & Out, newer 1986 Chevy 350 V-8 engine, and updated to include 4-speed automatic transmission, power steering, and power brakes. Repainted a 1992 Ford Lilac colour. This baby got bids as high as US$10,100. Nice car — sure would turn more heads than an SUV! Who'da thunk it? Maybe we should be selling hearses.

General Online Tips for Collectors

If you're just starting out on eBay, you probably like to shop and collect items that interest you. You'll find out pretty early in your eBay adventures that a lot of people online know as much about collecting as they do about bidding — and some are serious contenders.

How can you compete? Well, in addition to having a well-planned bidding strategy (which we cover in Chapter 7), knowing your stuff gives you a winning edge. We've gathered the opinions of two collecting experts to get the info you need about online collecting basics. (If you're already an expert collector but want some help finding that perfect something at eBay so you can get ready to bid, check out the section "Looking to Find an Item? Start Your eBay Search Engine," later in this chapter.) We also show you how one of those experts puts the information into practice, and we give you a crash course on how items for sale are (or should be) graded.

Although the tips from the experts in the following sections are targeted for collectors, much of the information is sound advice for those involved in any transaction online.

The experts speak out

John Snyder and Lisa Kennedy are a father and daughter team in the Waterloo Region of Ontario. They share a passion for collecting toys. John admits it started out just as a hobby more than 30 years ago, but it continued to grow as time passed. Lisa's interest developed by watching her father's hobby grow, eventually to become a substantial business. Although John has collected and sold many categories of toys over the years, Lisa, as many young girls have, developed a love of Barbie.

For several years, to earn some extra cash, John rented space at an Aberfoyle, Ontario, weekend flea market to sell parts of his collection. Lisa was, more often than not, right there at his side helping her dad with setup, sales, and tear-down. John gave Lisa her first vintage Barbie as a reward for her help at the flea market. That was all it took to get her hooked on collecting.

In 1999, John discovered eBay and began to buy and sell on the site routinely. Today, more than eight years later, John no longer rents space at the flea market, but he continues to sell all things related to toys and their collecting online. His eBay User ID, opa_sells_toys, has a positive feedback rating of more than 3,000. Lisa has also used eBay to grow her vintage Barbie collection over the years, with her User ID blonde1010_1. Although Lisa still has the collecting bug, she admits that she recently sold her large Barbie collection to help her new husband and herself finance the purchase of their first home. Lisa has now turned her attention to collecting Dollfie ball-jointed dolls. John and Lisa offer these tips to collectors new to eBay:

- ✔ **Get all the facts before you put your money down.** Study the description carefully. It's your job to analyze the description and make your bidding decisions accordingly. Find out whether all original parts are included and whether the item has any flaws. If the description says that the GI Joe figurine has a cracked back, e-mail the seller for more information on just how cracked Joe really is.

- ✔ **Don't get caught up in the emotional thrill of bidding.** First-time buyers (known as *Under-10s* or *newbies* because they have fewer than ten transactions under their belts) tend to bid wildly, using emotions rather than brains. If you're new to eBay, you can get burned if you bid just for the thrill of victory without thinking about what you're doing. John and Lisa both suggest that you put a watch on the listing and go back to it at a later time instead of immediately bidding.

We can't stress how important it is to determine an item's value, whether collectible or new. But because values are such flighty things (values depend on supply and demand, market trends, and all sorts of other variables), we recommend that you get a general idea of the item's value and use that ballpark figure to set a maximum amount of money you're willing to bid for that item. Then stick to your maximum and don't even think about bidding past it. If the bidding gets too hot, you can always find another auction. To find out more about bidding strategies, Chapter 7 is just the ticket.

✔ **Know what the item should cost.** Buyers used to depend on *price guides* — books on collectibles and their values — to help them bid. John and Lisa both think that price guides for eBay purchases are becoming a thing of the past because prices fluctuate so wildly based on availability of an item. Sure, you can find a guide that says an original *Lion King* Broadway poster in excellent condition has a book price of $150, but if you do a search at eBay, you'll see that those posters are actually selling for $65 to $75. Even though price guides can't help too much with eBay values, you may find the information about the production characteristics of collectibles in these guides invaluable.

When your search on eBay turns up what you're looking for, average out the current prices that you find. Also, check the completed listings. Looking over current and recent eBay auctions gives you a much better idea of what you need to spend than any price guide can.

✔ **Timing is everything, and being first costs.** If you're into movie posters, for example, consider this: If you can wait three to six months after a movie is released, you can get the poster for 40 to 50 percent less. The same goes for many new releases of collectibles. Sometimes, you're wiser to wait and save money.

✔ **Be careful of presell items.** Sometimes, you may run across vendors selling items that aren't in stock, which they promise to ship to you later. For example, before *Star Wars Episode I: The Phantom Menace* came out, some vendors ran auctions on movie posters they didn't have yet. If you bid and win on this sort of auction, and for some reason the vendor has a problem getting the poster, you're just out of luck. Don't bid on anything that can't be delivered as soon as you pay for the item. Learn more about eBay's presale rules in Chapter 10.

✔ **Being too late can also cost.** Many collectibles become more difficult to find as time goes by. Generally, as scarcity increases, so does desirability and value. Common sense tells you that if two original and identical collectibles are offered side by side, with one in like-new condition and the other in used condition, the like-new item will have the higher value.

✔ **Check out the seller.** Check the seller's feedback rating (the number in parentheses to the right of the person's User ID) before you buy. If the seller has a lot of feedback comments with only a minute number of negative ones, chances are good that he or she is a reputable seller. For more on feedback, check out Chapter 4.

✔ **Ask questions.** Some collectibles require a significant investment. Don't hesitate to contact the seller to ask for more information or additional pictures. A reliable seller will always try to accommodate your requests.

Although eBay forbids side deals, an unsuccessful bidder may (at his or her own risk) contact a seller after an auction is over to see if the seller has more of the item in stock. If the seller is an experienced eBay user (a high feedback rating is usually a tip-off) and is interested in the bidder's proposition, he or she may consider selling directly to a buyer. Suggest to the seller that if he or she puts the duplicate item up for sale on eBay, you'll purchase it immediately with a Buy-It-Now price. eBay strictly prohibits selling items off the site. If you conduct a side deal and are reported to eBay, you can be suspended. Not only that, but buyers who are ripped off by sellers in away-from-eBay transactions shouldn't look to eBay to bail them out. You're on your own. The eBay-legal way to purchase these items is by asking the seller to post another of the item for you — or if you were an underbidder in the auction, the seller can send you a Second Chance Offer. That way, you're also protected by the many eBay and PayPal buyer protections.

✔ **If an item you buy gets broken in the mail, contact the seller to work it out.** The best bet is to request shipping insurance (you have to pay for it) before the seller ships the item. But if you didn't ask for the item to be insured, it never hurts to ask for a discount (or a replacement item, if available) if you're not satisfied. Chapter 12 offers the lowdown on buying shipping insurance, and Chapter 16 provides pointers on dealing with transactions that go sour.

Go, Joe: Following an expert on the hunt

John looks for specific traits when he buys his very collectible GI Joe figures. Although his checklist is specific to the GI Joes from 1964 to 1969, the information here can help you determine your maximum bid on other collectibles (or whether an item is even *worth* bidding on) before an auction begins. As you can find out in Chapter 7, the more you know before you place a bid, the happier you're likely to be when you win. John's checklist can save you considerable hassle:

✔ **Find out the item's overall condition.** For GI Joe, look at the painted hair and eyebrows. Expect some wear, but overall, a collectible worth bidding on should look good.

✔ **Be sure the item's working parts are indeed working.** Many GI Joe action figures from this period have cracks on the legs and arms. But the joints should move, and any cracks shouldn't be so deep that the legs and arms fall apart easily. Serious collectors know that deep cracks are a sign of poor storage conditions over the years, and collectors will frequently avoid buying these figures.

✔ **Ask if the item has its original parts.** Because you can't really examine actual items in detail before buying, e-mail the seller with specific questions relating to original or replacement parts. Many GI Joe action figures are rebuilt from parts that aren't from 1964 to 1969. Sometimes, the figures even have two left or right hands or feet! If you make it clear to the seller before you buy that you want a toy with only original parts, you can make a good case for a refund if the item arrives rebuilt as the Six Million Dollar Man. Chapter 7 has plenty of tips on how to protect yourself before you bid, and Chapter 16 has tips on what to do if the deal goes bad.

✔ **Ask if the item has original accessories.** A GI Joe from 1964 to 1969 should have his original dog tags, boots, and uniform. If any of these items are missing, you have to pay around $25 to replace each missing item. If you're looking to bid on any other collectible, know in advance what accessories came as standard equipment with the item, or you may have to pay extra just to bring it back to its original version.

✔ **Know an item's value before you bid.** A 1964 to 1969 vintage GI Joe in decent shape, with all its parts, sells for $300 to $400 without its original box. (Mint-in-Box Joes can sell for thousands of dollars, and a GI Joe Nurse in excellent condition can fetch as much as $9,000.) If you're bidding on a GI Joe action figure at eBay, be aware that some unknowing eBay sellers may mistakenly offer a similar action figure as a genuine GI Joe. A series of figures that originated in the UK and are dubbed Action Man may fool the novice collector. All original GI Joe figures feature tags inside the clothing that indicate they're the genuine article. If you know the figure includes those tags and is within a realistic price range, you're okay. If you get the real item for less than $300, congratulations — you've nabbed a bargain.

✔ **If you have any questions, ask them *before* you bid.** Check collectors' guides, research similar auctions at eBay, and visit one of eBay's category chat rooms.

Making the grade

Welcome to our version of grade school (without the bad lunch). One of the keys to establishing value is knowing an item's condition, typically referred to as an item's *grade*. Table 5-1 lists the most common grading categories that collectors use. The information in this table is used with permission from (and appreciation to) Lee Bernstein, a columnist and collectibles dealer who operates Lee Bernstein Books and Collectibles from her home base in Schererville, Indiana, and who authors a monthly column for the *New England Antiques Journal*.

Table 5-1	Collectibles Grading Categories	
Category (Also Known As)	*Description*	*Example*
Mint (M, Fine, Mint-In-Box [MIB], 10)	A never-used collectible in perfect condition with complete packaging (including instructions, original attachments, tags, and so on), identical to how it appeared on the shelf in the original box.	Grandma got a soup tureen as a wedding present, never opened it, and stuck it in her closet for the next 50 years.
Near Mint (NM, Near Fine, Like-New, 9)	The collectible is perfect but no longer has the original packaging, or the original packaging is less than perfect. Possibly used but must appear to be new.	Grandma used the soup tureen on her 25th anniversary, washed it gently, and then put it back in the closet.
Excellent (EX, 8)	Used, but barely. Excellent is just a small step under Near Mint, and many sellers mistakenly interchange the two, but "excellent" can have very minor signs of wear. The wear must be a normal, desirable part of aging or so minor that it's barely noticeable and visible only upon close inspection. Wear or minor, normal factory flaws should be noted. (*Factory flaws* are small blemishes common at the time of manufacture — a tiny air bubble under paint, for example.)	Grandma liked to ring in the New Year with a cup of soup for everyone.
Very Good (VG, 7)	Looks very good but has defects, such as a minor chip or light color fading.	If you weren't looking for it, you might miss that Grandma's tureen survived the '64 earthquake, as well as Uncle Bob's infamous ladle episode.

(continued)

Table 5-1 *(continued)*		
Category (Also Known As)	*Description*	*Example*
Good (G, 6)	Used with defects. More than a small amount of color loss, chips, cracks, tears, dents, abrasions, missing parts, and so on.	Grandma had the ladies in the neighbourhood over for soup and bingo every month.
Poor (P or G-, 5)	Barely collectible, if at all. Severe damage or heavy use. Beyond repair.	Grandma ran a soup kitchen.

Grading is very subjective. Mint to one person may be Very Good to another. Always ask a seller to define the meaning of the terms he or she uses. Also, be aware that many amateur sellers may not really know the different definitions of grading and may arbitrarily add Mint or Excellent to their item descriptions.

Finding More Research Information

Hey, the experts have been buying, selling, and trading collectible items for years. But just because you're new to eBay doesn't mean you have to be a newbie for decades before you can start bartering with the collecting gods. We wouldn't leave you in the cold like that — and neither would eBay. You can get information on items you're interested in, as well as good collecting tips, right at the eBay Web site. Visit the Category Specific Discussion Boards in the Community area of the eBay.com site. You can also search the rest of the Web or go the old-fashioned route and check the library (yes, libraries are still around).

Keep in mind that every item truly has several prices. The retail (or manufacturer's suggested retail price — MSRP) price, the book value, the *secondary market price* (the price charged by resellers when an item is unavailable on the primary retail market), and the eBay selling price. The only way to ascertain the price an item will go for on eBay is to research completed auctions. In the section "eBay's Advanced Search" later in this chapter, we give you the skinny on how to research a completed auction.

Searching sites online

If you don't find the information you need at eBay, don't go ballistic — just go elsewhere. Even a site as vast as eBay doesn't have a monopoly on information.

Getting professional info from Marketplace Research

If you become an eBay fanatic someday, you may find yourself praising the genius of an amazing service offered by eBay. Marketplace Research allows you to research pricing further back than the 14 days of completed listings that the normal eBay search allows. If you come across a special or very old item, and not many are currently for sale on the site, you can use this tool to find out how much the item has sold for in the past couple of months. You can find Marketplace Research at `pages.ebay.ca/ marketplace_research/index.html`.

As with most of eBay's special features, you have to pay an extra charge to use the service. But the price is right, and you have to pay for the service only as long as you need it. eBay prices it as follows: A FastPass (good for two days) is $2.99; a monthly subscription costs $9.99 per month; and for extended history, you can get the pro version for $24.99. The main difference between the basic version and the pro version is that basic users can access up to 60 days of historical data, and pro users can access to up 90 days of historical data. In our (not so) humble opinion, 90 days is an eternity in Internet time — what sold well three months ago may be worth bupkis now. You can search for a lot of items by using the two-day, $2.99 FastPass version. That's the one we recommend.

The Internet is filled with Web sites and Internet auction sites that can give you price comparisons and information about cyberclubs.

Your home computer can connect to powerful outside servers (really big computers on the Internet) that have their own fast-searching systems called *search engines*. Remember, if something is out there and you need it, you can find it right from your home PC in just a matter of seconds. Here are the addresses of some of the Web's most highly regarded search engines or multi-search-engine sites:

- ✔ **AltaVista:** `ca.altavista.com`
- ✔ **Dogpile:** `www.dogpile.com`
- ✔ **Lycos:** `www.lycos.ca`
- ✔ **Google:** `www.google.ca`
- ✔ **Yahoo!:** `ca.yahoo.com`

The basic process for getting information from an Internet search engine is pretty simple. Just follow these steps:

1. **Type the address of the search-engine site in the Address box of your Web browser and press Enter on your keyboard.**

   You're taken to the search engine's home page.

2. **In the text box to the left of the button labelled Search (or something similar), type a few words indicating what interests you.**

Be specific when typing in search text. The more precise your entry, the better your chances of finding what you want. Look for tips, an advanced search option, or help pages on your search engine of choice for more information about how to narrow your search.

3. **Click the Search (or similar) button or press Enter on your keyboard.**

The search engine presents you with a list of how many Internet pages have the requested information. The list includes brief descriptions and links to the first group of pages. You can find links to additional listings at the bottom of the search results page if your search finds more listings than can fit on one page (and if you type in something popular in Step 2, such as Harry Potter, don't be surprised if you get millions of hits).

Always approach information on the Web with caution. Not everyone is the expert he or she wants to be. Your best bet is to get a lot of different opinions and then boil 'em down to what makes sense to you. And remember — *caveat emptor.* (Is there an echo in here?)

Many people throughout North America now buy cars on eBay. (Could it be because cars are so expensive? Maybe.) If you're researching prices to buy a car on eBay, look in your local newspaper to get a good idea of prices in your community. Several good sites exist on the Internet, but one of the very best Canadian sites is www.autotrader.ca. These folks have been putting those small AutoTrader magazines in your local convenience stores for years. You can now use their Web site as a very valuable research tool to determine local vehicle prices.

Finding other sources of information

If you're interested in collecting a particular item, you can get a lot of insider collecting information without digging too deep:

- ✔ **Go to other places at eBay.** eBay's chat rooms and message boards (covered in detail in Chapter 17) are full of insider info. The eBay community is always willing to educate a newbie.

- ✔ **Go to the library.** Books and magazines are great sources of info. At least one book or one magazine probably specializes in your chosen item. For example, if old furniture is your thing, *Antiquing For Dummies,* by Ron Zoglin and Deborah Shouse (Wiley Publishing, Inc.), can clue you in to what antiques collectors look for.

If you find an interesting specialty magazine at the library, try entering the title in your Internet search engine of choice. You may just find that the magazine has also gone paperless: You can read it online.

✔ **Go to someone else in the know.** Friends, clubs, and organizations in your area can give you a lot of info. Ask your local antiques dealer about clubs you can join and see how much info you end up with.

Looking to Find an Item? Start Your eBay Search Engine

The best part about shopping on eBay is that, aside from collectibles, you can find just about everything — from that esoteric lithium battery to new designer dresses (with matching shoes) to pneumatic jackhammers. New or used, it's all here — if you can find it hiding in the (get this!) 6 million new daily listings. (According to eBay, 100 million listings are on the site worldwide at any given time. That's a lot of gavels being banged!)

Finding the nuggets (deals) can be like searching for the proverbial needle in the haystack. The search secrets in this chapter can put you head and shoulders above your competition for the deals.

eBay has a lot of cool ways for you to search for items (sample 'em in Chapter 3). Although eBay allows you to search by item number, you saw what we said a couple of paragraphs back about the number of active listings. Some days, we can't remember our own phone numbers, let alone a 12-digit item number (and you can so easily write them down incorrectly). Those numbers are only going to get longer and longer as eBay continues to grow in popularity. Four main options are the most useful for researching:

✔ Find Items (by keyword or item number)

✔ Items by Seller

✔ Items by Bidder

✔ Items in eBay Stores

You can access the four search options by clicking the Advanced Search link to the right of the Search box at the top of any eBay page. Each search option can provide a different piece of information to help you find the right item from the right seller at the right price.

If you plan to repeat specific eBay searches, we recommend that you conduct searches often by saving them in your My eBay Favourite Searches area (see Chapter 18 to find out how). And when you find a particularly juicy item or subcategory, bookmark it. If it's an item, you can click Watch This Item (a link on the auction page just below the item number) or use your My eBay page for a summary of all of your watched items. (See Chapter 18 for more on eBay's personal shopper.)

Using the eBay Search page

When you click the Advanced Search link to the right of the Search box, the Search page appears. This page offers, by default, the most basic of searches (with only a few options), and you'll likely be using this one the most. To get the really advanced features, you must click the Advanced Search link at the bottom of the page. Once you've selected the Advanced Search page with more options, it will become your default choice.

When you use any of the Search options on eBay, the search engine will look for every listing (auction or fixed-price) that has the words you're looking for in the title or the description (you have to specifically include a search in the description by selecting that option). The *title* (as you may expect) is just another word or group of words describing what you call the item. For example, if you're looking for an antique sterling iced-tea spoon, just type `sterling iced tea spoon` into the Search text box (see Figure 5-1). If someone is selling a sterling iced-tea spoon and used exactly those words in his or her title or description, you're in Fat City.

Before you click the Search button, narrow down your search further. When you type in your search title, you have the option of choosing how you want the search engine to interpret your search entry. You can have the search engine search the title and description for

- All the words you type
- Any of the words you type
- The exact phrase in the order you've written it
- The exact match of the words you type

When you're familiar with the tricks listed in the section "Narrowing down your eBay search" later in this chapter, you'll be able to get most of these fancy Search results from one of the many search boxes you see littered around the eBay site.

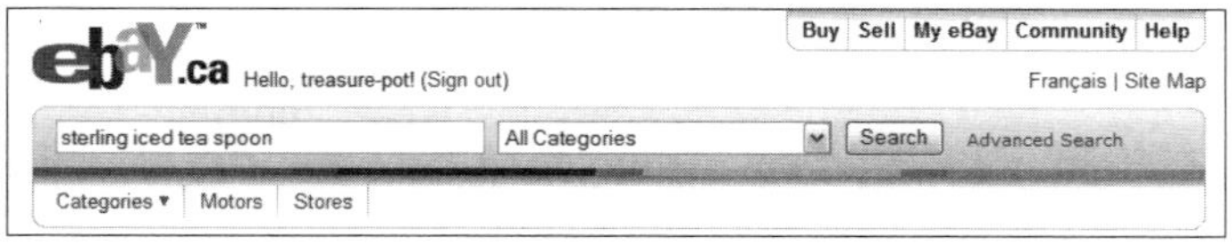

Figure 5-1:
Use the
Search
box to find
sterling
iced-tea
spoons.

| | | Buy | Sell | My eBay | Community | Help |

eb**Y**.ca   Hello, treasure-pot! (Sign out)   Français | Site Map

| sterling iced tea spoon | All Categories | ▼ | Search | Advanced Search |

Categories ▼ | Motors | Stores

In addition, you can find other useful criteria on the advanced version of the Advanced Search page:

- ✔ **Search title and description:** You can get more hits on your search if you select the Search titles and descriptions check box, but you may also get too many items that are out of your search range. See the section "Narrowing down your eBay search," later in this chapter, for some solid advice.

- ✔ **In this category:** Use this option if you want to limit your search to a particular main (or *top-level*) category, for example, instead of searching all eBay categories.

- ✔ **Completed listings only:** This option will return results from completed listings for the previous 14 days and is a valuable tool to be used to determine the eBay market value for an item.

- ✔ **Exclude these words:** If you want to find a sterling iced-tea spoon, but you don't want it to be plated silver, enter the word `plated` in the Exclude These Words text box.

- ✔ **Items priced:** Type in the price range you're looking for in the Items Priced section, and eBay searches the specific range between that low and high price. If money is no object, leave these boxes blank. If you don't want to spend more than $25 for your spoon, you can indicate that you want your search to ignore any items above that price by entering `25` in the Max box.

Testing, testing . . . How long does a search take at eBay?

Having a massive search engine is a matter of necessity at eBay — millions of items are up for auction at any given time — and often, an easy, fast search makes all the difference between winning an item and not winning an item. After all, time is money, and eBay members tend to be movers and shakers who don't like standing still.

So how long do searches really take at eBay? We decided to put it to the test. In the Search window of the eBay Canada Advanced Search page, we typed **Montreal Olympics Coin Set** in the Enter Keyword or Item Number text box,

selected Worldwide from the Preferred Locations drop-down list, and let 'er rip.

The search engine went through about 100 million general items and Montreal Olympics items (it found a grand total of 11 Montreal Olympics items), and, in less than three seconds, returned three listings that matched our specific keywords. (Now, if the wizards at eBay could only figure out a way to find that sock that always escapes from clothes dryers, they'd really be on to something.)

- ✔ **From sellers:** You can exclude (or include) particular sellers in the From Sellers section. If you want, you can search only sellers from your Favourite Sellers list (but why limit yourself?).

- ✔ **Location:** You can narrow your search to Canada only, North America, or worldwide.

- ✔ **Items near me:** Depending on your item, this search criteria can help weed out the most esoteric items. If you're looking for hefty items (such as an elliptical exercise machine that'll probably end up as a place to hang clothes) that would cost much too much to ship, you can specify how many kilometres from your postal code (or any postal code) you'll allow the search to extend. You can also choose a popular city if you happen to live in or near one of them.

- ✔ **Currency:** If you want, you can use this option to limit your search auctions offered in a specific currency. Selecting Canadian dollars will serve to exclude listings from most international sellers.

- ✔ **Multiple Item Listings:** If you are looking to buy a quantity of an item, be sure to make your choices here. Many eBay sellers use the "lots" search function to find items to sell on eBay.

- ✔ **Show Only:** You can really start to narrow your search results by making some selections here. You can choose to narrow your results to auctions or listings with a Buy it Now price. You can also choose to search for eBay Stores listings or exclude them entirely. If you are looking for real estate, you could limit your search to Classified Ads. You may decide you want to restrict your search to items that accept PayPal or that offer free shipping. Finally, you may decide that you want to limit your searches to auctions that are ending within a certain time frame. If that's the case, be sure to make a selection from the drop-down box.

- ✔ **Number of Bids:** Make selections here if you're looking for limited or minimum competition for an item.

- ✔ **Affiliate Tracking Information:** If you want your search criteria to generate an RSS feed, be certain to select your feed provider.

- ✔ **Sort By:** If you select Time: Ending Soonest from the Sort By drop-down list, the search engine gives you the results so that auctions closing soon appear first on the list. Selecting Time: Newly Listed lists all the newly listed auctions. Selecting Price: Lowest First or Price: Highest First lists the auctions just that way.

Okay, *now* click the Search button (see Figure 5-2). In a few seconds, you see the fruits of all the work you've been doing. (Wow, you're not even perspiring.)

If you feel that you really need even more search criteria, just click on the Customize Search Options link in the upper-right corner of the Advanced Search page. Even more options are available to allow you to fine tune your searches for the exact item and auction terms you're looking for.

You may notice that eBay has some Related Searches hyperlinks listed below the Search box on your Results page. Be sure to click the links because eBay's search functions can often be a bit temperamental — and you don't want to miss any great deals.

You often see pictures, or *icons,* to the left of item listings. A yellow rising sun picture means the listing is brand new (this icon stays on for the first 24 hours an item is listed), and a small camera means the seller has included a digital picture along with the item description; if you see a little picture, the seller chose to use the Gallery.

If you ever see a mysterious icon in a listing (eBay makes up new icons from time to time), just click the picture with your mouse. A help page appears, which describes the icon's meaning.

An easy way to keep track of an auction you're interested in is to click the Watch This Item link at the top-right of the auction page. The auction is then listed on your My eBay Items I'm Watching page, and you can keep your eyes on the action.

On the left side of the results page, you can find a list of categories that your search term is listed under, which is a great reference. To the right of each category, a number in parentheses tells you how many times your search item appears in that category. Figure 5-3 shows a sample of the category spread. To view the items appearing only in a particular category, click that category (or subcategory) title.

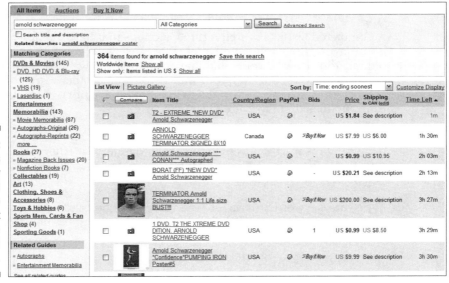

Figure 5-2: Use eBay's handy Related Searches to ferret out even more related listings.

Figure 5-3:
Search
results by all
categories
returns a
large
number of
listings.

eBay's Advanced Search

The Advanced Search page of the search area throws quite a few more options into the package. Don't be intimidated by this area; you need to understand just a few important bells and whistles.

A Completed Listings search

A Completed Listings search returns auctions that have already ended. This is our favourite search option at eBay because you can use it as a strategic bidding tool. How? If you're bidding on an item and want to know if the prices are likely to go too high for your wallet, you can use this search option to compare the current price of the item to the selling price of similar items from auctions that have already ended.

You can also use this tool if you want to sell an item and are trying to determine what it's worth, how high the demand is, and whether this is the right time to list the item. (Chapter 10 offers the nuts, bolts, and monkey wrenches you need to set up your auction.)

Type your keyword criteria into the Search text box and scroll down the page to the Completed Listings Only box. Follow these steps to do a Completed Listings Only search:

1. **In the title search field, type the title name or the keywords of the item you want to find.**

2. **Select the Completed Listings Only check box to see completed listings as far back as the eBay search engine will permit.**

   Currently, you can go back about two weeks.

3. **Tell eBay how you want the results arranged.**

   In the Sort By drop-down list, choose one of the available nine options. Some of the more popular options are:

   - **Items Ending First:** Include completed auctions starting with the oldest available (about two weeks).

   - **Newly Listed:** List the most recently completed auctions first.

   - **Lowest Prices First:** List auctions from the lowest price attained to the highest price paid for an item.

   - **Highest Prices First:** List completed items from highest to lowest. (This is a very useful option when you're searching for a 1967 Camaro, and you want to buy a car, not a Hot Wheels toy.)

4. **Click Search.**

   The search results appear in just a few seconds.

An alternate way to find completed items is to run a current auction search from any of the Search boxes at the top of almost any eBay page. When the results of your auction show up, scroll down to the Display box in the left column and click the Completed Listings check box. That way, you can scout out the active auction competition quickly before moving on to the completed sales.

An international search

You can select any country (from Afghanistan to Zimbabwe, no kidding!) or narrow your search to Canada or the United States. Don't forget that you have to pay for shipping, so if you don't want to pay to ship a heavy Victorian-style fainting sofa from Hungary to Vonda, Saskatchewan, stick close to home. The Location option lets you make an international search of eBay goodies. You have the choice of narrowing down your country search with the following options:

- ✔ **Items Located In:** The search engine looks for items from the specific country you select from the drop-down list.

- ✔ **Items Available To:** The search engine looks for items within your own country or from international sellers willing to ship to you.

A seller search

When you click the Items by Seller link on the left side of the search area, shown in Figure 5-4, a page opens that allows you to search by seller. This search method is a great way for you to keep tabs on people you have successfully done business with in the past. eBay users go to the Items by Seller page to assess the reputation of a particular seller. You can find out more about selling strategies in Chapter 9.

Viewing all items by a single seller

To use the Items by Seller search option to search for all of a single seller's items, follow these steps:

1. **In the Enter Seller's User ID search field, type the User ID of the person you want to find out about.**

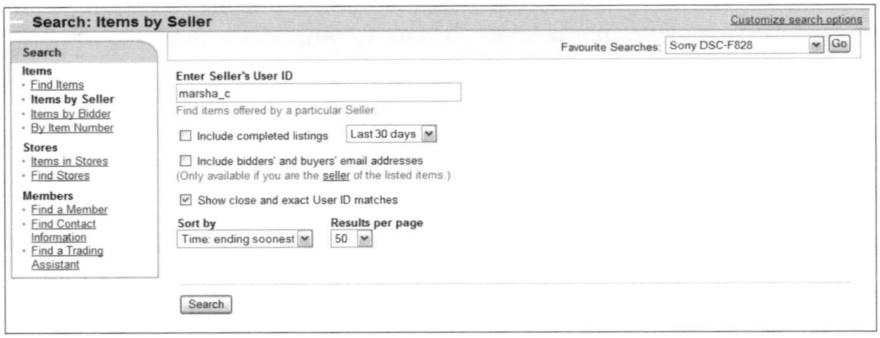

Figure 5-4:
You can search for all auctions by an individual on the Items by Seller page.

2. **If you don't want to see auctions that this specific seller has conducted in the past, don't select the Include Completed Listings check box.**

   You can choose to see all current and previous auctions, as well as auctions that have ended in the last day, last two days, last week, last two weeks, or last 30 days.

   eBay keeps past auction results active for only 30 days; if you're looking for something auctioned 31 days (or longer) ago, sorry — no dice.

3. **In the Sort By drop-down list, select an option to control how you want the results of your search to appear on-screen.**

   If you want to see the auctions that are closing right away, select Time: Ending Soonest.

4. **Select the number of results you want to see per page from the Results per Page drop-down list.**

   If the person you're looking up has 100 auctions running, you can limit the number of results to a manageable 25 listings on four separate pages to narrow down what you want to see.

5. **Click the Search button at the bottom of the Items by Seller search page.**

   Figure 5-5 shows the results page of an Items by Seller search.

Figure 5-5: The results of a By Seller search.

Finding items by keywords for multiple sellers

If you're looking for a specific item from a group of sellers, you'll have to go back to the Advanced Search page where you can fill the search information in the From Sellers section. You may need to perform this type of search after you settle into shopping on eBay and have several sellers that you like doing business with (or alternatively, you can exclude sellers you prefer not to do business with). With this method, you can limit the search for a particular item to just the sellers you want, rather than tens of thousands of sellers.

When you find a seller that you want to continue doing business with, you can add his or her link to your My eBay Favourite Sellers area. Just go to your My eBay page and, in the Favourites area, click the Add a Seller or Store link. You can add up to 30 sellers in this area and search their sales with a click of your mouse!

A bidder search

The Items by Bidder search option is unique because sellers and buyers alike use it when an auction is going on — to figure out their best strategies. After all, money is the name of the game. For information on conducting an Items by Bidder search, take a look at Chapter 7.

Narrowing down your eBay search

After you become familiar with each of eBay's search options, you need a crash course in what words to actually type into those nice little boxes. Enter too little information, and you may not find your item. Enter too much, and you're overwhelmed with listing returns that have little to do with what you're actually looking for. If you're really into bean-bag toys, for example, you may be looking for Ty's Tabasco the Bull. But if you search for just *Tabasco,* you get swamped with results ranging from hot sauce to advertisements.

Some simple tricks can help narrow your eBay search results when you're searching from pages other than the main Search page (where you don't find all the searching bells and whistles). Table 5-2 has the details.

Table 5-2	Symbols and Keywords for Conducting Searches with the eBay Search Engine	
Symbol	*Impact on Search*	*Example*
No symbol, multiple words	Returns auctions with all included words in the title	`trudeau letter` might return an auction for a mailed message from the former Canadian prime minister, or it might return an auction for a mailed message from Boris Yeltsin to Pierre Trudeau.

Symbol	Impact on Search	Example
Quotes, ""	Limits the search to items with the exact phrase inside the quotes	`"Wonder Woman"` returns items about the comic book/TV heroine. Quotes don't make the search term case sensitive. Using either upper- or lowercase in any eBay search gets you the same results.
Asterisk, *	Serves as a wild card	`budd*` returns items that start with budd, such as Beanie Buddy, Beanie Buddies, or Buddy Holly.
Separating comma without spaces, (a,b)	Finds items related to either the item before or after the comma	`gi joe,g.i. joe)` returns all GI Joe items, (whether the seller listed them as GI Joe or G.I. Joe.
Minus sign, −	Excludes results with the word after the −	Type in `box −lunch`, and you'd better not be hungry because you may find the box, but lunch won't be included.
Minus sign and parentheses, −()	Searches for auctions with words before the parentheses but excludes words inside the parentheses	`midge −(skipper, barbie)` means that auctions with the Midge doll won't have to compete with Skipper or Barbie dolls for Ken's attention.
Parentheses, ()	Searches for both versions of the word in parentheses	`political (pin, pins)` searches for political pin or political pins.

Here are additional tips to help you narrow down any eBay search:

- ✔ **Don't worry about capitalization.** You can capitalize proper names or leave them lowercase — the search engine doesn't care.

- ✔ **Don't use *and, a, an, or,* or *the.*** Called *noise words* in search lingo, these words are interpreted as part of your search. So if you want to find something from *The Sound of Music* and you type in `the sound of music`, you may not get any results. Most sellers drop noise words from the beginning of an item title when they list it, just like libraries drop noise words when they alphabetize books. So make your search for `sound music`. An even more precise search would be `"sound of music"` (in quotes).

✔ **Search within specific categories.** This type of search narrows down your results because you search only one niche of eBay — just the specific area you want. For example, if you want to find Tabasco the Bull, start at the home page and, under the Categories heading, click Toys & Hobbies, then click Beanbag Plush, Beanie Babies. The only problem with searching in a specific category is that sometimes an item can be in more than one place. For example, if you're searching for a Mickey Mouse infant snuggly in the Disney category, you may miss it because the item might be listed in Infant Wear. It's sometimes best not to limit yourself to a category because some of the best deals are wrongly categorized by sellers. What makes them such a good deal is that not everyone can find them. But you know better.

Use the asterisk symbol to locate misspellings. We've often found some great deals by finding items incorrectly posted by the sellers. Here are a few examples:

✔ **Rodri*:** In this search, we looked for items by the famous Cajun artist George Rodrigue. His Blue Dog paintings are world renowned and very valuable. By using this search, Marsha managed to purchase a signed Blue Dog lithograph for under US$200. (She resold it on eBay later that year for US$900!)

✔ **Alumi* tree:** Remember the old aluminum Christmas trees from the '60s? They've had quite a resurgence in popularity these days. You can buy these "antiques" in stores for hundreds of dollars . . . or you can buy one on eBay for half the price. You can find them even cheaper if the seller can't spell aluminum. . . .

✔ **Cemet* plot:** If you're looking for that final place to retire, eBay has some great deals. Unfortunately, sellers haven't narrowed down whether they want to spell it *cemetery* or *cemetary*. This search finds both spellings.

After studying these examples, we're sure you can think of many more instances in which your use of the asterisk can help you find deals. Be sure to e-mail both of us and let us know when you find something special in this way!

Finding eBay Members: The Gang's All Here

With millions of eBay users on the loose, you may think tracking folks down is hard. Nope. eBay's powerful search engine kicks into high gear to help you find other eBay members in seconds.

Here's how to find people or get info on them from eBay:

1. **From the top of most eBay pages, click the Advanced Search link.**

   The main Search page appears. You can see three links on the left side of the page under Members, including Find a Member.

2. **Click the Find a Member link in the box on the left side of the page.**

   This link takes you to the main Find a Member page, where you can search for other members of the community. Type in the User ID, click search, and eBay will return the exact match and some close matches (in case you were not certain of the spelling). When you find the member, you can access their My World page (by clicking on the ID), view their feedback (by clicking on the number that follows to the right of the ID — see Chapter 4 for details about feedback), visit their About Me page if they have one (by clicking on the Me link to the right of the feedback number or the link in the About Me column — see Chapter 14 to find out how to create your own personal eBay Web page), or visit their eBay Store if they have one (by clicking either the door symbol to the right of the User ID or the store name in the Stores column). You can also get a look at User ID histories of fellow eBay members (which comes in handy when you're bidding on items, as Chapter 7 avows) or view their current items by clicking the link (if provided) under Seller's Items.

If you're involved in a transaction with another eBay member and feel that you need to contact the individual by phone, click the Find Contact Information link, which is under the Members heading on the left side of the screen. On that page, you need to type in the transaction number, along with the other person's User ID. eBay compares this data with yours, and if you're indeed involved in a transaction with each other, eBay e-mails you the other person's phone number (along with the person's full name, and city and state of residence). Your contact information is, in turn, sent to the other party.

Clicking the arrow in the Favourite Searches drop-down box at the top-right of the page allows you to scroll through your My eBay Favourite Searches. You can tell eBay about the items you're looking for, and it does automatic searches for you. You can also have eBay e-mail you when auctions that match your descriptions crop up. (Chapter 18 gives you more info on how to go about ensuring that eBay sends you an e-mail whenever a new listing is posted for an item in your Favourite Searches.)

Chapter 6

Shopping eBay: The Basics

- -

- -

*B*rowsing different categories of eBay, looking for nothing in particular, you spot that must-have item lurking among other Elvis paraphernalia in the Collectables category. Sure, you *can* live without that faux-gold Elvis pocket watch, but life would be so much sweeter *with* it. And even if it doesn't keep good time, at least it'll be right twice a day.

When you bid for items on eBay, you can get that same thrill that you'd get at Sotheby's or Christie's for a lot less money, and the items you win are likely to be *slightly* more practical than an old Dutch masterpiece you're afraid to leave at the framer's. (Hey, you have to have a watch, and Elvis is the King.)

In this chapter, we give you the lowdown about the types of auctions and fixed-price listings available on eBay and a rundown of the nuts and bolts of bidding strategies. We also share some tried-and-true tips that can give you a leg up on the competition.

The Auction Item Page

Because, at any given point, you have more than 6 million pages of items that you can look at on eBay, auction item pages are the heart (better yet, the skeleton) of eBay listings. All item pages on eBay — whether auctions, fixed-price items, or Buy It Now items — look about the same. For example, Figure 6-1 shows a conventional auction item page, and Figure 6-2 shows a fixed-price sale. Both item pages show the listing title at the top, bidding or buying info in the middle, and seller info on the right. Below this area, you can find a complete description of the item, along with shipping information.

Of course, the two auction types have some subtle differences. Some auctions feature a picture at the top of the page, and some don't, depending on how the seller sets up his or her sale page. Some auctions include item specifics in the description, which appears below the listing details (as shown in Figure 6-2). This area is set up by eBay and filled in by the seller to give you a snapshot description of the item for sale. If you search for an item and end up finding it available in a fixed-price sale, you won't see the Place Bid button (see Figure 6-2). But overall, the look and feel of these pages is the same.

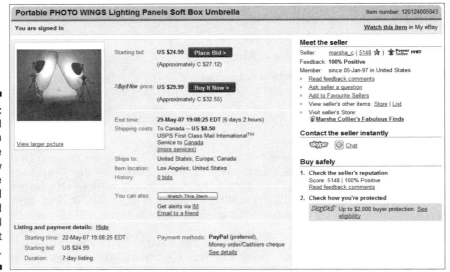

Figure 6-1:
This typical auction features the Buy It Now button, the Place Bid button, and PayPal payment options.

Figure 6-2:
A fixed-price sale has the Buy It Now button and info about buying through PayPal, but no Place Bid button.

Here's a list of information that a typical auction item page includes:

- **Item title and number:** The title and number identify the item. Keep track of this info for inquiries later on.

  If you're interested in a particular type of item, take note of the keywords used in the title (you're likely to see them again in future titles). Doing so helps you narrow down future searches.

- **Item category:** Located just above the item title and number bar, you can click the category listing and do some comparison shopping. (Chapter 5 gives more searching strategies.)

- **Current Bid:** This field indicates the dollar amount the bidding has reached, which changes throughout the auction as people place bids. If no bids have been placed on the item, this field is called Starting Bid.

  Sometimes, below the current dollar amount, you see (Reserve not met). This statement means that the seller has set a *reserve price* for the item — a secret price that must be reached before the seller will sell the item. If you don't see this note on an auction item page, don't be alarmed. Not all auctions have reserve prices. In fact, the majority don't. Also, the moment a reserve is met, the indicator disappears completely.

- **Buy It Now Price:** If you want the item immediately and the price quoted in this area is okay with you, click the Buy It Now button, which takes you to a page in which you can complete your purchase. This option is only visible if the seller has predetermined to include it and there are no previous bids or the item hasn't met the reserve price.

- **Quantity:** This field appears only in a multiple item, fixed-price sale or Dutch auction. It tells you how many items are available. If you see a number other than 1 in this field, you're looking at a Multiple Item (Dutch) auction, which we explain in the section "Placing Your Bid," later in this chapter. It may also be a multiple unit, fixed-price sale (which means that you can buy just one — you don't have to buy the entire lot). You can tell when it's a fixed-price sale because you have no opportunity to bid, you can use only the Buy It Now option for whatever quantity of the item you desire. You're prompted for a quantity when you buy. But if a seller is selling two Elvis watches for the price of one, the item quantity still shows up as 1 (as in one set of two watches).

- **End Time:** Although the clock never stops ticking at eBay, you must continue to refresh your browser to see the time remaining on the official clock. For most of the auction the time remaining will be displayed in days and hours, but when the auction gets down to the final hour, the time counts down in minutes and seconds. This field tells you the time remaining in this particular auction.

  Timing is key in an eBay bidding strategy (which we cover in Chapter 7). Because eBay's Canadian headquarters is in Toronto, eBay uses eastern standard time or eastern daylight saving time as the standard, depending on the season. Not a major deal if you live *"at the centre of the universe,"* but it can be an issue if you live anywhere else.

✔ **Item Location:** This field tells you, at the very least, the country in which the seller is located, and you may also see more specific info, such as the city and geographic area where the seller is. (What you see depends on how detailed the seller wants to be.)

Factor in the geographic location of a seller when you consider bidding on an item. Knowing exactly where the item is can help you quickly calculate approximately how long it will take for the item to get to you. (Chapter 10 tackles that subject.) Also, if you buy from someone within Canada, you may also have to pay GST, PST, or HST — depending on where you live — on your purchase. If the item is in Australia, for example, and you're in Quebec, you may decide that you don't really need that wrought-iron doorstop. (Remember, *you* pay the shipping charges.)

✔ **History:** This field tells you how many bids have been placed. To use the number of bids to your advantage, you have to read between the lines. You can determine just how hot an item is by comparing the number of bids the item has received over time. Based on the amount of interest in an item, you can create a time strategy (which we talk about in depth in Chapter 7). If you want to see the starting bid, you have to click the Show link to the right of Listing and Payment Details, as shown at the bottom of Figure 6-1. If you click the number of bids link to the right of the word History, you can find out who's bidding and at what date and time bids were placed on this item. The dollar amount of each bid is shown in the bidding history, but bidders' maximum bids are kept secret.

✔ **High Bidder:** This field shows you the User ID and feedback rating of the current high bidder — although eBay has made changes recently to protect bidders' identities on higher priced items. You could be in this honourable position if you've placed a bid!

Bidding is more an art than a science. Sometimes, an item gets no bids because everyone's waiting until the last minute. You see a flurry of activity as bidders all try to outbid each other (called *sniping,* which Chapter 7 explains). But that's all part of the fun of eBay.

✔ **Watch This Item:** Click this link to magically add the item to the All Buying section of your My eBay page. You can keep an eye on the progress of the auction from your My eBay page — without actually bidding. If you haven't signed in, you have to type in your User ID and password before you can save the auction to your My eBay page.

Be sure to use the Watch This Item feature. Organization is the name of the game at eBay, especially if you plan to bid on multiple auctions while you're running auctions of your own. We figure you're in the bidding game to win, so start keeping track of items now.

✔ **E-mail to a Friend:** You can tip off a friend on a good find, get some advice from an antiques or collecting expert, or run the auction by a friend who's been around the eBay block a few times and ask for strategy advice. (You can find this link at the top of the listing page below the Watch This Item link.)

✔ **Buying notifications:** Many of the big-time buyers use a sniping service, but eBay offers several buying notifications that are great for those do-it-yourselfers out there. So, if you really enjoy the thrill of the bid, set your eBay preferences to receive a notification if you're outbid and (or) when the auction is about to end. You can get a couple of types of notices:

- **E-mail messages:** You can get an e-mail message direct to your mailbox when one of your watched listings will end within the next five hours. Consider it a gentle reminder to get your bid in. You can also have eBay send you an e-mail if you're outbid on an active auction.

- **Instant messages:** You can opt to receive an IM sent to your AIM (AOL Instant Messenger), Yahoo! Messenger, Windows Live, or Skype account. You're not charged for the IM service, so if you have a Blackberry or a Sidekick and don't want to miss any bidding action, this could be a great option for you. Also, with the IM service, you can bid again from a link that comes along with the Outbid alert.

✔ **Meet the Seller box:** This area gives you information about the seller. *Know thy seller* ranks right after *caveat emptor* as a phrase that pays on eBay. As we tell you nearly a million times in this book, *read the feedback rating!* (Okay, maybe not a million — it would drive the editors bonkers.) Human beings come in all shapes, sizes, and levels of honesty, and like any community, eBay has its share of good folks and bad folks. Your best defence is to read the seller's feedback. The Meet the Seller box includes several bits of information about the seller (as shown in Figure 6-3):

Figure 6-3:
You can find a lot of data on the seller in the Meet the Seller box.

Meet the seller

Seller: marsha_c (5148 ⭐) 🏆 Power Seller me

Feedback: **100% Positive**

Member: since 05-Jan-97 in United States

- Read feedback comments
- Ask seller a question
- Add to Favourite Sellers
- View seller's other items: Store | List
- Visit seller's Store:
  🛒 Marsha Collier's Fabulous Finds

Contact the seller instantly

skype 🅾 Chat

Buy safely

1. **Check the seller's reputation**
   Score: 5148 | 100% Positive
   Read feedback comments

- **Feedback rating:** This is the number that's to the right of the seller's User ID. Click the number to view his or her eBay ID card and entire feedback history. Read, read, and reread all the feedback to make sure you feel comfortable doing business with this person.

- **Feedback percentage:** The eBay computers calculate this percentage from all the positive and negative feedback that a user receives.

- **Member since:** This line lists the date the seller registered on eBay and the country in which he or she registered.

- **Read Feedback Comments link:** This link does the same thing as clicking the Feedback Rating number.

- **Ask Seller a Question link:** Clicking this link hooks you up with eBay's e-mail system. You can ask the seller a question regarding the item through this system.

- **Add to Favourite Sellers link:** If you like what you see, don't hesitate to add the seller to Your Favourite Sellers list. Then you can visit them at a quick click of a link anytime you wish.

- **View Seller's Other Items link:** This link takes you to a page that lists all the seller's current auctions and fixed-price sales.

  If the seller has an eBay store, a link to it appears here, as well. We give you a step-by-step guide on how these links work in the section "Getting the scoop on the seller," later in this chapter.

  If the seller accepts PayPal, that option is indicated in a shaded area. Also, if the seller qualifies for Buyer Protection, that's indicated here.

✔ **Description bar:** Below this light blue shaded bar, you can find the item description. You must always read all the item description information *before* bidding. Check out the section "Reading the item description carefully," later in this chapter, to find out how to use this information.

On a typical auction item page, below the seller's description area, you can find some other important data, as shown in Figure 6-4:

✔ **Shipping and Handling:** Check here to see the details on shipping. You see

- Who pays (remember that on eBay, it's usually the buyer).

- Whether insurance is offered.

- Whether you have to pay applicable sales taxes.

- Whether the seller is willing to ship to your area. (Sometimes, sellers won't ship internationally, and they let you know in this section.)

Also, always check the item description for other shipping information and terms.

✔ **Return Policy:** If the seller has specified a return policy, you'll find it here.

✔ **Payment Details:** This field tells you the payment methods that the seller accepts: cheques, money orders, credit cards, or PayPal. Often, it tells you to read the item description for more details. We explain how to read item descriptions in the section "Reading the item description carefully," later in this chapter.

Figure 6-4:
Check
out the
shipping
and
payment
boxes to
find out
about
additional
costs that
may apply
when you
buy.

Shipping and handling

Ships to
Canada

Country: Canada

Shipping and Handling	To	Service
C $14.95	Canada	Canada Post Expedited Parcel

Domestic handling time
Will usually ship within 2 business days of receiving cleared payment.

Shipping insurance
Included (in the shipping and handling cost)

Sales tax
Seller charges sales tax for items shipped to: ON* (14.000%).
* Tax applies to subtotal + S&H for these states only

Return policy

Item must be returned within:	3 Days
Refund will be given as:	Exchange
Return policy details:	Unconditionally guaranteed to be as described and in working condition. Please email if there are any problems with your item on receipt and I'll be only too happy to make it right.
	I do not pay return shipping unless the item is not as described.

Learn about return policies

Beating the Devil in the Details

As with any sale — whether you find it at Joe's Hardware, Canadian Tire, or Zellers — carefully check out what you're buying. The item page gives you links to help you know what you're bidding on — and who you're potentially buying from. If you take advantage of these features, you won't have many problems. But, if you ignore these essential tips, you may end up unhappy with what you buy, who you buy it from, and how much you spend.

Reading the item description carefully

The *item description* is the most critical part of the auction item page. This is where the seller lists the details about the item being sold. Read this section carefully and pay very close attention to what is, and *isn't,* written.

Don't judge a book by its cover — but do judge a seller by his or her item description. If the sentences are succinct, detailed, and well structured, you're most likely dealing with an individual who planned and executed the auction with care. It takes time and effort to post a good auction. If you see huge lapses in grammar, convoluted sentences, and misspellings, you may be gonna get burnt! Make sure you feel comfortable dealing with this person; decide for yourself whether he or she is out to sell junk for a quick buck or is part of eBay for the long term.

If a picture of the item is available, take a good look. The majority of eBay sellers jazz up their auctions with photos of their items. The seller should answer a few general questions in the item description. If these questions aren't answered, that doesn't necessarily mean the seller's disreputable — only that if you're really interested, you should e-mail the seller and get those answers before you bid. In particular, ask questions such as these:

- ✔ Is the item new or used?

- ✔ Is the item a first edition or a reprint? An original or a reissue? (See Chapter 5 for tips on how to assess what you're buying.)

- ✔ Is the item in its original packaging? Does it still have the original tags?

- ✔ Is the item under warranty?

Most sellers spell out in their item descriptions exactly how the item should be paid for and shipped. Check both the Shipping and Handling box and the Payment Details box under the description to see whether an actual shipping charge applies — and if so, how much it'll cost you. Here are a few other questions to consider regarding the item you're thinking about buying:

- ✔ If you're in a hurry to get the item, are delays likely? If so, what sort and how long?

- ✔ Can the seller guarantee you a refund if the item is broken or doesn't work upon delivery?

- ✔ What condition is the item in? Is it broken, scratched, or flawed, or is it in mint condition?

Most experienced eBay buyers know that, depending on the item, a tiny scratch here or there may be worth the risk of making a bid. But a scratch or two may affect your bidding price. (Look at Chapter 5 for more expert advice on buying collectibles.)

- ✔ Is this item the genuine article or a reproduction, and if it's the real deal, does the seller have papers or labels certifying its authenticity?

- ✔ What size is the item, and how much does it weigh? (That life-size fibre-glass whale may not fit in your garage. That baby grand piano might cost a lot to ship from Peru, so you need to factor in the cost of shipping when you consider how much you're willing to bid.)

If you win the item and find out the seller lied in the description, you have the right to request to return the item. But, if you win the item and discover that _you_ overlooked a detail in the description, the seller isn't obligated to take the item back.

The seller is obligated to describe the item honestly and in detail, so if your questions aren't answered in the item description, then for goodness' sake, e-mail the seller for the facts. If a picture is available, is it clear enough that you can see any flaws? You can always ask the seller to e-mail you a picture taken from another angle.

Getting the scoop on the seller

We can't tell you enough that the single most important way you can make an auction go well is to know who you're dealing with. Apparently, the eBay folks agree; they enable you to get info on the seller right from the auction item page. We recommend that you take advantage of the links offered there. (Chapter 5 demonstrates how to conduct a thorough By Seller search.) To get the full scoop on a seller, here's what you need to do:

- ✔ Click the number to the right of the seller's User ID to get his or her feedback history. Click the Me link (if there is one) to the right of the seller's User ID to view the seller's About Me page. A seller's About Me page frequently gives you a good deal more information about the seller. (To set up your own free About Me page on eBay, check out Chapter 14.)

- ✔ The PowerSeller icon to the right of the seller's User ID means he or she is an eBay seller who has met certain stringent certifications. (For more on PowerSellers, see Chapter 20.)

- ✔ Click the View Seller's Other Auctions link to take a look at what else that person is selling. If the seller also has an eBay store, you will be offered a choice between viewing other items in a list or by the store view. (Frequently, if you win more than one auction from a seller, he or she will often combine the shipping costs — but be sure to ask if it isn't clearly mentioned in their listings.) Check the seller's feedback (does this message sound familiar?).

Check the seller's eBay ID card and feedback history. All together, now — _check the feedback._ (Is there an echo in here?) You'll find (for the most part) the honest thoughts and comments of buyers from previous transactions. With the introduction of eBay's Feedback v2.0, you may also find additional ratings on the accuracy of descriptions, communication with buyers, promptness of shipping, and fairness of shipping and handling charges. No eBay user has control over the comments that others make, and feedback sticks to you like your permanent record from high school.

Read the feedback — the good, the bad, and the neutral — and unless you're a big-time gambler, we've found it's safer not to buy from a seller who has a large percentage of negative comments.

eBay, like life, is full of shades of grey. Some sellers are unfairly hit with negative comments for something that wasn't their fault. A perfect example may be a negative comment for a delay in delivery caused by Canada Post. If you suspect that a seller's received a bum rap (after you've read his or her positive feedback), be sure to read the seller's response. (Check out Chapter 4 for more on reading and leaving feedback.)

Although scoping out an eBay Member Profile is *just that fast, just that simple,* you still need to take the time to read the feedback. (There's that echo again. Good thing it's a wise echo.) Someone with 500 positive feedback messages may look like a good seller, but if you take a closer look, you may find that his or her ten most recent feedback messages are negative. That may indicate the seller has decided that customer service is no longer a priority, or he or she may have fallen ill and can no longer honour shipping commitments. Hey — life happens!

Viewing the seller's other auctions

To find out what other auctions the seller has going at eBay, all you have to do is click the corresponding link on the item page; you're whisked away to a list of the other auction pies the seller has a finger in. If the seller has no other auctions going and has no current feedback, you may want to do a more thorough investigation and conduct a By Seller search to find all that person's completed auctions in the last 30 days. (See Chapter 5 for details.)

One man's trash . . .

One of Bill's earliest eBay purchases was for a vintage, mid-1970s Marantz model 2325 stereo receiver that the eBay seller described as simply "non-working." Marantz receivers from the '60s and '70s sell extremely well on eBay and are highly prized by stereo buffs. Bill contacted the seller to enquire about the nature of the defect and found out that the owner really had no idea what was wrong with the receiver and just wanted to be rid of it. Without an adequate description, few bidders made an offer, so Bill took a chance and managed to win the auction for a mere US$25 — and because the seller was local, he managed to arrange to pick the receiver up at the seller's home. In the end,

repairs basically amounted to the replacement of a couple of burnt mini-bulbs and a good cleaning. Bill spent about an hour finding information about the model on the Web, writing a good description, and taking abundant, clear photos before launching an auction on eBay for the same receiver. Bill figures his overall cost on the receiver was approximately US$40, plus a little of his time. Seven days later, that same receiver sold for US$565 on the same sight from which he'd purchased it. Certainly, it was a case of one man's trash being another's treasure. In fact, it led to the development of one of Bill's User ID's on eBay — treasure-pot.

Asking the seller a question

If anything about the auction is unclear to you, remember this one word: Ask. Find out all the details about that item before you bid. If you wait until you've won the item before you ask questions, you may get stuck with something you don't want. Double-checking may save you woe and hassle later.

You can find out more about payment options, shipping charges, insurance, and other fun stuff in Chapter 8 and Chapter 12.

If you're bidding on a reserve-price auction, don't be afraid to e-mail the seller and ask for the reserve price. Yeah, reserves are mostly kept secret, but there's no harm in asking — and many sellers gladly tell you.

To ask a seller a question, follow these steps:

1. **Click the Ask Seller a Question link under the Meet the Seller heading on the right side of the item page.**

   The Ask a Question form appears.

2. **Select a general topic from the drop-down list.**

3. **Fill in the message area and politely fire off your questions; then click Send.** You are also offered options to hide your return e-mail address from the seller and to receive a copy of the e-mail that eBay sends. We recommend selecting both these options. Hiding your e-mail address from someone you don't know might protect you from finding yourself on another spam e-mail list. The seller will still be able to respond through eBay. Receiving a copy of the e-mail sent assures you that it has not become a victim of a system failure. It stands to reason that if you can read it — so can the seller.

   Expect to hear back from the seller within a day. If it takes the seller more than a day or two to respond (unless it's over the weekend — eBay sellers are entitled to a little rest), and you get no explanation for the delay, think twice before putting in a bid.

Factoring in the Extras

Before you think about placing a bid on an item, you should factor in the financial obligation you have to make. In every case, the maximum bid you place won't be all you spend on an item. We recommend that you look closely at the payment methods that the seller is willing to accept and also factor in shipping, insurance, and escrow costs (if any). If you have only $50 to spend, you shouldn't place a $50 bid on a fragile item that will be shipped a long distance because the buyer (that would be you) often pays for shipping and insurance. In addition, if the seller also lives in Canada, you may have to pay applicable sales tax if the seller is running a legitimate business.

Payment methods

Several payment options are available, but the seller has the right to refuse some forms of payment. Usually, the accepted forms of payment are laid out in the item's Description, or in the Shipping and Handling area and Payment Details area (both below the Description area). If you don't see this payment info, ask the seller a question (as described in the section "Asking the seller a question," earlier in this chapter) and get a clear idea of your additional costs *before* you place a bid.

These are the forms of payment available to you:

- ✔ **Credit card:** Paying with a credit card is a favourite payment option for many buyers, one that's mainly offered by businesses and dealers. Although we like paying with credit cards because they're fast and efficient, you should have a pretty good idea of who you're dealing with before passing along your credit card information. One benefit to using a credit card is that it offers you another ally, your credit card company, if you're not completely satisfied with the transaction.

  Sometimes, sellers use a friend's company to run credit card payments for eBay auctions. So don't be surprised if you buy a vintage Tonka bulldozer and your credit card is billed from Holly's Hair-o-Rama.

- ✔ **PayPal:** We pay for almost all our eBay purchases through PayPal. Owned by eBay, PayPal is the largest Internet-wide payment network. Sellers who accept PayPal are identified with a special icon in the Meet the Seller box (as well as with a large PayPal logo in the Payment Methods area below the description) and accept American Express, Visa, and MasterCard, as well as electronic cheques and debits. The service is integrated directly into eBay auctions, so paying is a mouse click away.

  After you register with PayPal to pay for an item, PayPal debits your credit card or your bank chequing account (or your eBay account, if you've earned some money from sales) and sends the payment to the seller's account. PayPal doesn't charge buyers to use the service. Buyers can use PayPal to pay any seller within Canada and the U.S. (and around the world in more than 54 other countries). To see a current list of PayPal's international services, go to www.paypal.com/us/cgi-bin/webscr?cmd=_display-approved-signup-countries-outside.

  PayPal deposits the money directly into the seller's chequing or savings account. The service charges the seller a small transaction fee, so the seller absorbs the cost.

  One of the big reasons to consider using PayPal is that your credit card information is known only to the PayPal service. The seller never sees your credit card info. Another major advantage is that you have protection behind you when you use PayPal. And you have the right to dispute charges if the item arrives damaged or doesn't show up at all. When you use PayPal to pay for a qualified eBay item from a verified PayPal member, you may be covered by PayPal's Buyer Protection program for purchases up to $2,000. To find out whether your item is protected in this program, look for the information in the Buy Safely area, below the Meet the Seller box (refer to Figure 6-3).

For more details, check out the PayPal Web site (www.paypal.com).

✔ **Money order:** Our second-favourite method of payment — and the most popular non-electronic payment method at eBay — is the money order. Sellers love money orders because they don't have to wait for a cheque to clear.

Money orders are the same as cash. As soon as the seller gets your money order, he or she has no reason to wait to send the item. You can often buy money orders at banks, cheque-cashing businesses, and your local post office. The cost varies, but expect to pay $3.95 for a Canadian-dollar money order from Canada Post and $4.95 if you need it in U.S. funds. If you're purchasing an item from a seller in the U.S., be certain to send a Canada Post U.S. Funds money order. Many U.S. sellers have trouble cashing other forms of money orders.

✔ **Personal or certified cheque:** Paying by cheque is convenient, but it has its drawbacks. Most Canadian sellers won't ship you the goods until after your check clears, which means a lag time of a couple of weeks or more. If a seller takes personal cheques, the item's description usually states how long the seller will wait for the cheque to clear before shipping the item. Unfortunately, that means that while the seller is waiting for your cheque to clear, your merchandise is collecting dust in a box somewhere. That's no fun for you or the seller. Certified cheques are available at your bank, but they often cost much more than a money order. We don't think it's worth the extra money — have fun and buy more eBay items, instead. Just remember that you should never send a Canadian-dollar personal or certified cheque to a U.S. seller — U.S. banks convert Canadian-dollar cheques for a huge fee, and the seller will be none too fond of the experience.

Before you send a personal cheque, make sure that you have enough money to cover your purchase. A bounced cheque can earn you negative feedback — and too many negative transactions can bounce you off eBay.

The good news about cheques is that you can track whether they've been cashed. Personal cheques leave a paper trail that you can follow if a problem occurs later.

The bad news about cheques is that you're revealing personal information, such as your bank account number, to a stranger.

✔ **C.O.D.:** No, we're not talking about codfish. We're talking about *Cash on Delivery*. As a buyer, you may like the idea that you have to pay for an item only if it shows up. But paying C.O.D. has two problems:

• You have to have the money on hand — the exact amount. When was the last time any of us had exact change for anything?

- Even if you have exact change, if you're not around when the item's delivered, you're out of luck.

If you miss the C.O.D. delivery, the shipment heads back to Bolivia or Oblivion or wherever it came from, never to be seen again. And what do you get? A lot of angry e-mails and maybe some negative feedback. No wonder sellers rarely use this option.

Most business at eBay is conducted in U.S. dollars — even with Canadian sellers — so you'll probably have to convert Canadian dollars into U.S. dollars at some point. And if you happen to buy an item from an international seller, you may need to convert Canadian dollars into another currency. You can find one of the world's most popular online currency converters at www.xe.com.

Just type in the amount in the Convert This Amount box, select your choice of currencies from the drop-down menus, and click the Go! button.

Never use a form of payment that doesn't let you keep a paper trail. (Don't wire money, and never send cash in the mail!) If a seller asks for cash, quote that popular slogan from many years ago — just say no. Occasionally, we hear of buyers sending cash in the mail, and it always makes us cringe. If a seller asks for cash, chances are that you'll never see the item or your money again. In fact, eBay's Safe Payments policy no longer allows sellers to ask for cash or wire transfers as a form of payment for auctions. There's one exception — cash payments are permitted when the item is available for pickup. Oh, yeah, here's something else — if a seller asks you to send your payment to a post office box, get a phone number. Many legitimate sellers use post office boxes, but so do the bad guys.

Using an escrow service

Even though most sales at eBay are for items that cost $100 or less, using an escrow service comes in handy on occasion — such as when you buy a big-ticket item or something extremely rare. *Escrow* is a service that allows a buyer and seller to protect a transaction by placing the money in the hands of a neutral third party until a specified set of conditions are met. Sellers note in their item descriptions if they're willing to accept escrow. If you're nervous about sending a lot of money to someone you don't really know (such as a user named Clumsy who has only two feedback comments and is shipping you bone china from Broken Hill, Australia), consider using an escrow company.

Using an escrow company is worthwhile only if the item you're bidding on is expensive, rare, fragile, or travelling a long distance. If you're spending less than $200 for the item, we recommend that you purchase insurance from your shipper, instead — just in case. Remember, your purchases are protected against fraud if you pay by using PayPal. (You may be protected up to $2,000 by PayPal — see the preceding section for more on PayPal.)

eBay has a partnership with Escrow.com (www.escrow.com) to handle eBay auction escrow sales in Canada and the United States. After an auction closes, the buyer sends the payment to the escrow company. When the escrow company receives the money, it e-mails the seller, telling him or her to ship the merchandise. When the buyer receives the item, he or she has an agreed-upon period of time to look it over. If everything's okay, the buyer tells the escrow service to send the payment to the seller. If the buyer is unhappy with the item, he or she must ship the item back to the seller. If the buyer returns the item, when the escrow service receives word from the seller that the item has been returned, the service returns the payment to the buyer (minus the escrow company's handling fee, of course).

Before you start an escrow transaction, make sure that you and the seller agree on these terms (use e-mail to sort it out). Here are three questions about escrow that you should know the answers to before you bid:

- ✔ **Who pays the escrow fee?** Normally, the buyer pays the escrow fee, though sometimes the buyer and seller split the cost.
- ✔ **How long is the inspection period?** Routinely, the buyer can inspect the item for up to two business days after receipt of the merchandise.
- ✔ **Who pays for return shipping if the item is rejected?** The buyer usually pays return shipping costs.

Shipping and insurance costs

Don't let the sale go down with the shipping. Most auction descriptions end with, "Buyer to pay shipping charges." If the item isn't an odd shape, excessively large, or fragile, experienced sellers calculate the shipping based on Expedited Parcel through Canada Post (for shipments within Canada) or Global Priority through the U.S. Postal Service (for shipments from the U.S. to Canada), both of which are the unofficial eBay standards. Expect to pay a minimum of $7.50 for the first 750 grams, which includes delivery confirmation and the first $100 in insurance for shipments within Canada. Shipments from the U.S. to Canada can be substantially more expensive. Applicable taxes and a $5 service charge may also be added if the shipment exceeds $20 in value. Shipments by FedEx Ground or UPS from the U.S. to Canada may also have a surcharge of $25 or more for Customs clearance, depending on the value of the shipment. We recommend that you investigate your real costs before committing to a delivery service from a U.S. seller. Shipping from other countries to Canada can be very expensive, so be certain to thoroughly investigate the shipping costs before committing to the purchase.

It has also become somewhat routine for the seller to add a dollar or two for packing materials such as paper, bubble wrap, tape, and so on. This is a fair and reasonable handling charge because the cost of those items can add up over time.

You may come across sellers trying to nickel-and-dime their way to a fortune by jacking up the prices on shipping to ridiculous proportions. If you have a question about shipping costs, ask before you bid on the item.

Before bidding on big stuff, such as a barber's chair or a sofa, check for something in the item description that says, "Buyer pays actual shipping charges." When you see that, always e-mail the seller prior to your bid to find out what those shipping charges would be to your home. On larger items, you may need to factor in packing and crating charges. The seller may also suggest a specific shipping company.

As the bumper sticker says, (ahem) stuff happens — sometimes to the stuff you buy. But before you give up and just stuff it, consider insuring it. eBay transactions sometimes involve two types of insurance that may have an impact on your pocketbook:

- **Shipping insurance:** This insurance covers your item as it travels through Canada Post, the U.S. Postal Service, UPS, FedEx, or any of the other carriers.

  Although many sellers offer shipping insurance as an option, others don't bother because if the price of the item is low, they'd rather refund your money to keep you happy than go through all that insurance paperwork. Don't forget that if you want shipping insurance, in the end, you always pay for it. (See Chapter 12 for details on shipping insurance.)

- **Fraud protection:** Remember, if you pay via PayPal, you may be covered for purchases up to $2,000.

Placing Your Bid

Okay, so you've found the perfect item to track (say a really classy Elvis Presley wristwatch), and it's in your price range. You're more than interested — you're ready to bid. If this were a live auction, some stodgy-looking guy in a grey suit would see you nod your head and start the bidding at, say, $2. Then some woman with a severe hairdo would yank on her ear, and the Elvis watch would jump to $3.

eBay reality is more like this: You're sitting at home in your fuzzy slippers, sipping coffee in front of the computer; all the other bidders are cruising cyberspace in their pyjamas, too. You just can't see 'em. (Be really thankful for little favours.)

When you're ready to jump into the eBay fray, you can find the bidding form (shown in Figure 6-5) at the bottom of the auction item page (or click the Place Bid button at the top of the auction page which will take you rapidly to the bottom of the auction page). If the item includes a Buy It Now option, you see that option to the right of the bid form at the bottom of the item's auction page.

Take action on this item   Help

Item title: **Portable PHOTO WINGS Lighting Panels Soft Box Umbrella**

Place a bid	Buy It Now
Starting bid: US $24.99 (Approximately C $27.12)	*Buy It Now* : US $29.99 (Approximately C $32.55)
Your maximum bid: US $ [ ]	**Buy It Now >**
(Enter US $24.99 **or more**)	You will confirm in the next step.
Place Bid >	
You will confirm in the next step.	

(or)

eBay automatically bids on your behalf up to your maximum bid.   Purchase this item now without bidding.
Learn about bidding   Learn about Buy It Now

You can also [**Watch This Item**]

Figure 6-5: The bidding form appears at the bottom of every auction page.

To fill out the bidding form and place a bid, first make sure that you're registered (see Chapter 2 for details), and then follow these steps:

1. **Enter your maximum bid in the appropriate box.**

   Your bid needs to be an increment or more higher than the current minimum bid. The lowest amount you can bid is displayed to the right of the bidding box. (See the following section for more information about bidding increments.)

2. **If this is a Multiple Item auction, enter the quantity of items that you're bidding on.**

   Figure 6-6 shows a Multiple Item auction bidding form. If it's not a Multiple Item auction, the quantity is always 1.

Item title: **FDC SOUTH AFRICA 1960 2.5 CENTS, 7 FOR DUTCH AUCTION!**

Place a bid

Starting bid: US $3.55 (Approximately C $3.85)
Quantity: 7 available
Your maximum bid: US $ [   ]   (Enter US $3.55 **or more**)
Your quantity: x   [1]

Place Bid >   You will confirm in the next step.

Unlike a regular eBay auction, Multiple Item Auctions can have many winners. Learn about Multiple Item Auctions.

You can also [Watch This Item]

Figure 6-6: The Multiple Item auction bidding form requires you to enter the quantity of the items you want to bid on.

You don't need to put in the dollar sign, but you *do* need to use a decimal point — unless you really *want* to pay $1,049 rather than $10.49. If you make a mistake with an incorrect decimal point, you can retract your bid (see the section "Retracting your bid," later in this chapter).

3. **Click the Place Bid button.**

   The Review Bid page appears on your screen, filled with a wealth of
   legalese. This is your last chance to change your mind: Do you really
   want the item, and can you really buy it? The bottom line is this: If you
   bid on it and you win, you buy it. eBay really means it.

4. **At this point, you have to sign in if you haven't already.**

   If you're already signed in, skip to Step 5.

5. **If you agree to the terms, click Submit.**

   After you agree, the Bid Confirmation screen appears.

After you make your first bid on an item, you can instantly get to auctions
you're bidding on from your My eBay page. (If you need some tips on how to
set up My eBay, see Chapter 4.)

When you first start out on eBay, we suggest that you start with a *token bid* —
a small bid that won't win you the auction but that can help you keep tabs on
the auction's progress.

After you bid on an item, the item number and title appear on your My eBay
page, listed under (big surprise) Bidding, as shown in Figure 6-7. (See Chapter
4 for more information on My eBay.) The Items I'm Bidding On list makes
tracking your auction (or auctions, if you're bidding on multiple items) easy.

Figure 6-7:
Keep track
of items
you're
bidding on
right from
your My
eBay page.

eBay considers a bid on an item to be a binding contract. You can save yourself a lot of heartache if you make a promise to yourself — *never* bid on an
item you don't intend to buy — and keep to it. Don't make practice bids,
assuming that because you're new to eBay, you can't win; if you do that,
you'll probably win simply because you've left yourself open to Murphy's
Law. Therefore, before you go to the bidding form, be sure that you're in this
auction for the long haul and make yourself another promise — figure out the

maximum you're willing to spend, and stick to it. (Read the section "The Agony (?) of Buyer's Remorse," later in this chapter, for doleful accounts of what can happen if you bid idly or get buyer's remorse.)

Bidding to the Max: Proxy Bidding

When you make a maximum bid on the bidding form, you actually make several small bids — again and again — until the bidding reaches the price at which you want it to stop. For example, if the current bid is up to $19.99 and you put in a maximum of $45.02, your bid automatically increases incrementally so that you're ahead of the competition — at least until someone else's maximum bid exceeds yours. Basically, you bid by *proxy,* which means that your bid rises incrementally in response to other bidders' bids.

No one else knows for sure whether you're bidding by proxy, and no one knows how high your maximum bid is. And the best part is that you can be out having a life of your own while the proxy bid happens automatically. Buyers and sellers have no control over the increments (appropriately called *bid increments*) that eBay sets. The bid increment is the amount of money by which a bid is raised, and eBay's system can work in mysterious ways. The current maximum bid can jump up a nickel or a quarter or even $50, but there's a method to the madness, even though you may not think so. eBay uses a *bid-increment formula,* which uses the current high bid to determine how much to increase the bid increment. For example:

- ✔ A 5-quart bottle of cold cream has a current high bid of $14.95. The bid increment is $0.50 — meaning that if you bid by proxy, your proxy will bid $15.45.

- ✔ But a 5-ounce can of top-notch caviar has a high bid of $200. The bid increment is $2.50. If you choose to bid by proxy, your proxy will bid $202.50.

Table 6-1 shows you what kind of magic happens when you put the proxy system and a bid-increment formula together in the same cyber-room.

Table 6-1			Proxy Bidding and Bid Increments	
Current Bid	*Bid Increment*	*Minimum Bid*	*eBay Auctioneer*	*Bidders*
$2.50	$0.25	$2.75	"Do I hear $2.75?"	Joe Bidder tells his proxy that his maximum bid is $8. He's the current high bidder at $2.75.

(continued)

Table 6-1 *(continued)*

Current Bid	Bid Increment	Minimum Bid	eBay Auctioneer	Bidders
$2.75	$0.25	$3	"Do I hear $3?"	You tell your proxy your maximum bid is $25 and take a nice, relaxing bath while your proxy calls out your $3 bid, making you the current high bidder.
$3	$0.25	$3.25	"I hear $3 from proxy. Do I hear $3.25?"	Joe Bidder's proxy bids $3.25, and while Joe Bidder is out walking his dog, he becomes the high bidder.

A heated bidding war ensues between Joe Bidder's proxy and your proxy while the two of you go on with your lives. The bid increment inches from $0.25 to $0.50 as the current high bid increases.

Current Bid	Bid Increment	Minimum Bid	eBay Auctioneer	Bidders
$7.50	$0.50	$8	"Do I hear $8?"	Joe Bidder's proxy calls out $8, his final offer.
$8	$0.50	$8.50	"The bid is at $8. Do I hear $8.50?"	Your proxy calls out $8.50 on your behalf, and having outbid your opponent, you win the auction.

Specialized Auction Categories

After you get the hang of bidding at eBay, you may venture to the specialized auction areas. You can purchase fine art from eBay's Live Auctions, a car or car parts and accessories from eBay Motors, or your own piece of land or a new home in the Real Estate category. eBay is always adding new specialty areas, so be sure to check the announcements, as well as the home page.

Should you reach the big-time bidding, be aware that if you bid over $15,000 in an auction, you *must* register a credit card with eBay. All items in the special categories are searchable in eBay's search engine, so don't worry about missing your dream Corvette when you use the Search page.

eBay Motors

Visiting the automotive area of eBay is an auto enthusiast's dream. You can also find some great deals in used cars, and eBay offers these creative ways to make buying vehicles of all shapes and sizes (as well as the largest array of parts you'll find anywhere on the planet) easy for you. Visit eBay Motors by clicking the eBay Motors link on the home page or by going to `cars.ebay.ca`. Here are the main features of eBay Motors:

- **Search engine:** If you want to search for cars without coming up with hundreds of die-cast vehicles, eBay motors has its own search available from the eBay Motors home page.

- **Vehicle shipping:** If you don't want to drive across the country to pick up your new vehicle, you can have it shipped through Hansen's Vehicle Shipping. Check online for a free quote at `www.lhf.com/ebay/index.php`.

- **Inspections:** Many used-car sellers take advantage of inspection service vendors. These companies offer a comprehensive inspection covering the mechanical condition and cosmetic appearance, and they supply a detailed inspection report. Car auctions from sellers who have had their cars inspected include an Inspection icon.

- **Lemon Check:** With the vehicle's VIN (Vehicle Identification Number), you can get the entire vehicle history report through `www.autocheck.com`.

- **Escrow:** Escrow.com (`www.escrow.com`) is one of the safest ways to purchase a vehicle online. Escrow.com verifies and secures the buyer's payment and releases payment to the seller only after the buyer inspects and is completely satisfied with the vehicle.

eBay Live Auctions

If Marsha doesn't check out eBay Live Auctions (at `www.ebayliveauctions.com`) at least once a month, she feels like she's missing something. eBay Live Auctions is the very cool hub for auction houses and dealers from around the world. Here, you can find items that are so rare, you'll never find 'em anywhere else. You can easily waste (er, *enrich*) about half an hour of your life looking over some wonderful things up for auction. One day, you may find autographs from Abraham Lincoln or illuminated manuscripts from the 1700s, and the next day, you stumble on signed letters from Albert Schweitzer — how cool. It's great fun to look — even if you can't afford any of these items. Perusing eBay Live Auctions is like spending time in the fine galleries of the world — it's a virtual version of window shopping!

Live Auctions allows you to participate in real-time auctions as they happen at the finest auction houses around the world. Remember to read the terms carefully because you often must pay a bidder's premium (an additional amount of up to 20 percent added to your bid) on Live Auction items.

You may find yourself (or fantasize about) bidding against celebrities for amazing items — that, in itself, is a lot of fun! If you don't have the money at the moment to bid on Live Auction items, you can just click View Live, and your computer gives you a real-time view of the auction. Take a look at Figure 6-8; it's an item many would love to have, but few can afford!

If you think there's the slightest chance that you may want to bid on something, be sure to register for the auction in advance to participate in an eBay Live Auction. There's nothing worse than not being registered and seeing an item you'd love to have sell for a price within your range.

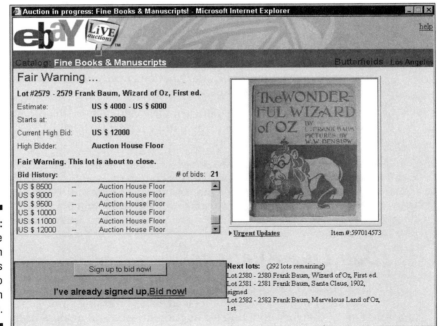

Figure 6-8: An old Live Auction item that was hard to refrain from bidding on.

Making purchases on the spot!

There's more to eBay than auctions. Aside from the Buy It Now offer available on some auctions, eBay holds venues for various items that you can buy *right now!*

eBay Stores

eBay Stores are a quick, easy, and convenient way to find items for sale that you can buy right now. A large number of eBay sellers have opened eBay Stores as an inexpensive way to display more items for sale. eBay sellers who open a Store are offered a much lower listing fee for their items, as low as six cents a month, and the items stay in their stores for as long as they want. The lower listing fees are quite a savings over the fees for listing an item for auction, and sellers often pass the savings onto you.

When you're perusing the auctions at eBay, look for the little red door icon to the right of a seller's User ID. If you click the door, you're magically transported to the seller's virtual eBay storefront. Figure 6-9 shows you the eBay Stores hub. You can get there by clicking the eBay Stores link on the upper-left side of the home page.

Figure 6-9: From the eBay Stores hub, you can browse categories, visit stores, or search all items in all eBay Stores.

eBay Stores have a separate search engine than the eBay auction search engine. If you don't find the item you're looking for at eBay auctions, look at the column on the left side of the page. The Shop eBay Stores section lists links to eBay Stores that may contain the item you're looking for, as well as a Search for Items in Stores link. Click the Search button and eBay performs the same search for you in all eBay Stores.

The Agony (?) of Buyer's Remorse

Maybe you're used to going into a shopping mall and purchasing something that you're not sure you like. What's the worst that could happen? You end up back at the mall, receipt in hand, returning the item. Not so on eBay. Even if you realize you already have a purple feather boa in your closet that's just like the one you won yesterday on eBay, deciding that you don't want to go through with a transaction *is* a big deal. Not only can it earn you some nasty feedback, but it can also give you the reputation of a deadbeat.

It would be a shame to float around eBay with the equivalent of a scarlet *D* (for *deadbeat*) above your User ID. Okay, eBay uses a kinder term — *non-paying bidder* — but for many members, it boils down to the same thing. If you win an auction and have to back out of your obligation as the winner — even through no fault of your own — you need to check out the following sections for some info that can keep you in good (well, okay, *better*) standing.

Retracting your bid

Remember, most jurisdictions consider your bid a binding contract, just like any other contract. You can't retract your bid unless one of these three outstandingly unusual circumstances applies:

- ✔ Your bid is clearly a typographical error (you submitted a bid for $4,567 when you really meant $45.67). If this occurs, you should re-enter the correct bid amount immediately.

 You won't get any sympathy if you try to retract an $18.25 bid by saying you meant to bid $15.25, so review your bid before you send it.

- ✔ You've tried to contact the seller to answer questions on the item, and he or she doesn't reply in a timely fashion.

- ✔ The seller substantially changes the description of an item after you place a bid (the description of the item changes from "can of tennis balls" to "a tennis ball," for example).

If you simply must retract a bid, try to do so long before the auction ends — and have a good reason for your retraction. eBay users are understanding, up to a point. If you have a good explanation, you should come out of the situation all right. So admit you've made a mistake.

If you've made an error and retract your bid prior to the last 12 hours of the auction, all bids you've placed in the auction are removed. Mistakes or not, when you retract a bid that was placed within the last 12 hours of the listing, only the most recent bid you made is retracted — your bids placed prior to the last 12 hours are still active.

To retract a bid while the auction's still going on, follow these steps (or you can just type `offer.ebay.ca/ws/eBayISAPI.dll?RetractBidShow` into your browser address field and skip to Step 6):

1. **Click the My eBay link on the main navigation bar.**

2. **Click the All Buying link on the left side of the screen.**

   The All Buying page appears.

3. **On the All Buying page, scroll down to Related Links (on the left side of the page) and click the More link.**

   The Buying-Related Links page appears.

4. **Click the Retracting a Bid link.**

5. **Read eBay's rules and legalese, then scroll down the page and click the Bid Retraction Form link.**

   The Bid Retractions page appears.

6. **On the Bid Retractions page, enter the item number of the auction from which you're retracting your bid in the box. Then select one of the three legitimate reasons for retracting your bid from the drop-down menu.**

7. **Click the Retract Bid button.**

   You receive a confirmation of your bid retraction via e-mail. Keep a copy of it until the auction is completed.

The seller may send you an e-mail to ask for a more lengthy explanation of your retraction, especially if the item was a hot seller that received a lot of bids. You may also get e-mails from other bidders. Keep your replies courteous. After you retract one bid on an item, all your lower bids on that item are also retracted (unless the retraction is done within the last 12 hours), and your retraction goes into the bidding history — so be sure you have a really good reason for the retraction. The number of bids you've retracted also goes on your feedback rating scorecard.

Buyer's remorse can pay off

Sometimes, buyer's remorse does pay off. We know one eBay buyer who got a serious case of remorse after winning an auction. She decided to do the right thing and pay for the item, even though she didn't want it. After receiving the item, she turned around and sold it on eBay for triple what she paid. If you really don't want the item, think like a seller — see whether you can turn a horrible mistake into a profitable venture. For more information on the benefits of selling, take a look at Chapter 9.

Avoiding deadbeat (non-paying bidder) status

Some bidders are more like kidders — they bid even though they have no intention of buying a thing. But those folks don't last long on eBay because of all the negative feedback they get. In fact, when honest eBay members spot these ne'er-do-wells, they often post the deadbeats' User IDs on eBay's message boards. Some eBay members have created entire Web sites to warn others about dealing with the deadbeats . . . ahem . . . *non-paying bidders.* (Civilized but chilly, isn't it?)

Exceptions to the deadbeat (er, sorry, non-paying bidder) rule may include the following human mishaps:

- A death in the family
- Computer failure
- A huge misunderstanding

If you have a good reason to call off your purchase, make sure that the seller knows about it. The seller is the only one who can excuse you from the sale.

If you receive a non-paying bidder warning but have paid for the item, eBay requires proof of payment. That can include a copy of the cheque (front and back) or money order, a copy of the payment confirmation from PayPal (or other online payment service), or an e-mail from the seller acknowledging receipt of payment. If the seller excused you from the auction, you need to forward the e-mail with all headers. Here's the contact info you need in order to remove a non-paying bidder warning from a user:

- ✔ **Fax:** Fax hard copies to eBay at 888-620-9497.

- ✔ **Snail mail:** Mail copies of the documents to Bay, Inc., Attn: Investigations Appeals, P.O. Box 30502, RPO Brentwood, Burnaby, BC, Canada V5C 6J5.

- ✔ **Online form:** Go to `pages.ebay.ca/help/tp/appeal-upi.html`, click the link to the online form, and plead your case.

There's no guarantee that your non-paying bidder appeal will be accepted. eBay will contact you after an investigation and let you know whether your appeal was successful.

eBay has a message for non-paying bidders: Three strikes and you're out. After the first complaint about a non-paying (deadbeat) bidder, eBay gives the bad guy or gal a warning. After the third offence, the non-paying bidder is suspended from eBay for good and becomes NARU (Not a Registered User). Nobody's tarred and feathered, but you probably won't see hide nor hair of that user again on eBay.

After the auction: Side deals or personal offers?

If a bidder is outbid on an item that he or she really wants, or if the auction's reserve price isn't met, the bidder can send an e-mail to the seller to see whether the seller is willing to make another deal. Maybe the seller has another similar item or is willing to sell the item directly rather than run a whole new auction. This kind of situation happens — but eBay doesn't sanction this outside activity.

If the seller has more than one of the item, or the original auction winner doesn't go through with the deal, the seller can make a Second Chance Offer. This is a legal eBay-sanctioned second chance for *underbidders* (unsuccessful bidders) who participated in the auction. Sellers can also make Second Chance Offers in reserve auctions if the reserve price wasn't met.

Any side deals other than Second Chance Offers are unprotected. Marsha tells the story of her friend Jack who collects autographed final scripts from hit television sitcoms. So when the curtain fell on *Seinfeld,* he had to have a script. Not surprisingly, he found one on eBay

with a final price tag that was way out of his league. But he knew that by placing a bid, someone else with a signed script to sell might see his name and try to make a deal. And he was right.

After the auction closed, he received an e-mail from a guy who claimed to have worked on the final show and had a script signed by all the actors. He offered it to Jack for $1,000 less than the final auction price at eBay. Tempted as he was to take the offer, Jack understood that eBay's rules and regulations wouldn't help him out if the deal turned sour. He was also aware that he wouldn't receive the benefit of feedback (which is the pillar of the eBay community).

If you even think about making a side deal, remember that not only does eBay *strictly* prohibit this activity, but eBay can also suspend you if you're reported for making a side deal. And if you're the victim of a side-deal scam, eBay's rules and regulations don't offer you any protection. Our advice? Watch out!

Chapter 7

Power-Bidding Strategies

. . . .

In This Chapter

▶ Knowing your competition

▶ Finding the hidden secrets in the bidding history

▶ Using canny strategies to win your auction

. . . .

*W*hile teaching our classes, we both speak to so many people who find an item at eBay, bid on it, and at the last minute — the last hour or the last day — are outbid. Sad and dejected, they find losing often cuts to the core and makes them feel like losers.

You're not a loser when you lose an auction on eBay. You just may not know the fine art of sneaky bidding (our way of saying *educated* bidding).

When the stakes are high and you really, really want the item, you have to resort to a higher form of strategy. Sports teams study their rivals, and political candidates scout out what the opposition is doing. Bidding in competition against other bidders is just as serious an enterprise. Follow the tips in this chapter and see if you can come up with a strong bidding strategy of your own. (Feel free to e-mail either of us with any scathingly brilliant plans; we're both always open to new theories.)

Getting to Know the High Bidder

The User ID of the person the item would belong to if the auction ended right now is usually listed on the auction item page (assuming someone has bid on the item). We say *usually* because eBay has recently made some changes that can mask the identity of the bidder in certain circumstances to protect him or her from scam artists. When the User ID is available, commit it to memory because you may see it again in auctions for similar items. If the high bidder has a lot of feedback, he or she may know the ropes — and be back to fight if you up the ante.

You can use the Items by Bidder search option on the eBay Search page, shown in Figure 7-1, to find out much of the bidder's recent auction experience. Again, recent changes by eBay may hide some of that bidder's activity, but hopefully, if he or she is a frequent buyer, you should still see enough to get an idea of his or her bidding habits. If you're bidding on an item, conducting a bidder search on your competition can be a valuable asset: With this information, you can size up your opponent's bidding style.

Figure 7-1:
Use an
Items by
Bidder
search to
get an idea
of the
competi-
tion's
bidding
patterns.

To get the skinny on a bidder, follow these steps:

1. **On the Items by Bidder Search page, type the User ID of the bidder you want to search for in the Enter Bidder's User ID box.**

2. **If you want to see auctions that this user has bid on in the past, check the Include Completed Listings check box.**

   You should check completed auctions. They give you a sense of how often and at what time of day the user participates in auctions. You can also see whether the opposition tends to bid in odd cents or round figures.

   Keep in mind that eBay has a 30-day limit on the auction information it returns, so don't expect to see results from a year ago. By clicking an item number in your search results, you can see at what times your main competition tends to bid — and then bid when you know those folks won't be looking.

3. **Select either the Even If Not the High Bidder option or the As High Bidder Only option.**

   Selecting Even If Not the High Bidder means that you want to see the bidder's activity in every auction, even if the person isn't the *current* high bidder. Selecting As High Bidder Only limits the search to auctions where the bidder is the current top dog. We think you should check all the bidder's auctions to see how aggressively he or she bids on items. You can also get a pretty good handle on how badly a bidder wants specific items — and how high that person will bid before dropping out.

If the bidder was bidding on the same item in the past that you're both interested in now, you can also get a fairly good idea of how high that person is willing to go for the item.

4. **Choose a number from the Results per Page drop-down list to specify how many items you want to see per page.**

5. **Click Search.**

You may be tempted to try to contact a bidder you're competing with so you can get information about the person more easily. This is not only bad form but could also get you suspended. Don't do it.

Finding Out an Item's Bidding History

An item's bidding *history,* shown on the item's auction page, lists everybody who's bidding on that item. You can see how often and at what time bids are placed, but you can't see how much each bidder bids until the auction ends. Figure 7-2 shows a typical bidding history list. You can see bid amounts because this auction has ended. Under new rules recently established by eBay to protect the privacy of bidders, if the bidding for an item exceeds US$200, the identities of the bidders aren't visible. Only the winning bidder's ID is visible after the auction ends.

Figure 7-2:
The bidding
history tells
you the date
and time
of day at
which the
bidders
placed
their bids.

Bid History		Item number: 180120767021
		Email to a friend | **Watch this item** in My eBay

Item title: Vintage A. TOURISTER "TIARA" Suitcase ROUND RETRO RED
Time left: 5 days, 4 hours 35 minutes 33 seconds
Reserve met.

Only actual bids (not automatic bids generated up to a bidder's maximum) are shown. Automatic bids may be placed days or hours before a listing ends. Learn more about bidding.

Bidder	Bid Amount	Date of bid
(405 ⭐)	US $45.00	22-May-07 22:35:59 EDT
(200 ⭐)	US $22.00	22-May-07 00:18:41 EDT
(405 ⭐)	US $20.00	22-May-07 22:34:28 EDT
(200 ⭐)	US $15.00	22-May-07 00:18:30 EDT
(5148 ⭐) me 🖼	US $12.51	22-May-07 02:13:27 EDT

If you and another bidder placed the same bid amount, the earlier bid takes priority.
You can retract your bid under certain circumstances only.

Pay attention to the times at which bidders are placing their bids; you may find that, like many eBay users, the people bidding in this auction seem to be creatures of habit — making their bids about once a day and at a particular time of day. They may be logging on before work, during lunch, or after work. Whatever their schedules, you have great info at your disposal in the event that a bidding war breaks out: Just bid after your competition traditionally logs out, and you increase your odds of winning the auction.

The tale of the dormant seller

Bill recently held a class in which a participant expressed his concern over not having yet received the plasma TV that he had bid on and won on eBay at a ridiculously low price. With a little questioning, the buyer explained that the seller had a feedback score of +12 that was 100 percent positive. However, on closer examination, feedback showed that the seller had never sold previously, and a search of the seller's User ID and completed sales showed that he or she sold two identical plasma TVs on the same day. The feedback scorecard also indicated that the account had been inactive for quite some time. Everything seemed to point to a case of a hijacked account. Fortunately for the buyer, the PayPal Buyer Protection Plan came to the rescue. Once again, repeat after us: *Always read the feedback comments! Be wary and ask questions!*

Early in an auction, an item may not have much of a bidding history, but that doesn't mean you can't still check out the dates and times a bidder places bids. You can also tell whether a bidder practices *sniping* (which we discuss in the section "Sniping to the finish: The final minutes," later in this chapter) if his or her bid zips in during the last few minutes (or even seconds!) of the auction. You may have a fight on your hands if the bidder practices sniping.

Strategies to Help You Outsmart the Competition

Your two cents do matter — at least at eBay. Here's why: Many eBay members tend to round off their bids to the nearest dollar figure. Some choose nice, familiar coin increments such as 25, 50, or 75 cents. But the most successful eBay bidders have found that adding two or three cents to a routine bid can mean the difference between winning and losing. So, we recommend that you make your bids in oddish figures (such as $15.02 or $45.57) as an inexpensive way to edge out your competition. If you have a proxy bid for, say, $22.57, and a sniper jumps in at the last second and places a bid for $22.50 — you still win! The highest bid placed always wins. For the first time ever, your two cents (or, in this case, seven cents) may actually pay off!

That's just one of the many strategies to get you ahead of the rest of the bidding pack without paying more than you should. ***Note:*** The strategies in the following sections are for bidders who are tracking an item over the course of a week or so, so be sure you have time to track the item and plan your next moves. Also, get a few auctions under your belt before you throw yourself into the middle of a bidding war.

Multiple Item (Dutch) auction strategy

Multiple Item (Dutch) auctions (which we explain in Chapter 1) are funky. Yes, that's a technical term that means that a Multiple Item auction strategy is a little . . . um . . . different. After all, each winner pays the same amount for the item, and Multiple Item auctions don't have a super-secret reserve price.

But winning a Multiple Item auction isn't all that different from winning other auctions. Therefore, wait until the closing minutes of the auction to bid, and then follow our sage advice for optimum success.

Here are the key things to remember about a Multiple Item auction:

- ✓ **The seller must sell all the items at the lowest winning price at the end of the auction, no matter what.** Whether there are higher bids or not, all winning bidders pay the same lowest winning price.

- ✓ **Winners are based on the highest bids received.** If you up the ante, you could win the auction and pay only the lowest winning price, which may be lower than your bid.

  Confused yet? Say the minimum bid for each of ten Groundhog Day watches is $10, and 20 people bid at $10, with each person bidding for one watch. The first ten bidders win the watch. But suppose you come along at the end of the auction and bid $15 as the 21st bidder. You get a watch (as do the first nine people who bid $10), *and* you get the watch for the lowest successful bid — which is $10! Get it?

- ✓ **Know where you stand in the pecking order.** A list of high bidders (and their bids) appears on the auction page, so you always know where you stand in the pecking order. Keep checking back during the progress of the auction so that you can adjust your bid appropriately.

- ✓ **Avoid being the lowest or the highest high bidder.** The highest bidder is sure to win, so the usual bidding strategy is to knock out the lowest high bidder. The lowest high bidder is said to be *on the bubble* or on the verge of losing the auction by a couple of pennies. To avoid being the bidder on the bubble, keep your bid just above the second-lowest winning bid.

- ✓ **If you want to buy more than one of an item up for auction, make sure you have that number of successful high bids as the auction draws to a close.** Huh? Remember, winners are based on the *highest* bids. If you're in a Multiple Item auction for ten items and place five $15 bids, nothing guarantees that you'll win five of that item. Nine other people who want the item could bid $20 apiece. Then they each win one of the items at $15, and you end up with only one of the item. (At least you still pay only $15 for it.) If you bid on all ten, your bid amount becomes the lowest successful bid amount, and that's how much you'll pay for all ten.

Pirates of the Caribbean . . . or Carribean?

Just before the movie *Pirates of the Caribbean* premiered, Disneyland gave out exclusive movie posters to its visitors. Some savvy eBayers snagged several copies to sell on the site. They typically listed the posters, after the movie opened, for a starting bid of US$9.99 each, but they rarely sold for more than the opening bid.

When we searched eBay for *pirates poster,* we found that the very same posters listed with a misspelled title, "Pirates of the Carribean,"

were selling for as high as US$30 each. Some sellers caught on quickly and changed their auctions to have the more popular misspelling *(Carribean)* in the title, and they quickly saw those dollar signs! Many of the posters listed with the misspelled title sold on the site for between US$15 and US$27!

The moral of this story is always search alternate spellings of your item; you might possibly eke out a gem without any competition.

Bidding strategies eBay doesn't talk about

Here's a list of do's and don'ts that can help you win your item (of course, some of these tips *are* eBay-endorsed, but we have to get you to notice what we have to say somehow):

- ✔ **Don't bid early and high.** Bidding early and high shows that you have a clear interest in the item. It also shows that you're a rookie, apt to make mistakes. If you bid early and high, you may give away just how much you want the item.

  Of course, a higher bid does mean more bucks for the seller and a healthy cut for the middleman. So it's no big mystery that many sellers recommend it. In fact, when you sell an item, you may want to encourage it, too.

  If you must bid early and can't follow the auction action (you mean you have a life?), use software or an online sniping service. Then feel free to place your highest possible bid! You can find out more about sniping services in Chapter 20.

- ✔ **Do wait and watch your auction.** If you're interested in an item, and you have the time to watch it from beginning to end, we say that the best strategy is to wait. Click the Watch This Item button on the item's auction page to place the item on your My eBay page, and remember to check the Items I'm Watching list on your My eBay page daily. But if you don't have the time, then go ahead — put in your maximum bid early and cross your fingers.

✔ **Don't freak out if you find yourself in a bidding war.** Don't keel over if, at the split second you're convinced that you're the high bidder with your $45.02, someone beats you out at $45.50.

You can increase your maximum bid to $46.02, but if your bidding foe also has a maximum of $46.02, the tie goes to the person who put in the highest bid first. Bid as high as you're willing to go, but bid at the very end of the auction.

✔ **Do check the item's bidding history.** If you find yourself in a bidding war and want an item badly enough, check the bidding history and identify your fiercest competitor; then refer to the section "Getting to Know the High Bidder," earlier in this chapter, for a pre-auction briefing.

To get a pretty exact picture of your opponent's bidding habits, make special note of the times of day when he or she has bid on other auctions. You can adjust your bidding times accordingly.

✔ **Do remember that most deals go through without a problem.** The overwhelming majority of deals at eBay are closed with no trouble, which means that if the auction you're bidding in is typical and you come in second place, you've lost. Or maybe not . . .

If the winning bidder backs out of the auction or the seller has more than one of the item, the seller *could* (but isn't obligated to) come to another bidder and offer to sell the item at the second bidder's price through eBay's Second Chance option. (See Chapter 13 for more details on this feature.)

Time Is Money: Strategy by the Clock

You can use different bidding strategies, depending on how much time is left in an auction. By paying attention to the clock, you can find out about your competition, beat them out, and end up paying less for your item.

Most auctions at eBay run for a week; the auction item page always lists how much time is left. However, sellers can run auctions for as short as one day or as long as ten days. eBay Canada (www.ebay.ca) bases listing times on the eastern time zone because its offices are in Toronto. eBay.com (www.ebay.com) bases all listings on the Pacific time zone because its corporate head office is in San Jose, California. So, synchronize your computer clock with the eBay site that you plan to do your bidding on and become the most precise eBay bidder around. Figure 7-3 shows eBay's official time page.

Figure 7-3:
eBay
Canada's
official time
page is
based on
the eastern
time zone.

To synchronize your clock, make sure that you're logged on to the Internet and can easily access the eBay Web site. Then follow these steps:

1. **Go into your computer's Control Panel and double-click the icon that represents your system's date and time functions.**

2. **On most every eBay.ca page you can find an eBay Official Time link at the bottom of the page. Clicking that link will take you to a page that will display the official time for both eBay.com and eBay.ca.**

3. **Check your computer's time against eBay's current time.**

4. **Click the minutes in your computer's clock and then click the Reload button (sometimes it's called Refresh) on your browser.**

    Clicking Reload ensures that you see the latest, correct time from eBay.

5. **Type the minutes displayed on the eBay Official Time page into your computer's clock as soon as the newly reloaded page appears.**

6. **Repeat Steps 5 and 6 to synchronize your computer's seconds display with eBay's.**

This process takes a little practice, but it can mean the difference between winning and losing an auction.

You don't need to worry about the hour display unless you mind your system clock possibly displaying a different time zone than eBay.

Most bidding at eBay goes on during East Coast work time and early evening hours, which gives you a leg up if you live out West. Night-owl bidders will find that after 10 p.m. Pacific time (about 1:00 a.m. eastern time), a lot of bargains are to be had. And believe it or not, a lot of auctions end in the wee hours of the morning. Monday holidays are also great for bargains, as are Thanksgiving and the day after. While everyone else is in the living room digesting and arguing about what to watch on TV (or getting up at 5:00 a.m. to buy the big discount deal at Wal-Mart), fire up eBay and be thankful for the great bargains you can win.

For simplicity's sake, go to Bill's Web site and print out his quick and easy eBay time-conversion chart. It's located at

`www.learningebayiseasy.com/canadian_time_zones.html`

Using the lounging-around strategy

Sometimes, the best strategy at the beginning of an auction is to do nothing at all. That's right: Relax, take off your shoes, and loaf. Go ahead. You may want to make a *token bid* (the very lowest you're allowed) or mark the page to watch in your My eBay area. We generally take this attitude through the first six days of a week-long auction that we may want to bid on, and it works pretty well. Of course, we both check in virtually every day, just to keep tabs on the items we're watching on our My eBay pages, and we revise our strategies as required.

The seller has the right to up his or her minimum bid — if his or her auction has received no bids — up to 12 hours before the auction ends. If the seller has set a ridiculously low minimum bid and then sees that the auction is getting no action, the seller may choose to up the minimum bid to protect his investment in the item that's up for sale. By placing the minimum token bid when you first see the auction, you can foil a Buy It Now from another bidder (because Buy It Now is disabled after a bid has been placed) or prevent the seller from upping the minimum. If it's important enough, you can see whether the seller has done this in the past by searching the Seller's completed auctions (see the section "Getting to Know the High Bidder," earlier in this chapter, to find out how to do this search). All preclosing changes are available for public view; just click the Revised link to the right of the Description title on the item page. See Figure 7-4 for a sample.

Figure 7-4:
This page shows the revisions made by the seller during this auction.

Item Revisions summary for item #270120893572		
The seller has revised the following item information:		
Date	**Time**	**Revised Information**
20-May-07	10:08:49 EDT	Reserve Price Buy It Now Price See Description

If you see an item that you *absolutely must* have, mark it to watch on your My eBay page (or make that token bid), then plan and revise your maximum bid as the auction goes on. We can't stress enough the benefits of adding items to your "watch" list if you really want to bid on and win those items. Not only does the watch feature allow you to find those items quickly in a vast sea of auctions, but it provides you with instant information on the bidding status of those auctions.

As you check back each day, take a look at the other bids and the high bidder. Is someone starting a bidding war? Look at the time the competition is bidding and note patterns. Maybe at noon, eastern time? During lunch? If you know what time your major competition is bidding, then — when the time is right — you can safely bid after he or she does (preferably when your foe is stuck in rush-hour traffic).

If you play the waiting game, you can decide if you really want to increase your bid or wait around for the item to show up again sometime. You may decide you really don't want this particular item after all. Or you may feel no rush because many sellers who offer multiple items put them up one at a time.

Using the beat-the-clock strategy

You should rev up your bidding strategy during the final 24 hours of an auction and decide, once and for all, whether you really *have* to have the item you've been eyeing. Maybe you put in a maximum bid of $45.02 earlier in the week. Now's the time to decide whether you're willing to go as high as $50.02. Maybe $56.03?

No one wants to spend the day in front of the computer (ask almost anyone who does). You can camp out by the refrigerator or at your desk or wherever you want to be. Just place a sticky note where you're likely to see it, reminding you of the exact time the auction ends. If you're not going to be near a computer when the auction closes, you can also use an automatic bidding site to bid for you; see Chapter 20 for details.

In the last half hour

With a half hour left before the auction becomes ancient history, head for the computer and dig in for the last battle of the bidding war. We recommend that you log on to eBay about five to ten minutes before the auction ends. The last thing you want to have happen is to get caught in Internet gridlock and not get access to the Web site. Go to the item you're watching and click the auction title.

With ten minutes to go, if there's a lot of action on your auction, click Reload (or Refresh) every 30 seconds to get the most current info on how many people are bidding. If the listing has a page view counter, it will be visible near the bottom of the auction page and it may give you some insight as to the general interest in the item.

Sniping to the finish: The final minutes

The rapid-fire, final flurry of bidding is called sniping. *Sniping* is the fine art of waiting until the very last seconds of an eBay auction and then outbidding the current high bidder just in time. Of course, you have to expect that the current high bidder is probably sniping back.

With a hot item, open a second window on your browser (in both Internet Explorer or Firefox, you can do that by pressing the Ctrl key and the N key together); keep one window open for bidding and the other open for constant reloading during the final few minutes. With the countdown at 60 seconds or less, make your final bid at the absolute highest amount you're willing to pay for the item. The longer you can hold off — we're talking down to around 20 seconds or less — the better. It all depends on the speed of your Internet connection (and how strong your stomach is). Practice on some small auctions so you know how much time to allow when you're bidding on your prize item. Keep reloading or refreshing your browser as fast as you can, and watch the time tick to the end of the auction.

The story of the Snipe sisters

Cory and Bonnie are sisters and avid eBay buyers. Bonnie collects vases. She had her eye on a Fenton Dragon Flies Ruby Verdena vase, but the auction closed while she was at work and didn't have access to a computer. Knowing that, her sister Cory decided to snipe for it. With 37 seconds to go, she inserted the high bid on behalf of her sister. Bang, she was high bidder at $63. But, with 17 seconds left, another bidder sniped back and raised the price to $73. It was, of course, Bonnie, who had found a way to get access to a computer from where she was. Bonnie got the vase, and they both had a good laugh.

If you want to be truly fancy, you can open a third window (see Figure 7-5) and have a back-up high bid in case you catch another sniper swooping in on your item immediately after your first snipe. (Marsha recently received an e-mail from one of her readers who used this somewhat paranoid method — the reader got the idea from the American version of this book — and by using the second snipe, she won her item!) You can avoid the third-window routine if you've bid your highest bid with the first snipe. Then, if you're outbid, you know the item went for more than you were willing to pay. (We know; it's some consolation, but not much.)

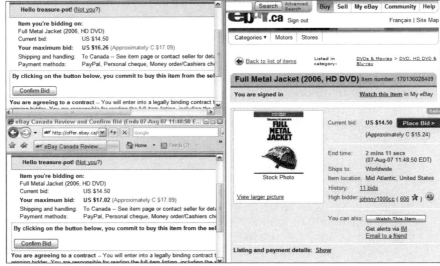

Figure 7-5:
An example of the dual-window sniping procedure in action!

Some eBay members consider the practice of sniping highly unseemly and uncivilized — it's like when hundreds of parents mobbed the department store clerks days before Christmas to get one of the handful of Sony PlayStation 3s that were just delivered. Of course, sometimes a little uncivilized behaviour can be a hoot.

We both consider sniping an addictive, fun part of life at eBay auctions. And it's a blast. So our recommendation is that you try sniping. You're likely to benefit from the results and enjoy your eBay experience even more — especially if you're an adrenaline junkie.

Here's a list of things to keep in mind when you get ready to place your last bid:

✔ Know how high you're willing to go.

If you know you're facing a lot of competition, figure out your highest bid to the penny. You should have already researched the item and know its value at this point. Raise your bid only to the level at which you're sure you're getting a good return on your investment; don't go overboard. Certainly, if the item has some emotional value to you and you just have to have it, bid as high as you want (and can afford — but you knew that). But remember, you'll have to pay the piper later. You win it, you own it!

✔ Know how fast (or slow) your Internet connection is.

✔ Remember, this is a game, and sometimes it's a game of chance — so don't lose heart if you lose the auction.

Although sellers love sniping because it drives up prices, and bidders love it because it's fun, a sniper can ruin a week's careful work on an auction strategy. The most skillful snipers sneak in a bid so close to the end of the auction that you have no chance to counter-bid, which means you lose. Losing too often, especially to the same sniper, can be a drag.

If your Internet connection is slower than most and you want to do some sniping, make your final bid two minutes before the auction ends — and adjust the amount of the bid as high as you feel comfortable so you can beat out the competition.

If you can make the highest bid with less than 20 seconds left, you most likely will win. With so many bids coming in the final seconds, your bid might be the last one eBay records.

This stuff is supposed to be fun, so don't lose perspective. If you can't afford an item, don't get caught up in a bidding war. Otherwise, the only person who wins is the seller. If you're losing sleep, barking at your cat, or biting your nails over any item, it's time to rethink what you're doing. Shopping at eBay is like being in a long line in a busy department store. If it's taking too much of your life or an item costs too much, be willing to walk away — or log off — and live to bid (or shop) another day.

When All Else Fails — Try Bid Assistant

eBay now offers a valuable tool to help you when you really must have an item but, it seems, the entire world bids against you at the last moment.

Recognizing that many buyers may become frustrated by repeated failure to win an auction, eBay created Bid Assistant as an automated bidding tool that bids on your behalf. However, unlike a sniping service (as we discuss in greater detail in Chapter 20), which places bids for you in the final few seconds of the listing, Bid Assistant places bids on your behalf throughout the duration of the listing. To use Bid Assistant, you must have a feedback score of five or more and follow these steps:

1. **Search for a group of products that you would be prepared to bid on and win.**

   Using the search function, find current auctions for items that are the same and offer similar terms. As you find each item, add it to your Watch list (as we discuss earlier in this chapter). You can add as many as ten items to any group with a limit of five active groups at any time.

2. **Create your group.**

Go to the Items I'm Watching view of My eBay and select the check box next to each of the items you want to add to this group; then click the Bid with Bid Assistant button. You must be willing to win and pay for any of the items within this group. You can only win one of the items with Bid Assistant, but you will be obligated to complete that transaction.

3. **Name your group and determine your highest bid for each item.**

   Bid Assistant allows you to compare current high bids and shipping costs (if they have been predetermined) to help you make your decisions. Enter your winning bids and click Continue. Your bids can be the same or different for each item.

4. **Review and finalize your bids.**

   Make any last-minute adjustments to your bids before clicking the Confirm Bid button.

Now that your bids are placed, Bid Assistant takes over and places the lowest possible bid on each item, starting with the item that ends first. Bid Assistant will continue to bid on your behalf until you win an auction, reach your maximum bid amount, or reach the end of your group. If Bid Assistant is successful in winning an auction, it will immediately stop bidding on your behalf. It will never bid on more than one item in a group at a time. If you are outbid on an item, Bid Assistant will always wait until that auction closes before moving on to bid on the next item in your group.

For more information about Bid Assistant and all of its features, visit:

```
http://pages.ebay.ca/help/buy/bid-
        assistant.html?fromFeature=My%20eBay
```

Chapter 8

After You Win the Item

In This Chapter

▶ Getting yourself organized

▶ Talking turkey with the seller

▶ Ironing out the details and sending your payment

▶ Dealing with a disappearing seller

▶ Finishing the transaction with feedback

The thrill of the chase is over, and you've won your first eBay item. Congratulations — now what do you do? You have to follow up on your victory and keep a sharp eye on what you're doing. The post-auction process can be loaded with pitfalls and potential headaches if you don't watch out. Remember, sometimes money, like a full moon, does strange things to people.

In this chapter, you can get a handle on what's in store for you after you win the auction. We clue you in on what the seller's supposed to do to make the transaction go smoothly, and show you how to grab hold of your responsibilities as a buyer. We give you info here about following proper post-auction etiquette, including the best way to get organized, communicate with the seller professionally, and send your payment without hazards. We also brief you on how to handle an imperfect transaction.

eBay Calling: You're a Winner

The All Buying section of your My eBay page highlights the titles of auctions you've won and indicates the amount of your winning bid. If you think you may have won the auction and don't want to wait around for eBay to contact you, check out the All Buying section for yourself and find out — are you a winner?

Throughout the bidding process, dollar amounts of items that you're winning appear in green on your My eBay page. If you've been outbid, they appear in red. After the auction ends, you get no marching band, no visit from Ed McMahon and his camera crew, no armful of roses, and no oversized cheque to duck behind. In fact, you're more likely to find out that you've won the auction from either the seller or the Bidding section of your My eBay page than you are to hear it right away from eBay. eBay tries to get its End of Auction e-mails (EOAs) out pronto, but sometimes there's a bit of lag time. For a look at all the contact information in the End of Auction e-mail, see Figure 8-1.

You can also receive EOA notices in the form of instant messages through AOL, Windows Live!, Or Yahoo! providers. (See Chapter 6 for more information on the types of eBay alerts available.) Go to your My eBay: My Account: Preferences page and click the Show link to the right of Notification Delivery. You can indicate just how you want to receive the various notifications from eBay here.

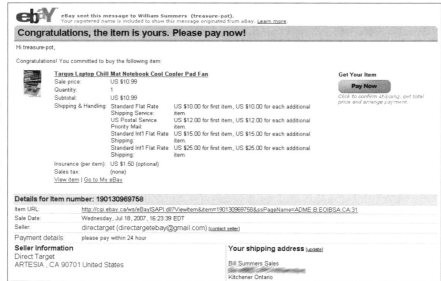

Figure 8-1: Everything you need to know about contacting your buyer or seller is included in eBay's End of Auction e-mail.

Getting Your Paperwork Together

Yeah, we know that PCs were supposed to create a paperless society, but cars were supposed to fly by the year 2000, too. Maybe it's just as well that some predictions don't come true (think of the way some people drive). Paper still has its uses; printing hard copies of your auction records can help you keep your transactions straight.

Your auction page shows the amount of your winning bid, the item's description, and other relevant information. The second you find out you've won the auction, click the Printer Version link in the upper-right corner of the listing — print *two* copies of the item page if you're mailing the payment to the seller. Keep a copy for your files. Send the second copy to the seller along with your payment; including this copy with your payment is not only efficient but also polite.

eBay displays auctions for only 30 days in the Bidder search, so don't put off printing that final auction page for your records. If you save the End of Auction e-mail that you get from eBay, you can access the auction for up to 90 days if you use the link in the e-mail.

Many sellers have multiple auctions going at the same time, so the more organized you are, the more likely you'll receive the correct item (and positive feedback) from the seller. Here's a list of the items you should keep in your auction purchases file:

- ✔ A copy of your EOA e-mail from eBay. *Don't* delete the EOA e-mail — at least, not until you print a copy and keep it for your records. You may need to refer to the EOA e-mail later, and you have no way to get another copy.
- ✔ Printed copies of any e-mail correspondence between you and the seller that details specific information about the item or special payment and shipping arrangements.
- ✔ A printed copy of the final auction page.

Sellers can edit and update their auctions even while those auctions are in progress, so keep your eyes peeled for changes in the auction as you monitor it. If the seller makes major changes in the auction, you're within your rights to withdraw your bid. (Check out Chapter 6 for more on the bidding process.)

Getting Contact Information

The eBay rules and regulations say that buyers and sellers must contact each other within three business days of the auction's end. So, if an item closes on a Saturday, you need to make contact by Wednesday.

If you've won an item and intend to pay through PayPal, it's *de rigueur* for you to go to the item as soon as possible after you've won and use the Pay Now link on the item page.

An order of fries with a menu on the side

In 1999, one seller auctioned off an old menu from Howard Johnson's, estimating its era as the 1950s based on the cars pictured on the cover — and the prices (fried clams were US$1.25). Also included was a separate menu card that listed fresh seafood and had a liquor menu (with Pieman logo) on the back — plus a list of locations in the New York City area. Except for a couple of staple holes at the top of the front cover (maybe evidence of daily specials past), the menu was in very good condition. The starting bid was US$5; the item sold for US$64. These menus are even harder to come by now, but are selling in the US$45 range.

(We wonder how much they want for fried clams in New York City these days. . . .)

So, What's Your Number?

If you don't hear from the seller after three business days and you've already tried sending an e-mail, you need to get more contact information. Remember back when you registered and eBay asked for a phone number? eBay keeps that information for times like this.

You may need to contact an eBay member by phone before you pay for your item. To get an eBay member's phone number, click the Advanced Search link below the Search box and then click the Members: Find Contact Information link on the left side of the screen. You need to enter the seller's User ID and the number of the item that you're buying from the other member; then click the Search button.

eBay automatically generates an e-mail for both you and the other user.

eBay's e-mail includes the seller's User ID, name, e-mail address, company, city, state, and country of residence, as well as the seller's phone number and date of initial registration. eBay sends this same information about you to the user you want to get in touch with.

Often, sellers jump to attention when they receive this e-mail from eBay and get the ball rolling to complete the transaction.

eBay doesn't tolerate any abuses of its contact system. Make sure that you use this resource only to communicate with another user about a specific transaction. To use contact information to complete a deal outside of eBay is an infringement of the rules. If you abuse the contact system, eBay can investigate you and kick you off the site.

If the seller doesn't contact you within three business days, you may have to do some nudging to complete the transaction. (The section "Keeping in Touch: Dealing with an AWOL Seller," later in this chapter, and Chapter 13 cover how to deal with a seller who's dragging his or her feet.)

Checking Out

When you buy something in a store, you need to check out to pay. eBay isn't much different. eBay's Checkout is a very convenient way to pay for your completed auctions, fixed-price sales, and Buy it Now sales with a credit card, existing balance, Instant Transfer, or eCheque through PayPal. You may also use Checkout to exchange your information with the seller and pay for your item in a way other than PayPal (such as by money order, cheque, or another payment service that the seller accepts).

Checkout is integrated directly onto the item page so that you can win and pay for an item in less than a minute. Some sellers indicate, in their descriptions, that they'll send you a link to their private checkout page. When the sale is over, the item page will have checkout information, as shown in Figure 8-2.

Figure 8-2: Click the Pay Now button to pay for the item through PayPal or to indicate your payment preferences.

When you click the Pay Now button, you're taken step-by-step through the checkout process. You pay for the item, and the seller is notified. You also get an e-mail confirming your payment, along with the seller's e-mail address.

You can make an immediate payment only if the seller chooses to accept PayPal. If the seller chooses to accept other forms of payment, such as personal cheques or money orders, you can still go through the process to send the seller your shipping information (but not your actual payment). If the shipping cost is based on your location, the seller can also use this information to send you an invoice or to update the checkout information on the item page. When that's done, you can go ahead and send payment.

Communicating with the Seller

Top-notch sellers know that communication is the absolute key to a successful transaction, and they do everything they can to set a positive tone for the entire process with speedy and courteous e-mails (or, at the very least, invoices).

Contact from a professional eBay seller should include the following information:

- Confirmation of the winning price
- The address for sending payment or a phone number for credit card processing
- A review of the shipping options and price (the fee you pay)
- Confirmation of escrow (if it was offered in the auction)
- The date the item will be shipped

When you read the seller's e-mail, be sure to compare the terms the seller lays out in his or her e-mail with the terms laid out on the auction page. And make sure that the form of payment and where it should be sent are clear to you.

You should pay immediately upon receipt of the invoice. If you have a question prior to payment, contact the seller immediately. He or she will be expecting your payment.

The e-mail you receive from the seller after the auction is over should be a confirmation of the options laid out on the auction item page. If you see significant differences between what the seller's saying now and what's on your printout of the auction item page, address those differences immediately with the seller before you proceed with the transaction. For more on clarifying payment options during the bidding process, see Chapter 6.

Sending the Payment Promptly and Securely

So how many times have you heard the saying "The cheque's in the mail"? Yeah, we've heard it about a thousand times, too. If you're on the selling end of a transaction, hearing this line from the buyer but not getting the money is frustrating. If you're on the buying end, it's very bad form and may also lead to bad feedback for you.

Being the good buyer that you are (you're here finding out how to do the right thing, right?), naturally, you'll get your payment out pronto. If you've purchased an item and intend to pay via PayPal, do it immediately — why wait? (The sooner you pay, the sooner you get that charming Flying Monkey decanter you won!)

Most sellers expect to get paid within seven to ten business days after the close of the auction. Although this timeline isn't mandatory, it makes good sense to let the seller know payment is on the way.

Send your payment promptly and in the correct currency. Some Canadian sellers allow you to send Canadian funds — even if the auction was listed in U.S. greenbacks — usually at the going rate of exchange. Make sure you ask the seller before sending your payment.

If you have to delay payment for any reason (you have to go out of town, you ran out of cheques, you broke your leg), let the seller know as soon as possible. Most sellers understand if you send them a kind and honest e-mail. Let the seller know what's up, give him or her a date by which the money can be expected, and then meet that deadline. If the wait is unreasonably long, the seller may cancel the transaction. In that case, you can expect to get some bad feedback.

Here are some tips on how to make sure that your payment reaches the seller promptly and safely:

- Have your name and address printed on your cheques. A cheque without a printed name or address sends up a big red flag to sellers that the cheque may not clear. For privacy and safety reasons, though, *never* put your driver's licence number or Social Insurance Number on your cheque.

- Always write the item title and your User ID on a cheque or money order, and enclose a printout of the final auction page in the envelope. The number one pet peeve of most eBay sellers is that they get a payment but don't know what it's for — buyers send cheques without any auction information.

- ✔ If you're paying with a credit card without using a payment service and you want to give the seller the number over the telephone, be sure to request the seller's phone number in your reply to the seller's initial e-mail and explain why you want it.

- ✔ You can safely e-mail your credit card information over the course of several e-mails, each containing four numbers from your credit card. Stagger your e-mails so that they're about 20 minutes apart and don't forget to let the seller know what kind of credit card you're using. Also, give the card's expiration date.

Buyers routinely send out payments without their name, their address, or a clue as to what they've purchased. No matter how you pay, be sure to include a copy of the eBay confirmation letter, a printout of the auction page, or a copy of the e-mail the seller sent you. If you pay with a credit card via e-mail or over the phone, you should still send this info through the mail, just to be on the safe side.

Using PayPal, a person-to-person payment service

Chapter 6 covers the pros and cons of using PayPal to pay for your auctions. In this section, we show you why PayPal is the safest way to pay on eBay. eBay sees to it that PayPal is incredibly easy to use because PayPal is the official payment service at eBay. After the auction is over, a link to pay appears. If you prefer, wait until you hear from the seller. (We much prefer to have the seller's full name and address for our records before sending payment — especially if the amount of the transaction exceeds PayPal's Buyer Protection Program limit.)

You can make your payment in four different ways:

- ✔ **Credit Card:** You can use your American Express, Visa, or MasterCard to make your payment through PayPal. The cost of the item is charged to your card, and your next credit card statement will reflect a PayPal payment with the seller's ID.

- ✔ **eCheque:** Sending money with an eCheque is easy. It debits your chequing account, just like a paper cheque. An eCheque doesn't clear immediately, and the seller probably won't ship until PayPal tells him or her it has cleared your bank.

✔ **Instant Transfer:** An Instant Transfer is just like an eCheque, except that it clears immediately and the money is directly posted to the seller's account. To send an Instant Transfer, you must have a credit card on file with PayPal as a backup (should the payment from your bank be denied).

✔ **Account Balance:** If you're a seller on eBay, you may already have funds in your PayPal account that you can use to pay for your purchases. This is PayPal's preferred payment method.

PayPal is our favourite payment service for another reason. PayPal has a buyer protection program, which covers your purchases up to $2,000. Read more about this protection program in Chapter 16.

When the auction is over, you can click the Pay Now button to check out and enter the PayPal site. If you don't pay immediately from the item page or seller's invoice, you can also go to your My eBay: All Buying: Won page and pay from the link to the right of the auction, or just type www.paypal.com in your browser's address box and press Enter. After you go to the PayPal home page, follow these steps:

1. **If this is your first visit to the PayPal site, register by clicking the Sign Up Now button and following the instructions on-screen.**

   If you're already a registered user, go ahead and log in by following the steps on-screen.

2. **Click the Auction Tools tab, then scroll down and click Pay for an Auction.**

   PayPal takes you step by step through the process of filling out a payment form to identify the auction you're paying for, as well as your shipping information.

You're all done. Your credit card information is held safely with PayPal, and the payment is deposited into the seller's PayPal account. The seller receives notice of your payment and notifies you about how quickly he or she will ship your item.

By paying with PayPal, you can instantly pay for an auction without hassle. Your credit card information is kept private, and your payment is deposited into the seller's PayPal account.

You can always view your checkout status by going to your My eBay: All Buying: Won area, shown in Figure 8-3. Click the drop-down menu in the Action column for the item in question.

ebaY.ca

Review Your Purchases From moviemagicusa   Help

You are paying for **2 items** totalling US $29.20 from **moviemagicusa**.
To continue payment for moviemagicusa, click the **Continue** button at the bottom of the page.

Review shipping address

Seller should ship to: **Bill Summers Sales**
                          Kitchener, Ontario N2E 4K6
                          Canada
                          Change shipping address

Review payment details

Want to save time?   Pay All Your PayPal Sellers At Once >

Seller: moviemagicusa (127315)   Power Seller   Top 5,000 Reviewer

Movie Magic USA
Thanks for shopping with Movie Magic USA! Be sure to check out even more specials in our store at www.moviemagicusa.com to save on shipping and handling. Shipping and handling is listed in every listing. Box sets S&H is listed for priority USA, Canada, and International. Email us if you have any questions. Enjoy your movies!

Item Title	Qty.	Price	Subtotal
TROY - Brad Pitt & Orlando Bloom - New Widescreen DVD (130125382797)	1	US $8.50	US $8.50
MAVERICK & WILD WILD WEST - New DVD 2 Pack (130134378071)	1	US $9.95	US $9.95

Payment Instructions
Payment may be made via PayPal. (PayPal name: info@moviemagicusa.com), Money Order, Cashier's Check, or Personal Check.
Payments may be mailed to:

Shipping and handling: USPS First Class Mail International US $10.75

Subtotal: US $18.45
Shipping and handling   US $10.75
Shipping insurance (included in S&H)   --
Seller discounts (-) or charges (+):

Figure 8-3:
Click the link in the Action column near the bottom of the screen to verify the status of your payment.

Keeping in Touch: Dealing with an AWOL Seller

The eBay community, like local towns and cities, isn't without its problems. With the millions of transactions that go on every week, transactional difficulties do pop up now and then.

The most common problem is the AWOL seller — the kind of person who pesters you for payment and then disappears. Just as you're obligated to hustle and get your payment off to the seller within a week, the seller also has an obligation to notify you within a week of receiving your payment with an e-mail that says the item has been shipped. If you sent the money but you haven't heard a peep in a while, *don't* jump the gun and assume the person is trying to cheat you, but *do* follow up.

Follow this week-by-week approach if you've already paid for the item but haven't heard from the seller:

✔ **Week one, the gentle-nudge approach:** Remind the seller with an e-mail about the auction item, its number, and the closing date. "Perhaps this slipped your mind and got lost in the shuffle of your other auctions" is a good way to broach the subject. Chances are good that you'll get an apologetic e-mail about some family emergency or last-minute business trip. The old saying "You can attract a lot more bees with honey than with vinegar" works great at eBay.

✔ **Week two, the civil-but-firm approach:** Send an e-mail again. Be civil but firm. Set a date for when you expect to be contacted. Meanwhile, tap into some of eBay's resources. See the section "Getting Contact Information," earlier in this chapter, to find out how to get an eBay user's phone number. After you have this information, you can send a follow-up letter or make direct contact and set a deadline for some sort of action.

✔ **Week three, take-action time:** If you still haven't heard from the seller, e-mail the seller once more and let him or her know that you're filing a complaint. Then go to Trust & Safety and file a grievance for Item Not Received. Explain in detail what has transpired. eBay will launch its own internal investigation. If your payment was through PayPal, you can also start the ball rolling with their dispute mechanism. Turn to Chapter 16 to find out more about filing complaints and using other tools to resolve problems.

You Get the Item (Uh-Oh, What's This?)

The vast majority of eBay transactions go without a hitch. You win, you send your payment, you get the item, you check it out, you're happy. If that's the case — a happy result for your auction — then skip this section and go leave some positive feedback for the seller!

On the other hand, if you're not happy with the item you receive, the seller may have some 'splaining to do. E-mail or call the seller immediately, and politely ask for an explanation if the item isn't as described. Some indications of a foul-up are pretty obvious:

✔ The item's colour, shape, or size doesn't match the description.

✔ The item's scratched, broken, or dented in ways that don't match the description (the doll's description was new, but the box is tattered and the doll's seen more than its share of action).

✔ You won an auction for a set of candlesticks and received a vase instead.

A snag in the transaction is annoying, but don't get steamed right away. Contact the seller and see whether you can work things out. Keep the conversation civilized. The majority of sellers want a clean track record and good feedback, so they'll respond to your concerns and make things right. Assume the best about the seller's honesty, unless you have a real reason to suspect foul play. Remember, you take some risks whenever you buy something that you can't touch. If the item has a slight problem that you can live with, leave it alone and don't go to the trouble of leaving negative feedback about an otherwise pleasant, honest eBay seller.

Of course, although we can give you advice on what you *deserve* from a seller, you're the one who has to live with the item. If you and the seller can't reach a compromise and you really think you deserve a refund, ask for one.

If you paid the seller to insure the item through Canada Post or the U.S. Postal Service, and it arrives at your home pretty well pulverized, e-mail or call the seller to alert him or her about the problem. Ask the seller to initiate a postal claim for damage. It's the seller's responsibility to process a claim on your behalf because he or she contracted for the delivery service. Check out Chapter 12 for more tips on how to deal with a shipping catastrophe. And jump over to Chapter 16 to find out how to file your eBay and/or PayPal insurance claim.

Don't Forget to Leave Feedback

Good sellers should be rewarded, and potential buyers should be informed. That's why no eBay transaction is complete until the buyer fills out the feedback form. Before leaving any feedback, though, remember that sometimes no one's really at fault when transactions get fouled up; communication meltdowns can happen to anyone. (For more info on leaving feedback, see Chapter 4.) Here are some scenarios that give you an idea of what kind of feedback to leave for a seller:

- ✔ **Positive:** If the transaction could have been a nightmare, but the seller really tried to make it right and meet you halfway, that's an easy call — give the seller the benefit of the doubt and leave positive feedback.

   Whenever possible, reward someone who seems honest or tried to fix a bad situation. For example, if the seller worked at a snail's pace, but you eventually got your item and you're thrilled with it, you may want to leave positive feedback with a caveat. Something like "Item as described, good seller, but very slow to deliver" sends the right feedback message.

- ✔ **Neutral:** If the seller worked at a snail's pace, did adequate packaging, and the item was kinda-sorta what you thought, you may want to leave neutral feedback; the transaction wasn't bad enough for negative feedback, but doesn't deserve praise, either. Here's an example of what you might say: "Slow to ship, didn't say item condition was good not excellent, but did deliver." Wishy-washy is okay as a response to so-so; at least the next buyer will know to ask very specific questions.

✔ **Negative:** If the seller never shipped your item, or if the item didn't match the description when it arrived, *and* if the seller won't make things right, you need to leave negative feedback. Make sure that both conditions apply. Never write negative feedback in the heat of the moment and never make it personal. Keep it mellow and just state the facts. Do expect a response, but don't get into a negative feedback war. Life's interesting enough without taking on extra hassles.

Part III

Are You Selling What They're Buying?

The 5th Wave   By Rich Tennant

@RICHTENNANT

"Oh, we're doing just great. Philip and I are selling decorative jelly jars on eBay. I manage the listings and Philip sort of controls the inventory."

In this part . . .

A lot of different factors are at work when a seller makes a nice profit on an item he or she has put up for sale.

If you're new to selling, you can find out all the benefits of selling and get pointed in the right direction to find items that could make you a tidy profit. In fact, you may be sitting on major profits hiding in your own home! eBay has its rules, though, so when you assess an item's value to prepare for your auction, you need to make sure the item isn't prohibited from being sold at the eBay site.

In this part, we walk you through the paperwork you need to fill out to list an item for selling, and we show you how to close the deal and ship the item without any hassles. But even though we're good, we can't stop problems from occurring, which is why we try to walk you through every conceivable mishap. There's also a chapter for those eBay newbies out there who already know that a picture's worth a thousand words. That's right — if you really want to make money at eBay, you can't miss the advanced strategies.

Chapter 9

Selling in Your Fuzzy Slippers for Fun and Profit

In This Chapter

▶ Discovering the benefits of selling

▶ Looking for inventory in your own backyard

▶ Knowing what to sell, when to sell, and how much to ask

▶ Staying out of trouble — what you can't sell at eBay

▶ Paying the piper with eBay fees

▶ Keeping the taxman happy (or at least friendly)

*F*inding items to sell can be as easy as opening up your closet and as challenging as acquiring antiques overseas (both of us have even taken a leap and imported custom items to sell on eBay). Either way, establishing yourself as an eBay seller isn't that difficult when you know the ropes. In this chapter, you can find out how to look for items under your own roof, figure out what they're worth, and turn them into instant cash. But before you pick your house clean (we know eBay can be habit forming, but, please, keep a *few* things for yourself!), read up on the eBay rules of the road — such as how to sell, when to sell, and what *not* to sell. If you're interested in finding out how to set up your auction page, get acquainted with Chapter 10; if you want to read up on advanced selling strategies, the Appendix is where to find them.

Why Should You Sell Stuff on eBay?

Whether you need to clear out 35 years of odd and wacky knickknacks cluttering your basement or you seriously want to earn extra money, the benefits of selling at eBay are as diverse as the people doing the selling. The biggest plus to selling at eBay is wheeling and dealing from your home in pyjamas and fuzzy slippers (every day is Casual Friday for most eBay sellers). But no matter where you conduct your business or how you dress, many more important big-time rewards exist for selling at eBay.

AUCTION ANECDOTE

Life lessons learned at eBay

If you have kids, get them involved with your eBay selling. They can learn real-life lessons that they can't learn in school. Give them a feel for meeting deadlines and fulfilling promises. Get them writing e-mails (if they aren't already) and helping pack the items. eBay is a great place to learn basic economics and how to handle money. When Marsha first started on eBay, she taught her pre-teen daughter about geography by using eBay. Every time she completed a transaction, her daughter would use a search engine to look up the city in which the buyer (or seller) lived — and then mark the city by placing a pin on a huge map. When Bill's daughter was 13, Bill encouraged her to appreciate the value of a dollar by helping her sell her childhood Disney VHS video collection. The resulting sales amounted to several hundred dollars that she then used to buy her own back-to-school wardrobe.

Get creative and make eBay a profitable learning experience, too. Remember, however, that eBay doesn't let anyone under the age of 18 register, buy, or sell — so make sure you're in charge of handling all transactions. Your kids can help out, but they need to be under your supervision at all times.

Most people starting a business have to worry about rounding up investment capital (start-up money they may lose), building inventory (buying stuff to sell), and finding a selling location such as a booth at a swap meet or even a small store. Today, even a little mom and pop start-up operation requires a major investment. eBay has helped to level the playing field a bit; everybody can get an equal chance to start a small business with just a little money. Anyone who wants to take a stab at doing business can get started with just enough money to cover the Insertion Fee.

Get a few transactions under your belt. Sell your old collection of postcards. See how you like the responsibilities of marketing, collecting money, shipping, and customer service. Continue to grow your business and you'll find yourself spotting trends, acquiring inventory, and marketing your items for maximum profit. In no time, you'll be making items disappear faster than David Copperfield (though you may have a little trouble with the Statue of Liberty — how'd he *do* that, anyway?). If you still want to go long on eBay, please take a look at our book, *Starting an eBay Business For Canadians For Dummies* (John Wiley & Sons Canada Ltd.). It gives you just what you need to ramp up from hobbyist to big-time eBay tycoon making a few hundred (or even thousand) dollars a month!

A fun way to get your feet wet on eBay is to buy some small items. When we say small, we mean it. Some of the least expensive items you can buy on eBay are recipes. Type `recipe` in the search box, click the Search button, and choose Price: Lowest First from the Sort By drop-down list that appears on the top-right of the results. You can find recipes for as little as a penny. You don't have to pay a shipping charge, either. The sellers usually e-mail the recipe directly to you after the auction. You can also begin selling your very own secret recipes. Selling your recipes is a great way to become familiar with how eBay works, and you can gain experience with leaving feedback — as well as building your own!

Mi Casa, Mi Cash-a: Finding Stuff to Sell

Finding merchandise to sell at eBay is as easy as opening up a closet and as tough as climbing up to the attic. Just about anything you bought and stashed away (because you didn't want it, you forgot about it, or it didn't fit) is fair game. Think about all those really awful birthday and holiday presents (hey, it was the thought that counted — and the giver may have forgotten about them, too). Now you have a place you can try to unload them. They could even make somebody happy.

In your closet, find what's just hanging around:

- ✔ Clothing that no longer fits or is out of fashion. Do you really want to keep it if you wouldn't be caught dead in it or you know it'll never fit? Don't forget that pair of shoes you wore once and put away.
- ✔ Any item with a designer label that's in new or almost-new condition.
- ✔ Kids' clothes. Kids outgrow things fast. Use profits from the old items to buy new clothes they can grow into. Now, that's recycling.

Have the articles of clothing in the best condition possible before you put them up for sale. For example, shoes can be cleaned and buffed up till they're like new. According to eBay's policies, clothing *must* be cleaned prior to shipping.

And consider what's parked in your basement, garage, or attic:

- ✔ **Old radios, stereo and video equipment, and 8-track systems:** Watch these items fly out of your house — especially the 8-track players (believe it or not, people love 'em). The very first items Bill sold on eBay were two old record turntables, and selling at eBay earned him far more than any yard sale would have.
- ✔ **Books you finished reading long ago and don't want to read again:** Some books with early copyright dates or first editions by famous authors earn big money at eBay. Be careful, though — books can be very expensive to ship by Canada Post, so be certain that the book has some real value before putting it up for auction.
- ✔ **Leftovers from an abandoned hobby:** Who knew that building miniature dollhouses was so much work?

✔ **Unwanted gifts:** Have a decade's worth of birthday, graduation, or holiday gifts collecting dust? Put them up for sale at eBay and hope Grandma or Grandpa doesn't bid on them because she or he thinks you need another moustache spoon!

Saleable stuff may even be lounging around in your living room or bedroom:

✔ **Home décor you want to change:** Lamps, chairs, and rugs (especially if they're antiques) sell quickly. If you think an item is valuable but you're not sure, get it appraised first.

✔ **Exercise equipment:** If you're like most people, you bought this stuff with every intention of getting in shape, but now all that's building up is dust. Get some exercise carrying all that equipment to the post office after you sell it at eBay. The very best time to sell your equipment is at the very beginning of the year — while people are still trying to stick to their New Year's resolutions.

✔ **Records, videotapes, and laser discs:** Sell them after you upgrade to new audio and video formats, such as DVD (Digital Versatile Disc) or DAT (Digital Audio Tape). (Think Betamax is dead? You may be surprised.)

✔ **Autographs:** All types of autographs — from sports figures, celebrities, and world leaders — are very popular at eBay. A word of caution, though: A lot of fakes are on the market, so make sure that what you're selling (or buying) is the real thing. If you're planning on selling autographs on eBay, be sure to review the special rules that apply to these items. Here's where to find them:

```
pages.ebay.ca/help/policies/autographs.html
```

Know When to Sell

Warning . . . warning . . . we're about to hit you with some of our clichés: *Timing is everything. Sell what you know and know when to sell. Buy low and sell high.*

Okay, granted, clichés may be painful to hear over and over again, but they do contain nuggets of good information. (Perhaps they're well known for a reason?)

Experienced eBay sellers know that when planning a sale, timing is almost everything. Fur coats don't sell very well in July, and as a collectible seller, you don't want to be caught with 200 Nintendo games during a run on Xbox. Superman action figures are traditionally good sellers unless a new Batman movie is coming out.

Snapping up profits

Way back in 1980, when Pac-Man ruled, Marsha's friend Ric decided to try his hand at photography. Hoping to be the next Ansel Adams — or to at least snap something in focus — he bought a 1/4 Kowa 66, one of those cameras you hold in front of your belt buckle while you look down into the viewfinder. Soon after he bought the camera, Ric's focus shifted. The camera sat in its box, instructions and all, for over 15 years until he threw a garage sale.

Ric and his wife didn't know much about his Kowa, but they knew that it was worth something. When he got an offer of $80 for it at the garage sale, his wife whispered "eBay!" in his ear, and he turned down the offer.

Ric and his wife posted the camera at eBay with the little information they had about its size and colour, and the couple was flooded with questions and information about the camera from knowledgeable bidders. One bidder said that the silver-toned lens made it more valuable. Another gave them the camera's history.

Ric and his wife added each new bit of information to their description and watched as the bids increased with their every addition — until that unused camera went for more than US$400 in a flurry of last-minute sniping in 1999. These days, when Ric posts an auction, he always asks for additional information and adds it to the auction page.

What difference does a year make? The values of all items on eBay trend up and down. In 2000, this camera sold at eBay for over US$600; in late 2001, it sold for US$455. In the winter of 2003, interest in it was waning; it sold in the US$375 to US$400 range. Now, they frequently sell for US$250 or less.

Some items — such as good antiques, rugs, baseball cards, and sports cars — are timeless. But timing still counts. Don't put your rare, antique paper cutter up for auction if someone else is selling one at the same time. We guarantee that the other auction will cut into your profits.

Timing is hardly an exact science. Rather, timing is a little bit of common sense, a dash of marketing, and a fair amount of information gathering. Do a little research among your friends. What are they interested in? Would they buy your item? Use eBay itself as a research tool. Search to see whether anyone's making money on the same type of item. If people are crazed for some fad item and you have a bunch, *yesterday* was the time to sell. (In other words, if you want your money out of 'em, get crackin' and get packin'.)

If the eBay market is already flooded with dozens of an item and no one is making money on them, you can afford to wait before you plan your auction.

Doing deep and thorough eBay research

eBay has a subscription service designed to help sellers set online prices and better understand the eBay marketplace. You don't need to pay for an outside company's high-priced products. The service, Marketplace Research, gives paid subscribers access to inside historical eBay data through charts and graphs that help you understand the demand for items you're planning to sell. When you subscribe, you can view top searches within a category or skim the entire site to see what buyers are searching for. The charts provide information on the average bids per item, the number of completed sales, and more. You can dip into the service for only US$2.99 for a two-day pass. The two-day pass enables you to go back and peruse up to 60 days of eBay records. With two days' access, you can easily look up bunches of items that you have to sell. Visit `pages.ebay.ca/marketplace_research` for more details.

Know Thy Stuff

At least, that's what Socrates would have said if he'd been an eBay seller. Haven't had to do a homework assignment in a while? Time to dust off those old skills. Before selling your merchandise, do some digging to find out as much as you can about it.

Getting the goods on your goods

Here are some ideas to help you flesh out your knowledge of what you have to sell:

- ✔ **Hit the books.** Check your local library for books about the item. Study price guides and collector magazines.

  Even though collectors still use published price guides when they put a value on an item, so much fast-moving e-commerce is on the Internet that price guides often lag behind the markets they cover. Take the price guides' prices with a grain of salt.

- ✔ **Go surfin'.** Conduct a Web search and look for info on the item on other Web sites. If you find a print magazine that strikes your fancy, check to see whether the magazine is available on the Web by typing the title of the magazine into your browser's search window. (For detailed information on using search engines to conduct a more thorough online search, check out Chapter 5.)

- ✔ **When the going gets tough, go shopping.** Browse local stores that specialize in your item. Price the item at several locations.

When you understand what the demand for your product is (whether it's a collectible or a commodity) and how much you can realistically ask for it, you're on the right track to a successful auction.

✔ **Call in the pros.** Need a quick way to find the value of an item you want to sell? Call a dealer or a collector and say you want to *buy* one. A merchant who smells a sale will give you a current selling price.

✔ **eBay to the rescue.** eBay offers some guidance for your research on its category pages. eBay offers special features for each main category. Click Buy on the navigation bar and select your favourite category from the list of links that appear. As you scroll the page, eBay places links to stories and features specifically for this category. Also, eBay has many category-specific chat rooms in which you can read what other collectors are writing about items in a particular category. (See Chapter 17 for more on eBay's Chat area.)

For information on how items are graded and valued by professional collectors, jump to Chapter 5, where we discuss grading your items.

Be certain you know what you have — not only what it is and what it's for, but also whether it's genuine. Make sure it's the real McCoy. You're responsible for your item's authenticity; counterfeits and knock-offs aren't welcome at eBay. In addition, manufacturers' legal beagles are on the hunt for counterfeit and stolen goods circulating on eBay — and they *will* tip off law enforcement.

Spy versus spy: Comparison selling

Back in the old days, successful retailers frequently spied on each other to figure out ways to get a leg up on the competition. Today, in the bustling world of e-commerce, the spying continues, and dipping into the intrigue of surveilling the competition is as easy as clicking your mouse.

Say that you're the biggest *Dukes of Hazzard* fan ever and you collect *Dukes of Hazzard* stuff, such as VHS tapes of the show, movie memorabilia, General Lee models, and lunchboxes. Well, good news: That piece of tin that holds your lunchtime PB&J may very well fetch a nice sum of money. To find out for sure, you can do some research at eBay. To find out the current market price for a *Dukes of Hazzard* lunchbox, you can conduct a Completed Items search on the Search page (as described in Chapter 5) and find out exactly how many *Dukes of Hazzard* lunchboxes have been on the auction block in the past couple of weeks. You can also find out their high selling prices and how many bids the lunchboxes received by the time the auctions were over. And repeating a completed auction search in a week or two isn't a bad idea — you can get at least a month's worth of data to price your item. Figure 9-1 shows the results of a Completed Items search.

You can easily save your searches on eBay. Just click the Save This Search link that appears above the list of results (you can also see it in Figure 9-1) to add this search to your favourite searches. Now, that search is on your My eBay Favourites page, and you can repeat the search with a click of your mouse.

Sometimes, sellers make spelling errors when they write item titles. In the case of a *Dukes of Hazzard* lunchbox, when you conduct a search for such an item, we suggest that you use one of our favourite search tricks featured in Chapter 5. The eBay search engine accommodates for one correction (as in *hazard* and *hazzard*), but when you want to check for two variations, you must input both. Type your search this way: `dukes (hazzard,hazard) ("lunch box",lunchbox)`. (Be sure that you drop the noise word *of*.) By using this search, you find all instances of *dukes hazzard lunchbox, dukes hazard lunchbox, dukes hazzard lunch box,* and *dukes hazard lunch box*.

Sure enough, when we tried this tactic, we found a considerable number of additional listings for a *Dukes of Hazzard Lunchbox*. Coincidentally, when we changed our search (remember, sellers *do* make mistakes) to `dukes (hazzard,hazard) ("lunch box",lunchbox)`, our search results went from 20 lunchboxes to 26! The best deals for buyers (and for sellers to resell) are always when the seller misspells a name or brand in the title.

Figure 9-1:
Use the
Completed
Items
search to
find out
what an
item is
selling for,
how many
bids it has
received,
and how
many have
been up for
sale in the
past two
weeks.

Look at the pictures on the individual auction item pages for each item that your Completed Items search turns up. That way, you can confirm that the items (lunchboxes, for example) are identical to the one you want to sell. And when you do your research, factor in your item's condition. Read the individual item descriptions. If your item is in better condition, expect (and ask for) more money for it; if your item is in worse condition, expect (and ask for) less. Also, note the categories the items are listed under; they may give you a clue about where eBay members are looking for items just like yours.

If you want to be extremely thorough in your comparison selling, go to a search engine to see whether the results of your eBay search mesh with what's going on elsewhere. If you find that no items like yours are for sale anywhere else online, and you're pretty sure people are looking for what you have, you may just find yourself in Fat City.

Always search for the same item with different word variations or spellings. This is about the only time "creative" spelling can actually help you.

Don't forget to factor in the history of an item when you assess its value. Getting an idea of what people are watching, listening to, and collecting can help you assess trends and figure out what's hot. For more about using trend-spotting skills to sniff out potential profits, take a look at the Appendix.

Know What You Can (And Can't) Sell

The majority of auctions found at eBay are aboveboard. But sometimes eBay finds out about auctions that are either illegal (in the eyes of law enforcement at the local, federal, or international level) or prohibited by eBay's rules and regulations. In either case, eBay steps in, calls a foul, and makes the auction invalid.

eBay doesn't have rules and regulations just for the heck of it. eBay wants to keep you educated so you won't unwittingly bid on — or sell — an item that has been misrepresented. eBay also wants you to know what's okay and what's prohibited so that if you run across an auction that looks fishy, you'll help out your fellow eBay members by reporting it. And eBay wants you to know that getting your auction shut down is the least of your worries: You can be suspended if you knowingly list items that are prohibited. And we won't even begin to talk about potential criminal prosecution.

You need to know about these three categories at eBay:

- ✔ **Prohibited:** Items that may *not* be sold at eBay under any circumstances
- ✔ **Questionable:** Items that may be sold under certain conditions
- ✔ **Potentially Infringing:** The types of items that may be in violation of copyrights, trademarks, or other rights

You can't even offer to give away for free a prohibited or infringing item, nor can you give away a questionable item that eBay disallows; giving it away doesn't relieve you of potential liability.

The items that you absolutely *can't* sell at eBay can fit into all three categories. Those items can be legally ambiguous at best — not to mention potentially risky and all kinds of sticky. To find a detailed description of which items are prohibited on the eBay Web site, follow these steps:

1. **Click the Policies link on the bottom of all eBay pages.**

   You arrive at the friendly eBay Policies page.

2. **Click the Rules for Sellers link on the bottom-right of the page.**

   The Rules for Sellers page appears.

3. **Click the Prohibited and Restricted Items & Services link.**

   Ta-da! Finally, you're presented with the lists and links that can help you decipher whether selling your item falls within eBay's boundaries.

   Or, if you don't mind typing, you can go directly to `pages.ebay.ca/help/policies/ia/prohibited_and_restricted_items.html`.

Sometimes, an item is okay to own but not to sell. Other times, the item is prohibited from being sold and possessed. To complicate matters even more, some items may be legal in one part of Canada or the United States but not in others — as is the case with radar detectors. Or an item may be legal in the United States but illegal in Canada (or vice versa).

Because eBay's base of operations is in California, United States law is enforced — even if both the buyer and seller are from other countries. Cuban cigars, for example, are legal to buy and sell in Canada, but even if the buyer *and* the seller are from Canada, eBay says *"No permiso"* and shuts down auctions of Havanas fast. Figure 9-2 shows an auction that was shut down soon after it was found.

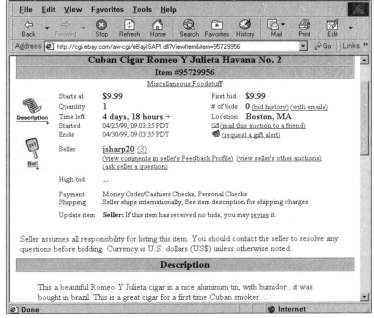

Figure 9-2:
We found
this auction
for a Cuban
cigar shortly
before the
eBay police
did (and
cancelled it)
in 1999.

Prohibited items

Even though possessing (and selling) many of the items in the following list may be legal in Canada, the United States, and elsewhere, you're absolutely, positively prohibited from buying and selling the following at eBay:

- ✔ **Firearms of all types:** This also means firearm accessories — including antique, collectible, sport, or hunting guns; air guns; BB guns; silencers; converters; kits for creating guns; gunpowder; high-capacity ammunition magazines (receptacles designed to feed ten rounds or more into a gun, not the publications about ammo); and armour-piercing bullets. You can't even sell a gun that doesn't work.

  You *can* buy and sell single bullets, shells, and even antique bombs and musket balls — as long as they have nothing explosive in them.

- ✔ **Firearms and military weapons:** No way can you sell any type of firearm that's designed to propel a metal (or similar) projectile, regardless of whether it works. Military weapons? Items included are bazookas, grenades, and mortars.

✔ **Police and other law-enforcement badges and IDs:** Stop in the name of the law if you're thinking about buying or selling any of these items, including badges or imitation badges. In fact, selling just about any government badge can get you in hot water.

You also can't own or sell government agencies' identification cards or credential cases, or those really cool jackets they use in raids. Selling a copy or reproduction of any of these items is prohibited, too, because these items are copyrighted (see the following section to find out about infringement).

If you find a badge that's legal to sell and own, you need to provide a letter of authorization from the agency. The same letter of authorization is required for fake badges, such as reproductions or movie props.

✔ **Replicas of official government identification documents or licences:** Birth certificates, drivers' licences, and passports fall into this category.

✔ **Current vehicle licence plates or plates that claim to resemble current ones:** Expired licence plates (at least five years old) are considered collectible — as long as they're no longer valid for use on a vehicle.

✔ **Locksmithing devices:** These items can be sold only to authorized recipients. Federal law prohibits the mailing of such devices.

✔ **Human parts and remains:** Hey, we all have two kidneys, but if you get the urge to sell one to pay off your bills, eBay isn't the place to sell it. You can't sell your sperm, eggs, blood, or anything else you manage to extricate from your body. What's more, you can't even give away any of these items as a free bonus with one of your auctions.

✔ **Drugs or drug paraphernalia:** Narcotics, steroids, or other controlled substances can't be listed, nor can gamma hydroxybutyrate (GHB). Drug paraphernalia includes all items that are primarily intended or designed for use in manufacturing, concealing, or using a controlled substance, including 1960s-vintage cigarette papers, bongs, and water pipes.

✔ **Anything that requires a prescription from a doctor, dentist, or optometrist to dispense:** Listen, just because it's legal to use doesn't mean it doesn't require special permission to get. For example, even though penicillin is legal to buy in Canada, only a doctor can prescribe it — which is why, when you get sick, you have to stand in that *loooong* line at the pharmacy sneezing on all the other sick people. And if you're looking for Viagra auctions at eBay, don't even *go* there.

✔ **Stocks, bonds, or negotiable securities:** Nope, you can't sell stock in your new pie-baking company or an investment in property you may own. And if you're thinking of offering credit to someone, you can't do that either. (Note that antiques and collectible items are permitted.)

✔ **Bulk e-mail lists:** No bulk e-mail or mailing lists that contain personal identifying information. You can't even sell tools or software designed to send unsolicited commercial e-mail.

✔ **Pets and wildlife, including animal parts from endangered species:** If you've had it with Buster, your pet ferret, don't look to eBay for help in finding him a new home. And you can't sell your stuffed spotted owls or rhino-horn love potions, either. If you're in the animal business — *any* animal business — eBay isn't the place for you.

✔ **Child pornography:** This material is strictly prohibited at eBay, but you can sell other forms of erotica. (See the section "Questionable items: Know the laws," later in this chapter, for the scoop on what can get you into trouble.)

✔ **Forged items:** Autographs from celebrities and sports figures are big business — and a big opportunity for forgers. Selling a forgery is a criminal act. Many jurisdictions are now actively investigating suspected forgery cases linked with online auctions.

If you're in the market for an autograph, don't even consider bidding on one unless it comes with a Certificate of Authenticity (COA). Many sellers take authenticity so seriously that they give buyers the right to a full refund if any doubt about authenticity crops ups. Figure 9-3 shows an item that comes with a COA from an auction at eBay. Find out more about authentication services in Chapter 16.

✔ **Items that infringe on someone else's copyright or trademark:** Take a look at the following section for details on infringing items.

✔ **Satellite and cable TV descramblers:** Although the Internet is loaded with hardware and instructions on how to get around cable TV scrambling, eBay prohibits the sales of anything in this arena. After all, it's illegal to get around these technologies.

✔ **Stolen items:** Need we say more? (Seems obvious, but you'd be surprised.) If what you're thinking about selling came to you by way of a five-finger discount, fell off a truck, or is hot, don't sell it at eBay.

Ignorance is no excuse. If you list an item that's in any way prohibited on eBay, eBay will end your auction. If you have any questions, always check eBay's Trust & Safety department at `pages.ebay.ca/help/sell/ questions/prohibited-items.html`.

Figure 9-3:
When bidding on an item with a COA, be sure that the seller is reputable (hint, hint — check the feedback).

The item you are bidding on is a 3x5 Card , Autographed by the late James Stewart ....

The card is white and in mint condition... Signed bold and clear , in black felt tip pen ...

This Autograph is 100% Genuine , and I will provide my COA that Guarantees it for life...

Infringing items

In school, if you copied someone's work, you were busted for plagiarism. Even if you've been out of school for a while, you can get busted for copying someone else's work. Profiting from a copy of someone else's legally owned intellectual property is an infringement violation. *Infringement,* also known as *piracy,* is the encroachment on another person's legal ownership rights on an item, a trademark, or a copyright. eBay prohibits the sale of infringing items at its site.

All the legal mumbo-jumbo, translated to English, comes down to this: Profiting from someone else's idea, original work, or patented invention is very, very bad and can get you in hot water.

Here's a checklist of no-no items commonly found at the centre of infringement violations:

- ✔ Music that's been recorded from an original compact disc, cassette tape, or record.
- ✔ Movies that have been recorded from an original DVD, laser disc, or commercial VHS tape.
- ✔ Television shows that have been recorded off the air, off cable, or from a satellite service.

Hot property busted

In 1961, a young jockey named John Sellers won his first Kentucky Derby on a horse named Carry Back. He was so emotional about the victory that he was crying as he crossed the finish line. Seventeen years later, someone broke into his California home and stole his priceless trophy. But more than two decades after it was stolen, it ended up back in his possession — thanks to an observant eBay member. The prized trophy was put up for auction in 1999 by a seller who had bought it legitimately. An eBay member who knows the history of the trophy saw that it was for sale and alerted the seller. The seller stopped the auction immediately, contacted the former jockey, and personally returned the trophy to him. Now that's a great finish!

Selling a used original CD, tape, commercial VHS movie cassette, DVD, or CD-ROM is perfectly legal. Some television shows sell episodes on tape or DVD; you can sell those originals, as well. But if you're tempted to sell a personal copy that you made of an original, you're committing an infringing violation.

✔ Software and computer games that have been copied from CD-ROMs or disks (and that includes hard drives — anybody's).

✔ Counterfeit items (also called *knock-offs*), such as clothes and jewellery, that have been produced, copied, or imitated without the permission of the manufacturer. (Bart Simpson knock-off T-shirts abounded in the early '90s.)

If you pick up a brand-name item dirt cheap from a discount store, you can check to see whether it's counterfeit by taking a look at the label. If something isn't quite right, the item is probably a knock-off.

Trademark and copyright protections don't cover just software, music, and movies. Clothing, toys, sunglasses, and books are among the items covered by law.

Intellectual property owners actively defend their rights and, along with help from average eBay users, continually tip off eBay to fraudulent and infringing auctions. Rights owners can use eBay's Verified Rights Owner (VeRO) program, as well as law-enforcement agencies. (See the section "VeRO to the Rescue," later in this chapter, for info about the VeRO program.)

Questionable items: Know the laws

Because some items are prohibited in one place and not another, eBay lists a few items that you can trade but that are restricted and regulated. As a member of eBay, you're responsible for knowing the restrictions in your area — as well as those on the eBay Web site.

Certain items are illegal in one geographic area and not another. This list mentions a few of the major questionables:

- ✔ **Event tickets:** Laws regarding the sale of event tickets vary from province to province in Canada and possibly even city to city within the United States. Some laws prohibit reselling the ticket for a price higher than the amount printed on the face of the ticket. Some jurisdictions may limit the amount you can add to the ticket's face value.

  If you're thinking of selling event tickets, you'd be wise to visit `pages.ebay.ca/help/policies/event-tickets.html` for restrictions. This page has details featuring the various provincial and state legal requirements. Be sure to double-check this page to be certain you're following the appropriate laws for your area.

- ✔ **Wine and alcohol:** Selling wine and alcohol at eBay — and anywhere else, for that matter — is tricky business. For starters, you have no business in this business unless you're at least 19 years old. eBay doesn't permit sales of any alcohol products by individuals unless those products are sold for their collectible containers. Some sellers in the United States may sell alcoholic beverages for consumption if they have a liquor licence and are pre-approved by eBay, but sales of alcohol in Canada are much more stringently regulated. In the case of collectible bottles, some strict rules apply:

  - The value must be in the collectible container, not in its contents. You can't auction off your uncle's Chateaux Margaux because the value is in the wine — not the bottle.

  - The bottle must be unopened, and your auction must state that the contents aren't meant for consumption.

  - The container's value must substantially exceed the price of the alcohol in the container, and must no longer be available at a retail outlet.

  - You must be sure that the buyer is at least 21 years old.

  - You must be sure that the sale complies with all laws and shipping rules. Every province and state has its own laws about shipping alcohol and wine. Some jurisdictions require licences to transport it; some limit the amount you can ship. You're responsible for knowing what your local laws are (and you're expected to conduct your auctions accordingly).

✔ **Erotica:** Some forms of erotica are allowed at eBay. To see what eBay allows and what it prohibits, type `pages.ebay.ca/help/policies/mature-audiences.html` into your browser's address box and press Enter.

One thing that's definitely illegal, wrong, and criminal is child pornography. If someone reports that you're selling child pornography, eBay forwards your registration information to law enforcement for criminal prosecution.

Forbidden auctions

The folks at eBay didn't just fall off the turnip truck. eBay staffers have seen just about every scam to get around paying fees or following policy guidelines. Chances are good that if you try one of these scams, you'll get caught. Then eBay cancels the auction. Do it once, and shame on you (don't count on getting the listing fee credited back to you). Do it a lot, and you're off of eBay.

The following items are definitely forbidden:

✔ **Raffles and prizes:** You need to sell something in your auction; you can't offer tickets or chances for a giveaway.

✔ **Want ads:** If you want something, you have to search for it. Don't try to run your needs as an ad thinly disguised as an auction. Visit eBay's Want-It-Now (`pages.ebay.ca/wantitnow`) section and legally post your wants and needs there.

✔ **Advertisements:** An eBay auction isn't the place to make a sales pitch (other than attractive copy describing your item, that is). Some eBay bad guys list an auction name and then use the auction to send bidders to some other auction or Web site. The Real Estate category is one exception. You can run an ad there for your property. Look out for eBay to expand its ads in the future.

✔ **Bait-and-switch tactics:** These tricks are a variation on the ugly old sales technique of pretending to sell what you're not really selling. Some eBay users who are selling an unfamiliar brand of item try to snag bidders by putting a more familiar brand in the title. For instance, writing *Designer Chanel purse — not really, but a lot like it!* is a fake-out. eBay calls it *keyword spamming*. We call it lousy.

✔ **Choice auctions:** These auctions are like Multiple Item (Dutch) auctions gone crazy. Normally, sellers can offer only one item per auction in a regular auction and multiples of the same item in a Multiple Item auction. Choice auctions offer a mishmash of multiple items from which bidders choose. For example, if you're selling T-shirts, an auction can be for only one particular size per sale. If you want to list small, medium, and large sizes, we suggest that you run an auction for one size and open an eBay store (see Chapter 11) in which you can list single sales for each size.

- ✔ **Mixing apples with oranges:** This gambit tries to attract more bidders to view an item by putting it in a high-traffic category in which it doesn't belong. Forget it. eBay will move it for you if necessary, but keeping that rutabaga recipe book away from the list of automotive repair manuals yourself is more considerate.

- ✔ **Catalogues:** "Buy my catalogue so you can buy more stuff from me!" Uh-huh. We don't know why anyone would put a *bid* on a catalogue (unless it's an Eaton's antique). If it's only a booklet that shows off all the cool junk you're selling, you can't offer it as an auction item.

Reporting a Problem Listing

You probably don't think that eBay can monitor millions of items for sale on a daily basis. You're right; it can't. eBay relies on eBay members like you to let it know when a shady listing is afoot. If you ever smell something fishy, for goodness' sake, report it to eBay. Sometimes, eBay takes a few days to cancel a listing, but rest assured that eBay invests a lot of time protecting its users from fraudulent auctions.

If you see something that just doesn't look right, you should report the auction via an online form at the following address (you can also find a Report This Item link at the bottom of every eBay item listing page):

```
pages.ebay.ca/help/contact_us/_base/index.html
```

eBay doesn't personally prosecute its users. However, eBay does have a stake in protecting its honest users — and will act as an intermediary between honest eBay users and law-enforcement agencies.

VeRO to the Rescue

If you own intellectual property that you think is being infringed upon on the eBay site, eBay has a program called the Verified Rights Owner (VeRO) program. Owners of trademarked or copyrighted items and logos, as well as other forms of intellectual property, can become members of this program for free.

You can find out more about the VeRO program by clicking the Help link on the main navigation bar. To get eBay's current VeRO policy, go to `pages.ebay.ca/help/tp/vero-rights-owner.html`. Read the information, and if you qualify, click the Download eBay's NOCI Form link to download the form, print a copy, fill it out, and fax it to eBay at the number provided on the VeRO Web page. Then you're on your way to protecting your intellectual property from being auctioned to the high bidder. Remember, only *you* can stop the infringement madness. If eBay agrees with you that your intellectual property is being infringed upon, it invalidates the auction and informs the seller by e-mail that the auction "is not authorized." The high bidders in the auction are also notified and warned that they may be breaking the law if they continue the transaction.

eBay understands that sometimes people don't know that they're selling infringing items, but it draws a hard line on repeat offenders. eBay not only shuts down the offenders' auctions, but also suspends repeat offenders of this ilk. Also, eBay cooperates with the proper authorities on behalf of its VeRO program members.

If eBay deems your auction invalid because the item doesn't meet eBay's policies and guidelines, you can find out why by checking `pages.ebay.ca/help/tp/listing-ended.html`. If you still feel you're in the right, scroll down the page to the Contact Us link. Click there to plead your case.

eBay Fees? What eBay Fees? Oops . . .

The Cliché Police are going to nab us sooner or later, but here's one we're poking a few holes in this time around: *You gotta spend it to make it.* This old-time business chestnut means that you need to invest a fair amount of money before you can turn a profit. Although the principle still holds true in the real world (at least, most of the time), at eBay, you don't have to spend much to run your business. This is one reason why eBay has become one of the most successful e-commerce companies on the Internet and a darling of Wall Street. eBay keeps fees low and volume high.

The eBay fees in the following list were current at the time of writing, but they've been known to change before our books actually make it into your hands. For the current fee structure, visit `pages.ebay.ca/help/sell/fees.html`. eBay charges the following types of fees for conducting auctions:

✔ **Regular auction and core fixed-price Insertion Fees:** $0.23 to $5.60.

✔ **Real estate Insertion Fee:** These fees can vary because you have the choice of listing your property as an ad rather than as an auction. Because eBay real estate auctions are non-binding (due to legalities), you may be better off running an ad. eBay charges these prices for Residential, Commercial, Manufactured Homes, Land, Timeshares, and Other Real Estate:

- **Auctions:** 1-, 3-, 5-, 7-, or 10-day listing, $41.00
- **Ad format:** 30-day listing, $175; 90-day listing, $350

✔ **Automotive or motorcycle Insertion Fee:** $5. A Transaction Services Fee (TSF) is also added after your vehicle receives a bid or when the reserve price (if applicable) is met. The TSF is $58 for passenger vehicles and $47 for motorcycles.

✔ **Additional reserve-auction fees:** $1.20 to $2.40. Auctions with reserves over $240 must pay 1 percent of the reserve, with a maximum of $70. (These fees are refundable if your item meets the reserve and sells.)

✔ **Final Value Fee:** A percentage of the sales price.

✔ **Optional fees and upgrades:** Vary widely.

Insertion Fees

Every auction is charged an Insertion Fee. There's no way around it. The Insertion Fee is calculated on a sliding scale that's based on your item's *minimum bid* (your starting price) or *reserve price* (the secret lowest price that you're willing to sell your item for). Take a look at Table 9-1 for eBay's Insertion Fee structure.

Table 9-1	Insertion Fee Charges
Starting (Or Reserve) Price	*The Insertion Fee*
$0.01–$0.99	$0.23
$1.00–$11.99	$0.47
$12.00–$29.99	$0.71
$30.00–$59.99	$1.40
$60.00–$239.99	$2.80
$240.00–$599.99	$4.20
$600–gazillions	$5.60

If you're running a reserve-price auction (explained in detail in Chapter 10), eBay bases its Insertion Fee on the reserve price, not the starting bid. eBay also charges a fee to run a reserve-price auction.

Here's a snapshot of how a reserve price affects your Insertion Fee. If you set a starting bid of $1 for a gold Rolex watch (say what?) but your reserve price is $5,000 (that's more like it), you're charged a $5.60 Insertion Fee based on the $5,000 reserve price, plus a $50 reserve fee (1 percent of the reserve price, up to a maximum of $70). The reserve fee is refundable if the item sells. (See Table 9-4 for the reserve auction fees.)

In a Multiple Item (Dutch) auction (explained in Chapter 10), the Insertion Fee is based on the starting bid — like in a regular auction — but then eBay multiplies it by the number of items you list. So, if you set a minimum bid of $1 for 300 glow-in-the-dark refrigerator magnets, you pay a $4.20 Insertion Fee for the listing as it has a $300 value.

So what does the Insertion Fee buy you at eBay? Here's what you're paying for:

- A really snazzy-looking auction page of your item that millions of eBay members can see, admire, and breathlessly respond to (Well, we can only hope.)

- The use of eBay services, such as the Trust & Safety program, which protects your auction experience. (Chapter 16 tells you how to use Trust & Safety during and after your auctions.)

Final Value Fees

If you follow the movie business, you hear about some big A-list stars who take a relatively small fee for making a film but negotiate a big percentage of the gross profits. This is known as a *back-end deal* — in effect, a commission based on how much the movie brings in. eBay does the same thing, taking a small Insertion Fee when you list your item and then a commission on the back end when you sell your item. This commission is called the *Final Value Fee* and is based on the final selling price of your item.

eBay doesn't charge a Final Value Fee on an advertisement in the Real Estate/Timeshares category like it does in other categories. You pay a flat Insertion Fee of $175 for 30 days of advertising for Residential, Commercial, Manufactured Homes, Land, Timeshares, and Other Real Estate. In the Automotive category, you pay a flat Transaction Services Fee of $58 for passenger vehicles and $47 for motorcycles if your auction ends with a winning bidder (and the reserve has been met).

In real life, when you pay sales commissions on a big purchase such as a house, you usually pay a fixed percentage. eBay's Final Value Fee structure is different: It's set up as a three-tiered system. Table 9-2 covers the calculation of Final Value Fees.

Table 9-2	Final Value Fees
Closing Bid	*To Find Your Final Value Fee*
$0.01–$30.00	Multiply the final sale price by 5.25 percent (0.0525). If the final sale price is $30, multiply 30 by 0.0525. You owe eBay $1.58.
$30.01–$1,200.00	You pay $1.58 for the first $30 of the final sale price (which is 5.25 percent). Subtract $30 from your final closing bid and then multiply this mount by 3.25 percent (0.0325). Add this total to the $1.58 you owe for the first $30. The sum is what you owe eBay. If the final sale price is $1,200, multiply 1,170 by 0.0325. (**Hint:** The answer is $38.03.) *Now*, add $38.03 and $1.58. You owe eBay $39.61.
$1,200.01 and over	You owe $1.58 for the first $30 of the final sale price (which is 5.25 percent). But you also have to pay $38.03 for the remainder of the price between $30.01 and $1,200.00 (which is 3.25 percent). This total amount is $39.61. Now, subtract $1,200 from the final sale price (you've already calculated those fees) and multiply the final sale amount that's over $1,200 by 1.5 percent (0.015). Add this amount to $39.61. The sum is the amount you owe eBay. If the final sales price is $3,000, multiply $1,800 by 0.015. (**Hint:** The answer is $27.) Add $39.61 to $27. The sum, $66.61, is what you owe eBay. (You won't be graded on this.)

So how do all these percentages translate to actual dollar amounts? Take a look at Table 9-3. We calculate the Final Value Fees on some sample selling prices.

Table 9-3	Sample Prices and Commissions	
Closing Bid Price	*Percentage*	*What You Owe eBay*
$10	5.25 percent of $10	$0.53
$260	5.25 percent of $30, plus 3.25 percent of $230	$9.05
$1,284.53	5.25 percent of $30, plus 3.25 percent of $1,170, plus 1.5 percent of $84.53	$40.87

Closing Bid Price	Percentage	What You Owe eBay
$1,000,000	5.25 percent of $30, plus 3.25 percent of $1,170, plus 1.5 percent of $998,800	$15,021.60 (yikes!)

If you try to work out your own Final Value Fees, you may get an extreme headache — and come up with fractional cents. eBay rounds up fees of $0.005 and more, and below $0.005, drops it. These roundings are done on a per-transaction basis and generally even out over time.

Always keep track of the exact amount. Here's why (you're gonna love this): An item that is sold for $37.89 shows a Final Value Fee of $1.83 on the View Account Status page (and in other areas where Final Value Fees are displayed), although the exact amount of the Final Value Fee is $1.831425. For display purposes, the additional digits are rounded to the closest cent on invoices and other pages. However, the *exact* amount ($1.831425) — not the displayed amount — is used to calculate the total amount due on your invoice. Therefore, if several items have been sold, multiple-line items showing final account fees that have been rounded to the nearest cent appear on invoices and other pages, and the correctly calculated total balance appears to be off by one or a few cents. (In other words, eBay charges you those fractions of a cent.) Here's where you can get further details:

```
pages.ebay.ca/help/account/rounding-account-balance.html
```

If you're starting to get dizzy just reading these examples, perhaps doing your own calculations isn't for you. It's certainly not for either of us — this stuff makes our eyes glaze over! Fortunately, you can use a very cool online calculator that can handle all these calculations for you. Check it out at

```
www.sellathon.com/ebay_calculator.html
```

Because of the sliding percentages, the higher the final selling price, the lower the commission eBay charges. (Maybe math *can* be a beautiful thing, if it's applied for our benefit.)

Optional fees

You don't have to pay a licence fee and destination charge, but setting up your auction can be like buying a car. eBay has all sorts of options to jazz up your auction. (Sorry, eBay is fresh out of two-tone metallic paint — but how about a nice pair of fuzzy dice for your mirror?) We explain how all these bells, whistles, and white sidewalls dress up your auction in Chapter 10.

Just to give you a taste of what Chapter 10 covers, Table 9-4 lists the eBay listing options and what they'll cost you.

Table 9-4	eBay Optional-Feature Fees
Option	*Fee*
Value Pack (Gallery, subtitle, and Listing Designer)	$0.77
Pro Pack (Bold, border, highlight, Gallery Featured, and Featured Plus!)	$35
Boldface title	$1.20
Border	$3.50
Featured Plus! (formerly Featured in Category)	$23.50
List in two categories	Double the listing and upgrade fees
10-Day auction	$0.47
Highlight	$5.90
Listing Designer	$0.12
Scheduled listings	$0.12
Subtitle	$0.59
Picture Services	First picture free, each additional $0.18
The Gallery (Featured Auction in Gallery); free Gallery for vehicles in Motors	$0.41 (standard) or $23.50
Gallery Plus	$0.88
Auction BIN (Buy It Now) fee	See Table 9-5
eBay Motors vehicle BIN fee	$1.20

Option	Fee
eBay Motors reserve fee	$0.01–$6,000.00: $5.90
	$6,000.01–12,100.00: 1% of the reserve
	12,100.01 or more: $12

eBay also charges an upgrade fee when you use the Buy-It-Now option on your listings. Table 9-5 shows you how Buy-It-Now upgrade fees break down.

Table 9-5	Buy-It-Now Fees
Buy-It-Now Price	**Fee**
$0.01–$11.99	$0.06
$12.00–$29.99	$0.12
$30.00–$59.99	$0.23
$60 or more	$0.29

Keep current on your cash flow

After you do all the legwork needed to make some money, do some eye-work to keep track of your results. The best place to keep watch on your eBay accounting is on your My eBay page, a great place to stay organized while you're conducting all your eBay business. (We describe all the functions of the My eBay page in Chapter 4.)

Here's a checklist of what to watch out for after the auction closes:

- ✔ **Keep an eye on how much you're spending to place items up for auction at eBay.** You don't want any nasty surprises, and you don't want to find out that you spent more money to set up your auction than you received selling your item.

- ✔ **If you decide to turn your eBay selling into a business, keep track of your expenses for your taxes.** We explain the Canadian Revenue Agency's tax position at eBay in the following section. Stay tuned.

- ✔ **Make sure that you get refunds and credits when they're due.** It's your money, and even the bookkeepers at eBay make mistakes.

- ✔ **Double-check your figures to make certain eBay hasn't made mistakes.** If you have any questions about the accounting, let eBay know.

Find an error or something that isn't quite right with your account? Use the form at `pages.ebay.ca/help/contact_us/_base/index.html` to get your questions answered.

The Taxman Wants You — to Pay Your Taxes

What would a chapter about money be without taxes? As a wise man once said (and we've all had a sneaking suspicion), "You can't escape death and taxes." (C'mon, it's not a cliché; it's traditional wisdom.) Whether in cyberspace or face-to-face life, never forget that the taxman is always your business partner.

As with offline transactions, knowledge is power. The more you know about buying and selling at eBay before you actually start doing it, the more savvy the impression you make — and the more satisfying your experience.

If you have a good accountant, give that esteemed individual a call. If you don't have one, find a tax professional in your area. Tax professionals actually do more than just process your income tax returns once a year; they can help you avoid major pitfalls even before income tax time rolls around.

For more details on taxes and bookkeeping, check out our book, *Starting an eBay Business For Canadians For Dummies* (John Wiley & Sons Canada Ltd.).

Two wild rumours about federal taxes

We've long heard rumours about not having to pay taxes on eBay profits. If you hear any variation on this theme, smile politely and don't believe a word of it. We discuss two of the more popular (and seriously mistaken) tax notions running around the eBay community these days.

The Canadian government has all the tools it needs to go after eBay outlaws. All Canadians are required to disclose income from all sources for the purpose of determining income tax due. If you have any doubt about whether the profit you make from eBay sales is taxable, our very best advice is to consult with a competent accountant or tax specialist. If you prefer to do a little research on your own, you can visit the Canada Revenue Agency — fondly referred to as CRA — Web site at `www.cra-arc.gc.ca`.

Rumour #1: E-commerce isn't taxed

One story claims that "there are no taxes on e-commerce sales (sales conducted online)." No one seems to know where this story started.

Some people confuse provincial sales tax issues with income tax issues. You may not always have to pay sales tax for purchases made on the Internet, but that's not the same as reporting income from sales you make on the Web.

CRA views selling on the Web in the same way as selling through a brick and mortar outlet. If you derive income from these sales, you're required to report it for the purposes of determining the amount of income tax due on an annual basis. Ordinarily, you can sell your personal belongings on eBay without declaring the proceeds as income if you don't make a profit. The rule of thumb is that if you purchase an item with a view to selling it at a profit, you should keep meticulous records and declare the income on your annual tax return.

Rumour #2: Profits from garage sales are tax-exempt

"eBay is like a garage sale, and you don't have to pay taxes on garage sales."

Uh-huh. And the calories in ice cream don't count if you eat it out of the carton. Who comes up with this stuff, anyway?

This notion is just an urban (or shall I say *suburban*) legend — somebody's wishful thinking that's become folklore. If you make money on a garage sale, you have to declare it as income — just like anything else you make money on. Most people never make any money on garage sales because they usually sell their personal belongings for far less than they bought them for. However, the exact opposite is frequently true of an eBay transaction.

Even if you lose money, you may have to prove it to CRA, especially if you're running a small business. You most definitely should have a heart-to-heart talk with your accountant or tax professional as to how to file your taxes. If something might look bad in an audit if you *don't* declare it, consider that a big hint.

To get the reliable word, Bill talked with a local CRA office. The good folks there told him that even if you make as little as a buck on any eBay sale after all your expenses (the cost of the item, eBay fees, shipping charges), you still have to declare it as income on your annual tax return.

If you have questions about eBay sales and your taxes, check with your personal accountant, or call the CRA at 800-959-8281 for individual income tax enquiries or 800-959-5525 for business or self-employed enquiries. You can also visit the CRA Web site at www.cra-arc.gc.ca. And remember to be friendly (just in case).

Goods and Services Tax (GST)

In Canada, the GST applies to almost all goods or services sold. Unlike Retail Sales Tax, which is paid only by the final consumer (except in Quebec), the GST is added at every step along the production and sale chain. Although everyone in this chain is charged the tax, the federal government wants to keep only the tax that's owed by the final consumer. All others can claim a refund of the tax paid (called an *input tax credit*).

You're required to register for the GST if your annual revenues are $30,000 or greater. Even if your sales fall short of this amount, you may still choose to register because doing so brings some distinct advantages. Because most of your sales will likely be shipped to the United States, and because you can't charge GST to American residents, registering for the program allows you to claw back all GST you pay for products that are shipped to the United States. You can also claim credit for GST paid for many items that are used in the day-to-day running of your business. All of these factors can lead to a substantial refund of the accumulated GST that you've paid. In fact, many sellers we know have yet to actually submit a payment of GST — they routinely claim a substantial refund.

Retail Sales Tax (RST)

Retail Sales Tax licences are the official-looking pieces of paper you see behind the register at local stores. Every retail business must have one, and if you plan to get serious about your eBay selling, it's in your best interests to obtain one, too. Yes, even if you're running a business out of your home and have no one coming to do business on-site, you may still need this licence. All provincial governments (except lucky Alberta) require that sales tax be charged to the consumer on most categories of merchandise.

In Newfoundland and Labrador, Nova Scotia, and New Brunswick, the Provincial Sales Tax has been "harmonized" with the Goods and Services Tax (GST) collected by the federal government. In the other provinces that still administer their own sales tax programs, you're required to collect sales tax from residents of the province in which you're licensed. If you don't, the authorities may charge you a bunch of penalties if they ever find out. Avoiding the step of getting the proper licence isn't worth the risk.

Your provincial government requires that you collect and remit RST on a regular basis (usually monthly or quarterly). You also have to keep accurate records of tax charged because you're subject to audit by the provincial watchdogs.

Securing an RST licence does offer an advantage: Having it can open many doors for you that would otherwise be closed. Most manufacturers and distributors won't consider selling their products to you unless you have this licence. Without it, you also wind up paying the provincial tax for items that you plan to resell, a cost you'd otherwise be exempt from.

Chapter 10

Time to Sell: Completing the Cyber Paperwork

*A*re you ready to make some money? Yes? (Call it an inspired guess.) You're on the threshold of adding your items to the hundreds of thousands that go up for sale on eBay every day. Some listings are so hot that the sellers quadruple their investments. Other items, unfortunately, are so stone cold that they may not even register a single bid.

In this chapter, we explain all the facets of the Sell Your Item page — the page you fill out to get your auction going at eBay. You can get some advice that can increase your odds of making money, and you can find out the best way to position your item so buyers can see it and bid on it. We also show you how to modify, relist, or end your auction whenever you need to.

In order to keep the marketplace vibrant, eBay's programmers are constantly working to improve the site. Improvement means change, and the form (as we describe in this chapter) can change from time to time. In fact, it has just undergone a major overhaul. But the basic decisions you need to make don't change. The selling philosophy laid out in this chapter should help you ride the waves of change on eBay — whatever they may be.

Getting Ready to List Your Item

After you decide what you want to sell, find out as much as you can about it and conduct a little market research. Then, you should have a good idea of the item's popularity and value. To get this info, check out Chapter 9.

Before you list your item, make sure that you have these bases covered:

- ✔ **The specific category under which you want the item listed:** Ask your friends or family where they'd look for such an item and remember the categories you saw most frequently when you conducted your market research with the eBay search function.

  To find out which category will pay off best for your item, run a Basic Advanced Search (get to this search page by clicking the Advanced Search link to the right of the search box at the top of most eBay pages). Enter your search keywords in the Enter Keyword or Item Number box, then click Search. See how many of the item are selling now (and if people are actually bidding on it). Then scroll down to the left of the page and click the Show Only Completed Listings box. Choose Price: Highest First from the drop-down menu at the top of the list of results, and then look over the sales to see which categories they're listed in. For more information on how to get ahead of the crowd through eBay's search, visit Chapter 5.

- ✔ **What you want to say in your item description:** Jot down your ideas. Take a good look at your item and make a list of keywords that describe it. Although this is hardly a complete list, keywords are single descriptive words that can include

  - Brand names

  - Size of the item (citing measurements, if appropriate)

  - Age or date of manufacture

  - Condition

  - Rarity

  - Colour

  - Size

  - Material

  We know all about writer's block. If you're daunted by the Sell Your Item page, struggle through it, anyway. Finishing this page means you've already done the hard work before you even begin.

- ✔ **Whether you want to attach a picture (or pictures) to your description via a Uniform Resource Locator (URL):** Pictures help sell items, but you don't have to use them. (This information won't be on the test, but if you want to know more about using pictures in your auctions, see Chapter 14.)

> ✔ **The price at which you think you can sell the item:** Be as realistic as you can. (That's where the market research comes in.)

Examining the Sell Your Item Page

The Sell Your Item form is where your listing is born. Filling out your online paperwork requires a couple of minutes of clicking, typing, and answering all kinds of questions. The good news is that when you're done, your listing is up and running and (hopefully) starting to earn you money.

Before you begin, you have to be a registered eBay user. If you still need to register, Chapter 2 explains how to fill out the preliminary online paperwork. If you've registered but haven't provided eBay with your financial information (credit card or chequing account), you're asked for this information to set up your seller account before you proceed. Fill in the data on the secure form. Then, you're ready to roll.

Just like the dizzying array of new car colours, you have four ways to sell an item on eBay. Four ways may not seem to be very dizzying, unless you're trying to decide just which format is the best for you. Here's what you need to know about each type:

> ✔ **Online Auction:** This is the tried-and-true traditional sale format on eBay. The newbies look for this type of sale, and you can combine an online auction with Buy It Now for those who want the item immediately. Often, if you're selling a collectible item, letting it go to auction may net you a much higher profit — remember to do your research before listing.

> ✔ **Fixed Price:** Just like shopping at the corner store, a fixed-price sale is easy for the buyer to complete. The only problem is that many potential buyers may lean toward an auction because of the perception that they *may* get a better deal.

> ✔ **Your eBay Store:** Chapter 11 covers eBay Stores — a convenient place to sell items related to your auctions or fixed-price sales.

> ✔ **Advertise:** If you don't want to put your property up for auction and want to correspond with the prospective buyers, this is the option for you. Although this option is currently available for only real estate on the Canadian eBay site, the ad format is growing in many categories on the U.S. eBay site. If you're interested in finding out about fees as they apply to categories other than real estate, check out this URL:

```
pages.ebay.com/help/sell/adformatfees.html
```

Say, for example, that you want to list a good, old-fashioned eBay auction. You want to sell your item for a fixed price but are willing to let it go to auction.

To find eBay's Sell Your Item form from the eBay Canada home page, you can use either of these methods:

- ✔ Click the Sell link on the navigation bar at the top-right of the page, and you're whisked there immediately. eBay allows you to select your category and download the Sell Your Item page in seconds.

- ✔ You can also start your auction from your My eBay page. Just click the Sell Similar link (on the All Selling page) to the right of one of your existing items. By using the form that appears, you can change the item data.

When listing your item, here's the info you're asked to fill out (each of these items is discussed in detail later in this chapter):

- ✔ **User ID and Password (required):** You need to sign in again before you begin listing items for sale.

- ✔ **Category (required):** The category in which you want to list your item.

- ✔ **Title (required):** The name of your item.

- ✔ **Description (required):** What you want to tell eBay buyers about your item.

- ✔ **eBay Picture Services or Image URL (optional):** The Web address of any pictures you want to add. To add the URL of an image to the Sell Your Item form, you must click the Customize Form link at the top of the page and select the radio button to include a URL (versus using eBay Picture Services). You get a free Preview picture at the top of your auction. Chapter 14 has more information on using images in your auction.

- ✔ **The Gallery (optional):** You can add your item's picture to eBay's photo gallery. eBay charges $0.41 extra to add the item to the Gallery, $0.88 to have a Gallery Plus image that gets larger when a user drags his or her mouse over it, and $23.50 to make your item a featured auction in the Gallery. (You can find more on the Gallery in the section "Put me in the Gallery," later in this chapter.)

- ✔ **Gallery Image URL (optional):** If you want to include a hosted image, you must include the Web address of the JPEG image you want to place in the Gallery. If you're using eBay Picture Services, the first photo you upload is resized for the Gallery. Check out Chapter 14 for the skinny on Gallery images.

- ✔ **Item Location (required):** The region, city, and country from which you'll ship the item.

- ✔ **Quantity (required):** The number of items you're offering in this auction is always listed as 1 unless you plan to run a Dutch (Multiple Item) auction.

- ✔ **Starting Price (required):** The starting price (sometimes called a *minimum bid*) that you set.

- ✔ **Duration (required):** The number of days you want the auction to run.

- ✔ **Reserve Price (optional):** The hidden target price you set, which must be met before this item can be sold. eBay charges you a fee for this feature.

- ✔ **Private Listing (optional):** You can keep the identity of all bidders secret with this option. This type of auction is used only in rare circumstances.

- ✔ **Buy It Now (optional):** You can sell your item directly to the first buyer who meets this price.

- ✔ **List Item in Two Categories (optional):** If you want to double your exposure, you can list your item in two different categories. Double exposure equals double listing fees.

- ✔ **Featured Plus! (optional):** You can have your auction appear at the top of the category in which you list it. eBay charges $23.50 extra for this feature.

- ✔ **Highlight (optional):** Your item title is highlighted in the auction listings and search listings with a lilac-coloured band, which may draw eBay members' eyes right to your auction. eBay charges $5.90 extra for this feature.

- ✔ **Boldface Title (optional):** A selling option to make your item listing stand out. eBay charges $1.20 extra for this feature.

- ✔ **Free Counter (optional):** If you want to avail yourself of a free page view counter, indicate so here.

- ✔ **Ship-to-Locations (optional):** You can indicate where you're willing to ship an item. If you don't want the hassle of shipping outside of Canada, check the Canada option only. You can individually select different countries, as well. Most Canadian sellers make their items available for both Canadian and U.S. buyers.

You may want to consider to what extent you *really* want to be in the international shipping business. Buyers pick up the tab, but you have to deal with Customs forms and post office paperwork. If time is money, you may want to skip it entirely — or at least have all the forms filled out before you get in line at the post office. Or, if you use PayPal to print your shipping labels, you can greatly streamline the amount of documentation required. If you don't ship internationally, you may be blocking out a bunch of possible high bidders, though. Depending on what you're selling, shipping internationally just may not be worth the investment in extra time.

- ✔ **Shipping and Handling Charges (optional):** When prospective buyers know the shipping cost in advance (assuming it's a realistic price), they're more likely to bid or buy right then and there. If they have to e-mail you with questions, they may find another listing for the same item — with reasonable shipping — and bid or buy that one. Also, if you list the shipping charges on the page, winning bidders can pay you instantly through PayPal.

- ✔ **Payment Instructions (optional):** You can put any after-sale information here. If you don't want buyers to use Checkout, state that here. If you want them to pay with a specific payment service, mention that, as well. This information appears at the top of your sale when the sale is completed, at the bottom of the auction while the sale is active, and in the End of Listing e-mail.

✔ **PayPal and Immediate Payment (optional):** Fill out this area if you want to require the high bidder to pay through PayPal immediately when using Buy It Now. Add the Immediate Payment option if you know the shipping amount and want the winner to pay with a click of the mouse.

✔ **Return Policy (optional):** If you're willing to accept returns, indicate it. You can give the customer as few as three days to return the item (that cuts down on spurious returns).

Filling in the Required Blanks

Yes, the Sell Your Item form looks daunting, but filling out its many sections doesn't take as long as you may think. Some of the questions you're asked aren't things you even have to think about; just click an answer and off you go. Other questions ask you to type in information. Don't sweat a thing; all the answers you need are right here. You can find info on all the required stuff in the following sections, and later in this chapter we talk about optional stuff.

Selecting a category

Many eBay sellers will tell you that selecting the exact category isn't crucial to achieving the highest price for your item — and they're right. The bulk of buyers (who know what they're looking for) just input search keywords into eBay's search box and look for their items. Potential buyers, though, may select a category and, just like when you go to the mall, peruse the items for sale and see if a particular one strikes their fancy.

On the first page of the Sell Your Item form, you need to select the main category for your item.

Here's where your creativity can come into play. Who says that a box of Cleaver (the beautiful illustrations from some of Canada's pre-eminent children's book illustrators) note cards belongs in Everything Else: Gifts & Occasions: Greeting Cards: Other Cards. If you look around, you may find a better category. The Find Categories tool appears the second you open the Sell Your Item page. Just click the associated link to browse for categories. Check to see if anyone else is selling the item (and in which category) or just let this tool help you pick a good category. Figure 10-1 shows you how easy it is to select a main category.

Figure 10-1:
Let eBay do some of the work in finding the proper category for your item.

After you select your main category, you need to select from the thousands of subcategories. eBay offers you this wealth of choices in a handy point-and-click way. If you're unfamiliar with the types of items you can actually find in those categories, you may want to pore over Chapter 3 before you choose a category to describe your item. Figure 10-2 shows you how to manually narrow down the subcategory listings on the Sell: Select a Category page.

To select a category, follow these steps:

1. **Click one of the main categories in the box on the far left.**

   A new box to the right of the main categories box will open to reveal a list of subcategories. Continue making selections to open additional sub-subcategory boxes until you have found an appropriate home for your auction.

2. **Select the most appropriate subcategory.**

   Sub-subcategories appear in the box to the right of this subcategory box.

3. **Continue selecting subcategories until you've narrowed down your item listing as much as possible.**

   You know you've come to the last subcategory when eBay gives you a message that says you've finished selecting your category.

Most bidders scan for specific items in subcategories. For example, if you're selling a Bakelite fruit pin, don't just list it under Jewellery; keep narrowing down your choices. In this case, you can put it in a costume jewellery category that's especially for Bakelite. We guarantee that the real Bakelite jewellery collectors out there know where to look to find the jewellery they love. To narrow down the category of your item, just keep clicking until you hit the end of the line.

Some subcategories aren't for everyone

If you choose to list an item, bid on an item, or even just browse in the Everything Else: Mature Audiences category, you need to follow separate, specific guidelines because that category contains graphic nudity or sexual content that may offend some community members. You must

✔ Be at least 18 years of age (but you already know that all eBay customers must be 18 or older).

✔ Have a valid credit card.

✔ Complete a waiver stating that you're voluntarily choosing to access adults-only materials. For more information and a handy primer on privacy issues, see Chapter 15.

If you have Adult/Erotica items that you want to sell in a private auction, study the section "I want to be alone: The private auction," later in this chapter, which details the private-auction option.

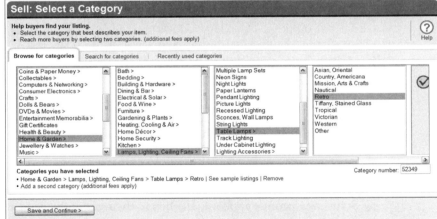

Figure 10-2: Narrow down your subcategories on the Sell: Select a Category page.

Creating the perfect item title

After you figure out in what category you want to list (which we talk about in the preceding section), eBay wants to get down to the nitty-gritty — what the heck to call that thing you're trying to sell.

Think of your item title as a great newspaper headline. The most valuable real estate on eBay is the 55-character title of your item. The majority of buyers do title searches, and that's where your item must come up to be sold! Give the most essential information right away to grab the eye of the reader who's just browsing. Be clear and informative enough to get noticed by eBay's search engine. Figure 10-3 shows examples of good titles. A couple of these titles contain subtitles (you can find more info on subtitles in the section "Giving the title punch with a subtitle," later in this chapter).

Here are some ideas to help you write your item title:

✔ Use the most common name for the item.

✔ If the item is rare, vintage, or hard to find, mention that.

✔ Mention the item's condition and whether it's new or old.

✔ Mention the item's special qualities, such as its style, model, or edition.

✔ Avoid fancy punctuation or unusual characters, such as $, hyphens, and L@@K, because they just clutter up the title — and buyers really don't search for them.

When you get into advanced selling mode, you should take a look at one of Marsha's other books, co-authored by Patti Louise Ruby, *eBay Listings that Sell For Dummies* (Wiley Publishing, Inc.). It covers eBay photography and HTML in depth.

Figure 10-3: These item titles are effective because they're clear, concise, and there's no question as to what the seller is selling.

Tactics Ogre Prima Strategy Guide PS GBA Battle Series
Model Trains Vol 14 No 6 December 1961 Magazine Vintage Pay Shipping on the first item only - all others free!
Gullwing Poster Mercedes Benz 300SL LARGE 28"x40" Print
New TRUE COLOR Photo Task Lamp LIGHT 13w 5000K w/BULB
White INFINITY Background Backdrop PORTABLE Photo STAGE Take Perfect eBay pictures anywhere in your home!
100% Egyptian Cotton 3-Packs Tank tops Large size White
2000 Château Montrose Bordeaux WS 96 points Red Wine
SANTA SHOPS ON EBAY Marsha Collier New 2006 Christmas SHOPPING HINTS FOR THE HOLIDAYS Direct from the Author
MEDIUM 10-13 lbs ~ CAT Soft Claws Paws ~ FREE TOY mice!

Ordinarily, we don't throw out French phrases just for the fun of it. But where making a profit is an issue, we definitely have to agree with the French that picking or not picking *le mot juste* (the best words) can mean the difference between having potential bidders merely see your auction and having an all-out bidding war on your hands. The following sections give you some tips about picking *le mot juste* to let your listing shine.

Look for a phrase that pays

Here's a crash course in eBay lingo that can help bring you up to speed on attracting buyers to your item. The following words are used frequently in eBay listings, and they can do wonders to jump-start your title:

- ✔ Mint
- ✔ One of a kind (OOAK — see the abbreviation list in Table 10-1)
- ✔ Vintage
- ✔ Collectible
- ✔ Rare
- ✔ Unique
- ✔ Primitive
- ✔ Well-loved

There's a whole science (called *grading*) to figuring out the value of a collectible. You're ahead of the game if you have a pretty good idea of what most eBay members mean. Do your homework before you assign a grade to your item. If you need more information on what these grades actually mean, Chapter 5 provides a translation.

eBay lingo at a glance

Common grading terms and the phrases in the preceding section aren't the only marketing standards you have at your eBay disposal. As eBay has grown, so has the lingo that members use as shortcuts to describe their merchandise.

Table 10-1 gives you a handy list of common abbreviations and phrases used to describe items. (***Hint:*** Mint means "may as well be brand new," not "tasty candy treat attached.")

Table 10-1	A Quick List of eBay Abbreviations	
eBay Code	*What It Abbreviates*	*What It Means*
COA	Certificate of Authenticity	Documentation that vouches for the genuineness of an item, such as an autograph or painting.
HTF, OOP	Hard to Find, Out of Print	Out of print, only a few ever made, or people grabbed up all there were. (HTF doesn't mean you spent a week looking for it in the attic.)

eBay Code	What It Abbreviates	What It Means
MIB	Mint in Box	The item is in the original box, in great shape, and just the way you'd expect to find it in a store.
MOC	Mint on Card	The item is mounted on its original display card, attached with the original fastenings, in store-new condition.
NR	No Reserve Price	A reserve price is the price you can set when you begin your auction. If bids don't meet the reserve, you don't have to sell. Many buyers don't like reserve prices because they don't think that they can get a bargain. (For tips on how to allay these fears and get those bids in reserve-price auctions, see the section "Writing your description," later in this chapter.) If you're not listing a reserve for your item, let bidders know.
NRFB	Never Removed from Box	Just what it says, as in "bought but never opened."
OEM	Original Equipment Manufacture	You're selling the item and all the equipment that originally came with it, but you don't have the original box, owner's manual, or instructions.
OOAK	One of a Kind	You're selling the only one in existence!

Often, you can rely on eBay slang to get your point across, but make sure you mean it and you're using it accurately. Don't label something MIB (Mint in Box) when it looks like it's been Mashed in Box by a meat grinder. You can find more abbreviations on Marsha's Web site, www.coolebaytools.com.

Don't let your title ruin your auction

Imagine going to a supermarket and asking someone to show you where the stringy stuff that you boil is, rather than asking where the spaghetti is. You might end up with mung bean sprouts — delicious to some but hardly what you had in mind. That's why you should check and recheck your spelling. Savvy buyers use the eBay search engine to find merchandise; if the name of your item is spelled wrong, the search engine can't find it. Poor spelling and incomprehensible grammar also reflect badly on you. If you're in competition with another seller, the buyer is likelier to trust the seller *hoo nose gud speling*.

If you've finished writing your item title and you have spaces left over, *please* fight the urge to dress it up with a lot of exclamation points and asterisks!!!!!!!!!!! (See how annoying that is?) No matter how gung-ho you are about your item, the eBay search engine may overlook your item if the title is encrusted with meaningless **** and !!!! symbols. If bidders do see your title, they may become annoyed by the virtual shrillness and ignore it anyway!!!!!!!! (It's even more annoying the second time around.)

Another distracting habit is overdoing capital letters. To buyers, seeing everything in caps is LIKE SEEING A CRAZED SALESMAN SCREAMING AT THEM TO BUY NOW! Using all caps is considered shouting, which is rude and tough on the eyes. Use capitalization SPARINGLY and only to stress a particular point.

Giving the title punch with a subtitle

A recently added feature at eBay is the availability of subtitles. eBay allows you to buy an additional 55 characters, which appear under your item title in a search. The fee for this extra promotion is $0.59, and in a few circumstances, it's definitely worth your while. Any text that you input really makes your item stand out in the crowd — but (you knew there would be a *but* didn't you?) these additional 55 characters won't come up in a title search. In other words, if the subtitle includes essential information ("NR NRFB," for example) that isn't in the main title, people searching for NR NRFB won't find your listing. Ensure that all essential keywords are included in your description so that people can find your auction. If you choose the subtitle option, pick attention-getting info that isn't absolutely needed for the title itself.

Writing your description

After you hook potential bidders with your title (check out the preceding sections for some title tips), reel 'em in with a fabulous description. Don't think Hemingway here; think infomercial (the classier the better). Figure 10-4 shows a great description of some American silver dollars. You can write a magnificent description, as well — all you have to do is click in the box and start typing.

Here's a list of suggestions for writing an item description:

> ✔ **Accentuate the positive.** Give the buyer a reason to buy your item, and be enthusiastic when you list all the reasons everyone should bid on it. Unlike the title, you can use as much space as you want. Even if you use a photo, be precise in your description — how big it is, what colour, what

kind of fabric, what design, and so on. Refer to the section "Creating the perfect item title," earlier in this chapter, as well as Table 10-1, for ideas on what to emphasize and how to word your description.

Figure 10-4:
Writing a good description can mean the difference between success and failure.

UNCIRCULATED MS63+ 1896 Morgan Silver Dollar

I recently purchased a group of MS63+ Morgan Silver Dollars from a long time collector to sell on ebay. The ones I've already sold have been very well received *(please look at my feedback)*. This is your chance to own a beautiful 1896 Morgan Silver Dollar in Premium Quality Brillliant Uncirculated Condition. Bright and well struck, it has very clean surfaces with very sharp features and details. The picture below doesn't do justice to this striking coin. It will make a lovely addition to any coin collection or a great start towards a new one.

Bid with confidence and bid whatever you feel this coin is worth to you as it is selling with NO RESERVE! Winning bidder to pay shipping & handling of $2.50, and must submit payment within a week of winning the auction. Credit cards are accepted through Paypal.com. Good luck!
Click below to...
Win another of my auctions and Save on shipping!

✓ **Include the negative.** Don't hide the truth of your item's condition. Trying to conceal flaws costs you in the long run: You'll get tagged with bad feedback. If the item has a scratch, a nick, a dent, a crack, a ding, a tear, a rip, missing pieces, replacement parts, faded color, dirty smudges, or a bad smell (especially if cleaning might damage the item), mention it in the description. If your item has been overhauled, rebuilt, repainted, or hot-rodded (say, a "Pentium computer" that was a 386 till you put in the new motherboard), say so. You don't want the buyer to send back your merchandise because you weren't truthful about imperfections or modifications. This type of omission can lead to a fraud investigation.

✓ **Be precise about all the logistical details of the post-auction transaction.** Even though you're not required to list any special S&H (shipping and handling) or payment requirements in your item description, the majority of eBay users do. Try to figure out the cost of shipping the item within Canada and to the United States, and add that to your description. If you offer shipping insurance, add that fact to your item description.

✓ **While you're at it, promote yourself, too.** As you accumulate positive feedback, tell potential bidders about your terrific track record. Add statements such as "I'm great to deal with. Check out my feedback section." You can even take it a step further by inviting prospective bidders to your About Me page (where you may also include a link to your personal Web site — if you have one). (Chapter 14 gives you some tips on how to make your auction seen by a wider audience.)

✓ **Wish your potential bidders well.** Communication is the key to a good transaction, and you can set the tone for your auction and post-auction exchanges by including some simple phrases that show your friendly side. Always end your description by wishing bidders good luck, inviting potential bidders to e-mail you with questions, and offering the option of providing additional photos of the item if you have them.

When you input your description, you have the option of jazzing things up with a bit of HTML coding, or you can use eBay's HTML text editor, shown in Figure 10-5. If you know how to use a word processor, you'll have no trouble touching up your text with this tool. Table 10-2 shows you a few additional codes to help you pretty things up.

You can go back and forth from the HTML text editor to the regular input and add additional codes here and there by clicking from the Standard form tab to the HTML entry form tab. Both of us often prepare our auctions ahead of time and save them as plain HTML files — that way, we can always retrieve them for use (it's easy to just copy and paste) — no matter what program or form we might be using to list our auctions. See Chapter 20 for more on software to help you with your auctions.

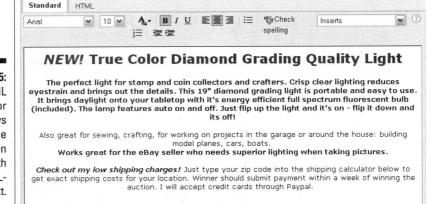

Figure 10-5: The HTML text editor shows you the description area with HTML-coded text.

Table 10-2	A Short List of HTML Codes	
HTML Code	*How to Use It*	*What It Does*
`<b></b>`	`<b>cool collectible</b>`	**cool collectible** (bold type)
`<i></i>`	`<i>cool collectible</i>`	*cool collectible* (italic type)

HTML Code	How to Use It	What It Does
`<b><i>` `</i></b>`	`<b><i>cool` `collectible</b></i>`	***cool collectible*** (bold and italic type)

`<font`
`color=red>`
`</font>`
	`<font color=red>`
	`cool collectible`
	`</font>`
		Selected text appears in red. (This book is in black and white, so you can't see it here.)

`<font`
`size=+1>`
`</font>`
	`<font size=+3>`
	`cool</font>`
	`collectible`
		cool collectible (font size normal +1–4, increases size 1–4 times)

` `	`cool ` `collectible`	cool collectible (inserts line break)
`<p>`	`cool<p>` `collectible`	cool collectible (inserts paragraph space)

`<hr>`	`cool`
	`collectible`
	`<hr>cheap`
		cool
		
		collectible
		
		————
		
		cheap
		
		(inserts horizontal rule)

`<h1><h1>`	`<h1>cool`
	`collectible`
	`</h1>`
		cool collectible
		(converts text to headline size)

Occasionally, sellers offer an item as a *presell,* or an item that the seller doesn't yet have in stock but expects to. If you're offering this kind of item, make sure that you spell out all the details in the description. eBay policy states that you must ship a presell item within 30 days of the auction's end, so be sure you'll have the item within that time span. Don't forget to include the actual shipping date. Putting an item up for sale without actually having it in hand is a practice fraught with risk. The item you're expecting may not arrive in time, or it may arrive damaged. We've heard of many sellers who have had to go out and purchase an item at retail for a buyer in order to preserve their feedback when caught in this situation. Many sellers have also wound up with unexpected negative feedback because they couldn't provide the item they sold.

Going Dutch

If you have five Barbie Wedding Day dolls, 37 Breathalyzers, or 2,000 Expo 67 commemorative pins, and you want to sell them all at once to as many bidders as quickly as possible, sell them as multiple quantities in a fixed-price sale. (You can also sell the whole shebang in one lot in the Wholesale Lot category.) If you're not sure how much you can get for the items, you can always try a Dutch (Multiple Item) auction. Dutch auctions are mainly used by dealers and businesses that want to move a lot of items fast.

eBay has requirements for starting a Dutch auction. You have to be an eBay member at least 14 days with a feedback rating of 30 or higher. Click the ? bubble to the right of the Quantity field on the Sell Your Item page for more information on how to conduct this type of auction, and check out Chapter 1 for more info on how a Dutch auction works. If you're interested in bidding on a Dutch auction, take a look at Chapter 6.

Listing the number of items for sale

Unless you're planning on holding a Multiple Item (Dutch) auction, the number of items is always 1, which means you're holding a traditional auction or listing a single item up for sale. If you need to change the quantity number from 1, just type the number in the box.

A matching set of cuff links is considered one item, as is the complete 37-volume set of *The Smith Family Ancestry and Genealogical History since 1270*. If you have more than one of the same item (two sets of identical cuff links), we suggest that you sell them one at a time. You're much more likely to get higher final bids for your items when you sell them individually. Never try to sell items that belong in a set as separate items.

Whether you list your items individually in auctions or together in a Multiple Item auction, eBay doesn't allow you to list the same item in more than 15 auctions at one time.

Setting a starting price — how low can you go?

What do a hockey puck autographed by Bobby Hull, a used walkie-talkie, and a Jaguar sports car all have in common? They all started with a $1 starting price. eBay requires you to set a *starting price*, also called a *minimum bid* — the lowest bid allowed in an auction. You may be surprised to see stuff worth tens of thousands of dollars starting at just a buck. These sellers haven't lost their minds. Neither are they worried someone could be tooling down the highway in a $100,000 sports car they bought for the price of a burger.

Setting an incredibly low minimum (just type it in the price box *without* the dollar sign but *with* the decimal point) is a subtle strategy that gives you more bang for your buck. You can use a low starting price to attract more bidders who will, in turn, drive up the price to the item's real value — especially if, after doing your research, you know that the item is particularly hot.

If you're worried about the outcome of the final bid, you can protect your item by using a *reserve price* (the price the bidding needs to reach before the item can be sold). Then you won't have to sell your item for a bargain-basement price because your reserve price protects your investment. The best advice is to set a reserve price that's the lowest amount you'll take for your item and then set a minimum bid that's ridiculously low. Use a reserve only when absolutely necessary because some bidders pass up reserve auctions. (For more info about setting a reserve price, see the section "Your secret safety net — reserve price," later in this chapter.)

Starting with a low starting price is also good for your pocketbook. eBay charges the seller an Insertion Fee — based on your opening bid. If you keep your opening bid low and set no reserve, you get to keep more of your money. (See Chapter 9 for more about eBay fees.)

The more bids you get, the more people will want to bid on your item because they perceive the item as hot. A hot item with a lot of bids draws even more bidders the way a magnet attracts paper clips.

Before you set any starting price, do your homework and make some savvy marketing decisions. If your auction isn't going as you hoped, you *could* end up selling Grandma Ethel's Ming vase for a dollar. Think about your strategy. See the section "Mid-Course Corrections: Fixing Current Auctions," later in this chapter, for how you can make changes in your listing if you've made some egregious error.

When entering a starting price, type in only the numbers and a decimal point. Don't use dollar signs ($) or cent signs (¢).

Buy It Now

eBay's Buy It Now (*BIN* in eBay-speak) is available for single-item auctions. This feature allows buyers who want to purchase an item *now* to do so. Have you ever wanted an item really badly and didn't want to wait until the end of an auction? If the seller offers Buy It Now, you can purchase that item immediately. If you're the seller, you can entice your bidders to pay just a tad more to have the satisfaction of walking away with the item free and clear. Just specify the amount the item can sell for in the Buy It Now price area — the amount can be whatever you want. If you choose to take advantage of selling a hot item, for example, during the holiday rush, you can make the BIN price as high as you think it can go. If you just want the item to move, make your BIN price the average price you see the item go for at eBay.

When your item receives a bid, the BIN option disappears, and the item goes through the normal auction process. If you have a reserve price on your item, the BIN feature doesn't disappear until a bidder meets your reserve price through the normal bidding process. To list an item with Buy It Now, you must have a feedback score of 10, or a feedback score of 30 for a multiple item, fixed-price sale.

Setting your auction time

How long do you want to run your auction? eBay gives you a choice — 1, 3, 5, 7, or 10 days. Just select the number you want from the drop-down box. If you choose a 10-day auction, you add $0.47 to your listing fee.

You can vary your auction-length strategy, depending on the time of year and the type of items you're selling. If you have an item that you think will sell pretty well, run a 7-day auction (be sure it'll cover a full weekend) so bidders have time to check it out before they decide to bid. However, if you know that you have a red-hot item that's going to fly off the shelves — such as a rare toy or a hard-to-get video game — choose a 3-day auction. This short-auction approach may certainly apply during the busy Christmas shopping season when popular items are in high demand. Eager bidders tend to bid higher and more often to beat out their competition if the item is hot and going fast. Three days is long enough to give trendy items exposure and to ring up bids.

No matter how many days you choose to run your auction, it ends at exactly the same time of day as it starts. A 7-day auction that starts on Thursday at 9:03:02 a.m. ends the following Thursday at 9:03:02 a.m.

Although the gang at eBay is a pretty laid-back group, they do run on military time. That means they use a 24-hour clock that's set to eastern time on the eBay Canada site, and Pacific time on the U.S. site. So, 3:30 in the afternoon is 15:30, and one minute after midnight is 00:01. Questions about time conversions? Check out www.timezoneconverter.com or look at the table on Bill's Web site, which has a printable conversion chart of eBay Canada times (www.learningebayiseasy.com). (And so you don't have to keep flipping back to this page, we also include these handy-dandy links on the Cheat Sheet at the front of this book.)

With auctions running 24 hours a day, seven days a week, you should know when the most bidders are around to take a gander at your wares. Here are some times to think about:

✔ **Saturday/Sunday:** Always run an auction over a weekend. People log on and off of eBay all day.

Don't start or end your auction on a Saturday or Sunday — *unless* your completed auction research indicates that you should. Certain types of bidders love sitting at their computers waiting for auctions to end on the weekends, but many bidders are busy having lives, and their schedules are unpredictable. Although a few eager bidders may log on and place a maximum bid on your auction, you can bet that they won't be sitting at a computer making a last-minute flurry of competitive bids if they have something better to do on a Saturday or Sunday.

✔ **Holiday weekends:** If a holiday weekend's coming up around the time you're setting up your auction, run your auction through the weekend and end it a day after the "holiday" Monday. This auction setup gives prospective bidders a chance to catch up with the items they perused over the weekend and plan their bidding strategies.

Don't end an auction on the last day of a three-day holiday. People in the mood to shop are generally at department stores collecting bargains. If eBay members aren't shopping, they're out enjoying an extra day off.

✔ **Time of day:** The best times of day to start and end your auction are during eBay's peak hours of operation, which are 8 p.m. to 12 p.m. eastern time, right after work on the West Coast. Perform your completed auction research, however, to be sure that this strategy applies to your item. Your timing depends on the item you're listing and whether 8 p.m. to 12 p.m. eastern time is the middle of the night where you live.

Unless you're an insomniac or a vampire and want to sell to werewolves, don't let your auctions close in the middle of the night — say, at 02:30. Not enough bidders are around to cause any last-minute bidding that would bump up the price.

Your secret safety net — reserve price

Here's a little secret: The reason sellers list big-ticket items such as Ferraris, grand pianos, and high-tech computer equipment with a starting bid of $1 is because they're protected from losing money with a reserve price. The *reserve price* is the lowest price that must be met before the item can be sold. It's not required by eBay, but it can protect you. eBay charges an additional fee for this feature that varies depending on how high your reserve is.

For example, say you list a first edition book of John Steinbeck's *The Grapes of Wrath*. You set the starting price at $1, and you set a reserve price at $80. That means that people can start bidding at $1, and if at the end of the auction the bidding hasn't reached the $80 reserve, you don't have to sell the book.

As with everything in life, using a reserve price for your auctions has an upside and a downside. Many choosy bidders and bargain hunters blast past reserve-price auctions because they see a reserve price as a sign that proclaims, "No bargains here!" Many bidders figure they can get a better deal on the same item with an auction that proudly declares *NR* (for *no reserve*) in its description. As an enticement to those bidders, you see a lot of NR listings in auction titles.

If you need to set a reserve on your item, help the bidder out. Many bidders shy away from an auction that has a reserve, but if they're really interested, they'll read the item description. To dispel their fears that the item is way too expensive or out of their price range, add a line in your description that states the amount of your reserve price. "I have put a reserve of $75 on this item to protect my investment; the highest bid over $75 will win the item." A phrase such as this takes away the vagueness of the reserve auction and allows you to place a reserve with a low opening bid. (You want to reel 'em in, remember?)

On lower-priced items, we suggest that you set a higher starting price and set no reserve. Otherwise, if you're not sure about the market, set a low minimum bid but set a high reserve to protect yourself.

If bids don't reach a set reserve price, some sellers e-mail the highest bidder and offer the item at what the seller thinks is a fair price. Sending a Second Chance Offer through the eBay system makes much more sense. Two caveats if you try to circumvent eBay fees and contact the bidders:

✔ eBay can suspend the seller *and* the buyer if the side deal is reported to Trust & Safety. This activity is strictly prohibited.

✔ eBay won't protect buyers or sellers if a side deal goes bad.

You can't use a reserve price in a Multiple Item (Dutch) auction.

I want to be alone: The private auction

In a private auction, bidders' User IDs are kept under wraps. Sellers typically use this option to protect the identities of bidders during auctions for high-priced big-ticket items (say, that restored World War II fighter). Wealthy eBay users may not want the world to know that they have the resources to buy expensive items. Private auctions are also held for items from the Adult/Erotica category. (Gee, there's a shocker.)

The famous sign that was pictured in almost every Disneyland promotion for the first 40 or so years of Disneyland's existence was put up for sale on eBay in 2000. Legend has it that the sign was purchased by actor John Stamos for a high bid of $30,700. Unfortunately for John, the Disney auction didn't use the private auction feature. After news of the winner's name hit the tabloids — the entire world knew John's eBay User ID! He had to change his ID in a hurry to end the throngs of lovey-dovey e-mail headed to his computer!

In private auctions, the seller's e-mail address is accessible to bidders in case questions arise. Bidders' e-mail addresses remain unseen.

Put me in the Gallery

The Gallery is a visually graphic auction area that lets you post pictures to a special photo gallery that's accessible from the listings. It also causes a postage-stamp-size version of your image to appear to the left of your listing in the category or search. Many buyers enjoy browsing the Gallery catalogue-style, and it's open to all categories. If you choose to go this route, your item is listed in both the Gallery and in the regular text listings. (We explain how to post your pictures in Chapter 14.)

The best thing about using a Gallery picture in your listings is that it increases the space your listing takes up on a search or category page. If you don't use a Gallery picture and just have an image in your auction, all that appears to the left of your listing is a teeny, tiny camera icon.

Filling out the item location

eBay wants you to list the general area and the country in which you live. The idea behind telling the bidder where you live is to give him or her a heads-up on what kind of shipping charges to expect. Don't be esoteric (listing where you live as *The Here and Now* isn't a whole lot of help), but don't go crazy with cross streets, landmarks, or degrees of latitude. Listing the city and province you live in is enough.

If you live in a big area — say, the Greater Toronto Area, which sprawls on for miles — you may want to think about narrowing down your region a little. You may find a bidder who lives close to you, which could swing your auction. If you do a face-to-face transaction, doing it in a public place is a good idea. (Bill has frequently met buyers at various Tim Hortons restaurants.)

A picture is worth a thousand words

Clichés again? Perhaps. But an item on eBay without a picture is almost a waste of time. If you haven't set up photo hosting elsewhere, you can list one picture with eBay's Pictures Service for free. Additional photos cost you $0.18 each.

Alternatively, you can put all the pictures you want in your auction description for free. See Chapter 14 for the necessary coding and instructions.

Listing Designer

How many times have you seen an item on eBay laid out on the page all pretty-like with a fancy border around the description? If that sort of thing appeals to you, eBay's Listing Designer can supply you with pretty borders for almost any type of item for $0.12. Selecting your design is as easy as clicking the menu (see Figure 10-6). You can designate where you want to place your image on the page relative to the description (left, right, top, or bottom).

Can the pretty borders increase the amount of bids your auction gets? It's doubtful. A clean item description with a couple of good, clear pictures of your item is really all you need.

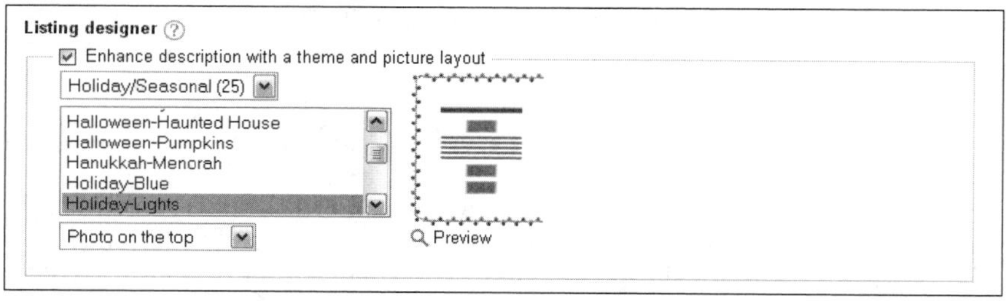

Figure 10-6:
Selecting a
graphic in
Listing
Designer is
as simple as
clicking
your mouse.

Listing designer (?)

☑ Enhance description with a theme and picture layout

Holiday/Seasonal (25) ▼

Halloween-Haunted House
Halloween-Pumpkins
Hanukkah-Menorah
Holiday-Blue
Holiday-Lights

Photo on the top ▼

🔍 Preview

eBay also offers a combination deal called the Value Pack on the review page of the Sell Your Item form. For $0.77, you can place a subtitle on your listing, add a Gallery picture, and doll things up with Listing Designer. All those features would normally cost $1.12, so the savings is clear if you run several auctions a week.

If you don't want to use the Listing Designer graphics to distract from your item, you can still get a discount. Just click the Enhance Description check box, but *don't* select a graphic pattern. You still save $0.23 over the price of a subtitle and Gallery (sneaky, huh?).

Listing the payment methods you accept

Yeah, sure, eBay is loads of fun, but the bottom line to selling is the phrase "Show me the money!" You make the call on what you're willing to take as money from the high bidder of your auction. eBay offers the following payment options — just select the ones that you like:

- **Money Order/Cashier's Cheque:** From a seller's point of view, this is the safest method of payment. It's the closest thing you can get to cash. As a seller, you want to get paid with as little risk as possible. The only drawback? You have to wait for the buyer to mail it.

- **Credit Cards:** If you accept credit cards, using PayPal is the cheapest and most convenient way to go. If you have a merchant account through a retail store, be sure to select the little check boxes to the left of the credit cards you accept.

  Offering a credit card payment option through PayPal or a merchant account often attracts higher bids to your auctions. These higher bids usually more than cover the small percentage that credit card payment services charge you to use them. See Chapter 8 for a more complete description on how to use these services.

  Some sellers who use credit card services try attaching an additional fee (to cover their credit card processing fees) to the final payment. However, that's against the law in California, home of eBay, and therefore against eBay's rules. So forget about it. eBay can end your auction if it catches you.

- **C.O.D. (Cash on Delivery):** We think that this option is the least attractive for both buyers and sellers. The buyer has to be home with the cash ready to go on the day the package arrives. Odds are that on the day the item's delivered, your buyer is taking his or her sick pet goldfish to the vet for a gill-cleaning. Then the item ends up back at your door, and you have no sale. It also often takes up to 30 days for you to get the money back in your hands.

- **See Item Description:** We think you should always state in your item description how you want to be paid. Why? Because there's no good reason not to and it takes away the mystery of shopping with you. If you're offering payment options that aren't specifically listed on the Sell Your Item form, select this option. Some buyers (mostly international) like to pay in cash, but we think paying in cash is way too risky, and we recommend that you never, ever deal in cash. If a problem arises — for either buyer or seller — no one has evidence that payment was made or received. Avoid it. In fact, soliciting a cash payment is against eBay rules unless you're doing a local pickup.

✔ **Personal Cheque:** This is an extremely popular option, but it comes with a risk: The cheque could bounce higher than a lob at Wimbledon. If you accept personal cheques, explain in your item description how long you plan to wait for the cheque to clear before sending the merchandise. The average hold is about ten business days. Some sellers wait as long as two full weeks. Accepting cheques from U.S. buyers may also mean substantially longer wait times for the cheque to clear. Accepting eCheques through PayPal leaves all the bookkeeping and waiting to PayPal; you don't have to call the bank for confirmation.

Cut down on the risk of bad cheques by reading the bidder's feedback when the auction's underway. Be wary of accepting cheques from people with negative comments. (We explain all about feedback in Chapter 4.) Never ship an item until you're certain the cheque has cleared the buyer's bank.

Most sellers offer buyers several ways to pay. You can choose as few or as many as you want. When the item page appears, your choices are noted at the top of the listing. Listing several payment options makes you look like a flexible, easygoing professional.

Setting shipping terms

Ahoy, matey! Hoist the bid! Okay, not quite. Before you run it up the mast, select your shipping options. Here are your choices:

✔ **Ship to Canada Only:** This option is selected by default; it means you ship only domestically.

✔ **Will Ship Worldwide:** The world is your oyster. But make sure that you can afford the time for the extra processing of Customs forms.

✔ **Will Ship to Canada and the Following:** If you're comfortable shipping to certain countries but not to others, make your selections here, and they show up on your auction page. Many Canadian sellers add the U.S. here to take advantage of potential sales to the huge market south of the border.

When you indicate that you ship internationally, your auction shows up on the international eBay sites, which is a fantastic way to attract new buyers! eBay has a lot of good international users, so you may want to consider selling your items around the world. If you do, be sure to clearly state in the description that all extra shipping costs and Customs charges are the responsibility of the winning bidder. (See Chapter 12 for more information on how to ship to customers abroad.)

Traditionally, the buyer pays for shipping, and this is the point of creating your listing at which you must decide how much to charge. You also have to calculate how much this item will cost you to ship. If it's a small item (weighing under a pound or so), you may decide to charge a flat rate to all buyers. To charge a flat rate, click the Flat Shipping Rates tab and fill in the shipping amount. Before you fill in the amount, be sure to include your charges for packing (see Chapter 12 for more info on how much to add for this task) and any insurance charges.

Check out Chapter 12 for more information on shipping options.

eBay Options: Ballyhoo on the Cheap

Although eBay's display options aren't quite as effective as a three-story neon sign in Times Square, they do bring greater attention to your auction. Here are your options:

- ✔ **Bold:** eBay fee: $1.20. Bold type does catch your attention, but don't bother using it on items that'll bring in less than $25. Do use it if you're in hot competition with similar items and you want yours to stand out.

- ✔ **Highlight:** eBay fee: $5.90. Yellow highlighter is what many of us use to point out the high points in the books we read. (You're using one now, aren't you?) The eBay highlight feature is lilac, but it can really make your item shine. Check out the category in which you choose to list before selecting this feature. Some categories are overwhelmed with sellers using the highlight option, and the pages look completely shaded in lilac. In these categories, *not* using highlight (and using perhaps a bold title instead) makes your auction stand out more.

- ✔ **Featured Plus!** eBay fee: $23.50. You want top billing? You can buy it here. This option puts you on the first page of your item category and on search results pages. This is a good option for moving special merchandise. Often, bidders just scan the top items; if you want to be seen, you gotta be there. eBay's statistics say that items listed as Featured Plus! are 58 percent more likely to sell — but it really depends on what you're selling and when. Ask yourself this: Is it worth $23.50 to have more people see my item? If yes, then go for it. Figure 10-7 shows how items are listed in the Featured Plus! listings.

You need a feedback rating of at least 10 to make it to the Featured Plus! auctions.

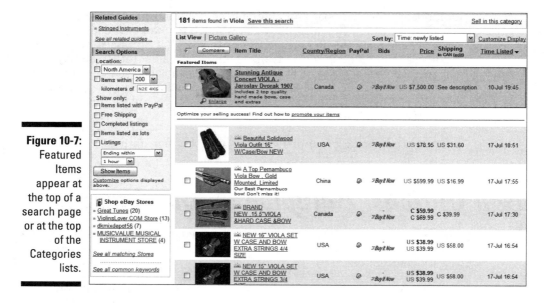

Figure 10-7:
Featured
Items
appear at
the top of a
search page
or at the top
of the
Categories
lists.

Checking Your Work and Starting the Auction

After you fill in all the blanks on the Sell Your Item form and think you're ready to join the world of e-commerce, follow these steps:

1. **Click the Review button at the bottom of the Sell Your Item page.**

   You waft to the Verification page (shown in Figure 10-8), the place where you can catch mistakes before your item is listed. The Verification page shows you a condensed version of all your information and tallies up how much eBay is charging you in fees and options to run this auction. You also see a preview of how your description and pictures will look on the site.

   You also may find the Verification page helpful as a last-minute chance to get your bearings. If you chose a very general category, eBay asks you whether you're certain there isn't a more appropriate category. You can go back to any of the pages that need correcting by clicking the Edit Listings links on the Verification page. Make any changes and additions, and then head for the Verification page again by clicking the Save and Continue button.

Figure 10-8:
The
Verification
page is the
last place
you can
double-
check for
errors
before the
listing
begins.

2. **Check for mistakes.**

   Nit-pick for common, careless errors; you won't be sorry. We've seen eBay members make goofs such as the wrong category listing; spelling and grammatical errors; and missing information about shipping, handling, insurance, and payment methods.

3. **When you're sure everything's accurate and you're happy with your item listing, click the Submit My Listing button.**

   A Confirmation page pops up from eBay. At that precise moment, your listing begins, even though it may be a couple of hours before it appears in eBay's search and listings updates. If you want to see your auction right away and check for bids, your Confirmation page provides a link for that purpose. Click the link, and you're there. You can also keep track of your auctions by using the My eBay page. (To find out how, see Chapter 4.)

All auction pages come with this friendly warning: `Seller assumes all responsibility for listing this item.`

Some eBay veterans just gloss over this warning after they've been wheeling and dealing for a while, but it's an important rule to remember. See Chapter 9 for details on the rules sellers must follow, and Chapter 12 for tips on your role in closing the deal and receiving good feedback.

For the first 24 hours after your sale is underway, eBay stamps the Item page with a funky sunrise icon to the left of the listing. This is just a little reminder for buyers to come take a look at the latest items up for sale.

Mid-Course Corrections: Fixing Current Auctions

Don't worry if you make a mistake filling out the Sell Your Item page, but don't notice it until after the auction is up and running. Pencils have erasers, and eBay allows revisions. You can make changes at two stages of the game: before the first bid is placed and after the bidding war is underway. The following sections explain what you can (and can't) correct — and when you have to accept the little imperfections of your Auction Item page.

Making changes before bidding begins

Here's what you can change about your listing before bids have been placed (provided your listing doesn't end within the next 12 hours):

- The title or description of your auction
- The item category
- The item's starting price
- The item's Buy It Now price
- The reserve price (you can add, change, or remove it)
- The duration of your listing
- The URL of the picture you're including with your auction
- A private listing designation (you can add or remove it)
- Accepted payment methods, checkout information, item location, and shipping terms

When you revise an auction, eBay puts a little notation on your auction page that reads: `Description(revised)`. (Think of it as automatic common courtesy.)

To revise a fixed-price listing or any auction before bids have been received, follow these steps:

1. **Go to the auction page and click the Revise Your Item link just under the item description.**

   This link appears only if you've signed in to eBay. If the item hasn't received any bids, a message appears on your screen to indicate that you may update the item.

   If you're already signed in, you go directly to the Revise Item page, which looks like the Sell Your Item form.

2. **Make changes to the item information on the Revise Item page and then click the Save and Continue button at the bottom of the page when you're finished.**

   A summary of your newly revised auction page appears on your screen.

3. **If you're happy with your revisions, click the Submit Revisions button.**

   If you're not happy, click one of the Edit Listing links and redo the Revise Your Listing page.

   You're taken to your newly revised item page, where you see a disclaimer from eBay that says you've revised the listing before the first bid.

Making changes after bidding begins

If your listing is up and running, and already receiving bids, you can still make some slight modifications to it. Newly added information is clearly separated from the original text and pictures. In addition, eBay puts a time stamp on the additional info in case questions from early bidders crop up later.

After your item receives bids, eBay allows you to add to your item's description. If you feel you were at a loss for words in writing your item's description, if you discover new information (that vase you thought was a reproduction is actually the real thing!), or if a lot of potential bidders are asking the same questions, go ahead and make all the additions you want. But whatever you put in the description the first time around stays there, as well.

Don't let an oversight grow into a failure to communicate, and don't ignore iffy communication until the auction is over. Correct any inaccuracies in your auction information now to avoid problems later on.

Always check your e-mail to see whether bidders have questions about your item. If a bidder wants to know about flaws, be truthful and courteous when returning e-mails. As you get more familiar with eBay (and with writing auction descriptions), the number of e-mail questions will decrease. If you enjoy good customer service in your day-to-day shopping, here's your chance to give some back.

Chapter 11

Forget the Car — Drive Your Mouse to an eBay Store

In This Chapter

▶ Shopping eBay Stores

▶ Opening your own eBay store

*S*ometimes, you just don't wanna buy in an auction. Sometimes, you want to buy your item *now*. No waiting for an auction to end — *now!* The easiest place to go for this type of transaction is the eBay Express site or the eBay Stores area, where you can find fixed-price items for sale. Visiting the stores can save you money — because buying from one seller allows several items to be shipped in the same box. Many sellers will combine shipping costs on multiple purchases.

All the fine merchandise that you can find on eBay can also be found in the eBay Stores area. eBay Stores is located in a separate area from the regular auctions, and regular eBay sellers run these stores. eBay Stores is a place where sellers can list as many additional items for sale as they want for a reduced Insertion Fee. Buyers are lured to the store by the small red eBay Stores icon that appears to the right of the seller's User ID.

Whenever you're looking at an item and see that the seller has a store, be sure to click the store icon. The seller may have the very same merchandise in his or her eBay store for a lower buy price.

If a seller has an eBay store, he or she can list individual items for different sizes of an article of clothing, different variations of items that he or she sells in regular auctions, or anything that falls within eBay's listing policies. The store items have a listing time of at least 30 days, so sellers can also put up specialty items that may not sell well in an auction that lasts only one to ten days.

We suggest that you transact business on the site for quite a while before you open a store. Operating a store requires a solid understanding of how eBay works and knowing how to handle all types of transactions. The requirements to open an eBay store are pretty basic:

- ✔ You must be registered as an eBay seller, with a credit card on file.

- ✔ You must have a feedback rating of 20 or more.

- ✔ You must accept credit card payments, either through PayPal or through a merchant account.

The eBay search engine doesn't directly search the eBay Stores area. If you perform a search on eBay, be sure to scroll to the bottom of the page to see whether the particular item is available in an eBay store. Store inventory listings appear in the search results when there are 30 or fewer listings for the item on the core eBay site.

To get to the eBay Stores main area, visit the eBay home page (`www.ebay.ca`), look for the Specialty Sites area on the lower-left side (see Figure 11-1), and click the eBay Stores link. Alternatively, you can type `http://stores.ebay.ca` in the address box of your Web browser and press Enter.

Figure 11-1: A quick click in the Specialty Sites box on the eBay home page takes you to the eBay Stores hub.

Unlimited Shopping from the Stores Page

Okay, you've arrived! You've come to the hub of power shopping online, the eBay Stores home page (see Figure 11-2). Just like the eBay home page, this is your gateway to many incredible bargains. In the following sections, you can find out what you can expect to find in eBay's stores, how to navigate the stores, and how to find the deals.

Figure 11-2: The eBay Stores home page, where you can search stores by item or store name.

Conducting an eBay Stores search

On the top-left of the eBay Stores home page is the search engine for eBay Stores. You can also access the store search link by clicking the Buy button in the navigation bar. (Just below the search box on the resulting page, you can find an eBay Stores Search link. Click that link to go to an eBay Stores search page.) You can perform your search in eBay Stores on different levels. You can search for Buy It Now items — seems a bit too obvious to us, isn't that why we're here? Anyway, if you type your keyword in the box and stay with the default search, you can find every piece of the fixed-price inventory in the stores that matches your keyword.

eBay Stores don't just list the fixed-price items. If sellers have current auctions on eBay, those auctions are listed in their stores, as well — only regular auctions don't come up in an eBay Stores item search. So if you find an auction that interests you at eBay, click the item to read the description and the condition of the item. If you want to buy the item, then click the Visit Seller's Store link below the seller's User ID or the Visit My eBay Store link to the left of the actual store name just above the item description to go to the seller's eBay store. You just may find some related items that you want. And the seller probably combines shipping so that you save some money!

If you remember a particular seller's store name (or part of it), you can also search eBay Stores by store name. All you have to do is type the store name (or part of the store name) in the Find a Store box, select the Search Store Name and Description option button, and click the Search Stores button to return your name matches (as shown in Figure 11-3).

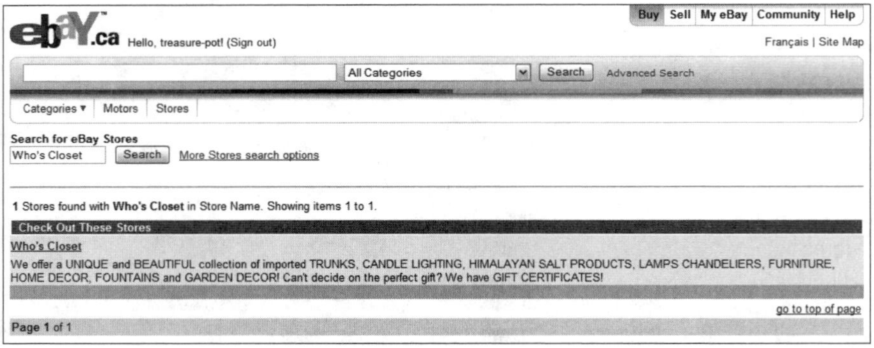

Figure 11-3: You can search for an eBay store by name.

If you can't remember the store name, but you can remember what it sells, type the keywords in the Find a Store box, select the Stores with Matching Items option, and click the Search Stores button. For example, you can search for `terrier t-shirts`. If the seller has used those words in his or her store description or title, it shows up in the search results listing. In Figure 11-4, we typed in the title of another book written by Marsha, then clicked the Search Stores button, and we were supplied direct links to all eBay stores carrying inventory.

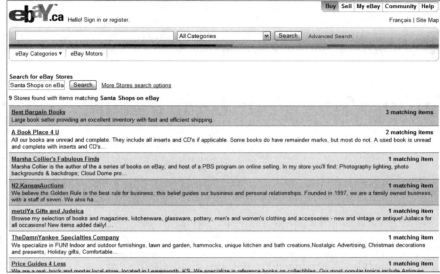

Figure 11-4:
This search
for Santa
Shops on
eBay
returned the
names of
several
stores.

Browsing the store categories

Browsing store categories is a great idea when you're looking for a specialist — you know, someone who carries a particular type of item that appeals to you. Perhaps you have an affinity for jewellery, art, limited edition books, or needlepoint. Whatever your interest, you can probably find a store here to suit your needs.

To browse eBay Stores, just click Buy in the navigation bar on any eBay page. Near the very bottom of the page on the bottom link area, click the Browse Stores link, and you travel to the eBay Stores hub. Look for a list of categories on the left side of the page; click a category that suits your fancy. When you do that, the left side of the page (surprise!) lists subcategories within that category. We clicked the Cameras & Photo category and then the Digital Cameras subcategory, and we ended up at that subcategory's hub page.

Browsing eBay Stores categories is like strolling down a mall filled with your favourite items. Stores with the highest inventories in the category are listed toward the top.

Just like in the brick-and-mortar world, more "general" stores at eBay carry a wide breadth of merchandise. By browsing individual categories, you may be missing those general stores. Try visiting the Everything Else category, and you can find, well, everything else.

Selling from Your Own Virtual Storefront

After you shop the eBay Stores, you may be thinking that this is a good place to open your own store. There's great news on that end because eBay stores have the most reasonable rent on the Internet. At an eBay store, you aren't constrained by the auction format of a 10-day maximum. You can list your fixed-price items in your eBay store on a "good till cancelled" basis.

We don't like to pull punches with our readers, so take our bit of advice: Opening an eBay store without a large stock of items, or many items that you stock in multiples, makes no sense. Opening an eBay store is really for true sellers — those who make a business on the eBay site selling merchandise they buy for the purpose of reselling. Retailers who come to the eBay site to expand their business can be successful with eBay Stores, but certainly it helps to know the e-commerce ropes already.

Too many readers (new to eBay) have e-mailed Marsha after reading previous editions of this book to tell her that they opened a store and have had no sales. You must sell buckets of items on eBay in the auction format to draw people to your store — simple as that.

Paying the landlord

Monthly rent for an eBay store is as low as $15.95 per month. Featured stores have a rent of $58.95, and anchor stores (just like your local department store) pay a lot more — $589.95 a month. Featured stores' listings are guaranteed to rotate through the special featured section on the eBay Stores home page. These listings also appear on the top level of their category's directory page. Anchor stores get extra promotion, and their logos are showcased in eBay Stores' directory pages. Owning a store also has other benefits: cost-per-click advertising, sales management tools, and a lot of promotional benefits for your merchandise.

The reasonable pricing behind eBay Stores is a remarkable bargain. For as little as $15.95 a month, you have the opportunity to sell your merchandise to over 222 million registered users! See Table 11-1 for eBay Stores listing fees.

Table 11-1	eBay Stores Listing Fees per 30 Days
Starting Price	*Listing Fee*
$0.01–$29.99	$0.06
$30 and higher	$0.12

Listing fees and monthly "rent" can be just the tip of the iceberg if you choose to get fancy by using all kinds of options. Our recommendation? Don't spend too much on those options until you're fully entrenched in an eBay business — by that time, you'll have the experience to know what to add and when. Stick with the basics. The Final Value Fees are charges calculated as a percentage of the sale price and are different in stores than on the regular eBay site. Check them out in Table 11-2.

Table 11-2	eBay Stores Final Value Fees	
Final Selling Price	*Final Value Fee*	*Calculation*
$0.01–$30.00	10%	10% of the selling price
$30.01–$120.00	7%	10% of the first $30, and 7% of the remaining amount, up to $120
$120.01–$1,200.00	5%	10% of the first $30, 7% of the amount from $30.01–$120.00, and 5% of the remaining amount up to $1,200
$1,200.01 and more	3%	10% of the first $30, 7% of the amount from $30.01–$120.00, 5% of the amount from $120.01 to $1,200.00, and 3% of the remaining amount

The photo Gallery option fee is reduced for use in store listings only. For example, the very valuable option of a Gallery picture adds only $0.01 to your listing cost!

Opening your eBay store

Because this book is your introduction to eBay, we give you just a few ideas about opening an eBay store. In our more advanced book, *Starting an eBay Business For Canadians For Dummies* (John Wiley & Sons Canada Ltd.), we take you step by step through the basics of opening your store.

Naming your store is your first challenge. Pick a name that describes the type of items your store will carry or one that includes your User ID. Don't pick a name that's so esoteric or overly creative that it doesn't give possible shoppers a clue as to what you carry. An informative, creative store name and graphic logo are pictured in Figure 11-5.

As you can see from Marsha's store page in Figure 11-5, each store can have its own categories. You get to make them up yourself so your customers can find items within your store in an organized manner. You can define up to 300 custom categories up to three levels deep. Each category can have a maximum of 29 characters for each name in your store.

Your eBay store home page has the links Store Policies and About the Seller under Store Pages on the lower-left of the page. The About the Store page is the same as your About Me page (which we discuss in Chapter 14).

Spend some serious time on eBay before you open the store. Study some of the very successful stores. You want to have enough know-how to make your store a success!

Figure 11-5: The eBay Stores page for Marsha's store.

Chapter 12

Closing the Deal and Shipping It Out

In This Chapter

▶ Organizing your sales

▶ Communicating with the buyer

▶ Packing and sending the item

▶ Purchasing stamps and shipping services online

*T*he auction's over, and you have a winning buyer who (you hope) is eager to send you money. Sounds perfect, doesn't it? It is if you watch your step, keep on top of things, and communicate like a professional.

In this chapter, we help you figure out how to stay organized by showing you what documents you need to keep and for how long. We also include tips and etiquette on communicating with the buyer so that you're most likely to come out with positive feedback. In addition, you can find out how to pack your item, assess costs, and make sure the item reaches the buyer when you say it will (oh, yeah . . . and in one piece).

Bookkeeping and Staying Organized

Although we don't recommend lining your nest with every scrap from every auction you run, you can safely keep some documents without mutating into a giant pack rat. Until you become an eBay expert and are comfortable with other ways to electronically store your information, you should print and file these essentials:

✔ **The listing page as it appeared when the auction closed:** This page gives you a record of the item name and number, the bidding history, and a lot of other useful information. The page also includes the auction item description (and any revisions you made to it), which is handy if the buyer argues that an item's disintegrating before his eyes and you honestly described it as just well loved.

You may think you don't need this information because you can always look it up, but here practicality rears its head: eBay makes completed auctions seem to disappear after 30 days. However, if you use the custom link that appears in your End of Auction e-mail (which we talk about in the following bullet), you can access the auction online for up to 90 days. Print your auction page before you forget about it, file it where you know you can find it, and *then* forget about it.

✔ **The End of Listing e-mail you receive from eBay that notifies you that the auction is over:** If you lose this e-mail, you can't get it back because eBay doesn't keep it.

You can easily set up a separate folder in your e-mail program for your End of Auction e-mails. When one of these e-mails comes in, you can read it and then drag it over to its special folder. That way, you can always check this folder for the information you need.

✔ **E-mail between you and the buyer:** In the virtual world, e-mail is as close to having a face-to-face conversation as most people get. Your e-mail correspondence is a living record of all the things you discuss with the buyer to complete the transaction. Even if you sell just a few items a month at eBay, keep track of who's paid up and who owes you money. And more importantly, if the buyer says, "I told you I'd be out of town," you can look through your e-mail and say, "Nope, it doesn't show up here," or "You're right! How was Tierra del Fuego? Is the payment on the way?" Or something more polite. Be sure to keep that e-mail with the headers and date on it so you can't be accused of (ahem) creative writing.

✔ **PayPal payment notices:** You get a notice from PayPal when the buyer pays for the item. The notice has the listing information and the buyer's shipping information. (When that e-mail arrives, the clock begins to tick on sending out the item.)

✔ **Any bank statements you receive that reflect a payment that doesn't clear:** Keep anything related to payments, especially payments that didn't go through. That way, if a buyer says she's sure she sent you a cheque, you can say, "Yes ma'am, Ms. X, you did send me a cheque, and it was made of the finest rubber." Or something kinder, especially if you want that payment.

✔ **Any insurance forms that you have:** Until the item has arrived and you're sure the customer is satisfied, keep those shipping and insurance receipts.

✔ **Refund requests you make:** If you make a request to eBay for a refund from a sale that doesn't go through, hold on to it until you can view the credit on your statement.

✔ **Receipts for items that you buy for the sole purpose of selling them on eBay:** These receipts come in handy as a reference so that you can see if you're making a profit. They can also be helpful at tax time.

Tales from the formerly Type A

Confession time. Both of us used to keep all our paperwork — listings, e-mails, the works. Now we keep only the e-mails and receipts sent to us until we're certain a transaction is complete. Then they go wafting off to our Recycle Bins so that we can still find a file in our Outlook Express programs.

These days, we stay on top of our eBay finances with online auction management that helps us keep track of who has paid and who hasn't. These programs also help us figure out expenses, profits, and other financial calculations, almost painlessly. (See Chapter 20 for more information on these programs.) They can also help jazz up the look of your auctions. Ah, progress.

Someday, the Canadian Revenue Agency may knock on your door. Scary, but true. Like hurricanes and asteroid strikes, audits happen. Any accountant worth his or her salt can tell you that the best way to handle the possibility of an audit is to be prepared for the worst — even if every eBay transaction you conduct runs smooth as silk and you keep your nose sparkling clean. See Chapter 9 for more tax information.

If you accept online payments by PayPal (PayPal Premier or Business members only), you can download your transaction history for use in QuickBooks, Quicken, or Excel. Additionally, these programs are excellent sources for your documentation.

When you're first starting your career as a seller, once a month conduct a By Seller search on yourself so that you can print out all the information on the bid histories of your most recent auctions. Do this independently of any auction software you use. Having the listings neatly printed easily helps you see what sold for how much and when. Chapter 5 gives you the lowdown on how to perform this search.

When it comes to printouts of e-mails and documents about transactions, as soon as the item arrives at the destination and you get your positive feedback, you can dump them. If you get negative feedback, hang on to your documentation a little longer (say, until you're sure the issues it raises are resolved and everyone's satisfied). If selling on eBay becomes a fairly regular source of income, save all receipts for items you purchase to sell; for tax purposes, that's inventory.

If you sell specialized items, you can keep track of trends and who your frequent buyers are by saving your paperwork. This prudent habit becomes an excellent marketing strategy when you discover that a segment of eBay users faithfully buys your items. An audience. Imagine that.

Talking to Buyers: The ABCs of Good Communication

You've heard it countless times — talk is cheap. Compared to what? Granted, empty promises are a dime a dozen, but honest-to-goodness talk and efficient e-mail are worth their weight in gold and good feedback — especially at eBay. Sometimes, *not* talking is costly.

A smooth exchange of money and merchandise really starts with you (the seller) and your attitude toward the transaction. Your listing description and then your first e-mail — soon after the auction is over and the sale is made — set the entire transaction in motion and set the tone for that transaction. If all goes well, no more than a few days should elapse between getting paid and sending the item.

Take a proactive approach and start the ball rolling yourself. We suggest contacting the buyer and sending an invoice even before you get eBay's e-mail. Just follow these steps (starting on the page of the item you sold):

1. **Click the Send Invoice Box that appears at the top of the item page.**

   You arrive at the Send Invoice page.

2. **Examine the invoice displayed on this page. Make any changes, if necessary.**

   If the buyer has purchased more than one item from you, click the link that becomes visible to combine the purchases.

3. **Double-check that the shipping amount is correct. When you're satisfied, click the Send Invoice button.**

   If you select the Copy Me check box on this invoice, you receive a copy of the invoice. The buyer's copy has a link in the invoice, enabling the buyer to pay directly to PayPal (if you accept PayPal for payment). Figure 12-1 shows what the invoice e-mail looks like.

 Signing in first puts a temporary cookie (a computer file that makes it easier to get around a Web site) in your computer so you don't have to go through this process again. You have to set your preferences to do this on your My eBay page. If you selected the Keep Me Signed In on This Computer for One Day Unless I Sign Out check box when you signed in to eBay, your password is saved even if you cut off your Internet connection. Your login is saved until you click the Sign Out link. For more yummy info on cookies, see Chapter 15.

 Another way to contact your buyer is to go to your My eBay page, scroll down to the Items I've Sold area, find the auction, and click the drop-down menu in the Action column. From there, you can click the Contact Buyer link from the drop-down menu to the right of the auction.

Thank you — I mean it

What do all the successful big-name department stores have in common? Yes, great prices, good merchandise, and nice displays. But with all things being equal, customer service always wins, hands down. One department store in the United States, Nordstrom, has such great customer service that the store happily took back a set of snow tires because a customer wasn't happy with them. No big deal, maybe — until you realize that Nordstrom doesn't even *sell* snow tires!

We've heard of this level of customer satisfaction being called the *Wow! effect.* If customers (no matter what they're buying) say, "Wow!" during or after the transaction — admiringly or happily — you've satisfied the customer. A good rule to go by: Give people the same level of service you expect when you're on the buying end. The best eBay sellers are regular eBay buyers.

The best way to start satisfying the buyer is with an introductory e-mail. Congratulate the person on winning the item — making him or her feel good about the purchase — and thank the buyer for bidding on your item. A good e-mail provides these important details:

- ✔ Item name and item number
- ✔ Winning bid amount
- ✔ Cost of shipping and packaging, and any shipping or insurance restrictions (We give pointers on determining shipping and packaging costs in the section, "Shopping for a shipper," later in this chapter.)
- ✔ Payment options (cheque, money order, credit cards, or PayPal)
- ✔ How long you'll hold the item waiting for a cheque to clear (usually 14 days)
- ✔ The shipping timetable

You should also mind a few vital details in the first e-mail:

- ✔ Confirm the address (and ask for a daytime phone number if you think you need to call); ask whether this is where you should ship the item. If not, ask for the correct shipping address.
- ✔ Include your name and the address to which you want the payment sent.
- ✔ Remind buyers to write the item name, item number, and shipping address on whatever form of payment they send. You'd be surprised how many buyers forget to give you the item number. Also, ask buyers to print and send a copy of your e-mail with the payment.
- ✔ If you're using an online payment service, such as PayPal, be sure to give buyers instructions on how they can pay for the auction online.

✔ Include your "customer service" phone number, if you want.

✔ Suggest that if all goes well, you'll be happy to leave positive feedback for the buyer. (See Chapter 4 for more on feedback.)

You can also send an invoice from your My eBay page, in the Items I've Sold area. Click the drop-down box in the Action column to the right of the item and click the Send Invoice link. On the next page, verify all the information and then click the Send Invoice button. Figure 12-1 shows what the invoice e-mail looks like.

Figure 12-1: An eBay invoice, as sent to a buyer.

Keep on e-mailing

If you have a good transaction going (and the majority of them are good), the buyer will reply to your e-mail within a couple of business days. Customarily, most replies come the next day. If your buyer has questions regarding anything you asked in your e-mail, you get those inquiries in this reply. Most of the time, all you get back is, "Thanks. Payment on the way." Hey, that's all we ask.

If any last-minute details need to be worked out, usually the buyer asks to set up a time to call or request further instructions about the transaction. Respond to this communication as soon as possible. If you can't deal with it at the moment, let the buyer know you're working on it and will shoot those answers back ASAP. *Never* let an e-mail go unanswered.

For sample e-mail letters and deeper information, get your hands on a copy of our book on more advanced eBay selling, *Starting an eBay Business For Canadians For Dummies* (John Wiley & Sons Canada Ltd.).

Shipping without Going Postal

Shipping can be the most time-consuming (and most dreaded) task for many eBay sellers. Even if the selling portion of your transaction goes flawlessly, the item has to get to the buyer in one piece. If it doesn't, the deal could be ruined — and so could your reputation.

This section briefs you on shipping etiquette, gives you details about the three most popular shipping options (Canada Post, UPS, and FedEx), and offers tips on how to make sure your package is ready to ride.

The best way to avoid shipping problems is to do your homework beforehand, determine which method is likely to work best, and spell out in your item description exactly how you intend to ship the item. If you want to try the way we handle the whole process, just follow these steps:

1. **After the listing is over, get the package ready to ship.**

   You don't have to seal the package right away, but you should have it ready to seal because the three critical factors in shipping are weight, physical size (often called *cube*), and time. The more a package weighs or the larger the cube, and the faster it has to be delivered, the higher the charge. (We cover packing materials and tips in the section "Getting the right (packing) stuff," later in this chapter.) The time to think about packing and shipping is *before* you put the item up for sale — that way, last-minute surprises are less likely to arise while your buyer waits impatiently for the item!

2. **Look into your carrier options.**

   In Canada, the three main shipping options for most eBay transactions are Canada Post, UPS, and FedEx. See the following section, "Shopping for a shipper" (try saying *that* five times fast), for how you can get rate options from each service, painlessly and online. Compare costs and services.

3. **Before quoting the shipping fees, make sure that you include all appropriate costs.**

   We recommend that you charge a nominal handling fee (up to $2 isn't out of line) to cover your packing materials, labels, and time, which can add up quickly as you start making multiple transactions. You should also include any insurance costs and any delivery-confirmation costs. See the sidebar "Insuring your peace of mind (and your shipment)," in this chapter, for more information.

   Some eBay scam artists inflate shipping and handling costs to make added profit. Shame, shame, shame on them. Purposely overcharging is tacky, ugly, and immature. (It's also a violation of eBay policy on circumventing fees.) The buyer also often figures it out after one look at the postage on the box.

It's best to post the shipping in the actual auction. This way, buyers can include this cost when they consider their bidding strategies. Figure out what the package's weight and dimensions will be, include a modest amount for your packaging costs (if you wish), and then calculate your shipping charges. If the item is particularly heavy and you need to use a shipping service that charges by weight, cube, and distance, be sure to say in your auction description that you're giving just an estimate, and that the final cost will be determined after the listing is over. Optionally, you can tell the bidder how much the item weighs, where you're shipping from, and what your handling charges are (a few bidders don't mind doing the math).

Occasionally, shipping calculations can be off-target, and you may not know that until after you take the buyer's money. If the mistake is in your favour and is a biggie, notify the buyer and offer a refund. But if shipping ends up costing you a bit more, take your lumps and pay it yourself. Consider it part of the cost of doing business. You can always let the buyer know what happened and that you paid the extra cost. Who knows, it may show up positively on your feedback from the buyer! (Even if it doesn't, spreading goodwill never hurts.)

4. **E-mail the buyer and congratulate him or her on winning; reiterate what your shipping choice is and how long you expect it to take.**

   Make sure you're both talking about the same timetable. If the buyer balks at either the price or the shipping time, try working out an option that will make the buyer happy.

5. **Send the package.**

   When should you ship the package? Common courtesy says it should go out as soon as the item and shipping charges are paid. If the buyer has followed through with his or her side of the bargain, you should do the same. Ship that package no more than a few days after payment (or after the cheque clears). If you can't, immediately e-mail the buyer and explain the delay. You should e-mail the buyer as soon as you send the package and ask for an e-mail to confirm arrival after the item gets there. (Don't forget to put in a plug for positive feedback.)

Send a prompt follow-up e-mail to let the buyer know the item's on the way. In this e-mail, be sure to include when the item was sent, how long it should take to arrive, any special tracking or delivery confirmation number (if you have one), and a request for a return e-mail confirming arrival after the item gets there. It's also good form to include a thank-you note (a receipt would be a business-like addition) in each package you send out. We both appreciate when we get thank-you notes in eBay packages, and it always brings a smile to the recipient's face. It never hurts to take every opportunity to promote goodwill (and future business and positive feedback).

Insuring your peace of mind (and your shipment)

Sure, "damaged in the mail" is an excuse we've all heard hundreds of times, but despite everyone's best efforts, sometimes things do get damaged or misplaced during shipment. The universe is a dangerous place; that's what insurance is for. Canada Post includes $100 of insurance for most of their services, so you can include the first $100 of insurance in all your listings if you use their services. Because eBay and PayPal consider it the responsibility of the seller to get the sold item safely to the buyer, regardless of whether insurance was purchased, it makes sense to build the cost of insuring into the shipping costs for all your auctions. You should spell out in your item descriptions that insurance is included.

The major shippers all offer insurance that's fairly reasonably priced, so check out their rates at their Web sites. But don't forget to read the details. For example, many items at eBay are sold MIMB (Mint in Mint Box). True, the condition of the original box often has a bearing on the final value of the item inside, but Canada Post insures only what's in the box. So, if you sold a Malibu Barbie mint in a mint box, Canada Post insures only the doll and not the original box. Pack carefully so that your buyer gets what he or she paid for. Shippers won't make good on insurance claims if they suspect you of causing the damage by doing a lousy job of packing.

Some sellers also offer their own form of self-insurance. We use the term "self-insurance" here as a descriptive phrase only. You may not charge your buyer for insurance unless you're actually paying for insurance from a licensed third-party insurance company. To charge a buyer for unlicensed insurance is frequently a violation of law. Here's what you might offer your buyers at no cost to them:

- On lower-priced items, consider refunding the buyer's money if the item is lost or damaged.

- On some items, you might have a risk reserve. A risk reserve comes into play if you have more than one of the item you sold. If the original item is lost or destroyed, you can send the backup item as a replacement.

More often than not, you do get an e-mail back from the buyer to let you know the item arrived safely. If you don't, it's a good idea to send another e-mail (in about two weeks) to ask whether the item arrived in good condition. It jogs the buyer's memory and demonstrates your professionalism as a seller. Use this opportunity to gently remind buyers that you'll be leaving positive feedback for them. Ask whether they're satisfied and don't be bashful about suggesting they do the same for you. Leave positive feedback right away so you don't forget.

Shopping for a shipper

If only you could transport your item the way they did on *Star Trek* — "Beam up that antique lamp, Scotty!" Alas, it's not so. Expedited Parcel via Canada Post is pretty much the eBay Canada standard if you're shipping within Canada and the United States. Many Canadians also rely on Canada Post to ship internationally, as well. FedEx and UPS are global alternatives that work well, too.

Many sellers think that they're unequivocally covered by requiring their buyers to purchase insurance. Even if your buyer opts not to pay for insurance, you're still responsible for making sure that the item arrives at the buyer's door. Many jurisdictions have laws that state that when an item is paid for, it must be delivered to the buyer within 30 days unless the buyer and seller have reached an agreement for other arrangements.

Whether you're at the post office, UPS, FedEx, or your doctor's office, be ready, willing, and able to wait in line. Many local postal or courier counters definitely have "rush hours" — everybody's in a rush, so everything moves at a glacial pace. Avoid both the noontime and post-work crunches (easier on the nerves). A good time to ship is around 10:30 a.m., when everyone is still in a good mood. If you do have to go in the afternoon, try about 3:00 p.m., when the clerks are back from their lunch breaks and friendly faces (you should always try to smile — especially if you plan to use that location regularly) can take the edge off those brusque lunchtime encounters. Better yet, if you can ship from home and are shipping many packages on a daily basis, you can also request a carrier pickup (limitations apply) from Canada Post, UPS, or FedEx for a nominal fee.

Canada Post

Canada Post is the butt of many unfair jokes and cheap shots, but when it comes right down to it, we think Canada Post is still the most efficient and inexpensive way to ship many items — eBay or otherwise. Here are some ways eBay members get their items from here to there via Canada Post:

- **Expedited Parcel or Regular Parcel:** These are the de facto standard methods of shipping for Canadian eBay users when shipping within Canada and the United States. Regular Parcel is available to anyone, but Expedited Parcel is available to businesses only. If you use the PayPal shipping tools, PayPal makes Expedited service available to you, regardless of whether you have a business name or not, and provides delivery confirmation and the first $100 of insurance at no additional charge. Rates for Expedited and Regular service are identical, but using PayPal shipping tools allows you a discount of up to 8 percent on Expedited service, depending on where you're shipping to. The delivery standards vary widely for service within Canada (from one to eight days). For most U.S. destinations, you can expect delivery in 6 to 12 days, although you may face additional delays of up to a week during peak holiday periods. Expedited Parcel to Canada or the United States qualifies for the PayPal Seller Protection Plan.

  Cost? As of this writing (rates are always subject to change), Expedited Parcel or Regular Parcel costs $7.06 or more for up to 750 grams within Canada. Rates to the United States. are applied to packages that exceed 1 kilogram and start at about $12. Rates are calculated according to weight, package dimensions, and distance.

✔ **Xpresspost:** If you need the item delivered quickly, use Xpresspost. Canada Post delivers the next business day locally and regionally, and two business days nationally between most major Canadian centres. To the United States, delivery standards are three to five business days. Service includes the first $100 of insurance and delivery confirmation. It meets the minimum requirements to qualify for the PayPal Seller Protection Plan.

Cost? Xpresspost runs $7.18 and up for packages 750 grams and under and $8.60 for up to 1 kilogram within Canada. Rates to the United States can be substantially more expensive. You can also get Xpresspost in flat-rate envelopes, but those envelopes are limited to shipping documents only. Xpresspost is also available for other international destinations.

You can save yourself waiting in lines at your local postal counter by printing your postage through PayPal. After you affix the postage to your package, you can simply drop your package into your local mailbox (if it'll fit) or just drop it on the counter at the post office.

✔ **Lettermail:** If your item weighs 200 ounces or less and contains documents only, you can use Lettermail. Lettermail is Canada Post's least expensive service — as low as $0.52 within Canada and $0.93 to the United States.

✔ **Light Packet — U.S.A. and International:** Canada Post now offers this new service that rivals Lettermail size and weight restrictions and delivery standards. Shippers selling CDs and DVDs most often use this service when the weight doesn't exceed 500 grams.

✔ **Small Packet — U.S.A. and International:** This service comes in two flavours — surface and air — and you use it primarily for small items (under 1 kg to the U.S. and 2 kg to other international destinations) of little value. Neither of these services offer delivery confirmation, but they do include the first $100 of insurance. Because they don't offer delivery confirmation, these services don't qualify for the PayPal Seller Protection Plan.

✔ **Other options:** Canada Post has additional services available for some of those in-between situations. If you need your package delivered within 24 hours, Purolator International can get your package there overnight — but it can be pricey. Registered and signature services are also available in certain circumstances.

If you're more than an occasional shipper (you sell more than you buy on eBay) and prefer not to use PayPal shipping services, you can still print bar-coded shipping labels with free delivery confirmation (for applicable services) at the Canada Post site by using their Electronic Shipping Tools. Just go to obc.canadapost.ca/orc/init.do?regType=1&sblid=sbuserid to register to use the Click-N-Ship service.

Delivery confirmation also comes in handy if you try to collect insurance for an item that was never delivered or if the buyer says the item was never delivered. It gives you the necessary proof from Canada Post that the item was sent. (We explain insuring shipments in the sidebar "Insuring your peace of mind (and your shipment)," earlier in this chapter.) But you can't accurately track your package. Delivery confirmation is merely proof that the package was mailed and delivered. If your package gets lost in the mail for a few weeks, this number rarely acts as a tracking number and won't reveal the location of your package until it's delivered.

The Canada Post Web site gives you an overview of their services and rates (at www.canadapost.ca/business/rates/default-e.asp) so you can see all your options. It sure beats standing in that endless line.

Even better, Canada Post has an online tool that can help you determine exactly what your item costs to mail (after you package and weigh it, of course). At the Web address given above, you'll find a Parcel Rate Calculator that will provide you with the total costs of the various service options available to you.

UPS

The folks in the brown UPS trucks love eBay. The options they offer vary, with everything from overnight service to UPS Ground service. UPS also takes many of the odd-shaped large boxes, such as those for computer equipment, that Canada Post won't.

UPS makes pickups, but you should preregister and establish an account with them prior to giving them a call or arranging the pickup online. UPS charges for this service unless you have a daily shipper account and ship a minimum number of packages with UPS per week.

At the time of writing, UPS is getting very aggressive with pricing from Canada to the United States. A flat rate promotion from Canada to any U.S. destination allows Canadian sellers to ship up to 10 pounds (4.5 kg) for $17 — regardless of the package size.

The rates for the same UPS shipment can vary based on whether you have a business account with UPS, whether the package goes to or is picked up at a residence, and whether you use the right kind of form. If you're going to use UPS regularly, be sure to set up an account directly with UPS. UPS is frequently guilty of charging very substantial Customs clearance fees to buyers, so be very certain that your U.S. or international customer understands that it's their responsibility to pay these fees.

You can find the UPS Canadian home page at www.ups.ca. For rates, click the Shipping tab and then click Calculate Time and Cost on the left side of the page, which gives you prices based on postal or zip codes and package weights. (Note the ominous "estimate" rates.)

Sí, oui, ja, yes! Shipping internationally

Money's good, no matter what country it comes from. We don't know why, but a lot of people seem to be afraid to ship internationally and list "I don't ship overseas" on the auction page. Of course, sending an item that far away may be a burden if you're selling a car or a street sweeper (they don't fit in boxes too well), but we've found that sending a package across the Atlantic can be just as easy as shipping across Canada. The only downside: Canada Post just can't seem to deliver to many international destinations in a reasonable amount of time unless your customer is prepared to pay for one of the higher-priced services. Shipping 1 to 2 kilograms by surface Small Packet to Australia can cost you $18.50, and delivery typically takes up to 12 weeks. If you do plan to ship internationally, be certain your buyers are aware of the extra time required to get packages to them.

Here are a couple of other timely notes about shipping internationally:

✔ **Tell what's inside the package.** Be truthful when declaring value on Customs forms. Be sure to use descriptions that Customs agents can figure out without knowing eBay shorthand terms. For example, instead of declaring the contents as "MIB Barbie," call it a "small doll." Some countries require buyers to pay special duties and taxes, depending on the item and the value. But that's the buyer's headache.

✔ **Neatness counts.** Wherever you send your package (especially if it's going to a country where English isn't the native language), be sure to write legibly. (Imagine getting a package from Russia and having to decipher a label written by a sloppy hand in the Cyrillic alphabet. 'Nuff said.)

The UPS.com Time and Cost Calculator prices are based on what UPS charges regular users. When you get to the counter, the price may be higher than what you find on the Web.

If you have a UPS account, you may want to buy the signature and delivery confirmation option for $2.45. As soon as the package gets to its destination and is signed for, UPS sends you a confirmation, so you have evidence that it's been delivered. But what's really cool is the free UPS online tracking. Every package is bar-coded, and that code is read everywhere your package stops along its shipping route. You can follow its progress by entering the package number at www.ups.com/WebTracking/track?loc=en_CA&WT.svl=PriNav.

FedEx

Many people use FedEx Express air all the time for rush business, but Express seems rather expensive for most eBay shipping. However, if the buyer wants it fast and is willing to pay, sending it by FedEx overnight is a sure bet.

FedEx Ground service has competitive prices and carries all the best features of FedEx. Using FedEx Ground for items that are heavy (say, antique barbells) or extremely large (such as a 1920s steamer trunk) makes a lot of sense because FedEx ships anything up to 68 kilograms in a single box — 38 more kilograms than Canada Post takes. Be prepared to drop your packages at the local FedEx counter because they don't pick up unless you establish an account with them.

The FedEx Ground Home Delivery service is a major competitor for UPS. The rates are very competitive, and FedEx offers a money-back guarantee (if it misses the delivery window) for residential ground delivery. For residential delivery, FedEx charges an additional $2 per package. A 2-kilogram package going from Kitchener to a residence in Vancouver takes four days and costs $14.62 (tax included). FedEx includes online package tracking and insurance up to $100 in this price. You have to be a business to avail yourself of home delivery — but plenty of home businesses exist.

The same 2-kilogram package sent by Canada Post Expedited with $100 insurance and a delivery confirmation costs you $12 (tax included), but delivery takes six to seven business days. For the same package, UPS came in at more than $24 (tax included).

You can find FedEx's Canadian home page at www.fedex.com/ca. The link for rates is conveniently located under the Ship tab at the top of the page.

Getting the right (packing) stuff

You can never think about packing materials too early. You may think you're jumping the gun, but by the law of averages, if you wait until the last minute, you won't find the right-size box, right tape, or labels you need. Start thinking about shipping even before you sell your first item.

Before you pack, give your item the once-over. Here's a list of what to consider about your item before you call it a wrap (gotta love that Hollywood lingo):

- ✔ **Is your item as you described it?** If the item has been dented or torn somehow, e-mail the winning bidder immediately and come clean. And if you sell an item with its original box or container, don't just check the item, make sure the box is in the same good condition as the item inside. Collectors place a high value on original boxes, so make sure the box lives up to what you described in your listing. Pack to protect it, as well.

- ✔ **Is the item dirty or dusty, or does it smell of smoke?** Some buyers may complain if the item they receive is dirty or smelly, especially from cigarette smoke. Make sure the item is fresh and clean, even if it's used or vintage. If something's dirty, check to make sure you know how to clean it properly (you want to take the dirt off, not the paint), and then give it a spritz with an appropriate cleaner or just soap and water. If you can't get rid of the smell or the dirt, say so in your item description. Let the buyer decide whether the item is still desirable.

If the item has a faint smell of smoke or is a bit musty, a product called Febreze may help. Just get a plastic bag, give your item a spritz, and keep it in the bag for a short while. _Note:_ This isn't recommended for cardboard. And, as with any solvent or cleaning agent, read the label before you spray. Or, if you're in a rush to mail the package, cut a 2-x-2-cm piece of sheet fabric softener and place it in a plastic bag with the product.

When the item's ready to go, you're ready to pack it up. The following sections give you suggestions on what you should consider using and where to find the right stuff.

Packing material: What to use

This may sound obvious, but you'd be surprised: Any list of packing material should start with a box. But you don't want just any box — you want a heavy cardboard type that's larger than the item. If the item is extremely fragile, we suggest you use two boxes, with the outer box about 7.5 centimetres (3 inches) larger on each side than the inner box that holds the item, to allow for extra padding. And if you still have the original shipping container for such things as electronic equipment, consider using the original, especially if it still has the original foam inserts (they were designed to protect the equipment, after all, and this way, they stay out of the environment awhile longer).

As for padding, Table 12-1 compares the most popular types of box-filler materials.

Table 12-1	Box-Filler Materials	
Type	**Pros and Cons**	**Suggestions**
Bubble wrap	**Pros:** Lightweight, clean, cushions well **Cons:** Cost	Don't go overboard taping the bubble wrap. If the buyer has to battle to get the tape off, the item may go flying and end up damaged. And for crying out loud, don't pop all the little bubbles, okay?
Newspaper	**Pros:** Cheap, cushions **Cons:** Messy, adds weight to the package	Seal your item securely in a plastic bag to protect it from the newspaper ink. Shredding the newspaper first works well. It's more manageable and doesn't seem to stain as much as wadded-up paper. You can buy a shredder at an office-supply store often for less than $30. (Or find one at eBay for much less.)

(continued)

Table 12-1 (continued)

Type	Pros and Cons	Suggestions
Cut-up cardboard	**Pros:** Handy, cheap **Cons:** Transmits some shocks to item, hard to cut up, heavy	If you have some old boxes that aren't sturdy enough to pack in, this is a pretty good use for them.
Styrofoam peanuts	**Pros:** Lightweight, absorb shock well, clean **Cons:** Environmentally unfriendly, annoying	Your item may shift if you don't put enough peanuts in the box, so make sure to fill the box. Also, don't buy these — instead, recycle them from stuff that was shipped to you (plastic trash bags are great for storing them). And never use plastic peanuts when packing electronic equipment because the peanuts can create static electricity. Even a little spark can trash a computer chip.
Air-popped popcorn	**Pros:** Lightweight, environmentally friendly, absorbs shock well, clean (as long as you don't use salt and butter, but you knew that), low in calories **Cons:** Cost, time to pop	You don't want to send it anywhere there may be varmints who like it. In fact, both Canada Post and the U.S. Postal Service recommend popcorn. Hey, at least you can eat the leftovers!

Whatever materials you use, make sure that you pack the item well and that you secure the box. Many shippers will contest insurance claims if they feel you did a lousy job of packing. Do all the little things that you'd want done if you were the buyer — using double boxes for really fragile items, wrapping lids separately from containers, and filling hollow breakables with some kind of padding. Here are a few other items you need:

- **Plastic bags:** Plastic bags protect your item from moisture and more. Marsha once shipped an MIB doll to the Northeast U.S., and the package obviously got caught in a snowstorm. The buyer e-mailed her afterwards with words of thanks for the extra plastic bag, which saved the item from being soaked along with the outer box. Plastic bags can also keep collectibles from potential soiling if you use shredded newspaper for packing. (Speaking of boxes, if you send an item in an original box, bag it.)

Storing those bags of plump packing peanuts

By now, you may have realized that we both have commandeered a large chunk of our homes for our eBay businesses, and you might think that we live in a giant swamp of packing materials. Not really. But we do have to store loads of packing peanuts. They're not heavy, but they sure are bulky!

If you have a house with a garage, you're set! Bear with us now, this plan isn't as crazy as it seems. Go to your local dollar store and purchase some large screw-in cup hooks. Then purchase the largest drawstring plastic bags

you can find. (Glad has a large 39-gallon Lawn & Leaf bag that works great.)

Screw the cup hooks into strategic locations on the ceiling rafters of your garage. Now, fill the drawstring bags to capacity with packing peanuts and hang. When you finish, your garage looks like some bizarre art installation, but it gets the packing peanuts off the floor and out of your hair. You can even set up a packing-peanuts barricade so you don't hit the end of your garage when you park — assuming you can still get your car into the garage!

For any small items, such as stuffed animals, you should always protect them in a lunch baggie. For slightly larger items, go to the 1-quart or 1-gallon size. Be sure to also wrap any paper or cloth products, such as clothing and linens, in plastic before you ship.

✔ **Bubble-padded mailers:** The shipping cost for a package that weighs less than 250 grams and qualifies for Light Packet U.S.A. is significantly cheaper than for Small Packet U.S.A. Many small items — CDs, DVDs, and so on — can fit comfortably into the many available sizes of padded envelopes. You can find them made of Kraft paper or extra sturdy polyethylene. A big plus is that they weigh considerably less than boxes — even when you use extra padding. See Table 12-2 for standard sizes.

✔ **Address labels:** You need extras because it's always a good idea to toss a duplicate address label inside the box, with the destination address and a return address, in case the outside label falls off or becomes illegible.

✔ **Two- or 3-inch shipping tape:** Use a strong shipping tape for the outside of the box. Clear plastic will do just fine. You can also find a box-color (beige) tape that works very well for recycling boxes (taping over old shipping information). Remember not to plaster every bit of box with tape; leave space for those "Fragile" rubber stamps or stickers.

✔ **Hand-held shipping tape dispensers:** It's quite a bit easier to zzzzzip tape from a tape dispenser than to unwind it and bite it off with your teeth. Have one dispenser for your special shipping tape and one for your clear tape.

✔ **Lightweight 2-inch clear tape:** For taping the padding around the inside items. You can also use a clear strip of tape over the address on the outside of the box so that it won't disappear in the rain.

- ✔ **Scissors:** A pair of large, sharp scissors. Having a hobby knife to trim boxes or shred newspaper is also a good idea.

- ✔ **Handy liquids:** Three that we like are GOO GONE (seen only occasionally at Home Depot and Grand & Toy stores within Canada); WD-40 (the unstick-everything standby that works great on getting stickers off plastic); and Un-Du (seen only online within Canada, but it's the best liquid we've found to take labels off cardboard). Lighter fluid also does the trick, but be very careful handling it and be sure to clean up thoroughly to remove any residue.

- ✔ **Rubber stamps/stickers:** Using custom rubber stamps or stickers can save you a bunch of time when preparing your packages. We've both purchased some return address self-inking rubber stamps (at an unbelievably low price) on eBay. You can use these stamps to stamp all kinds of things that require your identification.

- ✔ **Thermal label printer:** You might think this is a flagrant waste of money, but after you start shipping out a dozen (or more) packages a day, you won't want to be without one. You can find it far more convenient to use a separate label printer for addressing and delivery confirmations. Dymo offers one of the best deals for a quality printer, and you can find them on eBay for about $110. If you want to get industrial, try one of the Zebra (Marsha uses the LP2844) thermal printers. These printers can print labels for FedEx and UPS, as well as Canada Post (you can also get deals on these on eBay).

- ✔ **Black permanent marker:** These markers are handy for writing information ("Please leave on porch behind the planter") and the all-important "Fragile" all over the box or "Do Not Bend" on envelopes. We like the big, fat Sharpie markers.

Table 12-2	Standard Bubble-Padded Mailer Sizes	
Size	*Measurements*	*Suggested Items*
#000	4" x 8"	Collector trading cards, jewellery, computer diskettes, coins
#00	5" x 10"	Postcards, paper ephemera
#0	6" x 10"	CDs, DVDs, Xbox or PS2 games
#1	7¼" x 12"	Cardboard sleeve VHS tapes, jewel-cased CDs and DVDs
#2	8½" x 12"	Clamshell VHS tapes
#3	8½" x 14½"	Toys, clothing, stuffed animals
#4	9½" x 14½"	Small books, trade paperbacks

Size	Measurements	Suggested Items
#5	10½" x 16"	Hardcover books
#6	12½" x 19"	Clothing, soft boxed items
#7	14¼" x 20"	Much larger packaged items, framed items and plaques

If you plan to sell on eBay in earnest, consider adding a 5-kilogram weigh scale (for weighing packages) to your shipping department. You can find a lot of great, small scales available on eBay. Bill uses a small, handy 3-kilogram Sunbeam scale for smaller items and a larger 40-kilogram digital scale for those big, bulky packages.

When it comes to fragile items, such as dishes, pottery, porcelain, or china — anything that can chip, crack, or smash into a thousand pieces — double box. The boxes should be about 7.5 centimetres (3 inches) different on each side. Make sure that you use enough padding so that the interior box is snug. Just give it a big shake. If nothing rattles, ship away!

Packing material: Where to find it

The place to start looking for packing material is the same place you should start looking for things to sell at eBay: your house. Between us, we've shipped thousands of eBay transactions and not paid for cartons. Because we frequently buy stuff from catalogues and online companies (we're both e-commerce addicts), we save all the boxes, bubble wrap, padding, and packing peanuts we get in the mail. Just empty your boxes of packing peanuts into large plastic trash bags — that way, they don't take up much storage space. If you recently got a mail-order shipment box that was used only once — and it's a good, sturdy box with no dents or dings — there's nothing wrong with using it again. Just be sure to completely cover any old labels so the delivery company doesn't get confused.

Beyond the ol' homestead, here are a couple of other suggestions for places where you can rustle up some packing stuff:

✔ **Your local supermarket, department store, or drugstore:** You won't be the first person pleading with a store manager for boxes. (Ah, fond memories of moving days past . . .) Stores actually like giving them away because it saves them the extra work of compacting the boxes and throwing them away. Try to avoid using those big, waxed banana boxes, though.

We've found that drugstores and beauty supply stores have a better variety of smaller boxes. But make sure that you don't take dirty boxes reeking of food or medicinal smells.

✔ **Your local supermarket, department store, or drugstore:** Places such as Costco, Sam's Club, and office-supply stores often have good selections of packing supplies.

✔ **Shippers such as UPS, FedEx, and Canada Post:** These shippers offer all kinds of supplies as long as you use these supplies to ship things with their service. Avoid purchasing Canada Post shipping supplies through their retail outlets because they're dearly priced. Instead, visit their Web site (www.canadapost.ca) and order supplies through their online Business Centre.

✔ **Check the Yellow Pages:** After you start shipping with some regularity, it probably makes sense to start buying some of your supplies in case lots. Check your local phone directory for listings for Shipping Supplies or Paper Products.

✔ **eBay Sellers:** Many terrific eBay sellers are out to offer you really good deals. (You can't beat eBay sellers for quality goods, low prices, and great service.) We recommend the following family-run eBay stores:

- **Bubblefastca:** An eBay seller originally from the Chicago area that has now opened a Canadian operation in Etobicoke. Sells tons of reasonably priced bubble wrap, mailers, and more on eBay.

- **Melrose_Stamp:** Based in New York (but its items are tiny, so shipping isn't a huge issue). Melrose Stamp mainly sells custom and stock message rubber stamps. Also, rolls of package identification labels such as Fragile, Do Not Crush, First Class, Thank You, and Airmail.

We mention where these vendors are located for a reason. When ordering a large shipment, the distance it has to travel from the vendor's place to yours can tack on quite a bit of cash to your shipping costs (not to mention your delivery time)!

Buying Postage Online

Isn't technology great? You no longer have to schlep to the post office every time you need stamps. What's even better, with the new print-it-yourself postage, you can drop most of your packages directly into your local mailbox or arrange for regular Canada Post pickups. When you install Canada Post Electronic Shipping Tools (EST) software on your computer, you can print your own postage and shipping labels. If the service you choose allows, you can also print the bar code that allows Canada Post to provide delivery confirmation. Even if you choose not to install the software on your computer, you can use the EST online option. If you're an infrequent user, you can now also use a new service called Ship-in-a-Click, which allows you to purchase postage online in five easy steps and without registering.

By using EST, you can print postage for Expedited (Canada, U.S.A., and International), Light Packet (U.S.A. and International), Small Packet Surface and Air (U.S.A. and International), Xpresspost (Canada, U.S.A., and International), Purolator (Canada, U.S.A., and International), and insurance. If your printer mangles a sheet of labels or an envelope, you can reprint the postage. And if you need to cancel a label, you receive credit within 30 days. Other than through PayPal, Canada Post currently doesn't allow third parties to print online postage.

Shipping Directly from PayPal

We consider PayPal shipping to be required for all beginning eBay sellers. By using PayPal, a seller can streamline the buyer's shopping experience, making it simple to buy, click, and pay. Those out in the eBay world who haven't used PayPal find using the service to be a life-changing experience. Because you don't need to use additional software or sign up with an additional service, shipping with PayPal is a convenient system for those who don't have to ship many packages each week.

When you're ready to deal with shipping, you simply sign on to your PayPal account and handle it right on the site. You can also click the Print Label link from the item page to start the process. You don't have to pay a charge for the service, and you have a choice of Canada Post or UPS (sorry, no FedEx Ground). Recently, eBay Canada and both Canada Post and UPS have created special promotions that have extended large savings for sellers who purchase shipping services through PayPal. eBay Canada maintains ongoing negotiations with Canada Post, so watch for more deals in the future.

Chapter 13

Troubleshooting Your Transaction

· ·

· ·

*T*here's no getting around it: The more transactions you conduct at eBay, the more chances you have of facing some potential pitfalls. In this chapter, we give you pointers on how to handle an obnoxious buyer as if he or she is your new best friend (for a little while, anyway). In addition, we explain how to keep an honest misunderstanding from blowing up into a vitriolic e-mail war. You can find out how to handle a sale that's (shall we say) on a road to nowhere, how to get some attention, and if it all goes sour, how to sell to the next highest bidder legally, relist the item, and get back the Final Value Fee you paid eBay. There's no way that all of what we mention in this chapter will happen to you, but the more you know, the better prepared you'll be.

Dealing with a Buyer Who Doesn't Respond

Most of the time, the post-auction transaction between buyers and sellers goes smoothly. However, if you have difficulty communicating with the winner of your auction or store sale, you should know the best way to handle the situation.

You've come to the right place if you want help dealing with potential non-paying buyers (more commonly known as *deadbeat bidders,* which is how most experienced eBay sellers refer to them). Of course, you should start with good initial post-auction communication; see Chapter 12 for details. (For more information on how to deal with a fraudulent seller, see Chapter 16.)

Going into nudge mode

Despite all your best efforts, sometimes things fall through the cracks. Buyers who want to pay for their item through an online service should pay for the item without delay through PayPal. In the case of mail payments, buyers and sellers should contact each other within three business days of the close of the sale. Sometimes, winners contact sellers immediately, and some use Checkout to pay for the item immediately, which saves you any hassle. However, if you don't hear from the buyer within three business days of your initial contact, our advice is *don't panic.*

People are busy; they travel, they get sick, computers crash, or sometimes your auction simply slips the winner's mind. In short — life happens. After four days of no communication, you can go to your My eBay page and send out a payment reminder message. Just click the Contact Buyer link that appears near the top of the item's listing page, as shown in Figure 13-1.

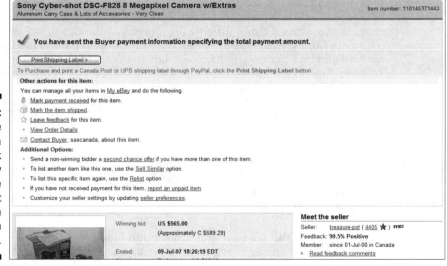

Figure 13-1: Send the buyer a quick reminder by using the Contact Buyer link in the item page.

You might also consider just resending the invoice. Go to the Selling area of your My eBay page and click the menu in the action column to the right of the item. Select the Send Invoice link to create a new copy of the invoice for your buyer.

If a couple more days pass and you haven't heard from the winner, you need to get into big-time nudge-nudge mode — as in, "Mr. X, remember me and your obligation to buy the Tiffany lamp you won at eBay last week?"

Send a polite-but-firm message letting Mr. X know that when he bid and won your auction, he became obligated to pay and complete the transaction. If Mr. X doesn't intend to buy your item for any reason, he needs to let you know immediately.

Don't threaten your buyer. The last thing you want to do is add insult to injury in case the buyer is facing a real problem. Besides, if the high bidder goes to sleep with the fishes, you'll *never* see your money.

Here's what to include in your nudge-nudge e-mail:

- ✔ A gentle admonishment, such as, "Perhaps this slipped your mind," "You may have missed my e-mail to you," or "I'm sure you didn't mean to ignore my first e-mail."

- ✔ A gentle reminder that eBay's policy states that every bid is a binding contract. You can even refer the buyer to eBay's rules and regulations, if you want.

- ✔ A statement that firmly (but gently) explains that, so far, you've held up your side of the deal and you'd appreciate it if he or she did the same.

- ✔ A date by which you expect to see payment. Gently explain that if the deadline isn't met, you'll have no other choice but to consider the deal invalid.

Technically, you can nullify the transaction if you don't hear from a buyer within three business days. However, eBay members are a forgiving bunch under the right circumstances. Give your buyer a one-week grace period after the auction ends to get in touch with you and set up a payment plan. If, at the end of the grace period, you don't see any real progress toward closing the deal, say goodnight, Gracie. Consider the deal kaput and go directly to the section "Auction Going Badly? Cut Your Losses," later in this chapter, to find out what recourse you have.

Be a secret agent, man

We want to say that history repeats itself, but that would be a cliché. (All right, you caught us, but clichés are memorable because they're so often true.) After you send your polite and gentle nudge-nudge e-mail, but before you decide that the transaction is a lost cause, take a look at the bidder's feedback history. Figure 13-2 shows you what feedback looks like. (Of course, virtually all Marsha's feedback is positive. It's tough — but possible — to be near perfect.)

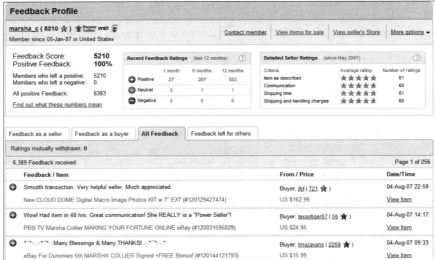

Figure 13-2:
You can get
a good idea
of whether a
buyer will
complete a
sale by
looking at
his or her
feedback
profile.

To check a bidder's feedback (starting at your item page), follow these steps:

1. **Click the number in parentheses to the right of your winner's User ID.**

   This action takes you to the member's feedback profile page.

2. **Scroll down the feedback profile page and read the comments.**

   Check to see if the bidder has gotten negative feedback from previous sellers. Make a note of it in case you need some support and background information (should you choose to block an unwanted bid and be chastised at a later date).

3. **Conduct a Bidder search.**

   Click Advanced Search and do an Items by Bidder search to see the buyer's conduct in previous transactions. How many items has the buyer won? Click the item number to see the history of the auction. For more info on Bidder searches, check out Chapter 5.

When all else fails, you may want to double-check with some of the bidder's previous sellers. It's okay to use eBay's e-mail system to contact previous sellers who've dealt with the bidder. They're often happy to give you details on how well (or badly) the transaction went.

If the buyer's feedback profile provides any indication that the buyer has gone AWOL in the past, start thinking about getting out of the transaction before too much time passes. If the buyer looks to be on the level, continue to give him or her the benefit of the doubt.

Be sure to ask previous sellers who dealt with the bidder the following questions (politely):

- ✔ Did Buyer X pay on time?
- ✔ Did his or her cheque clear?
- ✔ Did he or she communicate well?

When e-mailing a third party about any negative feedback he or she has left, choose your words carefully. There's no guarantee that if you trash the bidder, the third party will keep your e-mail private. Make sure that you stick to the facts. Writing false or malicious statements can put you in danger of being sued.

Stepping up your nudge a notch

If you don't hear from the winner after a week, your next course of action is to contact the winner by phone. To get the contact information of an eBay member for transaction purposes only, follow these steps:

1. **Click the Advanced Search link to the right of the search box at the top of most eBay pages.**

   You arrive at the Advanced Search area.

2. **Click the Find Contact Information link under the Members area in the link box on the left of the screen.**

   The Search: Find Contact Information page appears.

3. **In the box labelled Enter User ID of Member, enter the User ID of the person you're trying to contact. Then enter the item number of the transaction in question in the Item Number field of the Item You Are Trading with the Above Member box.**

4. **Click the Search button.**

   eBay e-mails you the registered contact information of the person with whom you want to be in touch, and also sends your contact information to that person.

Wait a day before calling the person. You might want to send a last-chance e-mail after seven days that says you want to put the item back up at eBay if the buyer is no longer interested. Also, mention that you want to apply for any credits you can get from eBay due to an incomplete transaction. If enough money is involved in the transaction, and you feel it's worth the investment, make the call to the winner. eBay automatically sends your request and your information to the winner, and that may be enough of a nudge to get some action.

If you do get the person on the phone, keep the conversation like your e-mail — friendly but business-like. Explain who you are and when the auction closed, and ask if any circumstances have delayed the bidder's reply. Often, the bidder will be so shocked to hear from you that you'll either receive payment immediately, or the phone call will likely let you know that this person is a complete deadbeat.

Try a last-ditch emergency effort

If e-mails and phoning the winner don't work, and you *really* want to give the buyer one last chance to complete the transaction, check out eBay's Emergency Contact Board. (You can get there from the Chat Rooms link on the main Community page on the U.S. eBay site only — www.ebay.com.) The Emergency Contact Board is where members who are having trouble contacting buyers and sellers leave word. Don't worry that the buyer may miss your message. A conscientious group of eBay pros man this area and try to help by passing on e-mails to the missing parties. Jump over to Chapter 17 for more information on this board and its group of regulars. Figure 13-3 shows you what the Emergency Contact Board looks like.

From personal experience, we can tell you that if you haven't heard from the buyer within seven days, you're not going to hear from him or her. No amount of e-mailing or phone calls can save the transaction. The information here is for those die-hards who really want to follow it through. After a week, which is eBay's minimum wait time, we file an Unpaid Item Dispute through eBay. (That definitely gets buyers' attention.)

Figure 13-3:
Post on the Emergency Contact Board on eBay.com in hopes that someone will see your post and help put you in contact with the buyer.

Posted by ▦▦▦ ☆ on 04/22/99 at 20:46:23 PDT	Auctions
WINTER ▦▦▦▦ - Feedback is all positive!! I will be entering negative feedback because I never received my item I paid for and there has been no response to my emails!!!	

Posted by ▦▦▦ ☆ on 04/22/99 at 20:29:43 PDT	Auctions
hello, if anyone knows anything about dotcomtoys please e-mail me. thanks, ▦▦▦▦	

Posted by ▦▦▦ 04/22/99 at 19:44:40 PDT	Auctions
LOOKING FOR JOAN IN CINCINNATI. KNOWS JER. IF YOUR OUT THERE E-MAIL ME.	

Posted by ▦▦▦ on 04/22/99 at 19:03:36 PDT	Auctions
Please if anyone knows the e-mail address of e-bay seller ▦▦▦ I need it I missed placed it I sent a 100.00 money order for a web tv unit over a month ago and havent heard from her yet I prob got ripped off Thanks ▦▦▦	

Posted by ▦▦ on 04/22/99 at 18:20:43 PDT	Auctions
I received an envelope from ▦▦▦, I think it may have to do with items I purchased a bit ago. Problem is the envelope was totally empty I need ▦▦ to contact me asap.....	

| Posted by mbotlf@earthlink.net (1) on 04/22/99 at 18:11:27 PDT | Auctions |

To post a message on the Emergency Contact Board, follow these steps:

1. **Click the Community link on the main navigation bar at the top of most U.S. eBay (www.ebay.com) pages.**

   You're taken to the Community hub page.

2. **Click the Chat Rooms link in the Connect area of the page.**

   You're taken to the Chat Rooms page, which lists all of eBay's chat boards.

3. **In the General Chat Rooms category, click the Emergency Contact link.**

   You're taken to the Emergency Contact Board.

   Before you post a message, scroll through the postings and look for messages from your AWOL buyer. Maybe he or she has been trying to get in touch with you, too.

4. **To access this chat board, you must sign in again. Click the Sign In link and type your User ID and password in the appropriate boxes and click the Sign In Securely button. Then type your message and click the Save My Message button.**

   Even though you may feel like the transaction is a lost cause when you get to the point of posting a message on the Emergency Contact Board, keep your message neutral and don't make accusations.

5. **Check your message for errors and click the Save My Message button.**

   Your message is instantly posted.

Not sure what to post on the Emergency Contact Board? Start off by sticking to the facts of the transaction and say what you want your buyer to do. Have the item number and the buyer's User ID handy before you start your posting. Don't post any personal information about the buyer, such as the buyer's real name and address. That's a violation of the eBay rules.

You can send messages to specific users or post a general cry for help. Here are two examples of short-but-sweet postings that get your message across:

 ✔ Dear Ms. X, I've been trying to reach you through e-mail and phone for two weeks about item number *(enter item number)* and have had no response. Please contact me by *(enter date),* or I'll invalidate the transaction and leave negative feedback.

 ✔ I've been trying to contact Ms. X for two weeks now regarding an auction. Does anybody know this person or have a new e-mail address for her? Did anybody get burned by this buyer in the past? Thanks.

For your postings to be useful, you need to check back often and read other eBay users' postings on the Emergency Contact Board. Check the board to see whether someone has responded to your message. Also, keep your eyes open as you scroll through the board. Don't trash anyone on this board — it's not good form — but many people do use the Emergency Contact Board to issue an all-points bulletin about bad eBay members.

Some Other Auction Problems

We're not quite sure why, but when money is involved, sometimes people act weird. Buyers may suddenly decide that they can't purchase an item after they've made a commitment, or you may have to deal with payment problems or shipping problems. Whatever the problem, look no further than the following sections to find out how to make things better.

The buyer backs out of the transaction

Every time eBay members place a bid or click Buy It Now, they make a commitment to purchase the item in question — in theory, anyway. In the real world, people have second thoughts, despite the rules. You have every right to be angry that you're losing money and wasting your time. Remind the buyer that making a bid is a binding contract. But, unfortunately, if the winner won't pay up, you can't do much except apply for a Final Value Fee refund and make the winner pay with negative feedback. Jump to Chapter 6 to find out more about buyer's remorse.

Keeping your cool

By all means, if the winner of your auction tells you that the transaction can't be completed, no matter what the reason, remain professional, despite your anger. For one thing, at least such a would-be buyer has the heart to break the news to you instead of ignoring your e-mails and phone calls.

When Plan A fails, try Plan B or even C — Second Chance Offer

You have several options if the winner backs out:

✔ **Make a Second Chance Offer: Offer the item to another bidder from the auction.** eBay offers a little-known feature called Second Chance Offer, which protects buyers just as if they were the winner of the auction. This is a great feature that turned the previously eBay-illegal practice of side deals into fair and approved auction deals. You can make a Second Chance Offer to any underbidder from your auction (at the amount of their high bid) for up to 60 days after the auction's end. The steps that follow this list detail how to make a Second Chance Offer.

✔ **Request a full or partial Final Value Fee credit, and then relist the item and hope it sells again.** We give you more information on requesting a Final Value Fee credit in the section "Filing for a Final Value Fee credit," and you can get the lowdown on relisting your item in the section "Déjà vu — relisting your item," both later in this chapter. Who knows? This bidder may actually *earn* you money in the long run if you relist the item and get a higher winning bid.

To make a Second Chance Offer, follow these steps:

1. **Go to the completed auction page.**

2. **Scroll to the bottom of the Seller Status area and click the Second Chance link.**

   You're taken to the Second Chance Offer page, which has the auction number already filled in.

3. **Click Continue.**

   The page shown in Figure 13-4 appears.

4. **Select an underbidder (or more than one underbidder if you have multiples of the item) to offer the item to and then click the Review Second Chance Offer link.**

   When you make a Second Chance Offer, you can give the recipient one, three, five, or seven days to take you up on the offer. You're not charged a listing fee for the item, but you are responsible for Final Value Fees if the transaction is completed.

5. **Check over the offer and then click Submit to send it to the underbidder.**

Figure 13-4: You can get out of a difficult situation by offering the item to one of the underbidders in an unsuccessful auction.

> **My Messages: Second Chance Offer**
>
> To send a Second Chance Offer for this item, select a duration and bidder(s) below.
>
> Item: PBS TV Marsha Collier MAKING YOUR FORTUNE ONLINE eBay (Original Item ID: 120006110254)
> Subject: **eBay Second Chance Offer for Item #120006110254: PBS TV Marsha Collier MAKING YOUR FORTUNE ONLINE eBay**
>
> 🛡 **Marketplace Safety Tip**
>
> You can be sure a Second Chance Offer is from your seller when you see it in My Messages.
>
> **Duration**
> 1 day ▾
>
> **Select bidders who will receive your offer**
> The number of bidders you select can't be more than the number of duplicate items you have to sell. The Second Chance Offer price is a Buy It Now price determined by each bidder's maximum bid. Learn more.
>
> | Select | User ID | Second Chance Offer Price |
> |--------|---------|---------------------------|
> | ☐ | ▬▬▬ (43 ☆) | US $23.00 |
>
> Bidders who have chosen not to receive Second Chance Offers or who have already been sent one are not displayed above.
>
> Continue >

Leaving feedback after an imperfect auction experience

If the buyer never materializes, backs out, bounces a cheque, or moves slower than a glacier to send your payment (but wants the item sent overnight from Boston to Khartoum at your expense), you need to think about how you want to word your feedback. You're well within your rights to leave negative feedback, but that doesn't mean you can go off the deep end. Remember to stick to the facts and don't get personal.

Here are a few feedback tips:

✔ If the transaction was shaky but everything turned out all right in the end, go ahead and leave positive or neutral feedback, depending on how tough things went.

✔ If a blizzard stopped planes out of Regina for three days and that's why it took a long time to get your cheque, take a deep breath, blame the fates, and leave positive feedback.

✔ If the buyer was a living nightmare, take a long break before leaving negative feedback — and have someone you love and trust read it before you send something into the virtual world that you can't take back.

For more information on leaving feedback, check out Chapter 4 and Chapter 6.

Houston, we have a payment problem

A lot of things can go wrong where money is concerned. Maybe you never receive the money or perhaps the cheque bounces. If the cheque bounces, contact the buyer immediately. Honest winners will be completely embarrassed and make good, whereas unscrupulous winners will offer lame excuses. Either way, insist on a more secure form of payment, such as a money order or payment with a credit card through PayPal. You can also require those who send bounced cheques to include an extra $20 with their payment. This extra money should cover your bank's bounced-cheque charges, with a little left over for your aggravation.

If the buyer pays by cheque, be sure to hang on to the item until you're positive the cheque cleared and then ship the item. Call your bank to make sure that you haven't received a return deposit item for the amount of the cheque.

The item you send is busted — and so are you

Uh-oh! Could it be true? Could you have sent the wrong item? Or is it possible that the crystal vase you thought you packed so well is a sad pile of shards at the bottom of a torn box? If so, read Chapter 12 as soon as you take care of this catastrophe so that you can get some hints on packing and insurance.

It's time to do some serious problem solving. If the buyer met his or her end of the deal, you need to do your best to fix the problem. Your communication skills are your number-one asset in this situation, so get to work.

Picking up the pieces

No matter how carefully you pack an item, sometimes it arrives on the buyer's doorstep mangled, broken, or squashed. News of this unfortunate event travels back to you fast. The buyer will let you know in about 30 seconds how unhappy he or she is in an e-mail. (Sometimes, they're not very polite, but keep your calm.) Tell the buyer that you'll immediately begin the process of filing an insurance claim. Ask the buyer to send you several pictures of the item and the mangled package by e-mail to support your claim. Also remind him or her to hold the packaging and item until you receive disposition instructions from the insurer. Canada Post occasionally asks that the package's recipient supply a letter that attests to the damage.

If a package is lost, you'll know it because the delivery confirmation never comes through, and the buyer tells you the package is a no-show. Canada Post has varying minimum delivery times before they'll begin a trace, depending on the service used. If your item isn't located within a reasonable time, Canada Post declares it lost, and you have to deal with another round of paperwork and processing before you get your money. You may be asked to support your claim with assorted documentation that may include an invoice that discloses your original cost — Canada Post is finicky about insuring the seller's cost and not the selling price. Canada Post will also refund postage paid if an item is undelivered.

A lot of eBay sellers seem to think that if a buyer doesn't pay for insurance and the package gets lost in transit, it's not the seller's problem. They couldn't be more wrong. Regardless of whether the buyer chose to pay for insurance, the seller is responsible for getting the goods to the buyer in good condition. Both PayPal and eBay require shippers to ensure that items are on their way to winning bidders within a reasonable amount of time after payment is received and cleared. The short version is that if your item doesn't get to the buyer within 30 days, you may be required to refund the payment.

Boxed out of a claim

In our experience, no shipping service (Canada Post, UPS, or FedEx) will pay on an insurance claim if they feel you did a lousy job of packing. So, don't be surprised if your claim is declined. Always use good packing products, wrap carefully, and get ready to plead your case.

Every shipping company has its own procedure for complaints. But here's the one thing they do have in common: No procedure is hassle-free. Call your shipper as soon as a problem arises.

You have regrets — seller's remorse

You've undoubtedly heard about buyer's remorse. Here's a new one for you — seller's remorse. If you're selling your velvet Elvis footstool because your spouse said, "It's me or that footstool!" and then you decide that your spouse should have known how much you revered the King when you went to Graceland on your honeymoon, you can end the auction. Check out the sections "Try cancelling bids first" and "If all else fails, end your auction early," both later in this chapter.

Auction Going Badly? Cut Your Losses

So your auction is cruising along just fine for a couple of days when you notice that the same eBay user who didn't pay up on a previous auction is your current high bidder. You don't want to get burned again, do you? Of course not; cancel this deadbeat's bid before it's too late. Although cancelling bids — or, for that matter, entire auctions — isn't easy (you have a load of explaining to do, pardner), eBay does allow it.

If you feel you have to wash your hands of an auction that's given you nothing but grief, it doesn't mean you have to lose money on the deal. Check out the following sections to find out the protocol for dumping untrustworthy bidders or (as a last resort) laying a bad auction to rest and beginning anew.

Many of these functions are also available from the Selling-Related Links area on the left side of your My eBay Selling page — just click the More link.

Try cancelling bids first

Face the facts: This auction is fast becoming a big-time loser. You did your very best, and things didn't work out. Before you kill an auction completely, see whether you can improve it by cancelling bids first. Cancelling a bid removes a bidder from your auction, but the auction continues running.

When you cancel a bid, you need to provide an explanation, which goes on record for all to see. You may have a million reasons for thinking your auction is a bust, but eBay says your explanation had better be good. Here are some eBay-approved reasons for cancelling a bid (or even an entire auction):

- ✔ The high bidder informs you that he or she is retracting the bid.

- ✔ Despite your best efforts to determine who your high bidder is, you can't find out — and you get no response to your e-mails or phone calls.

✔ The bidder makes a dollar-amount mistake in the bid. (The bidder bids $100, rather than $10.)

✔ You decide mid-auction that you can't sell your item due to the fact that it was sold in an outside venue — or the dog ate it. (You must cancel all bids and end the listing in this instance.)

We can't drive this point home hard enough: Explain why you're cancelling a bid, and your explanation had better be good. You can cancel any bid for any reason you want, but if you can't give a good explanation of why you did it, you'll be sorry. Citing past transaction problems with the current high bidder is okay, but cancelling a bidder who lives in Japan because you don't feel like shipping overseas after you said you'd ship internationally could give your feedback history the aroma of week-old sushi.

To cancel a bid (starting from most eBay pages), follow these steps:

1. **Click the My eBay link on the navigation bar at the top of the page.**

2. **In the Related Links area on the bottom-left, click the More link.**

   You're taken to the Selling-Related Links page.

3. **Click the Cancel Bids on My Item link.**

   The Cancelling Bids page appears, shown in Figure 13-5.

4. **Enter the item number and an explanation of why you're cancelling a bid, as well as the User ID of the person whose bid you're cancelling.**

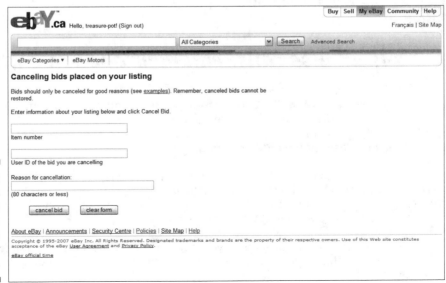

Figure 13-5: Use this form to remove a bidder from one of your auctions.

5. Click the Cancel Bid button.

> Be sure that you really want to cancel a bid before you click the Cancel Bid button. Cancelled bids can never be reinstated.

Cancelling bids means you remove an individual bidder (or several bidders) from your auction, but the auction itself continues running. If you want to end the auction completely, head to the section "If all else fails, end your auction early," later in this chapter.

Blocking bidders

If you have a bidder who just doesn't get the message and continually bids on your auctions, despite the fact that you've e-mailed and told him or her not to, you can block the bidder from ever participating in your auctions. You can create a list of bidders to prevent them from bidding temporarily or permanently, and you can edit the list at any time.

You can get to the Buyer/Bidder Management page from the same Selling-Related Links page we describe in the preceding section. Only this time, after clicking the More link, click Block or Pre-Approve Bidders and then create your list of User IDs. Alternatively, you can go directly to this address:

```
pages.ebay.ca/services/buyandsell/biddermanagement.html
```

eBay says you can't receive feedback on a transaction that wasn't completed. So, if something in your gut says not to deal with a particular bidder, then don't.

If all else fails, end your auction early

If you put your auction up for a week, and the following day, your boss says you have to go to China for a month or your landlord says you have to move out immediately so that he can fumigate for a week, you can end your auction early. But ending an auction early isn't a decision to be taken lightly. You miss all the last-minute bidding action.

eBay makes it clear that ending your auction early doesn't relieve you of the obligation to sell this item to the high bidder. To relieve your obligation, you must first cancel all the bids and then end the auction. Of course, if no one has bid, you have nothing to worry about.

When you cancel an auction, you have to write a short explanation (no more than 80 characters) that appears on the bidding history section of your auction page. Anyone who bid on the item may e-mail you for a written explanation. If bidders think your explanation doesn't hold water, don't be surprised if you get some nasty e-mails.

Bidding on your own item is against the rules. Once upon a time, you could cancel an auction by outbidding everyone on your own item and then ending the auction. But some eBay users abused this privilege by bidding on their own items merely to boost the sales price. Shame on them.

To end an auction early, go to the Selling-Related Links page (as described in the "Try cancelling bids first" section, earlier in this chapter) and click the End My Listing Early link. Then follow these steps:

1. **Enter the item number and then click Continue.**

2. **On the following page, shown in Figure 13-6, select a reason for ending your auction.**

3. **Click the End My Listing button.**

   An Ended Auction page appears.

   eBay sends an End of Auction Confirmation e-mail to you and to the high bidder.

Figure 13-6:
Select the reason for ending your auction early.

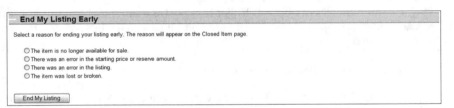

If you know when you list the item that you'll be away when the auction ends, let potential bidders know when you plan to contact them in your item description. Bidders who are willing to wait will still be willing to bid. Alerting them to your absence can save you from losing money if you have to cut your auction short.

Extending your auction (not)

Is your auction red hot? Bids coming in fast and furious? Wish you could have more time? Well, the answer is you can't. eBay won't extend auctions under normal conditions.

However, eBay on occasion experiences *hard outages*. That's when the system goes offline and no one can place bids. (Of course, Murphy's Law would put the next hard outage right in the thick of a furious bidding war in the final minutes of your auction. Or so it seems.) Outages can last anywhere from five minutes to a few hours. Because so many bidders wait until the last minute to bid, this can be a disaster. To make nice, eBay extends auctions by 24 hours if any of these three things happen:

✔ The outage is unscheduled and lasts two hours or more.

✔ The auction was scheduled to end during the outage.

✔ The auction was scheduled to end one hour after the outage.

If your auction was set to end Thursday at 20:10:09 (remember, eBay Canada uses military time, based on eastern time — which would make it 8:10 p.m., eastern time), the new ending time is Friday at 20:10:09. Same Bat-time, same Bat-channel, different day.

eBay also refunds all your auction fees for any hard outage that lasts more than two hours. That includes the Insertion Fee, Final Value Fee, and any optional fees. You don't have to apply for anything; eBay automatically refunds the appropriate fees.

You can read about any hard outages at eBay Canada's General Announcements Board. To get to an outage report, check the bottom of most eBay pages; an Announcements link takes you to the General Announcements Board.

If you can't find the Announcements link, follow these steps:

1. **Click Community on the main navigation bar at the top of most eBay pages.**

   The Community Overview page appears.

2. **In the News area, click the See All Announcements link.**

   You go to the General Announcements Board.

Make it standard operating procedure to check the General Announcements Board when you feel something is amiss. Checking the Announcements Board is sort of like checking the obituaries in the morning to make sure you're not listed. You can find more on the Announcements Board in Chapter 17.

Filing for a Final Value Fee credit

Hard outages aren't the only time you can collect a refund. If closing a successful auction is the thrill of victory, finding out that your buyer is a non-paying bidder or deadbeat is the agony of defeat. Adding insult to injury, eBay still charges you a Final Value Fee, even if the high bidder never sends you a cent. But you can do something about it. You can file for a Final Value Fee credit.

To qualify for a Final Value Fee credit, you must prove to eBay that one of the following events occurred:

✔ The winning bidder never responded after numerous e-mail contacts.

✔ The winning bidder backed out of the sale.

✔ The winning bidder's payment didn't clear or was never received.

✔ The winning bidder returned the item to you, and you refunded the payment.

If both you and the buyer decide that it's okay not to go through with the transaction, that's okay with eBay, too. eBay will allow you to get back your Final Value Fee by going through the refund process. You can find an option in the Reason for Refund area that absolves the buyer of any wrongdoing with eBay's Unpaid Item Police.

The instant you file for a Non-Paying Bidder Alert credit, eBay shoots off an e-mail to the winner of your item (copying you on the e-mail) and warns the eBay user of the non-paying bidder status.

If at least 7 days and no more than 45 days have elapsed since the end of the auction, you can apply for a full credit. First, you must file an Unpaid Item Alert. Just follow these steps:

1. **Click the My eBay link on the navigation bar at the top of most eBay pages.**

   You can report an unpaid item in one of two ways.

2. **At the bottom of your My eBay Views area, click the Dispute Console. On the page that appears, click the Report an Unpaid Item link.**

   You're taken to the Report an Unpaid Item Dispute page.

3. **Read all the current terms.**

4. **Enter the item number of the auction in question in the Item Number box, then click the Continue button.**

   The Unpaid Item Alert form appears, as shown in Figure 13-7.

5. **From the Reason for Unpaid Item Alert drop-down menu, select the reason for your request. Then click the Submit button.**

   If your reason is that you and the buyer mutually agreed not to complete the transaction, when you click Submit, you're taken immediately to the Final Value Fee Credit request page. In these instances, you don't have to wait for long to get your refund.

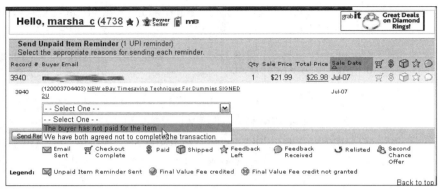

Figure 13-7:
Select your
reason for
filing a
Non-Paying
Bidder Alert
in the
Unpaid Item
Alert form.

After three non-payment warnings, eBay can boot a deadbeat from the site.

You and your non-paying bidder now have ten days to work out your problems.
If you make no progress after seven days, you can file for your Final Value Fee
credit.

You need to wait at least seven days after the auction ends to file a Non-Paying
Bidder Alert and then seven days more before you can apply for a Final Value
Fee credit. We think it's jumping the gun to label someone a non-paying bidder
after only seven days — try to contact the bidder again unless the bidder
sends you a message about backing out (or you have good cause to believe
you have a deadbeat on your hands). If you still want to file for your Final Value
Fee credit after seven days, follow these steps:

1. **On your My eBay All Selling page, either scroll down to the bottom of
   My eBay Views and click Dispute Console, or scroll further to the
   Related Links and click Unpaid Item Disputes.**

   You're taken to your Dispute Console page.

2. **Under the Unpaid Items heading, find the transaction in question.**

3. **Click the View Dispute link under the Dispute Status column.**

   You're now in the area in which you may respond to any comments the
   buyer has left regarding why he or she hasn't yet paid for your item.

4. **Enter your response to the buyer (if any) in the messages area and
   click Submit Response, or to get your Final Value Fee refund, click
   Close Dispute.**

5. **Click the Close Dispute button on the bottom of the page.**

   You're taken to the Credit Request Process Completed page, which con-
   firms your reasons for closing the dispute. When you close the dispute,
   you will receive confirmation that your refund is being processed by
   eBay, as shown in Figure 13-8.

When your listing ends, you have up to 45 days after the auction closes to request a credit. After 45 days, kiss your refund goodbye; eBay won't process it.

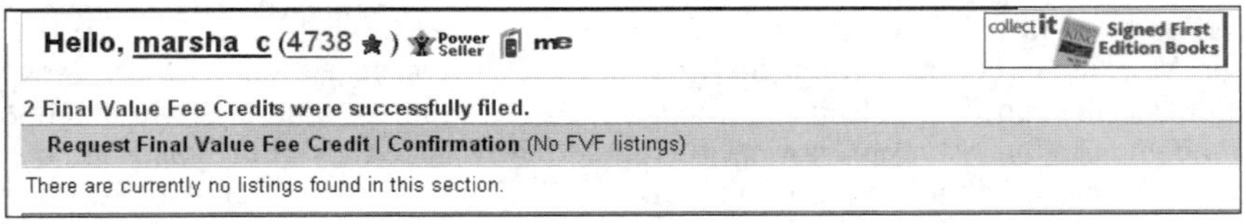

Figure 13-8:
eBay
processes
your Final
Value Fee
credit, and it
appears on
your
account
almost
immediately.

Hello, **marsha_c** (4738 ★) 🏆 Power Seller 📧 me ⎪ collect**it** Signed First Edition Books

2 Final Value Fee Credits were successfully filed.

Request Final Value Fee Credit | Confirmation (No FVF listings)

There are currently no listings found in this section.

Anyone caught applying for a refund on a successful item transaction can be suspended, or something worse — after all, this is a clear-cut case of fraud.

If you want to verify eBay's accounting, grab your calculator and use Table 9-2 in Chapter 9 to check the math. (Why couldn't we all have had one of those in high-school algebra class?)

Always print out a copy of any refund and credit requests you make. This paper trail can help bail you out later if eBay asks for documentation.

Déjà vu — relisting your item

Despite all your best efforts, sometimes your auction ends with no bids or bids that aren't even close to your reserve price. Or maybe a buyer won your auction, but the transaction didn't go through. eBay takes pity on you and offers you the chance to pick yourself up, dust yourself off, and start all over again.

The best way to improve your chances of selling a relisted item is by making changes to the auction. eBay says the majority of the items put up for auction sell. If you sell your item the second time around, eBay rewards you with a refund of your Insertion Fee (in most cases). You receive your refund after at least one billing cycle. Accept this refund as a reward for learning the ropes.

In the case of an unpaid item, you may (only in this situation) qualify for an Insertion Fee credit by relisting the item. If the item sells the second time, eBay will refund the Insertion Fee for relisting.

But is she a natural blonde?

Here's an example of an item that would have made the seller a bundle if she'd done a little more strategizing up front:

Platinum Mackie Barbie: Beautiful Platinum Bob Mackie Barbie. MIB (removed from box once only to scan). The doll comes with shoes, stand, booklet, and Mackie drawing. The original plastic protects her hair and earrings. Buyer adds $10 for shipping and insurance. Payment must be made within 10 days of auction by MO or cashier's check only.

The starting price was $9.99, and even though the bidding went to $256, the seller's reserve price wasn't met, so the item didn't sell. And the Second Chance Offer didn't bite.

When relisting this item, the seller should lower the reserve price and add much more to the description about the importance and rarity of the doll (unless, of course, $256 was far below what she wanted to make on the doll). Offering to accept credit cards through PayPal would have also helped her make the sale.

You must use eBay's Relist feature in order to receive the credit. After the item is filed as a UPI (un-paid item), you can use the Relist link on the unpaid item page or follow these steps:

1. **Go to your My eBay All Selling page.**
2. **On the left side of the page in the All Selling column, click the Unsold link.**

   You arrive at the page with Unsold Listings.

3. **Click the Relist link to the right of the unpaid item.**

To be eligible for a refund of your Insertion Fee, here's the scoop:

✔ You must relist no more than 90 days after closing the original auction.

✔ You can get credit only if you got no bids in your original auction or if the bids you got didn't equal the reserve in your reserve-price auction.

✔ You can change anything about your auction item description, price, duration, and minimum price, but you can't sell a different item.

✔ If you set a reserve price in your original auction, you must set the same reserve, lower it, or cancel the reserve altogether. If you set a higher reserve or add a reserve, you're not eligible for a relisting credit.

eBay's generosity has exceptions. It doesn't offer refunds for any listing options you paid for, such as **bold lettering** or use of Featured Plus! Also, Multiple Item (Dutch) auctions aren't covered by this offer. And if you have a deadbeat on your hands, you can relist, but you don't get a return of your

Insertion Fee. More bad news: If you don't sell the item the second time around, you're stuck paying *two* Insertion Fees. So work a little harder this time and give it your best shot!

To get your second shot at selling, follow these steps (starting at the Items I'm Selling section of your My eBay Selling page):

1. **Click the auction item listing that you want to relist.**

   You're taken to the main auction page of that item.

2. **Click the Relist link.**

   You're taken to the Relist Your Item form — basically, the Sell Your Item form with all the information filled in.

3. **Make your revisions to the original auction with the Sell Your Item form, launch it, and pray!**

Being as specific as possible with your item title improves your odds of being profitable. If you're selling an old Monopoly game, don't just title it Old Monopoly board game; call it Rare 1959 Monopoly Game Complete in Box. For more information about listing items, see Chapter 10.

Here's a list of ideas that you can use to improve your auction's odds for success:

- ✔ **Change the item category.** See if the item sells better in another category (see Chapter 3).

- ✔ **Add a picture.** If two identical items are up for auction at the same time, the item with a photo gets more and higher bids. Zoom in on Chapter 14.

- ✔ **Jazz up the title and description.** Make it enticing and grab those search engines. Breeze on over to Chapter 10.

- ✔ **Set a lower minimum bid.** The first bidders will think they're getting a bargain, and others will want a hot item. Mosey on over to Chapter 10.

- ✔ **Set a lower reserve price or cancel the reserve.** A reserve price often scares away bidders who fear it's too high. See (yup) Chapter 10 for ways to make your reserve more palatable to prospective bidders.

- ✔ **Offer more options for payment.** People may pop for an impulse item if they can put it on their credit card and pay for it later.

- ✔ **Change the duration of the auction.** Maybe you need some more time. Go to (you guessed it) Chapter 10.

Long-time eBay veterans say that reducing or cancelling your reserve price makes your auction very attractive to buyers.

Chapter 14

Using Pictures and Strategies to Increase Your Profits

*Y*ou may be enjoying most of what eBay has to offer, and you're probably having some good buying adventures. If you're selling, you're experiencing the excitement of making money. But there's more. Welcome to eBay, the advanced class.

In this chapter, you can go to the head of the class by discovering some insider tips on how to enhance your auctions by using images and spiffy text. Successful eBay vendors know that pictures (also called *images*) really help sell items. This chapter gives you the basics on how to create great images. We also give you advice on linking pictures to your auctions so that buyers around the world can view them.

Using Images in Your Auctions

Would you buy an item you couldn't see? Most people won't, especially if they're interested in purchasing items that they want to display — or clothes they intend to wear. Without a picture, you can't tell whether a seller's idea of good quality is anything like yours — or if the item is exactly what you're looking for.

Welcome to the cyberworld of *imaging,* where pictures aren't called pictures, they're *images,* and your monitor isn't a monitor, but a *display.* With a digital camera or a scanner and software, you can manipulate your images — spin, crop, and colour-correct — so that they grab viewers by the lapels. Even cooler: When you're happy with your creation, you can add it to your eBay auction for others to see.

Sellers, take heed and read these other reasons why you should use your own well-made digital images in your auction pages:

- ✔ If you don't have a picture, potential bidders may wonder whether you're deliberately hiding the item from view because you know something is wrong with it. Paranoid? Maybe. Practical? You bet.

- ✔ Fickle bidders don't even bother reading an item description if they can't see the item. Maybe they were traumatized in English class.

- ✔ Taking your own pictures shows that you actually have the item in your possession. Many scam artists take images from a manufacturer's Web site to illustrate their bogus sales on eBay. Why risk being suspect? Snap a quick picture!

- ✔ Everyone's doing it. We hate to pressure you, but digital images are the custom at eBay, so if you're not using them, you're not reaching the widest possible number of people who would bid on your item. From that point of view, you're not doing the most you can to serve your potential customers' needs. Hey, fads are driven by conformity. You may as well use them to your advantage.

So, which is better for capturing images: digital cameras or digital scanners? As with all gadgets, here's the classic answer: It depends. For our money, it's hard to beat a digital camera. But before you go snag one, decide what kind of (and how big) an investment you plan to make in your eBay auctions. If you're already comfortable with 35mm camera equipment, don't scrap it — scan (or find a digital SLR)! You can find the scoop on both of these alternatives in the following sections.

Be sure to check with a camera store to see if you can use older, traditional lenses on the digital SLR you buy. It's often the case with the major brands, although digital lenses don't have to be as good as the old lenses were — due to all the electronic manipulation that goes on inside the new cameras. Next, go to eBay and see what kind of deals you can find on compatible lenses.

Whether you buy new or used digital equipment at eBay, make sure it comes with a warranty. If you don't get a warranty, Murphy's Law practically ensures that your digital equipment will break the second time you use it.

Choosing a digital camera

If price isn't a factor, you should buy the highest-quality digital camera you can afford, especially if you plan to use images with a lot of your eBay auctions and the items you plan to sell vary in size and shape. By high-quality, we don't necessarily mean a camera with vast amounts of megapixels — we mean a camera from a quality manufacturer that has a high optical zoom and has a good (non-plastic) lens.

Sony, Canon, Kodak, and Nikon all make good basic digital cameras. You can find many models in retail stores for about $250 and up (and you can easily find them on eBay for even less). Middle-of-the-road new (and quality used) digital cameras sell for between $100 and $150. Compare prices at computer stores and in catalogues.

One of the most popular cameras used by eBay sellers are no longer produced — Sony Mavicas. They were made in two styles: the FD series used an everyday 3½-inch floppy disk as its memory; the CD series burns the images directly onto a rewritable mini-CD. The FD series was, by far, the more popular of the two.

The reason for their popularity is simple: Just take your pictures, and then pop out the floppy disk with the images and insert it into your computer. The images are immediately accessible from your floppy drive. No fuss, no muss — no cards to input, no software to install. The files can be easily read off the disks from the camera by your computer. The CD models are similar — only you insert the CD into your CD drive. Most recent computers have done away with the floppy disk drive, yet, surprisingly, the floppy-disk cameras are still commanding a fairly high price on eBay because they have a good optical zoom and are so easy to use.

A great place to buy digital cameras is (surprise!) eBay. Just do a search of some popular manufacturers, such as Canon, Kodak, Sony, and Nikon, and you'll find pages of listings — both new and used digital cameras that you can bid on and, if you win, buy.

When shopping for a digital camera, look for the following features:

✔ **Resolution:** Look for a camera that has a resolution of at least 800 x 600 pixels. This resolution isn't hard to find because new cameras tout their strength in megapixels (millions of pixels). You don't need that high a resolution for eBay because your pictures will ultimately be shown on a 72 dpi (dots per inch) monitor, not printed on paper. A *pixel* is a tiny dot of information that, when grouped with other pixels, forms an image. The more pixels an image has, the clearer and sharper the image is; the more memory the image scarfs up, the slower it shows up on-screen. An 800-x-600-pixel resolution may seem paltry next to the 6-million-pixel punch of a high-end digital camera, but trust us: No one bidding on your auctions will ever know the difference. And the lower-pixel picture will load a *lot* faster.

✔ **Optical Zoom:** Here's where the camera manufacturers try to pull the wool over the consumers' eyes. They sell their cameras with both an optical and a digital zoom. The *optical zoom* is a true zoom done by the camera, the lens, and its built-in *CCD* (the long name is a charge-coupled device, which is a computer chip in cameras that converts light into electronic data). A *digital zoom* is virtual; it's interpolated through software in the camera. That means it makes up data to fill in any holes it doesn't capture. You've seen this effect if you've ever tried to enlarge a picture from the Web in a software program — it gets all blurry.

If you ever plan on shooting close-ups, look for a high-quality optical zoom.

How we've been shooting on eBay

We've both been on eBay for years now, so we've taken a lot of pictures to promote our online sales. Generally, we're both pretty happy with the quality of our images. On occasion, when we've sold paper ephemera, our solution is to just lay the item on a scanner — and scan away. It's the best way to get a good image of that type of item.

Marsha started early on with an Olympus camera but quickly changed to the Sony Mavica FD-73 (after seeing that her cohorts at eBay University all used that model). The FD-73 was one of the first cameras that had a 10X digital zoom, which helps with intricate close-ups. Then she upgraded to a used FD-92 with an 8X optical zoom (a newer model that added a memory stick). And last year, she purchased a Sony DSC-H1 — a fancy 5-megapixel camera with a 12X zoom. To be perfectly honest, she finds it way too much camera for her eBay photo shoots. She still uses the FD-92 for most things. One excellent improvement on her most recent camera purchase is the addition of *image stabilization* — it holds the camera

steady when you zoom in for ultra macro close-ups. If you've ever taken a picture fully zoomed, you know that the slightest breath can make the resulting image a tad blurry.

Bill started out with a Sony CyberShot F505, a 2.1-megapixel camera, which he used for about a year before trading up to the Sony Mavica FD97 — a dual-media wonder with a 10X optical zoom. The FD97 worked well for more than two years — but then he upgraded his computer, and his new computer didn't have a floppy disk drive. He came across a great deal on the 8-megapixel Sony F828, sometimes called the Dark Angel. Although he was very satisfied with the images from this camera, he has recently purchased a 6-megapixel Canon PowerShot A540. The change was for simplicity's sake — the A540 is small and very easy to use. It takes great images in JPEG format, you can turn the flash off, and it has a macro setting. We've both found that, in the long run, a nice balance between new technological gadgets and familiar, easy-to-use equipment is the way to go.

✔ **Storage type:** Smart card? Secure Digital Card? CompactFlash card? Memory stick? Floppy disk? (Whew.) The instructions that come with your camera explain how to transfer images from your media type to your computer. (No instructions? Check the manufacturer's Web site.) Most newer computers have ports into which you can insert your camera's memory cards — the computer can read the disk like it's a teeny, tiny disk drive.

If you plan to sell small or detailed items that require extreme close-ups (such as jewellery, stamps, currency, coins, or Tibetan beads), you might want a digital camera that lets you change lenses.

A more versatile way to get the best images of these small items is to use a super invention called a Cloud Dome. When photographing complex items, no matter how good your camera is, you may find it difficult to capture the item cleanly and exactly (especially the colours and brightness of gems and metals). Your camera attaches to the top of this Cloud Dome, and pictures are taken inside a translucent plastic dome. The dome diffuses the light over the entire surface of the object to reveal all the intricate details of the item. You can purchase Cloud Domes on eBay or from the manufacturer's Web site at `www.clouddome.com`. Even in black and white, you can see the difference that a cloud dome can make when taking pictures of jewellery, as shown in Figure 14-1.

Figure 14-1:
Before and after pictures of items shot through a Cloud Dome.

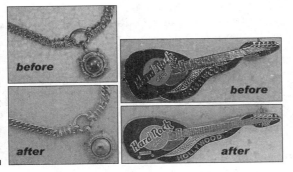

Choosing a scanner

If you plan to sell flat items, such as autographs, stamps, books, or documents — or if you need a good piece of business equipment that can double as a photocopier — consider getting a digital scanner. You can pick up a brand-new one for under $100; you can also find scanners at eBay.

Don't forget your camcorder!

The majority of eBay users use either a digital camera or scanner to dress up their auctions with images, but some just use what they already own — their handy-dandy camcorders! Yup, after videotaping your day at the beach, point your lens at that Victorian doll and shoot. With the help of a video-capturing device, you can create a still digital image right from the camera.

Here's what you need to look for when you buy a scanner:

- **Resolution:** As with printers and photocopiers, the resolution of digital scanning equipment is measured in dots per inch (dpi). The more dpi, the greater the resolution.

  Some scanners can provide resolutions as high as 12,800 dpi, which looks awesome when you print the image. But to dress up your eBay auctions, all you need is (are you ready?) 72 dpi! That's it. Your images will look great — and won't take up much storage space on your computer's hard drive. Basic scanners can scan images at resolutions of up to 1,200 dpi, so even they are far more powerful than you need for your eBay images.

- **Flatbed:** If you're planning to use your scanner to scan pictures of documents (or even items in boxes), a flatbed scanner is your best bet. Flatbeds work just like photocopiers. You simply lay your item or box on the glass and scan away.

Making Your Picture a Thing of Beauty

The idea behind using images in your auctions is to attract tons of potential buyers. With that goal in mind, you should try to create the best-looking images possible, no matter what kind of technology you're using to capture them.

Getting it on camera

Point-and-shoot may be okay for a group shot at some historical monument, but illustrating your auction is a whole different idea. Whether you're using a traditional film camera (in which case, you can scan your developed photographs later) or a digital camera to capture your item, some basic photographic guidelines can give you better results.

For more on using cameras and scanners, zoom ahead to the following section. Then c'mon back to these do's and don'ts to ensure that your digital image is a genuine enhancement to your auction:

- ✔ **Do** take the picture of your item outside, in daylight, whenever possible. In daylight the camera can catch all possible details and colour.

- ✔ **Do** forget about fancy backgrounds; they distract viewers from your item. Put small items on a neutral-coloured, non-reflective towel or cloth; put larger items in front of a neutral-coloured wall or curtain. You cut out almost all the background when you prepare the picture on your computer. (This chapter explains how to prepare your picture.)

- ✔ **Do** use extra lighting. You can add lighting by using your camera's flash mode or with extra photo lighting on stands. Use extra lighting even when you're taking the picture outside. The extra lighting acts as _fill light_ — it adds more light to the item, filling in some of the shadowed spots.

- ✔ **Don't** get so close to the item that the additional light washes out _(overexposes)_ the image. The easiest way to figure out the best distance is by trial and error. Start close and keep moving farther away until you get the results you want. This method can get pricey if you use film, but that's where digital cameras really shine: You can see the picture seconds after you shoot it, keep and modify it, erase it, and start again.

- ✔ **Do** take two or three acceptable versions of your image; you can pick the best one later on your computer.

- ✔ **Don't** use incandescent or fluorescent lighting to illuminate the photos you plan to scan. Incandescent lighting tends to make items look yellow-ish, and fluorescent lights lend a bluish tone to your photos. Some sellers use GE Reveal incandescent bulbs; they throw a good-quality light that, when combined with natural daylight, produces an even tone. The 5,000-degrees Kelvin full-spectrum bulbs are very popular. Yes, at $20 apiece, they're very expensive — but with a 10,000-hour life span, they should have you taking pictures into the next decade.

- ✔ **Do** take a wide shot of the entire item — and then take a close-up or two of the detailed areas that you want buyers to see — if your item relies on detail (for example, an engraved signature or detailed gold trim).

- ✔ **Do** make sure that you focus the camera; nothing is worse than a blurry picture. If your camera is a fixed-focus model (meaning you can't adjust it), get only as close as the manufacturer recommends. If you go beyond that distance, the item appears out of focus. (Automatic-focus cameras measure the distance and change the lens setting as needed.)

Taking pictures of your item from different angles gives the prospective buyer more information. When you have several images, use your photo-editing program to put them in one composite image, as shown in Figure 14-2.

Figure 14-2:
Making a composite image of pictures from several angles makes for a most attractive auction.

Some eBay creeps, whether out of laziness or deceit, steal images from other eBay members. (They simply make a digital copy of the image and use it in their own auctions. This is so uncool — because then the copied image doesn't represent the actual item being sold.) This pilfering has happened to both of us on several occasions. To prevent picture-snatching, you can add your User ID to all your photos. Then, the next time somebody lifts one of your pictures, it has your name on it. If you're familiar with adding HTML code to your auctions, Marsha offers a simple Java code on her Web site, www.coolebaytools.com, that you can insert into your auction descriptions to prevent scurrilous users from stealing your images.

Use traditional photos? Yes, we scan

If you use a scanner and a traditional (that is, non-digital) camera to create images for your eBay auction, you've come to the right place. (Also check out the tips in the preceding section.) Here goes:

- ✔ If the photo processor can scan your images for you, be sure you get that done. It saves you a lot of scanning time.

- ✔ If the photo processor can't or won't scan your images, have them print your photos on glossy paper; it scans best.

- ✔ When you take traditional photos for scanning, get as close to your item as your camera allows. Enlarging photos in the scanner only results in blurry (or worse, jagged) images.

✔ Scan the box that the item came in, or if a photo of the item appears on the box, scan that portion of the box.

✔ If you're scanning a three-dimensional item (such as a doll, jewellery item, or box) and you can't close the scanner lid, drape a black or white T-shirt over the item after you place it on the scanner's glass plate; that covering gives you a clean background and good light reflection from the scanner.

✔ If you want to scan an item that's too big to put on your scanner all at the same time, scan the item in sections and assemble the digital pieces with your image-editing software. The instructions that come with your software should explain how to put the images together.

Software that adds the artist's touch

After you take the picture (or scan it) and transfer it into your computer according to the camera or scanner manufacturer's instructions, the next step is to edit the picture. Much like a book or magazine editor, you get to cut, fix, resize, and reshape your picture until you think it's good enough to be seen by the public. If you're a non-techie type, don't get nervous — many of the programs have one-button magical corrections that make your pictures look great.

The software program that comes with your digital camera or scanner puts at your disposal an arsenal of editing tools that help you turn a basic image of your item into something special. Although each program has its own collection of features, these few basic tools and techniques are common to all:

✔ **Image quality:** Enables you to enhance or correct colours, sharpen images, remove dust spots, and increase or reduce brightness or contrast.

✔ **Size:** Reduces or increase the size or shape of the image.

✔ **Orientation:** Rotates the image left or right; flips it horizontally or vertically.

✔ **Crop:** Trims your picture to show the item, rather than extraneous background.

✔ **Create an image format:** Gives your edited picture a specific format, such as .JPG, .GIF, or others when you save it. The best format for putting photos on the Web (and thus the preferred format at eBay and the one we strongly recommend) is .JPG (pronounced "JAY-peg").

Every image-editing software program has its own system requirements and capabilities. Study the software that comes with your camera or scanner. If you feel the program is too complicated (or doesn't give you the editing tools you need), investigate some of the other popular programs. A simple-to-use program called Fast Photos was developed by an eBay seller with us in mind. It's incredibly simple to use, and you don't have to worry about much of a learning curve. You just have to click to change your image to picture-perfect form. Marsha uses it and loves it for its simplicity and speed — and it costs only US$24.95 (you can get a free 21-day trial at www.pixby.com).

If your camera didn't come with software, you can purchase commercial photo-editing software. The very complex Photoshop and the pared-down (but easier-to-use) Photoshop Elements are most widely used; both are made by Adobe. This is high-quality editing software — you can easily purchase Photoshop Elements on eBay for around US$50.

Copying someone else's auction text or images without permission can constitute copyright infringement — which ends your auction and could get you suspended from eBay.

Making Your Images Web-Friendly

Because digital images are made up of pixels — and every pixel has a set of instructions that has to be stored someplace — you have two difficulties facing you right after you take the picture:

- ✔ Digital images contain computer instructions, so bigger pictures take up more memory.

- ✔ Very large digital images take longer to *build* (appear) on the buyer's screen, and time can be precious in an auction.

To get around both these problems, think small. Here's a checklist of tried-and-true techniques for preparing your elegantly slender, fast-loading images to display at eBay:

- ✔ **Set your image resolution to 72 dots per inch (dpi).** You can also make this adjustment to the settings for your scanner. Although 72 dpi may seem like a low resolution, it only nibbles computer memory (instead of chomping), shows up fast on a buyer's screen, and looks great at eBay.

- ✔ **When using a digital camera, set the camera to no higher than the 800-x-600 format.** That's custom made for a monitor. You can always crop the picture if it's too large. You can even save the image at 640 x

480, and it can display well on eBay — plus, it takes up less space, so you can add more pictures!

✔ **Make the finished image no larger than 480 pixels wide.** When you size your picture in your image software, keep the image no larger than 480 x 480 pixels or 12.7 centimetres square, even if it's a snapshot of a classic 4 x 4 monster truck. These dimensions are big enough for people to see without squinting, and the details of your item show up nicely.

✔ **Crop any unnecessary areas of the photo.** You need to show only your item; everything else is a waste.

✔ **Use your software to darken or change the photo's contrast.** When the image looks good on your computer screen, the image looks good on your eBay auction page.

✔ **Save your image as a .JPG file.** When you finish editing your picture, save it as a .JPG. (To save your picture in this format, follow the instructions that come with your software.) .JPG is the best format for eBay; it compresses information into a small file that builds fast and reproduces nicely on the Internet.

✔ **Check the total size of your image.** After you save the image, check its total size. If the size hovers around 40K (kilobytes) or smaller, eBay users won't have to wait around forever to see the image.

✔ **Reduce the size of your image if it's larger than 50K.** Small is fast, efficient, and beautiful. Big is slow, sluggish, and dangerous. Impatient eBay users will move on to the next listing if they have to wait to see your image. Many eBay users still use a dial-up service for their Internet connection, which means slow downloads.

The Image Is Perfect — Now What?

After you complete your masterpiece, you want to emblazon it on your auction for all the world to see. When most people first get the urge to dazzle prospective buyers with a picture, they poke around the eBay site looking for a place to put it. Trade secret: You're not actually putting pictures on eBay; you're telling eBay's servers where to find your picture so that, like a good hunting dog, your auction points the buyers' browsers to the exact corner of the virtual universe where you've stored your picture. That's why the picture has to load fast — it's coming in from a different location. (Yeah, it confused us in the beginning, too, but now it makes perfect sense. Uh-huh. Sure.)

To help eBay find your image, just type the image's address into the Picture URL box of the Sell Your Item form — so don't forget to write down the Web address (URL) of your image.

If you use eBay's Picture Services, your photo is uploaded directly from your computer to eBay's servers where it is stored for inclusion in your auctions. We talk more about that in the section "Using eBay's Picture Services," later in this chapter.

You can highlight your image's URL with your cursor, right-click your mouse, and copy the URL to your computer's Clipboard. Then go to the auction page you're filling out at eBay, put your cursor in the Picture URL window, and paste the address into the box.

A typical address (for someone using AOL) looks something like this:

```
members.aol.com/ebay4dummy/rolexwatch.jpg
```

Because your image needs an address, you have to find it a good home online. You have several options:

- **Your ISP (Internet service provider):** Many big ISPs — such as Execulink, SureNet, Cogeco, and AOL — give you space to store your Internet stuff. You're already paying for an ISP, so you can park pictures there at no extra charge.

- **An image-hosting Web site:** Web sites that specialize in hosting pictures are popping up all over the Internet. Some charge a small fee; others are free. These services are generally very easy to use — even if you do wind up paying a small monthly fee.

- **Your server:** If you have your own server, you can store those images right in your own home.

- **eBay Picture Services:** You can find out about using eBay's photo-hosting service in the section "Using eBay's Picture Services," later in this chapter.

Using an ISP to store your images

Every ISP has its own rules and procedures. Go to the help area of your ISP for directions on how to *access your personal area* and how to *upload your images.* (No, we're not getting naughty — those are authentic computerese phrases!)

After you upload your images to your ISP, get the Web address of your item's location and type it into the Picture URL box of eBay's Sell Your Item page. Now, the picture appears within the item description whenever someone views your auction page. Figure 14-3 shows you an auction description with a picture.

Figure 14-3:
Including
pictures
in your
auctions
takes
practice, but
the results
are worth it.

Elegant Frosted & Clear
Floral Stopper Perfume Bottle

This charming and very Lalique style
perfume bottle stands approx. 4" tall. The
base features alternating swirls of frosted
and clear cut glass and has no markings of
any kind. The ground frosted stopper has
two lovely flowers at the top. A great item
for your vanity table, or a wonderful gift.
Bid with confidence and bid whatever you feel this bottle
is worth to you as he is selling with **NO RESERVE!** *(Feel
free to check my feedback!)* I pack all my items carefully.
Winning bidder to pay shipping & handling of $4.55 and
must submit payment within a week of winning the
auction. I will accept credit cards through paypal.com
(see below). Good luck on winning!

GOOD LUCK, HAPPY BIDDING!

Click below to...
*View my other auctions - Win more than one and $AVE on
shipping!*

Using image-hosting Web sites to store images

Okay, realistically, many people are combing cyberspace looking for the
next great thing. eBay's success has entrepreneurs all over the globe coming
up with different kinds of auction-support businesses. As usual, a lot of junk
pops up on the Internet in the wake of such trends — but one promising
development caught our attention recently — image-hosting Web sites.

Image-hosting Web sites have changed from one-stop shops to mega-markets
loaded with tons of services for your auctions. Some image-hosting sites let
you post your pictures without requiring you to use their auction-management
software. Not that we think such software is a bad thing — it's great! — we just
like to be able to choose what we use. (Flip to Chapter 20 for more about
auction-management software.)

Here are a few convenient image-hosting sites that allow you to post a few of
your images for free:

- **Auctiva:** www.auctiva.com
- **FreePictureHosting.com:** www.freepicturehosting.com
- **Filmloop:** filmloop.myfabrik.com

    This site enables you to make slide shows from all your eBay images.
    Take a look at Marsha's filmloop eBay store promotion on her MySpace
    page at www.myspace.com/marshacollier.

- **Photobucket:** www.photobucket.com

Using eBay's Picture Services

eBay hosts one image per auction — for free. If you want more images, it costs only $0.18 to add additional pictures. (You can have a maximum of 12 images per auction item.) If you're going to add a number of pictures, you may want to consider taking advantage of one of the two Picture Pack options that eBay offers — up to 6 images for $1.20 or from 7 to 12 images for $1.80. Picture Pack options also include Image Supersize (an $0.88 option that allows potential bidders to see your pictures enlarged to 800 x 800 pixels maximum) and Picture Show (which allows bidders to see all your images in a slide show).

If you use eBay's Picture Service, your photos appear on your auction in a pre-designed template. If you use more than one photo, the first photo shows up in a 400-x-300-pixel format. A miniature of the first image appears to the left of the larger image. The prospective bidder clicks the smaller picture, and it magically appears in the larger photo area.

When you prepare to list an item for your first auction, a page appears, and you're asked whether you want to use the photo service. If you don't want to use it, click the Your Own Web Hosting tab and input the URL of your picture. If you do want to use the service, follow the directions on-screen.

To post your photo, click the Add Pictures button or the first image box, and a new window will open to help you find and upload your image to the Sell Your Item form. By default, this window will open to eBay's Enhanced Picture Services, which will likely ask if it is okay to download and install an Active-X control to your computer. If it does, click Yes and the installation will take mere moments. If you prefer not to install the Active-X control, switch the top tab over to the Basic service.

If you choose to use the Enhanced service, click the Add Pictures button in the first picture window. An Open dialogue box appears to help you locate the picture file on your computer. Once you have found it, select it and click the Open button. Your file is now ready to upload to eBay's picture servers.

If you prefer to use the Basic service, click the Browse button and a Choose File window opens to locate the picture file on your computer. Once you have navigated to the file, click the Open button and the file is ready to upload. Whether you use Enhanced or Basic service, repeat the process to add additional photos as required. An Open File dialogue box appears. Find your image on your computer and click Open, and the image magically appears in the image box. Add more pictures if you want, then click Submit Pictures and Continue. Figure 14-4 shows the images uploaded section of the Describe Your Item page. Here are a few things to keep in mind:

✔ eBay keeps an image online for the duration of your listing and for up to 90 days (as long as you have the link available to access the page). After that, the image disappears (unless you relist the same auction).

✔ You can always post the image again if you need it later; be sure to leave a copy of the image on your computer.

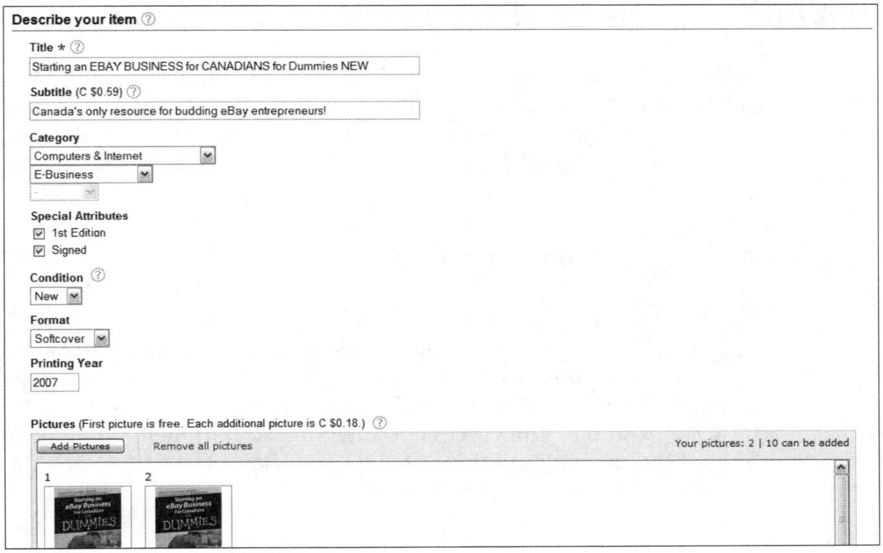

Figure 14-4:
Click the
Add
Pictures
button and
you're on
your way.

Using eBay's Gallery

Any discussion of images on eBay would be incomplete without a short discussion of eBay's Gallery pictures. Gallery pictures are the small pictures you see to the left of items in category listings or in your searches. Using eBay's Gallery option does draw more attention to your sales, but have you ever noticed that not all Gallery images show up crisp and clear? And that some are smaller than others? It's not by chance; eBay reduces the first image you uploaded for use in the Gallery. Occasionally the reduction can have a strange impact on the image quality.

The technology that allows eBay's Picture Services to do its magic resizes the seller's picture to fit the allotted space. In the case of the Gallery, a considerable amount of compression is applied to your image. The more compression that's applied, the fuzzier and more distorted your image can get.

When you use your own photo hosting on eBay, you can use a different photo for your Gallery image. Either use a different picture or reduce your main image to a tiny 110 x 120 pixels. If you reduce the picture yourself, you notice a big improvement in the way the Gallery picture looks.

Getting Your Item Noticed

Okay, you have a great auction at eBay and great images to go with it. Now, all you need to do is track the number of users peeking at your items and attract even more people to your auction. The following sections tell you how to make your auction even better.

Putting on the hits

Your auction is up and running at eBay, and you're dying to know how many people have stopped by to take a look. To easily monitor your auction's *hits* — the number of times visitors stop to look at the goods — you can use a free public counter program from an online source. A counter is a useful marketing tool; for example, you can check the number of times people have looked at, but not bid on, your auctions. If you have a lot more lookie-loos than bids, you may have a problem with your auction.

Multiple pictures in your descriptions

Here's the answer to the most-asked question when we teach a class on eBay. Many sellers have more than one picture within the auction description area. By putting extra images in the description, they don't have to pay extra for eBay's hosting services. This isn't magic; you can easily do it, too. Just add a tiny bit of HTML code to your auction description. Here's the HTML code you need to use to insert one picture in your auction:

```
<img
      src=http://www.yourserver.com/i
      magename.jpg/>
```

Be sure to use the brackets to open and close your code (they're the uppercase symbols located on the comma and the period keys on your keyboard). This code reflects the URL of your picture, and the coding img src= tells eBay's server to insert a picture.

When you want to insert two pictures, just insert code for each picture, one after the other. If you want one picture to appear below the other, use the HTML code for line break, <BR>. Here's how to write that:

```
<img
      src=http://www.yourserver.com/i
      magenumber1.jpg> <BR/>
<img
      src=http://www.yourserver.com/i
      magenumber2.jpg>
```

If your counter indicates that you're not getting many hits, consider the following potential problems so you can resurrect your auction:

- ✔ Does the picture take too long to load?
- ✔ Is the opening bid too high?
- ✔ Are those neon-orange-and-lime-green bell-bottoms just too funky to sell?

The eBay Sell Your Item form includes simple counters you can choose from. You can also find some highly intelligent and sophisticated counters elsewhere on the Net, at sites such as Sellathon (www.sellathon.com).

Secret links for fun and profit

By linking to your eBay auctions from your personal or business Web page, you can get even more people to look at what you're selling. eBay has a very specialized HTML that they'll give you for free — the only thing is very few people know about this HTML, and it's almost impossible to find on the eBay site. But not to worry — to get a cool display that shows off your eBay listings on your Web page, follow these steps:

1. **In your Web browser, go to**

   `affiliates.ebay.com/odcs/custom.htm?template=EditorKit`

   You're taken to the eBay Affiliate Editor Kit page.

2. **Scroll down the page and click the Create an Editor Kit button.**

   If you aren't already logged in, you're asked to do so. After you click Sign In, the Editor Kit License Agreement page appears.

3. **Look over the License Agreement and then click I Agree.**

   A page opens that asks you a bunch of basic questions.

4. **Answer the Editor Kit assembly questions to the best of your ability.**

   There really are no wrong answers (besides, eBay lets you preview your work).

5. **Customize your kit appearance by making your selections.**

6. **Click the Continue button.**

7. **On the page that appears, copy the handy HTML snippet that eBay generated for you; then use your computer's Clipboard to paste it into your Web site or text editor.**

Your eBay listings now appear on your personal or business Web page. Anyone who clicks one of the item links is transported directly to your item listing.

At the time of this writing, when you hit the big time and open your eBay store, eBay gives you 75 percent off your store's Final Value Fees when you bring in a sale from the eBay site.

The instant that you or another eBay user connects to a link that isn't owned or maintained by eBay, you're no longer protected by the eBay rules and regulations. eBay cancels any auctions that contain links to Web sites that offer to undersell an auction by touting the same item at a cheaper price — or offer to sell items forbidden at eBay.

It's against eBay policy to link to your Web site from your auction page, but you can link from your About Me page (see the following section for more on the About Me pages). To add a link to your About Me page that takes eBay users to your Web site, type the following HTML code at the end of your item description:

```
Click below...<br>
<a href=http://www.YourOwnISP.com/~yourUserID/sale.htm>
Visit my Web site</a>
```

It's All About Me!

Want to know more about the people behind those User IDs? Thousands of eBay members have created their own personal Web pages at eBay (called *About Me pages*). About Me pages are easy to create — and are as unique as each eBay member. eBay users with active About Me pages have a special ME icon to the right of their User IDs.

Take your time when you create your About Me page. A well-done About Me page improves your sales because people who come across your auctions and check out your About Me page can get a sense of who you are and how serious you are about your eBay activities. They see instantly that you're no fly-by-night seller.

Before you create your About Me page, look at what other users have done. eBay members often include pictures, links to other Web sites (including their personal or business home pages), and links to just about any Web location that reflects their personalities — which is why these pages are so entertaining. If your purpose is to generate more business, we recommend that you keep your About Me page focused on your auction listings, with a link to your Web site.

Sellers with many auctions running at the same time often add a message to their About Me pages that indicates they're willing to reduce shipping charges if bidders also bid on their other auctions. This direct tactic may lack nuance, but it increases the number of people who look at (and bid on) your auctions.

To create your About Me page, follow these steps:

1. **Go to any eBay user's About Me page, scroll to the very bottom, and click the Create My About Me Page link.**

   If you can't find the link, go to
   `members.ebay.ca/ws2/eBayISAPI.dll?AboutMeLogin.`

   If you haven't signed in, the Sign In page appears.

2. **If the Sign In page appears, type your User ID and password in the appropriate boxes.**

   You're taken to Step 1 of the About Me page creation process.

3. **Choose between using eBay's Step-by-Step process or entering your own HTML.**

   For this discussion we'll assume you want to use eBay's nifty layout creator. Click the Continue button and the About Me: Enter Page Content page appears.

4. **Enter your About Me page content.**

   Add your text and images in the spaces provided. You can also choose other content to include your recent feedback, your items for sale, and your favourite links to sites off eBay. The key elements to your page are:

   - **Page Title:** Type the title of your About Me page (for example, `Larry's Lunchboxes`).

   - **Paragraph 1:** Type a personal attention-grabbing headline, such as `Welcome to Larry Lunch's Lunchbox Place`, and then include a short paragraph that greets your visitors (something such as, `Hey, I like lunchboxes a lot` — only more exciting).

   - **Paragraph 2:** Type another paragraph about yourself or your collection (such as, `I used to stare at lunchboxes in the school cafeteria` ... only more, you know, *normal*).

   - **Add Your Pictures:** If you're adding a picture, type a sentence describing it in the Label for Picture 1 text box. For example, you can label a picture `This is my wife Loretta with our lunchbox collection`. You can add up to two pictures in the Add Pictures section of the page.

- **Show Your eBay Activity:** Here you can select how many of your feedback postings you want to appear on your About Me page from a drop-down list. (You can opt not to show any feedback, but we think you should put in a few comments, especially if they're complimentary — as in, "Larry sent my lunchbox promptly, and it makes lunchtime a blast! Everybody stares at it. . . .") You can also select how many of your current auctions you want to appear on your About Me page from the drop-down list. If you don't have any auctions running at the moment, you can select the Show No Items option.

- **Add Links:** In these text boxes, type the names and URLs of any Web links you want visitors to see (for example, a Web site that appraises lunchboxes — "It's in excellent condition, except for that petrified ham sandwich. . . .").

When your content is complete, click the Continue button.

5. **Click the radio button next to the layout design that you want and preview your page.**

    You can see a sample of a completed About Me page in Figure 14-5.

6. **Click the Back button.**

    If you don't like your current layout, click the Back button to go back to make the necessary corrections. Otherwise, if your new About Me page looks ready to go, click the Submit button. Your About Me page is now visible to the world.

Welcome to *Marsha Collier's* Home on Ebay!
Ebay Member since January 5, 1997

Author of "eBay® for Dummies" and "Starting an eBay® Business for Dummies" and "eBay Bargain Shopping". Click on the link to visit my website! CoolEbayTools.com™

A little bit of eBay history...
In 1997, eBay sent these Pierre "signed" certificates out to their leading sellers. I was lucky enough to get one.

Figure 14-5: Make your About Me page your home at eBay.

I *love* eBay, don't you?...
I love eBay and all the wonderful people who visit this site. I discovered eBay in 1996, and quickly figured out that this would be the marketplace of the future. Although I had a successful business, The Collier Company, (a home based retail marketing and advertising firm) I enjoyed buying and selling on eBay. My business was awarded the "Small Business of the Year" award from the

Don't forget to update your About Me page often. A good About Me page makes bidders eager to know more about your auctions. An out-of-date About Me page turns off potential bidders. If you choose to update, you need to edit it by selecting to enter your own HTML, otherwise, if you use eBay's Step-by-Step process, you will have to create a whole new page.

You can link to your About Me page from your Web site or from your e-mail because all About Me pages have their own personal URLs. The address ends with your User ID. For example, here's the URL for Marsha's page:

```
cgi3.ebay.ca/ws/eBayISAPI.dll?ViewUserPage&userid=marsha_c
```

Welcome to My World

As an eBay registered user, you get publishing space to tell the community what makes you . . . *you*. eBay My World lets you tell anyone who visits about all of your favourite things — what you sell, what you buy, and a whole lot more. In many respects, it's a lot like your About Me page, but many users claim it's easier to update My World content because you don't need to know HTML to do it.

eBay breaks the My World page down into modules — each of which adds different content. You may decide to add the Favourites module but skip adding the Blog module. Or, you might decide to add the Reviews and Guides module or the Guest Book module — it's all up to you.

You can go back and add, change, or delete information on your My World page anytime you want. Give some thought as to how much you want the world to know about you, and add or remove accordingly. As with your About Me page, allowing people to see that you're a legitimate seller gives them a better feeling about doing business with you and frequently translates into more profitable sales.

To access the My World setup page, you can click the My World link in the Related Links box at the bottom-left of your My eBay page, or you can simply click your User ID anytime it appears as a link. You can find links to add content, to change the theme, or to change the layout near the top of your My World page, which allow you to personalize your page.

Part IV
Oy Vey, More eBay! Special Features

The 5th Wave   By Rich Tennant

"He saw your laptop and wants to know if he can check his feedback ratings."

In this part . . .

So you want to protect yourself from bad apples, not just at eBay, but all over the Internet? You're not alone. We want to keep safe, as well, and that's why we tip you off to the information in this part.

This part is the place to come if you want to know just what eBay knows about you and is willing to share with other eBay members. We also introduce you to Trust & Safety (SafeHarbor), the next best thing to a superhero when it comes to protecting you from people who don't qualify for the eBay User of the Year Award.

eBay is a community, so you need to be let in on some of the ways you can commune with other collectors and get into the social scene. In this part, you can find out about the special features that make eBay such a unique environment. Where else can you buy an item you really want and also help out a charity, all with the click of a mouse?

Chapter 15

Privacy: To Protect and to Serve

In This Chapter

▶ Digging up what eBay knows about you

▶ Finding out what eBay does with your info

▶ Avoiding spam

▶ Protecting your privacy

. . . .

*O*n the Internet, as in real life, you should never take your personal privacy for granted. Sure, you're ecstatic that you can shop and sell at eBay from the privacy of your home, but remember: Just because your front door is locked doesn't mean that your privacy is being protected. If you're new to the Internet, you may be surprised to find out what you reveal about yourself to the world, no matter how many precautions you take. (Yes, we all know about that neon green exfoliating mask you wear when you're bidding . . . just kidding . . . honest.)

In this chapter, you can find out how much eBay knows about you and who eBay shares your information with. We explain what you can do to protect your privacy and tell you some simple steps you can take to increase not only your Internet privacy but also your safety.

What (And How) eBay Knows about You

The irony of the Internet is that although you think you're sitting at home working anonymously, third parties such as advertisers and marketing companies are secretly getting to know you. (All together now: *Get-ting-to-know all a-bout youuu . . .*)

While you're busy collecting World's Fair memorabilia and buying that hot new Kate Spade purse, eBay is busy collecting nuggets of information about you. eBay gets some of this information from you and some of it from your computer. All the data eBay gets is stored in the mammoth eBay memory bank.

What you tell eBay

eBay gets much of what it knows about you *from* you. When you sign up, you voluntarily tell eBay important and personal information about yourself. Right off the bat, you give eBay these juicy tidbits:

- Name
- E-mail address
- Snail-mail address
- Phone number
- Date of birth
- Password

"Okay, that's no big deal," you say, but if you're using your credit card to settle your eBay fees, you're also giving out the following personal financial information:

- Credit card number
- Expiration date
- Credit card billing address
- Credit card history

If you make a one-time payment with a personal cheque or register to pay by cheque through PayPal, you give eBay even more information about yourself. eBay instantly knows your bank's name and your chequing account number. The bottom line is that every time you pay by cheque, you give away personal info about yourself. eBay carefully locks up this information (in a high-tech Alcatraz, of sorts), but other companies or individuals may not be so protective. Before you put the cheque in the mail, make sure you're comfortable with where it's going.

What cookies gather

Web sites collect information about you by using cookies. No, they don't bribe you with oatmeal-raisin goodies. *Cookies* are nothing more than tiny files that companies (such as eBay) put on your hard drive to store data about your surfing habits.

Most Web site designers install cookies to help you navigate their sites. Sometimes, the cookie becomes sort of an admission ticket so that you don't need to register every time you log on.

eBay has partnerships both with companies that provide page-view and data-tracking technology and with advertisers who display advertising banners on eBay pages, whether you want to see the banners or not. If you click a banner, a cookie from that particular advertiser *may* go onto your computer, usually to prevent you from seeing that banner again.

Cookies can't steal information from other files on your computer. A cookie can access only the information that you provide to its Web site.

DoubleClick, a major player in the cookie-tracking field, says that it uses your information to limit the number of times that you see the same advertisement. DoubleClick also measures the kinds of ads that you respond to and tracks which member Web sites you visit and how often. The bottom line is that DoubleClick is just trying to sell you stuff with ads based on your personal interests. The upside is that you get to see stuff that you may like.

You can find out more about cookies at `www.cookiecentral.com/faq`. This site gives you simple instructions on how to handle cookies on your computer.

If you want to keep your information private, you can remove yourself from the DoubleClick cookie system by going to this Web site:

```
www.doubleclick.com/us/about_doubleclick/privacy/dart_
            adserving.asp
```

Your eBay sign-in cookie

When you visit eBay and sign in, eBay gives you a special kind of cookie — not pecan shortbread — an end-of-session or permanent cookie. Here's a description of the two types of cookies:

✔ **End of session:** This cookie type remains on your computer as long as your browser is open. When you close your Internet browser (Internet Explorer, Firefox, Netscape, Safari, or Opera), the cookie disappears as if you downed it with icy cold milk.

✔ **Permanent:** This flavour is perfect if you don't share your computer with anyone else; it permits your computer to always remain signed in to a particular Web site.

eBay's permanent "keep me signed in" sign-in cookie is a good thing. It means you don't have to repeatedly type your User ID and password at every turn. This cookie simplifies your participation in chats, bidding, watching items, viewing e-mail addresses, and so on. Because you don't have to sign in every moment that you're doing business on eBay, it's a real timesaver.

Web beacons

Web beacons are clear, 1-x-1-pixel images that are placed in the HTML (Internet page code) for individual pages. They're also commonly called *pixel tags*. Web beacons, like cookies, are used mainly for collecting marketing information. They track the traffic patterns of users from one page to another.

Web beacons are sneaky little things. They're invisible as cookies, but they're incorporated into Web pages without your knowing. Turning off cookies won't disable Web beacons, but this action does protect your anonymity. Web beacons aren't as ominous as they may seem because the information they collect isn't personally identifiable, they just track your passage along the site.

What Web servers collect

Every time you log on to the Internet, you leave an electronic trail of information, just like Hansel and Gretel's breadcrumbs. eBay, like zillions of other Web sites, uses *servers,* which are immense programs that do nothing but collect and transfer bits (and bytes) of information day and night. Your Internet connection has a special address that identifies you to all servers when you surf the Net. This address is called an *IP (Internet Protocol) address,* and authorities often use it to track those whose shenanigans wreak havoc on Web sites or other users.

Web servers all over the Internet track some or all of the following information:

- ✔ What Web site you came from
- ✔ The ISP (Internet service provider) that you use
- ✔ The items that you're selling on eBay
- ✔ The Web sites you linked your listings to
- ✔ Your favourite Web sites (if you link them to your About Me page)

eBay collects the following information while you visit the eBay site (After you log off, the server discards the data.):

✔ What you do while logged on to the site

✔ Which categories you tend to browse

✔ What times you log on and log off

Like incredible Internet archivists, eBay's servers keep a record of everything you bid on, win, and sell, which is great news if you have a problem with a transaction and need eBay to investigate. Also, eBay couldn't display feedback about you and other users if its servers didn't store all the feedback you write and receive. Have you ever sent an e-mail to eBay? eBay's servers record it and keep it in some murky recess of eBay's memory. Remember, we live in the age of electronic commerce, and the people at eBay run a serious business that depends on e-commerce. They have to keep everything in case they need it later.

To see a chart on what personal information is accessible by third parties, check out this address:

```
pages.ebay.ca/help/policies/privacy-appendix.html
```

Be sure to visit the page; you may be shocked by the amount of information that exists on the eBay servers about you and your habits.

For examples of how this type of information can be used against you while you surf the Internet, visit this Web site:

```
www.anonymizer.com/consumer/threat_center
```

Cookie removal-ware

Not long ago, Bill's daughter complained that the laptop computer she uses at college was getting slower and slower. He sat down to have a look at it and noticed that it was opening extra windows and accessing the Internet spuriously. After running the software to determine whether she had a virus (no, she didn't), he went to the Internet to get her spyware removal software. Perhaps her problem was that too many people had inserted information-gathering cookies on her computer.

That was certainly the case. After installing and running the software, he found that she had several hundred cookies pulling information from her computer as she surfed. After he deleted those cookies, her computer ran much faster.

She certainly didn't give these people permission to spy on her comings and goings on the Internet. These cookies were placed on her computer without her knowledge. If you want to purge these uninvited spies from your computer, download any of the free spyware or malware software from the Internet. Two good free ones are Ad-Aware from www.lavasoft.com/products/ad_ aware_free.php and Spybot Search and Destroy, available from www. safer-networking.org/en/spybotsd/index.html.

If you're apprehensive about all the information that Web servers can collect about you while you innocently roam the Internet, we understand. But before you start looking out for Big Brother watching over your shoulder, consider this: On the Web, everybody's collecting information.

The odds are excellent that all the information that eBay knows about you is already in the hands of many other folks, too — your bank, your grocer, the staffs of any magazines you subscribe to, clubs you belong to, any airlines you've flown, and any insurance agencies you use. That's life these days. And if you're thinking, "Just because everybody knows all this stuff about me, that doesn't make it right," all we can say is, "You're right." But maybe you'll sleep better knowing that eBay is one place where folks take the privacy issue seriously. See the following section for details.

eBay's Privacy Policy

eBay had a Privacy Policy for all its users before privacy policies were even in vogue, not to mention the law. Now eBay maintains the safety standards set forth by the pioneer in online safeguarding: TRUSTe.

TRUSTe (www.truste.org) sets a list of standards that its member Web sites have to follow to earn a "seal of approval." The thousands of Web sites that subscribe to this watchdog group must adhere to its guidelines and set policies to protect privacy. eBay has been a member of TRUSTe since the privacy watchdog group was founded in 1997.

Do seals bite back?

Because eBay pays to display the TRUSTe mark, some online critics say that the seal is nothing more than window dressing. These critics wonder whether it would be in the Web watchdog's best financial interest to bite the hand that feeds it all those display fees. Critics complain that the seal offers a false sense of security — and suggest that you view the seal as nothing more than a disclaimer to be careful in your Internet dealings.

Technically, TRUSTe can pull its seal whenever a Web site becomes careless in its handling of privacy issues. However, the critics make a good point: Always be careful in your Internet dealings, no matter how much protection a site has. If you ever feel your personal information has been compromised, file a complaint at the TRUSTe Web site, www.truste.org/ consumers/watchdog_complaint. php.

Grateful Dead cookie jar

In 1999, an auction description read: "This is one of the grooviest jars I have ever come across — a real find for the die-hard Grateful Dead fan or for the cookie jar collector who has it all. Made by Vandor, this Grateful Dead bus cookie jar looks like something the Dead *would* drive. Beautiful detailing on the peace signs; the roses are running lights. Painted windows. You have just got to see this piece. Only 10,000 made, and I have only seen one other. Comes with box that has Grateful Dead logos on it. Buyer pays all shipping and insurance."

The cookie jar started at US$1 and sold at eBay for US$102.50. When Marsha updated this book

in 2002, it sold on eBay for US$125. The Grateful Dead's bus cookie jar is even more valuable these days; in 2004, an auction closed with the final bid at US$150. The price of the original has skyrocketed, so much so that Vandor just came out with a 40th anniversary replica. Buy it now for your Deadhead friends — and buy it quick. Only 1,200 were made, and the price is already edging up to the US$100 mark.

Oh wow, dude — that's some far-out cookie jar. (Cue the band: *Keep truckin'....*)

To review the policy that's earned eBay the TRUSTe seal of approval, click the Policies link that appears at the bottom of every eBay page.

In addition to setting and displaying a Privacy Policy, eBay follows these guidelines, as well:

- eBay must make its Privacy Policy links easily accessible to users. You can find a Policies link on virtually every eBay page. Clicking on that link will take you to the eBay Policies page, where you will find a combined User Agreement and Privacy Policy link. One more click of that link and you will find the page that houses the User Agreement at the top of the page and the Privacy Policy on the lower portion of the page. Take advantage of this opportunity to find out how your data is being protected.

- eBay must disclose what personal information it collects and how it's using that info.

- Users must have an easy way to review the personal information that eBay has about them.

- Users must have an option — *opting out* — that lets them decline to share information.

✔ eBay must follow industry standards to make its Web site and database secure so that hackers and non-members have no access to the information. eBay uses *Secure Sockets Layer (SSL),* which is an encryption program that scrambles data while it's in transit to eBay. Unfortunately, no Web site, including Revenue Canada's Web site, is completely secure, so you still have to be on your guard while you're online.

What Does eBay Do with Information about Me, Anyway?

Although eBay knows a good chunk of information about you, it puts the information to good use. The fact that it knows so much about you actually helps you in the long run.

Here's what eBay uses personal information for:

✔ **Upgrading eBay:** Like most e-commerce companies, eBay tracks members' use and habits to improve the Web site. For instance, if a particular item generates a lot of activity, eBay may add a category or a subcategory.

✔ **Clearing the way for transactions:** If eBay didn't collect personal information (such as your e-mail address, your snail-mail address, and your phone number), after an auction was over, you couldn't complete the transaction you started. Bummer.

✔ **Billing:** You think it's important to keep track of your merchandise and money, don't you? So does eBay. It uses your personal information to keep an eye on your account and your paying habits — and on everybody else's. (Call it a gentle encouragement of honest trading habits.)

✔ **Policing the site:** Never forget that eBay tries to be tough on cybercrime, and that if you break the rules or regulations, eBay will hunt you down and boot you out. Personal information is used to find eBay delinquents, and eBay makes it clear that it cooperates with law enforcement and with third parties whose merchandise you may be selling illegally. For more about this topic, read up on the VeRO program in Chapter 9.

Periodically, eBay runs surveys asking specific questions about your use of the site. It uses your answers to upgrade eBay. In addition, eBay asks whether it can forward your information to a marketing firm. eBay says that it doesn't forward any personally identifiable information, which means that any info you provide is given to third parties as raw data. However, if you're nervous about privacy, we suggest that you make it clear that you don't want your comments to leave eBay if you decide to participate in eBay surveys. If you don't participate in the surveys, you won't have any hand in creating new eBay features, though, so you can't complain if you don't like how the site looks. Sometimes, eBay advertises surveys that users can take part in on the eBay home page.

What Do Other eBay Members Know about Me?

eBay functions under the premise that eBay's members are buying, selling, working, and playing in an honest and open way. That means that anyone surfing can immediately find out some limited information about you:

- ✔ Your User ID and history.
- ✔ Your feedback history.
- ✔ All the auctions and eBay store sales you run.
- ✔ Many of your current bids and any bids you've made within a given 30-day period. (eBay no longer reveals bids you've made on items with a final value that exceeds $200.)

eBay clearly states in its policies and guidelines that the use of e-mail addresses between members should be used only for eBay business. If you abuse this policy, you can be suspended or even kicked off for good.

eBay provides limited eBay member registration information to its users. If another member involved in a transaction with you wants to know the following facts about you, he or she can get them:

- ✔ Your name (and business name if you've provided that information)
- ✔ Your e-mail address
- ✔ The city, province or state, and country that you provided to eBay
- ✔ The telephone number that you provided to eBay

Following the transaction, buyers and sellers exchange some real-world information. As we explain in Chapter 6 and Chapter 12, members initiate the exchange of merchandise and money by e-mail, providing personal addresses for both payments and shipments. Make sure that you're comfortable giving out your home address. If you're not, we explain alternatives in the section "I Vant to Be Alone — and Vat You Can Do to Stay That Vay," later in this chapter.

Spam — Not Just a Tasty Treat

Although you can find plenty of places to socialize and have fun at eBay, when it comes to business, eBay is . . . well, all business.

eBay's policy says that you can make requests for registration information only for people with whom you're transacting business on eBay. The contact information request form requires that you type in the item number of the transaction you're involved in, as well as the User ID of the person whose contact info you want. If you're not involved in a transaction, as either a bidder or a seller in the specified item number, you can't access the user information.

When it comes to e-mail addresses, your secret is safe. If you bid on an auction, your e-mail is visible only to the seller. The end of listing notice contains your e-mail address so that the person on the other end of the transaction can contact you. After the other user has your e-mail address, eBay rules state that the user can use it only for eBay business.

Here's a list of business reasons for e-mail communication, generally accepted by all at eBay:

- ✔ Responding to feedback that you left
- ✔ Responding to feedback that you received
- ✔ Communicating with sellers or buyers during and after transactions
- ✔ Suggesting to other eBay members items that buyers may be interested in via the Mail This Auction to a Friend feature
- ✔ Leaving chat-room comments
- ✔ Discussing common interests with other members, such as shared hometowns, interesting collections, and past or current auctions

Sending spam versus eating it

Sending e-mail to other members is a great way to do business and make friends. But don't cross the line into spam. *Spam,* a Hormel canned meat product (we've given Spam its own sidebar), now has an alternate meaning. When you spell it with a small s, *spam* is unsolicited e-mail — most often, advertising — sent to multiple e-mail addresses gleaned from marketing lists. Eventually, it fills up your inbox the way "Spam, Spam, Spam, and Spam" filled up the menu in an old *Monty Python* restaurant skit.

Spam I am

Spam, the unwanted electronic junk mail, is named after Spam, the canned meat product. (Spam collectibles at eBay are another matter entirely.) According to the Spam Web site (www.spam.com), more than 6 billion cans of Spam have been consumed worldwide. Spam is made from a secret recipe of pork shoulder, ham, and special spices. It was first produced in 1937 and got its name from the *sp* in *spice* and the *am* in *ham*.

It's widely believed that spam (junk e-mail) got its name from the old *Monty Python* sketch because the refrain "Spam-Spam-Spam-Spam" drowned out all other conversation, and one of the participants kept saying, "I don't want any Spam. I don't like Spam." Others say that it came from a bunch of computer geeks at the University of Southern California who thought that junk e-mail was about as satisfying as a Spam sandwich. Perhaps they've never enjoyed a Spam luau in Hawaii under the moonlight — aloha!

Think of spam as the electronic version of the junk mail that you get via Canada Post. Spam may be okay for eating (if you're into that kind of thing), but sending it can get you banned from eBay.

If you send an e-mail that advertises a product or service to people who haven't agreed that they wanted this sort of e-mail (meaning they haven't *opted in*), you're guilty of spamming.

Trashing your junk mail

Sometimes, spam can come in the form of mail from people you know and expect mail from. Your closest friend's computer may have been abducted by some weird Internet virus and replicated the virus to everyone in his or her e-mail address book. Obviously, this isn't a good thing for those who receive and open the e-mail.

Don't open e-mail from anyone you don't know, especially if a file is attached to it. Sometimes, if a spammer is really slick, it's hard to tell that you've received spam. If you receive an e-mail with no subject line, however — or if the e-mail has an addressee name that isn't yours or is coming from someone you never heard of — delete it. You never know; it could be just annoying spam — or worse, it could contain a computer virus as an attachment, just waiting for you to open and activate it.

Speaking of e-mail, if you're new to the technology, we recommend getting a good antivirus program that can scan e-mail attachments and rid your system of some annoying — and increasingly dangerous — computer bugs.

For some interesting general anti-spam tips, drop in at `spam.abuse.net`. This Web site offers helpful advice for doing battle with spam artists. Also, we've come across a very handy software program called MailWasher, which allows you to preview your e-mail before it's downloaded to your computer. It even bounces spam back to the sender on command — as if your e-mail address didn't exist. Best of all, this program is free and available from `www.mailwasher.net`.

E-mail spoofing

E-mail spoofing has become the bane of the online community and can really wreak havoc. Spoofing is accomplished when crafty techno-geeks send out e-mail and make it appear to come from someone other than themselves — someone you know and expect e-mail from. Most often, this type of e-mail is programmed to invade your privacy or, even worse, bilk you out of confidential information.

A spate of e-mails have purportedly been sent from eBay, PayPal, and other major e-commerce sites, claiming that your membership is about to be or has been suspended — or that your records need updating. The opportunistic e-mail then asks you to click a link to a page on the site, which then asks you to input your personal information. Don't do it!

Most sites will *never* ask you to provide sensitive information through e-mail, so don't do it. If you receive an e-mail saying your account has been suspended, close the e-mail and go directly to the site in question — *without* using the supplied link in the e-mail. You'll know soon enough if there's really a problem with your account.

If you get this sort of e-mail from eBay and want to confirm whether it's really from eBay, visit this eBay security page:

```
pages.ebay.ca/help/confidence/isgw-account-theft-
          spoof.html
```

To help eBay in its investigation of these information thieves, send a copy of the e-mail (along with all identification headers) to `spoof@ebay.com`. When forwarding the e-mail, don't alter it in any way. You can send PayPal spoof messages (also with the headers) to `spoof@paypal.com`.

My Messages safeguard your privacy

Being the conscientious company it is, eBay has set up a private area, accessible only through your My eBay page, called My Messages. (You can find it on the left side of your My eBay page in the long column of links.) My Messages enables you to communicate with other eBay members without revealing your e-mail address. All your missives with other members, such as Ask the Seller a Question communications, appear in this area. You can answer messages you receive, send new mail, and delete communications from this area, just as if it was your own e-mail software.

This service can protect you from many of the most dangerous forms of spam. For safety's sake, whenever you receive an e-mail sent (in reality or purportedly) from eBay or an eBay member, don't click the e-mail link to Respond Now. Open your Internet browser, if it isn't already open, and go directly to your My eBay page's My Messages area. If the e-mail is legitimate, it appears here. Simply click the e-mail to open it, read it, and reply. Your privacy (in the form of your e-mail address) isn't exposed to the receiving party.

I Vant to Be Alone — and Vat You Can Do to Stay That Vay

The Internet has a long reach. Don't be surprised if you furnish your personal information freely on one Web site, and it turns up somewhere else. If you don't mind people knowing things about you (your name, your hobbies, where you live, and your phone number, for example), by all means, share. But we think you should give only as much information as needed in order to do business on the site.

Privacy isn't secrecy. Don't feel obligated to reveal anything about yourself that isn't absolutely necessary. (Some personal facts are in the same league as body weight — private, even if hardly a secret.)

Although you can't prevent privacy leaks entirely, you can take some precautions to protect yourself. Here are some tips to keep your online information as safe and secure as possible:

> ✔ **User ID:** When eBay first started, members used their e-mail addresses to buy and sell; today, users appear on the site with a *nom de plume* (okay, User ID, but *nom de plume* sounds oh-so chic). Your first line of defence against everyone who surfs the eBay site is to choose a User ID that doesn't reveal too much about you. Chapter 2 gives you some pointers on how to choose your User ID.

✔ **Passwords:** Guard your password as if it were the key to your home. Don't give any buyers or sellers your password. If a window requesting your password pops up in an auction, skip it — it's somebody who's up to no good. Use your password only on official eBay screens. (See Chapter 2 for tips on choosing passwords.)

If you're concerned that someone may have your password, change it immediately by following these steps:

1. **Go to your My eBay page.**

2. **Find the My Account area on the left side of the screen and click the Personal Information link.**

3. **On the Personal Information page that appears, click the Edit link in the Password area and follow the instructions.**

   Your password is immediately changed.

If some dastardly evil-doer has changed your password, and you can't sign in to your account, go to the eBay home page. On the eBay home page, click the Live Help link (in the upper-right corner). A chat window opens, in which you can communicate with a live human being who can help you secure your account before damage can be done.

✔ **Credit card information:** Whenever you use your credit card at eBay, you can make sure that your private information is safe. Look for an SSL (SSL stands for *Security Sockets Layer*) link or check box. Sometimes, you may see a link that says `You may also sign in securely`. This encryption program scrambles the information so that hackers have almost no chance of getting your information. (We explain more about SSL in Chapter 2.)

When buying from an auction that accepts credit cards, check the seller's feedback and carefully weigh the risks of giving your credit card number to someone you don't know versus the added time of paying by money order or personal cheque. An even safer way to pay is through PayPal, where your credit card number is never released to the seller.

Never give anyone your Social Insurance Number online. Guard it as if it were your bank account number.

✔ **Registration information:** When you first register, eBay requests a phone number and address for billing and contact purposes. Neither of us have ever had a problem with anyone requesting our registration information and then misusing it. However, many people want an added measure of anonymity. You can give eBay the information it wants in several ways without compromising your privacy:

- Rather than your home phone number, provide eBay with a cell-phone number, a work phone number, or a SkypeIn number. (See Chapter 18 for more information on Skype.) Screen your calls with an answering machine.

- Use a post office box, rather than your home address.

- Start a bank account solely for eBay transactions. Make it a DBA account — as in *Doing Business As* — so that you can use an alternate name. Your bank can help you with this process.

✔ **Chat rooms:** eBay has a multitude of chat rooms in which members exchange information and sometimes heated arguments. (Chat rooms are thoroughly discussed in Chapter 17.) But heed this advice: Be careful what you reveal about yourself in a chat room. Don't expect that "just between us" means that at all. Anyone who visits the eBay site, not just eBay members, can view chat rooms.

Never say anything online that you wouldn't feel comfortable saying to the next person who passes you on the street. Basically, that's who you're talking to. You can find stories of romances blossoming at eBay — and we're delighted for the happy couples, we swear — but come on, that doesn't mean you should lose your head. Don't give out any personal information to strangers; too often, that's asking for trouble. Have fun at eBay, but hang on to your common sense.

Skim some of the category chat rooms, especially the New to eBay's Discussion Boards room, for policy guidelines and tips about staying safe in the chat rooms and boards. A great bunch of users and eBay staffers frequent that board, and they're sure to give you good information.

✔ **Check feedback:** Yep, we sound like a broken record (in case you don't remember, *records* were the large, black, prone-to-breaking disks used by people to play music before iPods and CDs were invented), but here it is again: Check feedback. eBay works because it's policed by its participants. The best way to find out about the folks whom you're dealing with is to see how others felt about them. If you take only one thing away from this book, it's to check feedback *before* you bid!

In the virtual world, as in the real world, cyberstalking is scary and illegal. If you think someone is using information from eBay to harass you, contact eBay immediately — as well as your local police. Chapter 16 gives you the ins and outs of contacting eBay's security team.

Fighting back

Robbin was minding her own business, selling software at eBay, when she ran into one of the world's nastiest eBay outlaws. He was a one-stop-shopping outlet of rule-breaking behaviours. First, he ruined her auctions by bidding ridiculously high amounts and then retracting bids at the last legal minute. He e-mailed her bidders, offering the same item but cheaper. He contacted Robbin's winning bidders to say he was accepting her payments. Then he started leaving messages on her answering machine. When she finally had enough, she contacted Trust & Safety, which suspended him.

But like a bad lunch, he came back up — with a new name. So Robbin fought back on her own.

She got his registration information and sent him a letter. She also informed the support area at his ISP about what he was doing, and because he used his work e-mail address, she also contacted his boss.

Her efforts must have done the trick. He finally slipped out of eBay and slithered out of her life. The lesson: Don't rely completely on eBay to pick up the pieces. If you're being abused, stand up for your rights and fight back through the proper channels!

Chapter 16

eBay's Trust & Safety Program

In This Chapter

▶ Keeping eBay members safe

▶ Staying current with the rules

▶ Filing complaints against eBay bad guys

▶ Trying to resolve problems by using mediation

▶ Knowing your items through authentication

▶ Saving yourself: Where to go when eBay can't help

Millions of people transact business every day on eBay. If you're new to the Internet, however, you may need a reality check. With around 100 million listings worldwide, and 6.6 million new listings every day, the law of averages dictates that you're bound to run into some rough seas eventually. If you do, know that you can get the answers you need from eBay's Trust & Safety Department. In this chapter, we take you through the Trust & Safety resources — from reporting abuses to resolving insurance issues. This chapter explains how eBay enforces its rules and regulations, shows how you can use third-party bonding and mediation services, and even points out how to go outside eBay for help if you run into some really big-time problems.

Keeping eBay Safe with Trust & Safety

Trust & Safety is the eBay area that focuses on protecting eBay buyers and sellers from members who aren't playing by the rules. Through this department, eBay issues warnings and policy changes — and in some cases, it gives eBay bad guys the heave-ho.

You can find eBay's Trust & Safety by clicking the Community link in the navigation bar. Scroll down the page to the Security & Resolution Centre. (If eBay ever moves this link, just type pages.ebay.ca/securitycentre into your browser, press Enter, and you're there.)

The Security & Resolution Centre is more than just a link to policies and information. It also connects you with a group of eBay staffers who handle complaints, field incoming tips about possible infractions, and dole out warnings and suspensions. These dedicated employees investigate infractions and send out e-mails in response to tips. eBay staffers look at complaints on a case-by-case basis, in the order they receive them. Most complaints they receive are about these problems:

- Shill bidders (see the section "Selling abuses," later in this chapter)
- Feedback issues and abuses (see the section "Feedback abuses," later in this chapter)

Keep in mind that eBay is a community of people, most of whom have never met each other. No matter what you buy or sell at eBay, don't expect eBay transactions to be any safer than buying or selling from a complete stranger. If you go in with this attitude, you can't be disappointed.

If you've read any of the other chapters in this book, you probably know about eBay's rules and regulations. For a closer online look at them, click the Policies link on the bottom of most eBay pages, and then click the User Agreement and Privacy Policy link in the Rules and Policies page that appears. The User Agreement and Privacy Policy page appears, in all its glory. (The agreement is revised regularly, so check it often.)

Another helpful page is the Rules for Everyone Overview, which explains the legalese in clearer English. To find it, go to

```
pages.ebay.ca/help/policies/everyone-ov.html
```

If you plan on being an active eBay member, it's probably worth your while to opt-in to receive eBay's User Agreement update e-mail. Go to your My eBay page and follow these steps:

1. **Click the Preferences link under the My Account heading on the left side of the screen.**

   The Preferences page appears.

2. **Click the Show link to the right of Legal and Policy Notifications.**

   The Legal and Policy Notifications options appear.

3. **Click the Edit link to the right of User Agreement Changes.**

   After you click the Edit link, you're taken to a sign-in page.

To go to the eBay Security & Resolution Centre (see Figure 16-1) for tips on current security issues on eBay, click the Security Centre link that you can find at the bottom of most eBay pages.

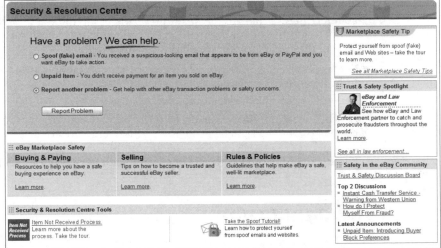

Figure 16-1:
The
Security &
Resolution
Centre.

Abuses You Should Report to Trust & Safety

Before you even consider blowing the whistle on the guy who (gasp!) gave you negative feedback by reporting him to Trust & Safety, make sure that what you're encountering is actually a misuse of eBay. Some behaviour isn't nice (no argument there), but it *also* isn't a violation of eBay rules — in which case, eBay can't do much about it. The following sections list the primary reasons you can start Trust & Safety investigations.

Selling abuses

If you're on eBay long enough, you're bound to find an abuse of the service. It may happen on an auction you're bidding on, or a seller whose listings compete with your auctions may do something really, really wrong. Be a good community member and be on the lookout for the following:

✔ **Shill bidding:** A seller uses multiple User IDs to bid or has accomplices place bids to boost the price of his or her auction items. eBay investigators look for six telltale signs, including a single bidder putting in a really high bid, a bidder with really low feedback but a really high number of bids on items, a bidder with low feedback who has been an eBay member for a while but who's never won an auction, or excessive bids between two users.

✔ **Auction interception:** An unscrupulous user, pretending to be the actual seller, contacts the winner to set up terms of payment and shipping in an effort to get the buyer's payment. You can easily avoid this violation by paying directly through the eBay site with PayPal.

✔ **Fee avoidance:** A user reports a lower-than-actual final price and/or illegally submits a Final Value Fee credit. Final Value Fee credits are explained in Chapter 13.

✔ **Hot bid manipulation:** A user, with the help of accomplices, enters dozens of phoney bids to make the auction appear to have a lot of bidding action. Let the experts at eBay decide on this one; but you may wonder if loads of bids come in rapid succession with very little price movement.

Bidding abuses

If you want to know more about bidding in general, see Chapter 6. Here's a list of bidding abuses that eBay wants to know about:

✔ **Bid shielding:** Two users working in tandem: One of the users, with the help of accomplices, intentionally bids an unreasonably high amount and then retracts the bid prior to the 12-hour cancellation deadline of the auction — leaving a lower bid (which the offender or an accomplice places) as the winning bid.

✔ **Bid siphoning:** Users send e-mail to bidders of a current auction to offer the same merchandise for a lower price elsewhere.

✔ **Auction interference:** Users warn other bidders through e-mail to stay clear of a seller during a current auction, presumably to decrease the number of bids and keep the prices low.

✔ **Bid manipulation (or Invalid Bid Retraction):** A user bids a ridiculously high amount, raising the next highest bidder to the maximum bid. The manipulator then retracts the bid and rebids *slightly* over the previous high bidder's maximum.

✔ **Non-paying bidders:** We frequently call them deadbeats; the bottom line is that these people win auctions but never pay up. Your bid on eBay is a legal contract to buy if you win, it is *not* a game.

✔ **Unwelcome bidders:** A user bids on a specific seller's auction, despite the seller's warning that he or she won't accept that user's bids (such as in the case of not selling internationally and receiving international bids). This practice is impolite and obnoxious. If you want to bar specific bidders from your auctions, you can exclude them. See Chapter 13 for the scoop on how to block bidders.

Feedback abuses

All you have at eBay is your reputation, and that reputation is made up of your feedback history. eBay takes any violation of its Feedback system very seriously. Because eBay's feedback is now transaction related, unscrupulous eBay members have less opportunity to take advantage of this system. Here's a checklist of feedback abuses that you should report to Trust & Safety:

- ✔ **Feedback extortion:** A member threatens to post negative feedback if another eBay member doesn't follow through on some unwarranted demand. Typical extortion attempts include demanding a refund or demanding that you give a generous discount after the bad buyer has won the item.

- ✔ **Personal exposure:** A member leaves feedback for a user that exposes personal information that doesn't relate to transactions at eBay.

- ✔ **Malicious feedback:** Sometimes called *feedback bombing.* Writing malicious feedback is a sick game played by those who have very little to do with their time except upset upstanding eBay sellers. These sickies register on eBay with a new User ID and use the Buy It Now function to buy many items from a seller who has a high positive feedback rating. A few hours later, they leave dastardly negative feedback. The only goal of this action is to ruin the seller's reputation.

- ✔ **–4 feedback:** Any user reaching a net feedback score of –4 is subject to suspension.

Identity abuses

Who you are at eBay is as important as what you sell (or buy). eBay monitors the identities of its members closely — and asks that you report any great pretenders in this area to Trust & Safety. Here's a checklist of identity abuses:

- ✔ **Identity misrepresentation:** A user claims to be an eBay staff member or another eBay user, or he or she registers under the name of another user.

- ✔ **False or missing contact information:** A user deliberately registers with fraudulent contact information or an invalid e-mail address. If you come across someone on eBay who has false information registered on eBay, that member can be suspended.

- ✔ **Under age:** A user falsely claims to be 18 or older. (You must be at least 18 to enter into a legally binding contract.)

- ✔ **Dead/invalid e-mail addresses:** When e-mails bounce repeatedly (single bounces are almost a fact of life on the Internet) from a user's registered e-mail address, chances are good that the address may be dead — and it's doing nobody any good. If you send a message to a dead e-mail address, you usually receive return e-mail indicating that the address is unknown.

✔ **Contact information:** One user publishes another user's contact information on the eBay site.

Operational abuses

If you see somebody trying to interfere with eBay's operation, eBay staffers want you to tell them about it. Here are two roguish operational abuses:

✔ **Hacking:** A user purposely interferes with eBay's computer operations (for example, by breaking into unauthorized files). If someone attempts to alter any of the eBay-generated information in a listing, such as a feedback rating or User ID, the person is violating important eBay rules.

✔ **Spamming:** The user sends unsolicited e-mail to eBay users. Just because you're in a transaction with someone doesn't give you the right to e-mail the person after the auction is over to solicit future business. You can send a newsletter or solicitations only if your recipients opted in to your list. And no one has the right to send you e-mail unrelated to your transaction without your permission.

Miscellaneous abuses

The following are additional problems that you should alert eBay about:

✔ A user is threatening physical harm to another eBay member.

✔ A person uses racist, obscene, or harassing language in a public area of eBay.

For a complete list of offences and how eBay runs each investigation, go to `pages.ebay.ca/help/tp/programs-investigations.html`.

Reporting Abuses to Trust & Safety

If you suspect someone of abusing eBay's rules and regulations, go to the Security & Resolution Centre (you can find a Security Centre link at the bottom of any eBay page) and click the radio button to the left of the topic that best represents your issue. After that, click the Report Problem button. After you click this button, a Contact Us page appears, as shown in Figure 16-2. On this page, several scrollable windows categorize violations by topic and subtopic. Click the topic and subtopics that best represent the issue you're reporting.

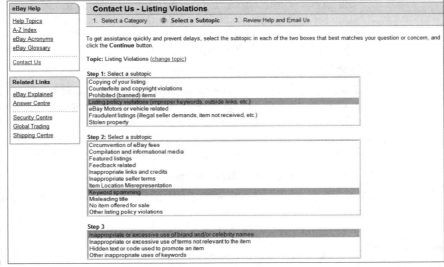

Figure 16-2:
Use this
handy-
dandy form
to report
violations
directly to
the Trust &
Safety
division of
eBay.

If you encounter any of the abuses outlined in this chapter, be sure to report the problem. Community policing is what makes eBay work.

The Security & Resolution Centre offers a wealth of good general information that can help you prevent something from going wrong in a future transaction. Be sure to use these pages regularly as a resource to help prevent problems.

If you're involved in a troubled transaction and need to launch a report, follow these steps:

1. **Read all the information on the Investigations page (pages.ebay.ca/help/tp/programs-investigations.html) before filing a complaint.**

2. **Click any of the many informational links on this page.**

   No matter which link you click, you're taken to an area that instructs you further and provides answers about what offences eBay can and can't investigate.

3. **If you find out that you have a legitimate case that should be investigated, click the Contact Us link on the left side of the page, under eBay Help.**

   You're taken to the Contact Us page that asks you to select a main topic of concern. After selecting the radio button to the left of the item that relates to your situation, click Continue and you will be taken to the handy form shown in Figure 16-2. After each selection is made, another window may open to help in further narrowing down your concern. Once the final topic is determined, click the Continue button and eBay will present you with a page with several links to tell you about their policies and some possible solutions to your issue. After reviewing them, and if you still need to contact Trust & Safety, click the Email Us link under Contact Customer Support.

4. **You're now at the Contact eBay Customer Support form. (Whew!)**

   Figure 16-3 shows you the form. Just type in the item number (or numbers if they're all part of a related problem) and give a thorough description of what transpired, if that information is requested.

   Before you send your message to Customer Support, be sure to review what you've written to confirm that your report is accurate.

5. **Send the report by clicking Send.**

   Be sure you send only one report per case — and one case per report.

Figure 16-3:
Here's where you spill the beans on policy violators to Trust & Safety.

> **My Messages: Contact eBay Customer Support**
>
> **Step 1:** Confirm that your email is about **"Misleading Titles"**
> **Step 2:** If the "Subject" is incorrect, please <u>select a new subject</u> to ensure prompt and accurate processing.
> **Step 3:** After completing all fields in the form, press the **Send** button.
>
> To: **eBay.ca Customer Support**
> From: treasure-pot
> Subject: **Misleading Titles**
>
> **Enter the item number(s) that you wish to report:**
> 110149268290,110149799650
>
> Up to 10 items separated by commas
> (example: 1365609580 , 1748176843)
>
> ☐ Send a copy to my email address.
>
> Send   Cancel

If you file a report, make your message clear and concise by including everything that happened — but don't editorialize. (Calling someone a "lowdown mud-sucking cretin" may make you feel better, but it doesn't provide any useful info to anyone who can help you; it doesn't make you seem un-cretin-like, either.) Keep it business-like — just the facts, ma'am. Do include all pertinent documentation, such as e-mails, receipts, and cancelled cheques — and don't forget the transaction/item number.

Here's a checklist of what you should include in your report to Trust & Safety:

- ✔ Write only the facts as you know them.

- ✔ Attach any pertinent e-mails with complete headers, if required. (*Headers* contain all the information that precedes an e-mail message.) Trust & Safety uses the headers to verify how the e-mail was sent and to follow the trail back to the originator of the message. See the sidebar "Finding the hidden headers in an e-mail message," in this chapter, to decipher this information.

- ✔ Be sure that the subject line of your report precisely names the violation.

Finding the hidden headers in an e-mail message

Most of the time, your e-mail program hides the headers in an e-mail message. If you're using Outlook Express (a free program included with every Windows-enabled personal computer), follow these steps to find them:

1. **Open an e-mail message by double-clicking the Subject line.**

2. **In the open message, choose File⇨ Properties.**

The Properties dialogue box appears.

3. **Click the Details tab.**

Bingo! The headers appear. Copy and paste these into the eBay form whenever you need to report any spurious e-mail.

This information is vital not just to eBay, but to any online entity you might need to report an e-mail abuse to.

If the clock is running out on your case (for example, you suspect bidding offences in a current auction), we suggest that you avail yourself of the Live Help link that appears at the top-right of the eBay home page.

After eBay receives your report via the Customer Service form, you usually get an automatic response that your e-mail was received — although in practice, several days may go crawling by before eBay actually investigates your allegations. (The Customer Service Department must look at a *lot* of transactions.)

Depending on the outcome of the probe, eBay may contact you with the results. If your problem becomes a legal matter, eBay may not let you know what's going on. The only indication you may get that some action was taken is that the auction in question ends before it was due and is no longer visible on the site, or the eBay member you reported is suspended — or NARU *(Not A Registered User)*.

If your complaint doesn't warrant an investigation by the folks at Trust & Safety, they pass it along to someone at the overworked Customer Support staff, who then contacts you. (Don't bawl out the person if the attention you get is tardy.)

Unfortunately, NARU members can show up again on the eBay site. Typically nefarious sorts as these just use a different name. In fact, this practice is fairly common, so beware! If you suspect that someone who broke the rules once is back under another User ID, alert Trust & Safety. If you're a seller, you can refuse to accept bids from that person. If the person persists, alert Trust & Safety Customer Support by using the reporting process previously described in this chapter.

As eBay has grown, so has the number of complaints about slow response from Customer Support. We don't doubt that eBay staffers are doing their best. Although slow response can get frustrating, avoid the temptation to initiate a reporting blitzkrieg by sending reports over and over until eBay can't ignore you. This practice is risky at best and inconsiderate at worst, and it just slows down the process for everyone — and won't endear the e-mail bombardier to the folks who could help. It's better to just grin and bear it — and wait for action to be taken.

If you're desperate for help and can't get satisfaction at the Live Help link, you can post a message with your problem in one of the eBay chat rooms. eBay members participating in chat rooms often share the names of helpful staffers. Often, you can find some eBay members who faced the same problem (sometimes with the same member) and can offer advice — or at the very least, compassion and a virtual ear. (Jump to Chapter 17 for more info on discussion boards and chat rooms.)

If you're a PowerSeller, you can always contact PowerSeller support through the PowerSeller Portal with your immediate problem.

Make sure that you don't violate any eBay rules by sharing any member's contact information when you share your story in a chat room. In addition, make sure that you don't threaten or libel (that is, say untrue things or spread rumours about) the person in your posting.

For general, all-purpose help, eBay has a Customer Support e-mail response form that will get you an answer within 12 to 36 hours. You can find Customer Support creatively tucked away at

```
pages.ebay.ca/help/contact_us/_base/index.html
```

Stuff eBay Won't Do Anything About

People are imperfect everywhere, even online. (Ya think?) You probably won't agree with some of the behaviour that you run into at eBay (ranging from slightly annoying to just plain rotten). Although much of that conduct is detestable, it can (and does) go on as long as it doesn't break eBay rules.

In some cases, you may need to bite your tongue and chalk up someone's annoying behaviour to ignorance of the unwritten rules of eBay etiquette. Just because people have computers and some things to sell or buy doesn't mean that they possess grown-up social skills. (But you knew that.)

Here's a gang of annoying issues that crop up pretty regularly but *aren't* against eBay's rules and regulations:

- **You receive unwarranted or retaliatory feedback.** The biggest fear that haunts members who consider leaving negative feedback is that the recipient will retaliate with some negative feedback of his or her own. Remember that you can respond to negative feedback. However, eBay won't remove a negative comment — no matter how unjustified you may think it is. eBay has agreed that two parties can work through Mutual Feedback Removal to remove feedback if both parties agree that the feedback was left in haste and is unwarranted. See the section "Negative feedback can be removed!" later in this chapter.

  Often, people who leave retaliatory feedback are also breaking some heftier eBay rules, and (sooner or later) they disappear from the site, never to rant again.

- **A seller sets astronomical shipping costs.** eBay policy says that shipping costs must be reasonable. Basically, eBay is wagging its finger and saying, "Don't gouge your buyers." Some sellers are trying to avoid fees or may be disappointed that a sale didn't make enough money, so they jack up shipping costs to increase their profit.

  While eBay will not necessarily step in if the seller is charging more than actual shipping costs, under the rules, eBay can stop someone from charging excessive amounts for shipping if they deem it to be a form of fee avoidance. For more information on eBay's Excessive Shipping policy, go to `pages.ebay.ca/help/policies/listing-shipping.html`.

  Bidders should always check shipping terms in the Item description. Bidders must decide whether to agree to those terms before they bid. The best way to protect yourself from being swindled is to agree with a seller on shipping costs and terms in writing — *before* you bid.

- **A seller or buyer refuses to meet the terms that you mutually set.** eBay has the power only to warn or suspend members. It can't make anyone do anything — even someone who's violating a policy. If you want to make someone fulfill a transaction, you're more or less on your own.

  We've heard one story of a seller who refused to send a product after being paid. The seller said, "Come and get it." The buyer happened to be in town on business and did just that!

  Often, reluctant eBay users just need a nudge from eBay in the form of a warning-to-comply. So go ahead and file a Final Value Fee credit request (we explain how to do that in Chapter 13) and, if necessary, a fraud report (more on fraud reports in the section "Launching a Fraud Report," later in this chapter).

> ✔ **An eBay member sends unwanted e-mail messages (spam).** In fact, members can send spam by using eBay's own tools. All the user has to do is access the Contact a Member form by clicking a member's User ID. eBay sees non-transaction-related communication as spam; you need to report any member who abuses this system, and eBay will investigate and take appropriate action. Although the items spammers are selling may be perfectly good, eBay won't offer you any protection if you participate in "off-the-site" deals. We suggest that you ignore these deals and avoid doing business with the spammers in the future.

New eBay users are often the unwitting perpetrators of annoying behaviour, but you're ahead of the pack now that you know what *not* to do. You can afford to cut the other newbies some slack and help them learn the ropes before you report them.

Using Mediation and Dispute Resolution Services

Even the best of friends sometimes have misunderstandings that can escalate to all-out war if they don't resolve their problems early enough. If the going gets tough, you need to call in the heavy artillery: a *mediator.* Just as pro boxing has its referees, auctions may need a level head to intervene in any squabble. eBay joins with SquareTrade, an online problem-solving service, and you can access the service directly at www.squaretrade.com. Acting as a third party with no axe to grind, a mediator such as SquareTrade can often hammer out an agreement or act as judge to resolve disputes. You do have to pay for the services of a mediator, so we suggest you exhaust your direct negotiation options before you involve SquareTrade.

SquareTrade offers online sellers the opportunity to get a SquareTrade Seal (like an online version of the Better Business Bureau) to post with your auctions. The SquareTrade Seal represents that the seller is committed to participating in online problem solving, dedicated to superior customer service, is in compliance with SquareTrade standards, and has been verified by SquareTrade. Find out more about obtaining the SquareTrade Seal by going to www.squaretrade.com.

Resolving a transaction dispute

If you file a complaint through the SquareTrade link, the service asks you to supply information regarding the offending transaction on an online form. SquareTrade then sends an e-mail to the offending party, outlining the situation. Both the complaint and the response from the other party appear on a secure Web page that only the offender, the mediator, and you can access.

SquareTrade uses a patent-pending technology to help smooth the mediation process. The mediator listens to both points of view and, if the parties can't reach an agreement, suggests a solution that he or she bases on the rules of fair play and good conduct. The use of a mediator doesn't, however, preclude the use of a lawyer if things truly hit an impasse.

Negative feedback can be removed!

You may find yourself in a situation in which you've received unjustified feedback (such as in the case of the nervous Nellie who left negative feedback because the item hadn't arrived, but it was just hung up in the mail). If the problem gets resolved between the two of you, you can get that feedback removed. eBay has agreed to nullify the feedback if the two parties agree that the feedback was unwarranted, and the feedback rating will be expunged from your record. The comment will still appear in your member profile, but it will no longer count toward your feedback score.

You must initiate your application for Mutual Feedback Withdrawal within 30 days of either person leaving feedback or within 90 days of the transaction end date, whichever is later. To file for this service, click Community in the eBay navigation bar at the top-right of most pages. When the Community page opens, click the Feedback Forum link. On the Feedback Forum page, click the Feedback Disputes link. In the middle of the page that pops up, you can find the link for Mutual Feedback Withdrawal. Alternatively, you can save time by typing this URL into your browser:

```
feedback.ebay.ca/ws/eBayISAPI.dll?MFWRequest
```

Walking the Plank: Knowing the Deeds That Can Get You Suspended

Playing by eBay's rules keeps you off the Trust & Safety radar screen. If you start violating eBay policy, the company's going to keep a close eye on you. Depending on the infraction, eBay may be all over you like jelly on peanut butter. Or you may safely lurk in the fringes until your feedback rating is lower than the temperature in Whitehorse in January.

Here's a docket of eBay no-no's that can get members flogged and keel-hauled — or at least suspended:

- ✔ Feedback rating of –4
- ✔ Three instances of deadbeat bidding with three different sellers
- ✔ Repeated warnings for the same infraction

- Feedback extortion
- Bid shielding
- Unwelcome bidding after a warning from the seller
- Shill bidding
- Auction interception
- Fee avoidance
- Fraudulent selling
- Identity misrepresentation
- Bidding when younger than age 18
- Hacking
- Physical threats

If you get a suspension but think you're innocent, respond directly to the person who suspended you to plead your case. Reversals do occur. Don't broadcast your suspicions on chat boards. If you're wrong, you may regret it. Even if you're right, it's oh-so-gauche.

Be careful about accusing members of cheating. Unless you're involved in a transaction, you don't know all the facts. Perry Mason moments are great on television, but they're fictional for a reason. In real life, drawing yourself into a possible confrontation is senseless. Start the complaint process, keep it business-like, and let eBay's staff figure out what's going on.

Tossing a Lifesaver: Getting Buyer Protection

One thing's for sure in this world: Nothing's for sure. That's why insurance companies exist. Several types of insurance are available for eBay users:

- Insurance that buyers purchase to cover shipping (see Chapter 12)
- PayPal's Buyer Protection
- eBay Motors Vehicle Protection Program
- SquareTrade warranties

PayPal Buyer Protection

Aside from safety, PayPal now offers an even better reason to pay for your eBay purchases by using its service. If you've purchased your item through a PayPal-verified seller, your purchase is covered for up to $2,000. This protection covers you only for non-delivery of tangible items and tangible items that you receive "significantly not as described" — not if you're simply disappointed with the item.

If you pay with a credit card through PayPal, be sure to make your claim with them. Don't make a claim with your credit card company. PayPal Buyer Protection is for PayPal purchases, and you're not covered if you make a claim with your credit card company.

For the latest information on this program, go to `pages.ebay.ca/help/tp/paypal-protection.html`.

eBay Motors Vehicle Protection Program

eBay's Vehicle Protection Program offers a free limited warranty to anyone who purchases a car on eBay. Look for the Vehicle Protection Program Shield at the bottom of the seller's information box to see whether the vehicle you're interested in is covered. Qualified cars are identified in the listing description in the Item Specifics box with the words `Vehicle Protection Program up to C$25,000` or `US$20,000` (depending on the listing currency).

Your vehicle purchase is protected for up to C$25,000 or the vehicle purchase price, whichever is lower. You can find more information at the eBay Motors Passenger Vehicle Purchase Protection page:

```
pages.ebay.ca/ebaymotors/help/education/buying/
            purchase-protection.html
```

Launching a Fraud Report

If you're ready to complain to eBay about a seller who's taken money but hasn't delivered the goods, you can choose from a variety of remedies. To begin the process of filing a Fraud Alert for misrepresented or non-delivered items prior to eBay's suggested 30-day waiting period, start by going to

```
pages.ebay.ca/help/confidence/programs-protection-on-ebay.
        html
```

Follow the links to determine your best course of action. Click the appropriate link in the Information for Buyers area to find out more about eBay's protection programs.

 To file a complaint with eBay, you must initiate the process no sooner than 10 days, and no later than 60 days, after the close of the listing. Be careful not to jump the gun and register a complaint too soon. We suggest waiting about two or three weeks before you register your complaint about an Item Not Received (an item lost in the mail can often take as long as 30 days or more to arrive — especially if it's shipped internationally); double-check first to make sure that your e-mail is working and that you have the correct contact information of the person with whom you're having difficulties. After all, neither eBay nor your ISP is infallible.

Even if your claim isn't worth a nickel after 90 days, you can still register a fraud report and help the investigation of a lousy, terrible, *allegedly* fraudulent eBay user. That's payment enough, ain't it?

After you register a complaint, eBay informs the other party that you're making a fraud claim. eBay contacts both parties by e-mail, and frequently will work with both buyer and seller to reach a resolution.

If you've clearly been ripped off, use the Item Not Received or Significantly Not as Described process to file a complaint. Just scroll to the bottom of any eBay page and click the Security Centre link to start the process.

 To file an Item Not Received or Significantly Not as Described complaint, go directly to the form at feedback.ebay.ca/ws/eBayISAPI.dll? InrCreateDispute.

 If the accusation you're registering is a clear violation, eBay gives you information on the kind of third-party assistance you can get to help resolve the problem. If eBay deems the problem a violation of the law, it reports the crime to the appropriate law-enforcement agency.

Getting the Real Deal? Authentication and Appraising

Despite eBay's attempts to keep the buying and selling community honest, some people just refuse to play nice. After the New York City Department of Consumer Affairs launched an investigation into counterfeit sports memorabilia sold on the Web site, errant eBay outlaws experienced some anxious moments. We can always hope they mend their ways, but at the same time, don't bet on it. Fortunately, eBay offers a proactive approach to preventing such occurrences from happening again.

Topmost among the countermeasures is easy member access to several services that can authenticate specific types of merchandise. The good news here is that you know what kind of item you're getting; the bad news is that, as does everything else in life, it costs you money.

Have a good working knowledge of what you're buying or selling. Before you bid, do some homework and get more information. And check the seller's or bidder's feedback. (Does this advice sound familiar?) See Chapter 5 and Chapter 9 for more information about conducting research.

Before you spend the money to have your item appraised and authenticated, ask yourself a few practical questions (regardless of whether you're buying or selling):

- ✔ **Is this item quality merchandise?** Am I selling/buying merchandise whose condition is subjective but important to its value — meaning, is it really well loved or just busted? Is this item graded by some professionally accepted standard that I need to know about?

- ✔ **Is this item the real thing?** Am I sure that I'm selling/buying a genuine item? Do I need an expert to tell me whether it's the real McCoy?

- ✔ **Do I know the value of the merchandise?** Do I have a good understanding of what this item's worth in the marketplace at this time, considering its condition?

- ✔ **Is the merchandise worth the price?** Is the risk of selling/buying a counterfeit, a fake, or an item I don't completely understand worth the cost of an appraisal?

If you answer "yes" to any of these questions, consider calling in a professional appraiser.

As for *selling* a counterfeit item — otherwise known as a knock-off, phoney, or five-finger-discount item — that's a no-brainer: No way. Don't do it.

If you need items appraised, consider using an appraisal agency. You can access several agencies by visiting `pages.ebay.ca/help/community/auth-overview.html`. eBay offers links to various appraising agencies that offer their services at a discount to eBay members:

- ✔ The **PCGS** (Professional Coin Grading Service) and **NGC** (Numismatic Guaranty Corporation) serve coin collectors. Visit `www.pcgs.com` and `www.ngccoin.com/ebay_ngcvalue.cfm`.

✔ **PSA/DNA** (a service of Professional Sports Authenticators) and **Online Authentics** authenticate your autographs. Both keep online databases of thousands of certified autographs for you to compare your purchases against. Their respective online addresses are www.psadna.com and www.onlineauthentics.com.

✔ **Global Authentication, Inc.** specializes in authenticating autographs and memorabilia from the sports world. See gacard.net/ebay/authmain.asp.

✔ **PSE** (Professional Stamp Experts) authenticates your postal stamps: www.psestamp.com.

✔ **CGC** (Comics Guaranty) grades and restores comic books. Visit www.cgccomics.com/ebay_comic_book_grading.cfm.

✔ **IGI** (International Gemmological Institute) grades, authenticates, and identifies loose gemstones and jewellery. Visit www.e-igi.com/ebay.

✔ **PSA** (Professional Sports Authenticators) and **SGC** (Sportscard Guaranty) help guard against counterfeiting and fraud with sports memorabilia and trading cards. eBay has teamed up with these services to grade and authenticate trading cards. You can visit the respective addresses of these agencies at www.psacard.com and www.sgccard.com/ebay.

Even if you use an appraiser or an authentication service, do some legwork yourself. Often, two experts can come up with wildly different opinions on the same item. The more you know, the better the questions you can ask.

If a seller isn't sure whether the item he or she is auctioning is authentic, you may find an appropriate comment (such as Can't verify authenticity) in the item description. Knowledgeable eBay gurus always like to share what they know, and we have no doubt that someone on the appropriate chat board may be able to supply you with scads of helpful information. But be careful — some blarney artist (one of *those* is born every minute, too) may try to make a sucker out of you.

You should consider all of eBay's current and future programs for protecting you from problematic transactions and people, but we think the undisputed heavyweight champ for finding out if someone is legit (and keeping you out of trouble) is the first program eBay created. That's right, folks, *feedback* can show you other eBay members' track records and give you the best information on whether you want to do business with them or take a pass. Feedback is especially effective if you analyze it in conjunction with eBay's other protection programs. We suggest taking the time to read all about feedback in Chapter 4.

If It's Clearly Fraud

After filing a fraud report, you can do more on your own. If the deal looks as though it's beyond salvaging — if you sent a cheque or money order payment and got nothing in return, or the seller sends you merchandise that's completely wrong and refuses to make good — you can file a fraud complaint with other agencies that will take up your fight.

If you mailed your payment and the seller is in the United States, you can file a fraud complaint through the United States Postal Service by visiting www.usps.com/postalinspectors/fraud and clicking the Mail Fraud Complain Form link near the bottom of the page. You're taken to a page that contains a form you can fill out. After you complete the form and click Submit, the USPS sends the eBay bad guy a notice that you've filed a fraud complaint. Perhaps that'll get his or her attention.

If you're interested in finding out about the U.S. mail-fraud laws, go to the following Web site:

www.usps.com/websites/depart/inspect/usc18

Although Canada Post doesn't deal as aggressively with fraudsters as the USPS, you can turn to some other agencies for help:

- **Law enforcement agencies:** Contact the seller's local police department within Canada, the district attorney, or the state Attorney General's office. Also contact the local and state Consumer Affairs Department if the seller is in the United States. (Look online for contact information.)

- **Reporting Economic Crime On-Line (RECOL):** An initiative administered by the RCMP, contact these folks if you're convinced that you're a victim of fraud. You can report the fraudster by calling 888-495-8501 or by visiting www.recol.ca.

- **Internet service provider:** Contact the member's ISP. You can get this bit of info from the person's e-mail address, just after the @ symbol. (See? This easy access to information does have its advantages.) Let the ISP know whom you've filed a complaint against, the nature of the problem, and the agencies that you've contacted.

A great Canadian Web site exists to further help you in your quest for justice. The Cyber Criminals Most Wanted site is packed with links to law enforcement and reporting agencies. They'll even assist you in determining the most suitable agency to file a report with. You can find their list of links at www.ccmostwanted.com/report/report2.htm.

Any time you contact another agency for help, keep eBay's Trust & Safety up to date on your progress by writing to its representatives the old-fashioned way. Address your letter to eBay, ATTN: Fraud Prevention, 2145 Hamilton Ave., San Jose, CA 95125.

A very thin line separates alerting other members to a particular person's poor behaviour and breaking an eBay cardinal rule by interfering with an auction. Don't make unfounded and/or vitriolic accusations — especially if you're counting on those accusations never getting back to the person they're about (or, for that matter, if you hoped they wouldn't). Trample the poison out of the gripes of wrath before you have your say. We recommend that you hunt for facts, but don't do any finger pointing on public message boards or chat rooms. If it turns out that you're wrong, you can be sued for libel.

Communication and compromise are the keys to successful transactions. If you have a difference of opinion, write a polite e-mail outlining your expectations and offering to settle any dispute by phone. See Chapter 12 and Chapter 13 for tips on communicating after the auction ends — and solving disputes *before* they turn wicked, aggressive, or unprintable.

Chapter 17

The eBay Community: Joining In with Other eBay Members

*e*Bay is more than just an Internet location for buying and selling great stuff. eBay wants the world to know that it has created (and works hard to maintain) a community. It's not a bad deal — prime real estate in *this* community costs only pennies! As in real-life communities, you can participate as much as works for you. You can get involved in all sorts of neighbourhood activities, or you can just sit back, mind your own business, and watch the world go by. eBay works exactly the same way.

As you've probably heard by now, one of the main ways to participate in the eBay community is through feedback (which we explain in detail in Chapter 4 and Chapter 6). In this chapter, we show you some other ways to become part of the community. You can socialize (making friends who live in your community or who live across the planet), get useful info from other members, post messages, or just read what everybody's talking about on eBay's discussion boards, groups, chat boards, and the corporate Announcements Board. We include tips on how to use all these places to your benefit, and then we give you a change of scenery by surfing through some off-site message boards that can help you with your buying and selling.

On eBay's navigation bar, the clickable Community link connects you to the happenings on eBay; we use it regularly to check on proposed changes to the site, which are listed on the General Announcements page. But you can find a whole lot more in the Community area of eBay. Take a little time to explore it for yourself.

News and Chat, This and That

It's not quite like *The New York Times* ("All the News That's Fit to Print"), but you can find all the links to news, chat boards, groups, and discussion boards on the Community overview page. Figure 17-1 shows you what the page looks like.

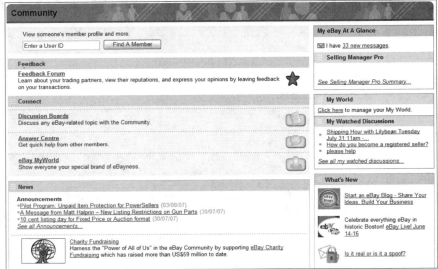

Figure 17-1: Part of the main Community page features links to many informative places on eBay, including areas to chat and post messages.

Here's a list of all the main headings on the Community page. Each heading offers you links to the following specific eBay areas:

- ✔ **Feedback:** Find a handy link to the Feedback Forum. (More on feedback in Chapter 4 and Chapter 6.)

- ✔ **Connect:** Click the links in this section to be whisked to eBay's discussion boards, the Answer Centre, or eBay MyWorld.

- ✔ **News:** This area contains links to the Announcements page, which covers general news, policy changes, technology updates, system announcements, and more. You can also find links to Charity Fundraising, Kijiji.ca (eBay's free local want ads), The Chatter (eBay's community newspaper), and Meet the Community (stories about how eBay has affected the lives of normal Canadians).

- ✔ **Education:** Under this heading, you can find important links for eBay Explained, the Help Centre, and the Workshop Calendar.

- ✔ **Marketplace Safety:** This link provides a handy shortcut to the Security & Resolution Centre.

✔ **More Community Programs:** Links here can teleport you to pages for Charity Fundraising, the Education Specialist program, Create an About Me Page, Participate in the eBay Developers Community, and Send in Your Suggestions.

Hear Ye, Hear Ye! eBay's Announcements Boards

If you were living in the 1700s, you'd see a strangely dressed guy in a funny hat ringing a bell and yelling, "Hear ye, hear ye!" every time you opened eBay's announcements boards. (Then again, if you were living in the 1700s, you'd have no electricity, computers, fast food, or anything else you probably consider fun.) In any case, eBay's announcements boards are the most important place to find out what's going on (directly from the home office) on the Web site. And no one even needs to ring a bell.

You have your choice of two boards. First, the General Announcements Board, on which eBay lists any new features and policy changes. And second, the System Announcements Board. Visiting the General Announcements Board is like reading your morning eBay newspaper because eBay adds comments to this page almost every day. You can find out about upcoming changes in categories, new promotions, and eBay goings-on. eBay also uses it to help users become aware of critical changes in policies and procedures. Reach this page at `www2.ebay.com/aw/marketing-ca.shtml`. Figure 17-2 shows you eBay's General Announcements Board, which contains information that could affect your sales.

eBay also tips you off to the system status (if you wonder whether a glitch is on your computer or on the eBay system). The System Announcements Board is available only on the eBay.com site at `www2.ebay.com/aw/announce.shtml` and is where eBay reports outages. eBay uses this board to update users on glitches in the system and when they hope to have those glitches rectified.

We suggest a weekly (at least) stop at the Announcements Boards as a standard part of your eBay routine.

eBay now has close to 230 million members — a bigger population than many countries — but it can still have that small-town feel through groups, chat boards, and discussion boards. Start by clicking Community on the navigation bar (at the top of most eBay pages). Then click any of the links that you want to. At the time of writing, you can access 17 different chat and help discussion boards on the Canadian eBay site. And if that isn't enough, head on over to the U.S. site (`pages.ebay.com/community/boards/index.html`), where you can find more than two dozen category-specific discussion boards, as well as a bunch of general chats, discussion boards, and help discussion boards.

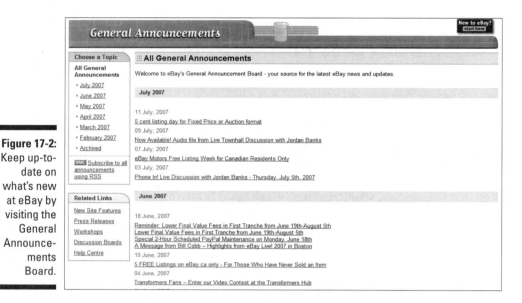

Figure 17-2:
Keep up-to-
date on
what's new
at eBay by
visiting the
General
Announce-
ments
Board.

Help! I Need Somebody

If you ever have specific eBay questions to which you need answers, several eBay discussion boards on the Community page, under the Connect heading, can help you. You can also go directly to the chat rooms to pose your question to the eBay members currently in residence.

Boards work differently than chat rooms. Chat rooms are full of people who are hanging out talking to each other all at the same time, whereas users of discussion boards tend to go in, leave a message or ask a question, and pop out again. Also, in a discussion board, you need to start a thread by asking a question. Title your thread with your question, and you'll no doubt get a swift answer to your query. Take a look at the eBay Stores Discussion Board in Figure 17-3.

You can answer many questions by going to eBay's Answer Centre, which you can get to by clicking the Answer Centre link in the Connect area of the Community page. The Answer Centre page that appears has boards covering almost any topic regarding selling and buying on eBay. Just post your question, and hopefully some kind eBay member will suggest an answer (but remember to take that advice with a grain of salt, just as you would any advice from someone with unknown credentials).

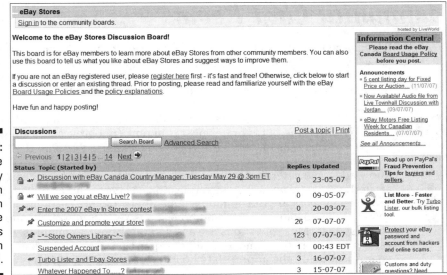

eBay newbies often find that the boards are good places to add to their knowledge of eBay. As you scroll on by, read the Q & A postings from the past; your question may already be answered in an earlier posting. You can even ask someone on this board to look at your auction listing and provide an opinion on your descriptions or pictures.

Rating the member chat rooms and boards

You know you need help, but you don't know which area is best for you. Here's our take on which boards are most helpful:

✔ **User to User Help:** This discussion board is a catchall for many subjects. If you don't see a board specific to your question (or if you post to another board and get no reply), try this one — it's always hopping with a lot of peeps.

✔ **Selling on eBay:** Good help from other eBay members for those with specific questions about eBay's selling policies, selling tools,

and listing preparation. This board can be a great resource for new sellers or users thinking of starting to sell on the site.

✔ **Buying and Bidding:** This board is for eBay members who want to find out more about bidding and buying from other community members and get the occasional answer from eBay staff.

You can access a new board from any other board by scrolling down the links list at the top of each board page.

Community Chat Rooms

Because sending e-mail to eBay's Customer Service people can be frustratingly slow if you need an answer right away (they get bombarded with a gazillion questions a day), you may want to try for a faster answer by posting your question on one of the Community discussion boards.

You can always tell if an eBay staff member is replying on a board because the top border line of his or her post is in pink (not grey, as with regular users). For this reason, they've earned the nickname Pinks on the boards.

Knowledgeable veteran eBay members or Customer Service Pinks (if they're around) generally answer posted questions as best (and as quickly) as they can. The answers are the opinions of members and are certainly not eBay gospel. But you can get a fast and honest answer; often, you get more than one response. Most questions are answered in about 15 minutes. If you don't get a response in that time, repost your question. Make sure that you post your question on the appropriate board because each board has a specific topic of discussion.

If a new policy or some sort of big change occurs, the boards are most likely going to quickly fill with discussion about it. On slow days, however, you may need to wade through endless personal messages and chat that has no connection to eBay. Many of the people who post on these boards are long-time members with histories (as well as feuds) that can rival any soap opera. On a rare occasion, the personal postings can get rather nasty. Getting involved in personality clashes or verbal warfare gains nothing and wastes your valuable time.

One cardinal rule for eBay chat boards and message boards exists: no business. No advertising items for sale! Not now. Not ever. eBay bans any repeat offenders who break this rule from participating on these boards.

Remember that you're visiting eBay and that you're a member. It's not Speakers' Corner — no cameras are set up to capture your vents and replay them on television later that week. If you feel the need to viciously complain about eBay, take it outside, as the bar bouncers say.

User-to-User Discussion Boards

eBay has some other boards that take a different tack on things. They're *discussion* boards, as opposed to *chat* boards, which basically means that the topics are deliberately open ended — just like the topics of discussions in coffee houses tend to vary depending on who happens to be in them at any given time. Check out these areas and read ongoing discussions about eBay's latest buzz. It's a lot of fun and good reading. Post your opinions to the category that suits you. You can find a lot of discussion boards on various topics relating to doing business on eBay, but many chatters seem to favour the General Discussion area. Each discussion board carries as many topics as you can imagine. Here are few of our favourites:

- ✔ **Canada Town Square:** Largely a social gathering with a potpourri of various subjects and topics.
- ✔ **Hockey Board:** The place to voice your views about your favourite team and discuss all things related to Canada's game.
- ✔ **Collector's Board:** Where Canadian users can discuss everything collectible. Whether it's a Spiderman #1 comic, a rare World War II Canadian helmet, your prized plate collection, or a rare stamp you finally found to complete your collection, this is the place to talk about it.
- ✔ **Crafts & Hobbies:** Share your views and suggestions about the Crafts & Hobbies category here. Whether you enjoy scrapbooking or crocheting, you're sure to find someone who shares your interests.
- ✔ **Canadian Motors Speedway:** Where Canadian eBay auto buffs hang out. Thinking of buying or selling on eBay Motors? This is the spot to get some great advice.

Other Chat Rooms (Message Boards)

Over on the U.S. eBay site, about a dozen chat rooms specialize in everything from pure chat to charity work. Even if the crowd on these boards is largely American, they're still friendly and helpful. To access the U.S. chat rooms, go to www.ebay.com and log in as you normally would. From your My eBay page, click the Community link in the top-left corner, and then click the Chat Rooms link. The following sections describe a few of these boards.

Café society

The eBay Café (eBay's first message board from back when they were just selling Pez candy dispensers) and AOL Café message boards attract mostly regulars chatting about eBay gossip. Frequent postings include the sharing of personal milestones and whatever else is on people's minds. You can also find useful information about eBay and warnings about potential scams here.

Holiday Board

Although eBay suggests that this is the place to share your favourite holiday memories and thoughts, it's really a friendly place where people meet and chat about home and family. Stop by for cybermilk and cookies the next time you have a few minutes and want to visit with your fellow auction addicts.

Giving Board

eBay isn't only about making money. On the Giving Board, it's also about making a difference. Members in need post their stories and requests for assistance. Other members with items to donate post offers for everything from school supplies to clothing on this board.

For information on how to participate, visit the Giving Board at `chatboards.ebay.com/chat.jsp?forum=1&thread=59`. If you feel like doing a good deed and want to conduct a member benefit auction, click the eBay Giving Works link on the Discussion Board page. For more on charity auctions, see Chapter 18.

Emergency Contact Board

This board doesn't have any sirens or flashing lights, but if your computer crashes and you lose all your info, this board is the place to put out an all-points bulletin for help. If your ISP goes on vacation, your Internet access is on the fritz, or you're abducted by aliens and can't connect to your buyers or sellers, use a friend's computer to post a message on the Emergency Contact Board. A dedicated group of eBay users frequent this board; they'll try to help you by passing on your e-mails to the intended parties. Talk about a bunch of *givers!*

The Emergency Contact Board can really be a tremendous help. A few years ago, we recall a posting from a bidder saying that her computer had crashed *and* that she was in the process of moving. She asked her sellers to be patient and told them she'd get to them as soon as possible. The friendly regulars of the Emergency Contact Board looked up her bidding history and e-mailed the sellers whose auctions she'd won in the previous week. Then they forwarded her the e-mails they'd sent on her behalf. The sellers understood the situation and didn't leave negative feedback for the user because of lack of communication. Talk about community.

If you're having trouble contacting another eBay member, posting for help from other members to track 'em down often gets the job done.

If you think you may be the victim of a rip-off, check the Emergency Contact Board. The buyer or seller may have left word about an e-mail problem. On the flip side, you may find out that you're not alone in trying to track down an eBay delinquent who seems to have skipped town. Posting information about a *potentially* bad eBay guy is (at the least) bad manners on most boards. If you wrap it in the guise of an emergency contact, however, you can clue in other members about a potential problem. Stick to the facts and make the post as honest and useful as you can.

To access the Emergency Contact Board, follow these steps:

1. **On the eBay.com site, click the Community link on the eBay navigation bar.**

   The main Community page appears.

2. **Click the Chat Rooms link in the Connect area.**

   The main Chat page appears.

3. **In the General Chat link area, click Emergency Contact.**

   A message board appears, filled with messages from all the desperate sellers and buyers trying to locate each other.

The eBay Friends From All Over Discussion Board

People from all around the world enjoy eBay. If you're considering buying or selling globally, visit the eBay Friends From All Over Board. It's a great place to post questions about shipping and payments for international transactions. Along with eBay chat, this board turns up discussions about current events and international politics.

Got a seller or bidder in Italy? Spain? France? Translate your English messages into the appropriate language through the following Web site:

```
babelfish.altavista.digital.com
```

Category-Specific Chat Boards

Want to talk about Elvis, Louis XV, Sammy Sosa, or Howard the Duck? Over on the eBay.com site, over 25 category-specific chat boards enable you to tell eBay members what's on your mind about merchandise and auctions. You can reach these boards by clicking Community on the main navigation bar and then clicking Chat Rooms in the Connect area. The Category-Specific Chat Rooms list appears on the right of the main Chat Rooms page.

Of course, you can buy and sell without ever going on a chat board, but you can certainly figure out a lot from looking one over. Discussions mainly focus on merchandise, and the nuts and bolts of transactions. In category-specific chat boards, you can post questions about items that you don't know much about.

At eBay, you get all kinds of responses from all kinds of people. Take some of the help you get with a grain of salt because some of the folks who help you may be buyers or competitors.

Don't be shy. As your second-grade teacher said, "No questions are dumb." Most eBay members love to share their knowledge of items.

eBay Groups

If you're the friendly type and want an instant group of new friends, we suggest that you go to the eBay.com site and click the Groups link in the Connect area. On the eBay Groups page, you can find thousands of user groups hosted on eBay — but run by eBay community members. These groups may consist of people from the same geographic area, those with similar hobbies, or those interested in buying or selling in particular categories.

eBay Groups may be public (open to all) or private clubs with their own private boards. Only invited members of the groups can access the private boards.

Joining a group is easy: Just click any of the Groups links near the bottom of the main eBay Groups page, and you're presented with a dizzying array of groups to join. Your best bet, though, is to participate in chats or discussions, and find other members that you want to join up with.

Blog It on eBay

A recent addition to the eBay Community page is the eBay Blogs area. Any eBay member can start his or her own online posting page, or *blog*. You can share your opinions and ideas with the entire Internet universe, directly from eBay. Reading other members' blogs can be a fun pastime; plus, you get to find out a little more about the faces behind the User IDs. Blogs don't replace the all-important About Me page, but you can have fun starting a blog, and all your friends can have fun reading it.

Blogs are a fun and friendly pastime. Keep in mind, we said a pastime. If your plan is to learn to sell on eBay, study this book and a lot of PowerSeller listings on the site. Go and list some test items instead of spending precious moments playing on your blog. But if time isn't of the essence, have some fun.

Chapter 18

Fun Stuff and Features

● ●

In This Chapter

▶ Bidding for a good cause

▶ Using eBay's membership features

▶ Calling free with Skype

● ●

*N*o one can say that eBay isn't fun! The eBay staff is always trying to work with the community by filling needs and finding fun stuff to keep us happy. In this chapter, we show you how eBay members can get great inside deals from manufacturers. We also show you how you can help your favourite charity earn some well-deserved cash at eBay's charity auctions.

Over and over, eBay members show what big hearts they have. Yes, you actually can pocket some nice-sized profits from selling at the eBay Web site, but (just as in real life) people usually take the time to give a little back for worthy causes. But because we're talking about eBay, giving back means getting something fabulous in return.

Truly Righteous Stuff for Charity

Most of us have donated to charity in one form or another. But here at eBay, charities really rock. Do you need a *Jurassic Park* helmet signed by Steven Spielberg to round out your collection (and deflect the odd dino tooth)? Post a bid on one of the charity auctions. How about a signed original photograph of Jerry Seinfeld from *People* magazine? Yup, you can get that, too. All these items and more have turned up in charity auctions. In short, having a big heart for charities has gotten a whole lot easier thanks to eBay. You can get to the Featured Canadian Charities page by going to `pages.ebay.ca/charity`.

eBay Charity Fundraising

November 2003 was a lucky time for charities. That's the month that eBay launched the eBay Giving Works Charity auction area on the U.S. site. Smartly, the folks at eBay teamed up with one of the finest charity sites on the Internet, MissionFish. MissionFish, a service of the Points of Light Foundation, has been around since early 2000 and has enabled charities to raise hundreds of thousands of dollars by turning in-kind donations into cash.

eBay Canada added its efforts shortly after the U.S. eBay site. In Canada, the program is called Charity Fundraising, and it's administered differently than in the United States. In Canada, charities interested in running auctions have to register with eBay, submitting proof of their status as a registered Canadian charity. After they're accepted to the program, eBay.ca allows them to run auctions on the site with all Insertion, Gallery, and Final Value Fees credited back.

Individuals are welcome to participate in raising funds for charitable causes, provided they receive written consent from the charity and include a copy of that consent in all listings. eBay doesn't refund fees to individuals raising funds for charitable causes.

You can find a current listing of eBay-accepted registered Canadian charitable organizations at `pages.ebay.ca/charity`. You can also get to this page by clicking the Charity Auctions link on the left side of the eBay home page.

When you visit different areas of eBay, you can recognize the U.S. charity auctions by the small blue ribbon icon that appears to the left of the listing's title in searches and the Category list. At this time, Canada does not employ use of the ribbon icon, but that may change as the program grows.

Creative charity auctions

New charities are popping up all the time at eBay. To see what auctions it's running, go to the Charity page. To get there, start at eBay's home page and click the Charity Auctions link on the left side of the screen. Here are some of the more creative charity auctions being held at eBay:

- ✔ CTV and the cast of Canadian Idol have joined forces with McDonald's Restaurants of Canada to raise funds for Ronald McDonald House. Items available include signed and game-worn sports memorabilia; unique Canadian Idol memorabilia; a meet-and-greet with the show host, Brian Mulroney; and a chance to attend Canada's favourite high school — Degrassi.

Auction for America

In mid-September of 2001, eBay took on one of its most ambitious attempts at fundraising: the Auction for America. In response to requests by New York Governor George E. Pataki and Mayor Rudolph Giuliani, eBay called on the community to raise $100 million in 100 days. eBay and Billpoint (eBay's payment service at the time) waived all fees, and community members gave their all, donating and buying all kinds of items benefiting the New York State World Trade Center Relief Fund, the Twin Towers Fund, the American Red Cross, and the September 11 Fund.

Community member Jay Leno sold his celebrity-autographed Harley Davidson for over $360,260; Tim Allen sold his 1956 Chevrolet Nomad for $46,000; and countless corporate sponsors joined in with the person-to-person community to raise funds. Over 100,000 sellers participated, and over 230,000 items were listed.

The auction ended on December 25, raising $10 million. This is an amazing tribute to the eBay members and their community spirit.

✔ The SickKids Foundation routinely runs auctions for everything from Toronto Raptors' and Leafs' tickets to kayaks to rare Disney collectibles, with 100 percent of the net proceeds going to this very worthy cause.

✔ The March of Dimes frequently runs auctions to benefit children and adults with physical disabilities. Recent items have included a kitchen-makeover package, hotel packages, and valuable artwork.

If you go to the About Me page of any of the charities on the Featured Canadian Charities page (by clicking the charity's link), you can find out exactly where the money that eBay users bid goes.

And Now for Our Feature Presentation

As an eBay member, you're entitled to some features offered on the Web site. The perks aren't quite as high-end as you may receive with, say, a country club membership, but hey, your non-existent membership dues are a lot less! With about 230 million confirmed registered users, eBay can get outside companies and manufacturers to listen to what it has to say. You know the old saying about power in numbers? At eBay, you find "savings in numbers" on items or services that you can buy outside the Web site.

The following sections explain some of the savings and other services you can find at eBay.

Member specials

As eBay gains popularity, more and more outside companies are offering special deals exclusively for members. These deals aren't auctions, they're conventional "pay the price and get the item or services" transactions.

Finding the member specials can be tricky. Our advice is to visit eBay's General Announcements Board frequently because most offers are posted there at some time or another. You can access the board directly at www2.ebay.com/aw/marketing-ca.shtml.

The special deals change all the time, but here's a small sampling of perks available to you as a member:

- ✔ **Shipping discounts:** Wow! It doesn't get much better than this. When was the last time Canada Post told you that they were going to discount postage for you? eBay.ca has been negotiating on a continuous basis to solicit discounts on behalf of Canadian eBay sellers. At the time of writing, Canada Post was offering a 25-percent discount on Xpresspost service within Canada and a 15-percent discount for Xpresspost service to the United States.

    And it doesn't stop there. Not to be outdone, UPS is offering flat-rate bargains to the United States that are far below their normal prices. You can find out more about current shipping discounts by visiting the eBay.ca Shipping Centre at pages.ebay.ca/help/sellerguide/shipping.

- ✔ **PayPal:** Occasionally, PayPal offers promotions that include discounts for purchases made on eBay and paid through PayPal. Normally, you need a redemption code that you have to supply when making your payment. Watch the PayPal and eBay Web sites for news about promotions and the necessary redemption codes.

- ✔ **Authentication services:** Get a special discount (usually 10 percent) if you authenticate coins through Professional Coin Grading Service (PCGS) or trading cards through Professional Sports Authenticator (PSA). See Chapter 16 for tips on authenticating your items.

As time passes, you can see additional benefits and programs that eBay creates for the community. The folks at eBay are aggressively searching out new and helpful affiliations to help you take care of your auction business. But don't leave the task of maintaining your listings entirely to eBay — take it upon yourself to find new ways to make your listings easier to manage.

A successful seller takes advantage of every program and service he or she can. The less time you spend tied to your computer, the more time you have to plan new auctions and find new items to sell. Investigate these programs and try them out for yourself.

eBay's Favourite Searches e-mail service

If you're too busy to explore the nooks and crannies of eBay on a daily basis (or you're the type who wants to cut to the chase), sign up for eBay's personal shopper through your My eBay Favourite Searches.

This service is one of eBay's better ideas. It enables you to find what you're looking for and still have a life because it sifts through the new listings for you 24 hours a day, looking for the items that meet your personalized description. eBay sniffs 'em out like a bloodhound. Then eBay sends you an e-mail containing a list of items that you may want to bid on, complete with links that take you right to those items. Hey, best of all, the service is free!

To register for the personal shopper e-mail service, follow these steps:

1. **Type keywords into the Search box on the top of any eBay page, then click Search.**

   The results of your search appear.

2. **Click the Save This Search link that appears above the results.**

   A dialog box pops up asking you to name the search and to select a time frame to continue searching.

3. **Make sure the check box to the left of Email Me Daily When New Items Match My Search For area is checked, then select a time period (from 7 days to 12 months) during which you want to receive e-mails about newly listed items.**

4. **(Optional) Click the Show link to the right of More Options.**

   The dialogue box expands to reveal more options. You can further refine your search parameters.

5. **Click the Save button.**

6. **The search is now added to your My eBay Favourite Searches page.**

   Go to that page to see a list of your current searches.

   You can save up to 100 searches, about which you'll receive e-mail notifications. Yikes, don't do 100! All you'll get is e-mail after e-mail from eBay!

The new search appears in your Favourite Searches page. Clicking the search on that page immediately sends eBay looking for your keywords.

Getting Free Calls over the Internet with Skype

eBay has purchased an Internet-based communication service called Skype (pronounced *sky-yp*). You can bet that in the near future, eBay will be integrating the Skype technology with its other services. (Imagine the possibilities!) You need to have a broadband Internet connection to use Skype, but after you have that, you can call other Skype users long distance for free.

Skype is controlled by software that you download to your computer. It allows you to communicate with the rest of the world at no additional cost (over the expense of your high-speed Internet connection). To download the software for PC, Mac, or Linux, just go to www.skype.com and click the Download Skype link.

eBay has now incorporated Skype into auction listings. We're not sure that it will replace the Ask the Seller a Question feature, but it certainly raises possibilities. Sellers offering big-ticket items can certainly offer Skype as a way to inexpensively and quickly satisfy questions from potential bidders. Figure 18-1 shows the options that bidders now have to communicate with sellers.

Figure 18-1:
Click the Skype Chat link as another way to contact the seller with your questions.

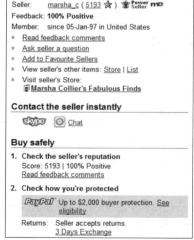

Meet the seller

Seller: marsha_c (5193 ☆) ⚡Power Seller me
Feedback: **100% Positive**
Member: since 05-Jan-97 in United States
- Read feedback comments
- Ask seller a question
- Add to Favourite Sellers
- View seller's other items: Store | List
- Visit seller's Store:
  📕 Marsha Collier's Fabulous Finds

Contact the seller instantly

skype ◎ Chat

Buy safely

1. **Check the seller's reputation**
   Score: 5193 | 100% Positive
   Read feedback comments

2. **Check how you're protected**
   PayPal Up to $2,000 buyer protection. See eligibility
   Returns: Seller accepts returns.
   3 Days Exchange

After you download the software, you can install the program with a click of your mouse. Skype allows you to use your computer (along with a microphone and your regular computer speakers) as a telephone. You can contact anyone who's a member of Skype at no charge — wherever in the world they reside or do business. (You can call regular phone numbers for a low, discounted per-minute fee.) All Skype-to-Skype calls are free. As wonderful (and simple) as that is, Skype has other revolutionary features that can really expand your business:

- ✔ **SkypeIn:** This is a great feature. With SkypeIn, you can purchase a special phone number for US$60 a year for your Skype computer so that people not set up with Skype can contact you on your Skype account. If you live in Edmonton but do a lot of business in, say, Halifax, you can get a local number in Halifax so your Halifax customers have to make only a local call (without incurring long-distance charges) to reach you. Unfortunately, SkypeIn doesn't do anything about the time difference, so you may still get calls from your Maritime customers in the very early morning if you live in Vancouver. But this feature does make your business look pretty big time — you have a remote office across the country! You can get up to ten different SkypeIn numbers.

- ✔ **Skype Voicemail:** If you're not at your computer when another user attempts to call you, your account can receive and store voice mail. Skype Voicemail is free when you purchase a SkypeIn telephone number. If you purchase it separately, the annual cost is US$20.

- ✔ **SkypeOut:** You can make unlimited calls to any number in Canada and the United States (mobile or land line) for just US$3 per month. Skype also has very reasonable charges for calls made to foreign countries through SkypeOut. For example, here are some per-minute charges: Belgium is US$.021, Japan is US$.023, and Australia is US$.021. For a complete and up-to-date listing of international per-minute rates, go to `www.skype.com/products/skypeout`. To make international calls, you are required to purchase Skype Credit in US$10 denominations, and your international calls are deducted from your balance. Skype requires that you make at least one call every six months to maintain your credit balance.

Marsha recently got a Skype DUALphone. The DUALphone carries her office land line as well as her Skype line wirelessly to anywhere she carries the phone. It plugs into her computer with a USB connection to pick up her Skype calls, and a phone line wire plugs into the wall jack to access the land line. It also uses a new technology that expands the strength and range of the wireless phone. See Figure 18-2 to get a glimpse at her contacts.

Marsha's home was built after the Northridge, California, earthquake, and it has a good deal of steel in the structure to prevent it from collapsing. This structural element had precluded her using a wireless phone from one end of the house to the other — until she got the DUALphone. Now, she can access Skype and get free long distance from anywhere in her home or office. (For more information, check the Web site at www.dualphone.net.)

Skype is adding interesting features all the time. The PC version of the software even allows for free video calls on your computer (assuming you have a Web cam or other camera PC set up). You can also add a Skype button to your e-mails, allowing your contacts to just click to call you.

Figure 18-2:
Skype
becomes
part of your
desktop.

Part V
The Part of Tens

The 5th Wave   By Rich Tennant

"Come on Walt — we need a shot of the product to bring in more bids."

In this part . . .

In keeping with a longstanding (yawn) tradition, this part gives you the short version of the facts, somewhat like downloadable class notes. Check here for the golden rules every eBay user needs to know, whether you buy or sell (or, like most eBay members, do both).

In this part, you can also get information on a few of the software programs available to help simplify your auction experience — from creating a catchy auction item page to helping you snipe the final bid while you're sleeping, walking Fido, washing your hair, or otherwise occupied. The best thing about some of these programs is that the price is right — you can get started for free.

Following the Part of Tens, you get an appendix. The Appendix gives you eBay fanatics exactly what you've been looking for — tips to help you acquire stock and take your auction habit to the next level by thinking strategically.

Chapter 19

Ten (Or So) Golden Rules for eBay Buyers and Sellers

*N*o matter how much experience an airplane pilot may have, he or she always keeps a checklist to go over. The same is true at eBay (although the only crashing that you need to worry about is on your computer). No matter how many times you buy, the advice in this chapter can help you survive and thrive at eBay.

Although conducting business at eBay is relatively smooth overall, any venture is bound to have a few bumps here and there. A certain etiquette goes along with everything we do in life. If you follow these simple rules, your time on the site will be a whole lot more pleasant for everyone. That said, here are ten (or so) easy, important golden rules for eBay. We note which tips are geared toward buyers or sellers. Happy hunting and gathering!

After a while, posting auctions and bidding become rote. You can all too easily forget the basics, so look at this chapter every now and again, and remember that, as an eBay member, you're part of a very special person-to-person community.

Buyer: Investigate Your Treasure before You Buy

In the excitement of finding just what you want, you may develop a tendency to leap before you look. Even if the item is closing soon, carefully read the item description. Does the item have any flaws? Can you live with those flaws? Is something missing from the description that should be there? Did you read the terms of payment and shipping?

You can also communicate with the seller of the item that you're longing for. Don't be too shy or embarrassed. If you have any questions, send an e-mail! You're better off covering your bases before you place a bid than facing disappointment after making a purchase. Remember that when you click the bid or buy button, you are *legally and morally obligated* to go through with the transaction if you win. Make sure that everything is as you want it and check for a warranty or return policy. Clarify everything upfront. If the seller doesn't answer back, consider that non-response an early warning that dealing with this person may be a mistake!

Buyer: Check the Seller's Feedback

Never bid without checking the seller's feedback. You need to be able to trust the person you're buying from. Don't just evaluate the Feedback percentage: Investigate the seller's feedback by clicking the number to the right of his or her User ID. Be sure to read the comments left by other users Also, check the feedback left by the seller for his or her customers to get an idea of how the seller responds to the occasional difficulty that may arise with their transactions. Checking some of the seller's other listings, past and present, to get an idea of the seller's history also can't hurt. As badly as you may want something, sending a payment to someone with a high feedback rating but who recently got a bunch of negatives could be risky business.

Buyer: Understand Post-Auction Charges and Payment Methods

Before you bid on an item, make sure that you and the seller have similar ideas on the shipping and handling, insurance, and escrow fees (if applicable — see Chapter 6). Buying a $10 item and finding out that shipping and handling are going to cost more than your winning bid is a real bummer. Don't forget to ask about any handling charges.

Also, make sure that you and the seller can agree on the form of payment before the deal closes. While most international sellers will not consider a personal cheque because of extensive delays in bank clearing, if the seller is in Canada, is he or she willing to accept a cheque as payment? Are you willing to wait to receive your purchase until a cheque clears? Does the seller accept credit card payments? Is the seller using a secure method of accepting credit cards, such as PayPal?

Buyer: Check the Item Price Tag and Bid Wisely

Before you bid, make sure that you have some knowledge of the item, even if you limit your search to completed auctions to get an idea of how much the item went for in the past.

If a deal sounds too good to be true, it may well be.

We love eBay — but not for every single thing that we buy. Make sure that you can't get the item cheaper at the store or from another online seller.

Beware of getting caught up in the frenzy of last-minute bidding: It's an easy thing to do. Whether you choose proxy bidding or sniping (see Chapter 7 for our discussion on sniping), decide how much you're willing to pay before bidding. If you set a limit, you aren't overcome with the urge to spend more than an item is worth — or, worse, more than you have in your bank account.

Although eBay is a lot of fun, it's also serious business. Bidding is a legal and binding contract. Don't get a bad reputation by retracting bids or becoming a deadbeat.

Buyer: Be a Good Buyer Bee

Always leave feedback after you put the finishing touches on a transaction. Leaving feedback about how a seller performs, and thereby helping other members, is your responsibility. Remember your manners, too, when sending off your payment. You like to be paid on time, right? And, speaking practically, the sooner you send in the dough, the sooner you get your stuff.

Keep in mind that the transaction isn't complete until the buyer receives the merchandise and is happy with the purchase. Don't automatically expect positive feedback because you paid for your item in a timely manner.

Buyer: Cover Your Assets

Just because you're conducting transactions from the privacy of your home doesn't mean that you're doing everything you can to protect your privacy. Legitimate buyers and sellers *never* need to know your eBay password or Social Insurance Number. Don't respond to this sort of e-mail. See Chapter 15 to find out how to handle these kinds of e-mails.

Seller: Know Your Stuff

Do some homework. Know the value of your item. At the very least, get an idea of your item's value by searching completed listings for similar items. If it's a new item, check out other online sites and see what your item is selling for by running a Google product search at www.google.com/products. Knowing your product also means that you can accurately describe what you have and will never, ever pass off a fake as the real McCoy. Make sure that your item isn't prohibited, illegal, questionable, or infringing. It's your responsibility!

Before posting your listing, you should take the following actions:

- ✔ Establish what kinds of payment you're willing to accept.
- ✔ Set your cheque-holding policy (usually seven to ten business days).
- ✔ Spell out your shipping and handling charges.

Add each of the preceding pieces of info to your item's description to avoid any unnecessary disputes later.

Seller: Polish and Shine

Make sure that your title is descriptive enough to catch the eye of someone browsing a category and detailed enough for eBay's search engine to identify. Don't just write 1960s Board Game. Instead, give some details: Tiny Tim Vintage '60s Board Game MIB. That gets 'em tiptoeing to your auction.

Play editor and scrutinize your text for grammar mistakes and misspellings. Typos in either your title or description can cost you money. For example, a search engine will keep skipping over your Mikky Mouce Cokie Jare. Spelling counts — and pays. Double-check your work!

Seller: Picture-Perfect Facts

Photos can be a boon or a bust at eBay. Double-check the photo of your item before you post it. Is the lighting okay? Does the photo paint a flattering image of the item? Crop out unnecessary backgrounds. Would *you* buy this item?

Take your picture as if you didn't have a description; be sure it totally illustrates the item. Also, write your description as if you didn't have a photo. With a thorough written description, if the photo server crashes, the prospective buyer will still have a good idea of what you're selling.

Be factual and honest. At eBay, all you have is your reputation, so don't jeopardize it by lying about your item or terms. Tell potential buyers about any flaws. Give as complete a description as possible, with all the facts about the item that you can include.

Seller: Communication Is Key

Respond quickly and honestly to all questions sent via the My eBay My Messages page, and use the contact to establish a good relationship. Don't let more than 24 hours pass without sending a response. If a bidder makes a reasonable request about payment or shipping, going along with that request is usually worth it to make a sale. *Note:* The customer is always right! (Well, some of the time, anyway.)

Be upfront and fair when charging for sending merchandise to your buyer. You don't make a fortune overcharging for shipping and handling. (Besides, charging outrageous handling fees is a violation of eBay's policies and could get you suspended from the site.) After the item arrives, the buyer may realize what it costs to ship. Unreasonable charges inevitably lead to bad feelings and negative feedback.

Seller: Be a Buyer's Dream

Just because you're transacting through the computer doesn't mean that you can forget your manners. Live by the golden rule: Do unto others as you would have others do unto you. Contact the buyer within three business days — within 24 hours is even better. (Better yet, why not ship the item that quickly? We do.) And keep all your correspondence polite.

Ship the goods as soon as you can (in accordance with the shipping terms you outline in the item description, of course). An e-mail stating that the item is on its way is always a nice touch, too. That way, buyers can eagerly anticipate the arrival of their goods.

And, when shipping your items, use quality packing materials and sturdy boxes to prevent disaster. Broken or damaged items can lead to reputation-damaging negative feedback. Pack as if someone's out to destroy your package (or as if *you* had made this purchase). Your buyers are sure to appreciate the effort.

Seller: Listen to the Music

As we state in the golden rules for buyers earlier in this chapter, don't under-estimate the power of positive feedback. Your reputation is at stake. Always generously dole out feedback when you complete a transaction. Your buyers will appreciate it and should return the favour. What should you do if you get slammed unfairly with negative feedback? Don't freak out! Don't retaliate. Do, however, post a response to the feedback by clicking the Respond to Feedback link on your My eBay page. Those who read your feedback can often see past a single disgruntled message.

Keep in mind that many negative feedback reports result from misunderstand-ings. Contact the buyer and see if you can work things out to your satisfaction. Then apply for a Mutual Feedback Removal to keep your eBay reputation pristine.

Buyers and Sellers: Keep Current, Keep Cool

You'd be surprised at the number of users who get suspended even though they have automatic credit card payment. Maybe they move. Or their e-mail address changes because they change Internet service providers. Regardless, if you don't update your contact and credit card information, and eBay and other users can't contact you as a result, you can be suspended.

If you make any major moves (home address, billing address, ISP provider), let eBay know this new contact information. As soon as you know your new credit card number, mailing address, e-mail address, or contact phone number, click My eBay on the main navigation bar, then click the Personal Information link on the left side of the page. On the Personal Information page that appears, update the appropriate information by using the Edit links to the right of the information eBay currently has about you.

Chapter 20

Ten (Or So) Programs and Services to Ease Your Way on eBay

*R*eady to take your auctions to the next level? Are you looking for cool text or fancy layouts to make your auctions scream out, "Buy me!"? Need to slip in a bid in the middle of the night without losing sleep? If so, here's a list of ten (or so) software programs and services to make your bidding life easier and help put your auctions ahead of the pack.

As online auctions grow in popularity, software developers are constantly upgrading and developing new auction software to meet eBay's changes. Many of these programs even look for new versions of themselves — and update themselves as you start them. (Aladdin never had things so good.)

You don't *have* to use any of these programs or services to run an eBay auction successfully. But when you're running more than several auctions a week, the addition of a helper makes things go ever so much smoother.

A massive amount of companies out there are offering online management service and offline programs. We can't cover them all, so the software that we mention in this chapter has been tried and tested by one or both of us at some time or another. You may know of others, and we'd love to hear about them. We do know that the pieces of software in this chapter work, and they're good tools if you choose to expand your eBay sales.

This chapter talks about several auction-management Web sites. Each site has its own distinct personality. We also provide the names of some terrific offline software programs that you can use to help manage your auctions, make your e-auctions elegant and eye-catching, find the best prices, and snatch up that bargain at the last minute.

Be sure to check Marsha's Web site, www.coolebaytools.com, for updates on software and services, as well as special discounts that are offered to her site's visitors.

Online Services

You're comfortable transacting your auctions online, so why not manage them online, as well? These sites offer incredibly useful services that save time in both posting your auctions and wrapping them up. Unfortunately, many of the sites available are developed in the United States and are designed for use with the U.S. eBay site. For most Canadian sellers, this isn't a problem because they recognize the importance of selling in U.S. currency and the market share the U.S. represents. Selling on eBay.com represents a very little obstacle for most Canadian sellers.

Auctiva

If you're new on eBay and want to try a little automation to get yourself started, Auctiva is your entry-level choice. First, let us tell you our favourite thing about Auctiva: It's free. That's right, *free* (our favourite four-letter word). Now, we always say you get what you pay for, but with Auctiva, you get a bit more than that.

The service is run on Class A servers, just like the big guys. So you don't have to worry about a lot of downtime for your images.

Auctiva has been serving eBay sellers since Marsha published her first edition of *eBay For Dummies* in 1999. Auctiva gives small merchants the power of large companies by helping them build their brands, merchandise their products, and sell efficiently through eBay. This is the only completely free and simple solution for eBay sellers — and it continues to improve its site.

Auctiva offers online auction management software and image hosting for eBay sellers. The easy-to-use site guides you through the process: creating auction listings, posting them on eBay, communicating with buyers, collecting payments, organizing shipments, keeping records of sales, marketing your listings, and much more.

Unfortunately, at the time of writing, Auctiva doesn't yet post listings to the Canadian eBay site. You can, however, post your listings to the eBay.com site and ensure that they're available to Canadian buyers if you want to take advantage of the following Auctiva features:

✔ **A one-page listing tool:** You can create your professional-looking listings with a complete one-page listing tool — and if you like variety, you can choose from 500 template options.

✔ **Unlimited image hosting:** Auctiva enables you to upload hundreds of images at a time, and you can keep your account organized by managing your images within Auctiva's online folder structure.

✔ **Profiles:** After you generate your profile information, your Auctiva profile will be set to automatically appear in all your listings by default.

For these features and more, visit the Auctiva Web site at `www.auctiva.com`.

ChannelAdvisor

ChannelAdvisor is a very popular, professional-grade management service for all levels of eBay sellers. The site supplies listing and management services to everyone from Fortune 1,000 companies to the little old lady next door. (Her name is Sadie, and she sells antique china.)

ChannelAdvisor offers three levels of software:

✔ **Enterprise:** For large companies that want to outsource their online business

✔ **Merchant:** For mid-size businesses and higher-level PowerSellers

✔ **Pro:** For small businesses and individual sellers

Most eBay users can comfortably use the Pro version, which costs US$29.95 a month for as long as you use its service. The downside to the Pro software is that you can't use it to list on the Canadian eBay site. As with Auctiva (which we discuss in the preceding section), you can list to only the eBay.com site. But be certain to add Canada as a country to which you'll ship. You can generally get the Pro software for a two-week free trial, but as a reader of this book, you can get an additional 30 days of its service free by typing in the code `ebaydummiespro` when you register.

Here's a portion of what you get from ChannelAdvisor:

✔ **Listing design and launching:** Create your listings by using ChannelAdvisor's standard templates, or use your own HTML skills to design auction descriptions. List your items immediately, or schedule a listing. ChannelAdvisor launches the auction when you tell it to.

✔ **Item and inventory management:** If you want to keep your inventory online, you can create an inventory listing on ChannelAdvisor's system or import an Excel template that you create offline. You can also import open auctions or store listings to your ChannelAdvisor account for relisting or servicing.

✔ **Image hosting:** You get 250MB of space to host your images. You can upload them to the site four at a time or use FTP to upload a large quantity.

✔ **Post-auction management:** This function merges your winning auction information and generates customized e-mails and invoices to your buyers. You can print mailing labels, too.

To tour the various offerings of ChannelAdvisor and to sign up for its free trial period, visit `pro.channeladvisor.com/pro/default.asp`.

InkFrog

InkFrog is another Web-based service that's been helping eBay sellers since 1999. In 2006, InkFrog bought out another respected service, SpareDollar. InkFrog represents a super bargain in Web-based management services. The best part about its service is that you pay a flat monthly fee of only US$9.95. With its easy-to-use service, little guys can get the same benefits as large-volume sellers — and pay smaller fees. InkFrog doesn't yet allow sellers to list to the Canadian eBay site, so you must use InkFrog through the U.S. version of eBay.

With InkFrog, you can manage every aspect of your eBay sales, including image hosting, ad design, automated e-mail management, and report tracking. If you want to get fancy, you can design your item listing by using any of InkFrog's templates. Here are some more features:

✔ **Image hosting:** InkFrog hosts your images and has a very handy uploader that allows you to insert your images with a click of your mouse.

✔ **One-step lister:** Create your listings (with as many images as you want) by using a simple form. InkFrog also lets you schedule your listings to start at a future time at no additional cost.

✔ **Checkout system and tracking:** InkFrog has a checkout system that integrates with eBay's checkout system. You can track which items have yet to be paid for, which items you need to ship, and for which of your customers you need to leave feedback. You can then update these items in bulk. You can also automatically send out custom e-mails to your customers.

For more information, and even more features, visit the InkFrog Web site at `www.inkfrog.com`.

Marketworks

Marketworks (formerly called Auctionworks) was one of eBay's first preferred providers in 1999 and has been serving thousands of professional sellers since. The company facilitates over $30 million in monthly sales on eBay in the United States, Canada, the United Kingdom, Australia, and Germany — not to mention eBay Motors. Many top PowerSellers who have to manage large inventories and launch a lot of listings use Marketworks. It's one of the very few third-party service providers that lists directly to the Canadian eBay site, and it's a very professional and automated way to handle auctions.

Here are just a few of its many advanced features:

- **Advanced Inventory Management:** Marketworks has an easy-to-use inventory-management system that enables you to post items in your own area on the site and list them at eBay whenever you want. You can organize them in individual folders that you create.

- **Robust Business Management:** Marketworks tracks all functions relating to the selling process: notifications, payments, shipments, and feedback — all of which the system can automate to save you time. It also integrates with PayPal to facilitate auction payments.

By using Marketworks's tools, sellers can manage inventory, images, customers, financial data, and post-auction tasks. Of course, Marketworks also offers professionally designed description templates, image hosting, and a wide variety of counters. All sellers get a storefront, too — your very own e-commerce site.

Marketworks is a pay-as-you-go service, so be sure that you know what's new on the Marketworks Web site (www.marketworks.com). You can sign up for a free two-week trial from this site, too.

BidRobot

As you can tell by reading Chapter 7, we're both big fans of sniping. It's our favourite way to win an auction. It makes the entire auction experience even more entertaining. Sadly, if you have a schedule like ours, you may find it difficult to be at your computer when the auctions close.

BidRobot to the rescue! When you find an auction that you're serious about, you can simply go to the BidRobot Web site, log in, and place your future snipe bids. All you have to do is type in the item number and your high bid, and that's it. You can shut off your computer knowing that BidRobot will do your bidding for you. Nobody on eBay knows what item you're desperate to have because the magical BidRobot doesn't place your bid until a few seconds before the auction closes. If you're the high bidder, no one will have the chance to bid against you!

BidRobot's services are reasonably priced, based on the amount of time that you want to use the service. As of this writing, BidRobot has placed bids for more than 100,000 eBay users since 1998! It works on all eBay international sites, too. You pay a flat rate of US$35 for 4 months for all the snipes you can handle after the initial two-week, free, trial period. BidRobot's Web site is at `www.bidrobot.com`.

Software for Offline Use

Software for offline use can handily reside on your computer after a simple download from a Web site. As with online services, this software comes in a variety of flavours, so take a look and decide which program works best for you. You may be able to find downloadable software from Web sites that offer auction management services, and you can use that software whether you're online or not. Offline software enables you to handle auctions in your spare time, without the limitations of ISPs or servers.

Auction Wizard 2000

Auction Wizard 2000 is a full-service, professional, management software package developed by eBay sellers. The software is fairly simple and amazingly powerful even if it is restricted to use on the eBay.com site. It expedites all the seller functions for running and completing eBay sales, including automating the following tasks:

- ✔ Inputting your inventory on the software's HTML templates and uploading auctions in bulk onto eBay.
- ✔ Automatically updating the software with the current status of your auctions, including who won, who's a runner-up, and the auction bidding history. The preformatted e-mail and feedback files automatically fill in the values from each auction and send them to the people you do business with directly through the software.
- ✔ Tracking income and expenses, as well as creating a full set of reports.

If you choose to become a Trading Assistant — that is, sell items for other people — Auction Wizard 2000 has a separate tracking area in which you can keep track of your consignment sales by consignee. It even computes the fees that you're charging for your services.

Finally, for the Mac!

Rejoice! You Mac users out there now have a couple of eBay listing services that can help you expedite your listings on eBay. eLister 2 is a full-powered offline listing program that allows you the freedom to write up auctions on your own time and includes a group of good-looking auction templates. It also includes an automatic HTML generator and an automatic listing fee calculator. Visit www.blackmagik.com; the program is updated regularly to conform to any changes in eBay listing procedures.

A very robust Mac solution is AuctionGenie, which not only gives you listing capabilities, but gives you advanced management software and a lot of extras. It also works with your Mac e-mail program and provides FTP services for uploading your photos to your Web site. Check out its services at www.luxcentral.com/auctiongenie.

Download a fully functional 60-day test drive (with no inactive features and no restrictions) from www.auctionwizard2000.com. After this free trial period, Auction Wizard 2000 costs US$100 for the first year of use, and there is an annual US$50 renewal fee.

Shooting Star

A super desktop software program from Foodogsoftware, Shooting Star works for sellers on multiple eBay sites: the United States, Canada, Australia, and the United Kingdom. Download the software to your computer, install it, and you're set to perform all listing and management procedures without being online. Check out this e-commerce software at www.foodogsoftware.com.

eBay's Software and Services

When the users call, eBay answers! As eBay grew, the need for additional services and software also grew. eBay answered the need with Turbo Lister software and its PowerSeller program. The following sections tell you how these services, tailored for the eBay user, may benefit you.

eBay's Turbo Lister

Turbo Lister is free software that enables you to upload many auctions simultaneously. After you prepare your auctions offline, the software uploads your auctions to eBay with just the click of a button. You can edit, preview, and (whenever you're ready) launch all your auctions at the same time, or you can schedule them to launch at different times (which costs you $0.12 for each scheduled auction). Your items can incorporate eBay's built-in templates, and the items remain archived on your computer for later use. The software is very convenient and simple to use. You can put Turbo Lister to use, even if you have only a few auctions at one time — although Turbo Lister will let you launch thousands of auctions at a time!

The program is free, and you can download it at `pages.ebay.ca/turbo_lister`.

Selling Manager and Selling Manager Pro

We've both used Selling Manager Pro for our eBay sales for the past few years, and we find it to be a very convenient way to quickly relist singly (or in bulk), track the progress of our sales, send e-mails, leave feedback, and keep track of what has and hasn't sold.

You also get a nice selection of reports to help you keep track of how your listings are performing. With these reports, you can tell whether your sales are on target or not.

As you can see from Figure 20-1, Selling Manager Pro (or Selling Manager) replaces the normal All Selling page of My eBay. This thorough data is updated automatically from eBay's servers and PayPal, so you have up-to-the-minute info.

eBay offers Selling Manager for $5.99 a month. The Pro version, which adds inventory management and reporting features, is tailored to high-volume sellers, and it costs $18.99 a month. Both versions are available for a 30-day free trial, Selling Manager at `pages.ebay.ca/selling_manager` and Selling Manager Pro at `pages.ebay.ca/sell/tools/allinone`.

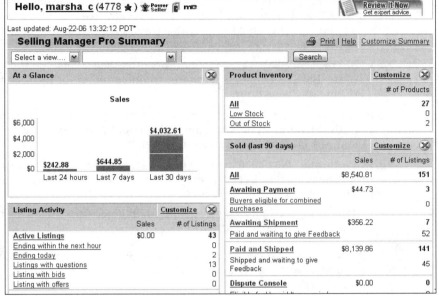

Figure 20-1:
Marsha's
Selling
Manager
Pro home
page.

eBay PowerSellers program

eBay offers an elite club for PowerSellers who fulfill the following requirements:

- ✔ Maintain a 98-percent positive feedback average with 100 or more feedback comments and an excellent sales performance record.

- ✔ List a minimum of four items average per month over the past three months.

- ✔ Maintain minimum monthly average of US$1,000 in gross sales.

No, you don't need to wear an ugly tie. PowerSellers get a special icon to the right of their User IDs on the eBay site, thereby giving potential bidders the assurance that they're dealing with a seller of good repute who stands behind each sale. PowerSellers who meet or exceed eBay's requirements can receive the following rankings (and the benefits that come with those rankings):

- **Bronze:** At the Bronze level and higher, you get a PowerSeller logo posted on the site next to your User ID, identifying you as an eBay PowerSeller. You also have access to a private PowerSeller discussion board and have 24/7 e-mail tech support with a very fast response time.

- **Silver:** US$3,000 average in monthly gross sales gets you the benefits of the Bronze level plus a toll-free phone number for priority support during business hours.

- **Gold:** US$10,000 average in monthly gross sales gets you the benefits of the Silver level plus a dedicated account manager and a dedicated support hotline, 24 hours a day, seven days a week!

- **Platinum:** US$25,000 average month in gross sales gets you Gold level benefits, plus we bet you get quicker callbacks from your account manager than at the Gold level.

- **Titanium:** US$150,000 average month in gross sales probably gets you a whole lot of special attention!

If you feel that you qualify for eBay's PowerSellers service (eBay knows who you are!), apply at `pages.ebay.ca/services/buyandsell/ powersellers.html`.

Trading Assistant program

For experienced eBay sellers who have a feedback rating of 97 percent or greater and a minimum feedback score of 50, the Trading Assistant program is the place to be! With the Trading Assistant program, you can register to sell items for others who don't have the time or inclination to figure out how to sell on eBay.

All the knowledge you gain by reading this book can help you get items to sell. People with items to sell go to `tradingassistant.ebay.ca/ws/ eBayISAPI.dll?TradingAssistant` and search for Trading Assistants by postal or area codes. After they click the Search button, they're presented with a list of sellers who are ready and willing to sell their goods (that's you, right?). Take a look at some of the sellers in your area that act as Trading Assistants to get an idea of what you should charge for your services.

For full information, go to `pages.ebay.ca/tradingassistants/ becoming-trading-assistant`.

Appendix

Answers for the Fanatic: Finding More Stuff to Sell

After you pick through everything that's not nailed down in your house, you may want to broaden your horizons. The key to successfully selling items at eBay is to find things people actually want to buy at the right price. (Wow, what an incredible observation.) We know it seems obvious, but having stuff to sell isn't always the same as having things people want to buy. Using this concept, you can figure out all kinds of effective marketing strategies. Finding the item that may be "the next big thing" takes a lot of work, timing, and sometimes a dose of good luck.

As an eBay seller, no doubt you'll receive tons of spam (unsolicited e-mails) guaranteeing that the sender has the hottest-selling items for you to sell on eBay. Think about this for a second. If you had the hot ticket to riches, wouldn't you be selling the product on eBay and making the fortune yourself? These people aren't big-hearted millionaires; they make money by preying on those who think there's a magic way to make money on eBay. There isn't. It takes old-fashioned elbow grease and research.

Knowing the Market

Just as successful stockbrokers know about individual companies, they also need to know about the marketplace, as a whole. Sure, we know about the top designer purses out there, and so does nearly everyone else. To get a leg up on your competition, you need to know the big picture, as well. Here are some questions you should ask yourself as you contemplate making serious buckets of money (well, we hope) by selling items at eBay:

✔ **What items are currently hot?** If you see everyone around you rushing to the store to buy a particular item, chances are good that the item will become more valuable as stocks of it diminish. (iPod accessories?) The simple rule of supply and demand says that whoever has something everyone else wants stands to gain major profits. Big-box warehouse stores such as Costco usually have a full stock of popular items because their very savvy buyers purchase by the truckload months in advance — how about visiting a warehouse store to find items at discount?

✔ **Do I see a growing interest in a specific item that might make it a big seller?** If you're starting to hear talk about a particular item, or even an era ('70s nostalgia? '60s aluminum Christmas trees? Who knew?), listen carefully and think of what you already own (or can get your hands on) that can help you catch a piece of the trend's action.

✔ **Should I hold on to this item and wait for its value to increase, or should I sell now?** Knowing when to sell an item that you think people may want is a tricky business. Sometimes, you can catch the trend too early and find out that you could have commanded a better price if only you had waited. Other times, you may invest in a fad that's already passé and find that no one's interested anymore. It's best to test the market with a small quantity of your hoard, dribbling items individually into the market until you make back the money you spent to acquire them. When you have your cash back, the rest will be gravy.

Marsha's a huge fan of the artist George Rodrigue. While building her collection of his famous Blue Dog items years ago, she came across a seller who had liberated some early museum exhibition catalogues from a dumpster. The old catalogues had been tossed in the trash, but they were boxed and bundled — and in perfect condition. Being a true-blue Rodrigue fan, she thought perhaps these catalogues might make good future eBay items. She asked the seller if he had 30 to sell, he said yes, and he sold them to her for $4 each. She resold them over the following four years, for between $15 and $30 each. Spotting the trends and seeing the value in items is what it's all about.

✔ **Is a company discontinuing an item that I should stockpile now and sell later?** Pay attention to items that are discontinued, especially toys and novelty items. If you find an item that a manufacturer has a limited supply of, you could make a tidy profit. If the manufacturer ends up reissuing the item, don't forget that the original run is still the most coveted — and valuable. Bill once bought several dozen of a 900 MHz cordless telephone (shortly after Microsoft discontinued it) at a huge discount from normal wholesale price. He then sold them one at a time, often at a 300 percent profit, for almost a year.

✔ **Was there a recall, an error, or a legal proceeding associated with my item?** If so, how it affects the value of the item takes a backseat to eBay policy: Items that have been recalled can't be sold on eBay (for details, go to `pages.ebay.ca/help/policies/recalled.html`). For example, a toy recalled for safety reasons may no longer be appropriate for your kids, but even if it's rare and collectible, you still can't sell it on eBay.

But here's another angle: Consider that shares of (and any paperwork to do with) the now-defunct U.S. energy corporation, Enron, became highly prized collectibles after the scandal hit.

Some people like to go with their gut feelings about when and what to buy for resale at eBay. By all means, if instinct has worked for you in the past, factor instinct in here, too. If you've done some research that looks optimistic but your gut says, "I'm not sure," listen to it; don't assume you're just hearing that lunchtime burger talking. Try testing the waters by purchasing only one of the prospective item for resale at eBay. If that sale doesn't work out, you haven't invested a lot of money, and you can credit your gut with saving you some bucks.

Do You Have a Talent?

If you're talented in any way, you can sell your services on eBay. Home artisans, chefs, and even stay-at-home psychics are transacting business daily on the site. What a great way to make money on eBay — make your own product!

Personalized and custom items do well on eBay. There's a demand for personalized invitations, cards, and announcements — and even return address labels (and you thought you had all you needed). Calligraphic work or computer-designed (customized with Fido's picture, awww) items are in big demand today, but no one seems to have the time to make them. Savvy sellers with talent can fill this market niche.

People go to trendy places (when they have the time) such as Toronto's Kensington, Montreal's Rue Ste-Catherine, and Vancouver's Gastown to find unique custom jewellery. They also go to eBay.

The world is your oyster on eBay, and the sky is the limit. Use your imagination, and you might be surprised at what your new business will be!

Catching Trends in the Media

Catching trends is all about listening and looking. You can find all kinds of inside information from newspapers, magazines, television, and of course, the Internet. Believe it or not, you can even find out what people are interested in these days by bribing a kid. Keep your eyes and ears open. When people say, "Those Bell Canada beavers are everywhere," instead of nodding your head vacantly, start getting ideas. What can you sell that takes advantage of what is popular in the media right now?

In newspapers

Newspapers are bombarded with press releases and inside information from companies the world over. Pay close attention to the various sections of the newspaper. Look for stories on celebrities and upcoming movies, and see if any old fads are making a resurgence (you can sell items as "retro chic" — lava lamps, anyone?).

Read the stories about trade conventions, such as the Canadian Gift and Tableware Association or the Canadian Consumer Electronics show. New products are introduced and given the thumbs-up or -down by journalists. With this information, you can start to think about the direction your area of expertise is heading.

On television

No matter what you think of television, it has an enormous impact on which trends come and go, and which ones stick. Why else would advertisers sink billions of dollars into TV commercials? And look at the impact of Oprah's Book Club. Just one Oprah appearance for an author can turn a book into an overnight bestseller. More and more celebrities (even Homer Simpson) are talking about eBay on television. The buzz brings people to the site.

Tune in to morning news shows and afternoon talk shows. See what's being featured on the programs. The producers of these shows are on top of pop culture and move fast to be the first to bring you the next big thing. Take what they feature, and think of a marketing angle. If you don't, you can be sure somebody else will.

Catch up with youth culture . . .

. . . or at least keep good tabs on it. If you can remember cranking up The Beatles, James Brown, or The Partridge Family (say what?) until your parents screamed, "Shut that awful noise off!" you may, like us, be at that awkward time of life when its difficult to see the appeal of what young people are doing or listening to. But if you want tips for hot-selling items, tolerate the awful noise of today's music (how *did* that happen?) and listen to the kids around you. (Try to watch a little MuchMusic, too.) Children, especially preteens and teens, may be the best trend-spotters on the planet. See what kind of marketing tips you get when you ask a kid questions such as these:

- ✔ **What's cool at the moment?** Or "rad" if you want to sound cool — whoops, that was '80s-speak, wasn't it?
- ✔ **What's totally uncool that was cool two months ago?** Their world moves at warp speed!
- ✔ **What music are you buying?** Jay-Z, Babyface, Sum 41, and Timbaland — yup, all the hot bands with big hits — may be *ewww-that's-so-five-minutes-ago* by the time you read this.
- ✔ **What could I buy you that would make you really happy?** *Hint:* If the kid says, "A red BMW Z-3" or "Liposuction," look for a younger kid.

Check out eBay

The staff at eBay sends out reports regarding the up-and-coming items by category. Visit eBay Canada's Seller Central at `pages.ebay.ca/seller-central` for tips and inside news. Additionally, to see what's been selling well on eBay over the past 30 days, go to eBay's What's Hot page at `pages.ebay.com/sellercentral/whatshot.html` and get a wealth of information.

Click the link to Hot Items by Category, and a huge document in Adobe PDF format appears. The document outlines the hot, hotter, and hottest items selling on eBay (by category) during the past month. If you follow this data, you can't go wrong.

Another important link goes to the eBay Pulse. Visit the Pulse page, and you can find the most-searched-for items in each category by keyword. This is usually pretty amusing reading — you'd be surprised how many people are watching eBay listings for get-rich-quick schemes, right along with expensive real estate! You can also reach the eBay Pulse page by going directly to `pulse.ebay.ca`.

Collecting magazines

Though not quite a plethora, the number of magazines geared to collectors is definitely approaching a slew. Although these magazines can't help you catch a trend (by the time it gets into one of these magazines, somebody's already caught it), they can give you great information on pricing, availability, and general collecting information. And you can follow the course of a trend for a real-life example of how it works. Here's a list of collectors' magazines that we like:

✔ **Antique Trader:** The bible of the antique collecting industry for over 40 years. Visit its online home at www.antiquetrader.com for more articles and other information.

✔ **Collect.com:** A Web site (www.collect.com) from Krause publications. It gives you info on over 35 different collectors' publications for everything from stamps to toys to muscle cars.

✔ **Barbie Bazaar:** Has info on everything related to Barbie. Go to www.hautedoll.com.

✔ **Canadian Coin News:** This standard has been around for more than 40 years now. Check them out on the Web at www.canadiancoinnews.ca.

Use the drop-down menu at the top of the page to see the most-searched-for items in the main categories.

Check out magazines

Magazines geared to the 18- to 34-year-old age group (and sometimes to younger teens — they call them *tweens*) can help you stay on top of what's hot. See what the big companies are pitching to this target audience (and whether they're succeeding). If a celebrity's suddenly visible in every other headline or magazine, be on the lookout for merchandise relating to that person. (Are we talking hysteria-plus-cash-flow here, or just hysteria?)

The Hunt for eBay Inventory

If you're not sure what you want to sell for profit at eBay — but you're a shop-till-you-drop person by nature — then you have an edge. Incorporate your advanced shopping techniques into your daily routine. If you find a bargain that interests you, chances are, you have a knack for spotting stuff that other shoppers would love to get their hands on.

The goods are out there

When you shop to sell at eBay, don't rule out any shopping venue. From the trendiest boutique to the smallest second-hand store, from garage sales to Wal-Mart, keep your eye out for eBay inventory. The items people look for at eBay are out there; you just have to find them.

Check your favourite eBay category and see what the hot-selling items are. Better yet, go to your favourite store and make friends with the manager. Store managers are often privy to this type of information a couple of months in advance of a product release. If you ask, they can tell you what's going to be the hot new item next month. After you're armed with the information you need, seek out that item for the lowest price you can, and then you can give it a shot on eBay.

Keep these shopping locales in mind when you go on the eBay hunt:

- Upscale department stores, trendy boutiques, outlet stores, or flagship designer stores are good places to do some market research. Check out the newest items — and then head to the clearance area or outlet store and scrutinize the bargain racks for brand-name items.

- Tour some of the discount and dollar stores in your area. Many of the items these places carry are *overruns* (too many of something that didn't sell), *small runs* (too little of something that the big guys weren't interested in stocking), or out-of-date fad items that need a good home at eBay.

- Garage sales, tag sales, and moving sales offer some of the biggest bargains you'll ever come across. Check for vintage kitchen pieces, designer goods, and old toys, and make 'em an offer they can't refuse.

- Thrift stores are packed with used but usually good-quality items. And you can feel good knowing that the money you spend in a nonprofit thrift shop is going to a good cause.

- Find going-out-of-business sales. You can pick up bargains by the case if a shopkeeper just wants to empty the shelves so the store can close.

- Take advantage of any flea markets or swap meets in your area.

- Gift shops at museums, monuments, national parks, and theme parks can provide eBay inventory — but think about where to sell the items. Part of your selling success on eBay is access. People who can't get to Halifax may pay handsomely for a velour wall hanging of the Citadel. Or maybe not?

✔ Hang on to the freebies you get. If you receive handouts (lapel pins, pencils, pamphlets, books, interesting napkins, flashlights, towels, stuffed toys) from a sporting event, premiere, or historic event — or even a collectible freebie from a fast-food restaurant — any of them could be your ticket to some eBay sales.

Tips for the modest investor

If you're interested in making money in your eBay ventures, but you're starting with limited cash, follow this list of eBay inventory do's and don'ts:

✔ **Don't spend more than you can afford to lose.** If you shop at boutiques and expensive department stores, buy things that you like to wear yourself (or give as gifts) in case they don't sell.

✔ **Do try to find something local that's unavailable in a wider area.** For example, if you live in an out-of-the-way place that has a local specialty, try selling that at eBay.

✔ **Don't go overboard and buy something really cheap just because it's cheap.** Figure out who would *want* the item first.

✔ **Do consider buying in bulk, especially if you know the item sells well at eBay or if the item is inexpensive.** Chances are good that if you buy one and it sells well at eBay, by the time you try to buy more, the item's sold out. If an item is inexpensive (say, 99¢), it makes sense to always buy at least five of it. If no one bids on the item when you hold your auction, you're out only $5. (Anyone out there need any Calgary Winter Olympics Commemorative coffee mugs?)

Index

• F •

• G •

Walter Harris
Memorial Library

WALTER HARRIS MEMORIAL LIBRARY

33436008058705

Dakotaful

eBay ~~Canada~~ For Dummies

Cheat Sheet

eBay Time and Updates

eBay Canada's clocks are set to military time in the Eastern Time zone, and eBay's USA site is set to the Pacific Time zone. A conversion chart of eBay times is available at Bill's site shown below. You can also keep abreast of changes at eBay by visiting Marsha's Web site and subscribing to her free newsletter. Here are the respective Web addresses:

www.learningebayiseasy.com

www.coolebaytools.com

Tips for Sellers

- Find out as much as you can about the item's value, history, and condition.

- Answer all questions posed by prospective bidders via e-mail within several hours. Don't let too much time pass by, lest you appear uninterested in their queries.

- Check out your eBay competition. If a ton of other auctions are taking place at the same time for the same kind of item and the bidding is competitive, wait until the competition is fierce for a few select items.

- Make sure your item isn't prohibited or considered questionable by eBay. If you're not sure, read eBay's guidelines and check your local laws.

- Be sure to add a picture to spruce up your auction, and make sure that your title highlights the item's keywords — but don't gloss over its flaws in the description. Being direct, informative, and concise shows potential buyers that you're honest and easy to work with.

Tips for Buyers

Before you bid on an item in an auction, follow these tips:

- Research the item before you bid, and search completed auctions to see what price similar items have sold for in the past. If the item is new and can be bought in a store, do some online research to find out what the stores are selling the item for. Don't overbid!

- Make a mental note of the cost of shipping prior to bidding on an item. Add the shipping cost to your total bid to get a clear idea of the total amount you will be paying.

- Check the seller's feedback. No matter how high the feedback rating is, be sure the latest feedback isn't negative.

- Bid in odd increments. Bidders often bid in round numbers (like 25-cent increments). If you bid in 27-cent increments, you can win by just 2 cents!

- Have fun and be prepared to pay for whatever you bid on. **Remember:** On eBay, placing a bid is a binding contract.

Walter Harris
Memorial Library

For Dummies: Bestselling Book Series for Beginners

eBay® For Canadians For Dummies®

Know Your Auction Terms

- **Starting bid:** The lowest acceptable bid for an item, set by the seller. This amount must be determined by the seller and is not kept secret. Starting bid amounts are generally lower than reserve prices.

- **Reserve price:** The minimum price a seller is willing to accept for an item up for auction. Setting a reserve is optional, and only the seller knows the reserve price. If the bidding doesn't extend the reserve, the seller has the option to keep the item. eBay charges the seller a small fee for this option.

- **Multiple item (Dutch) auction:** An auction that allows a seller to put multiple items up for sale instead of holding multiple separate auctions. The seller must sell all items at the *lowest winning price*. You can bid on one, some, or all of the items.

- **BIN (Buy It Now):** You have the option of purchasing an item with the BIN option. If you feel the BIN price is a bit more than you want to pay, place a bid at the minimum bid level (or the most you'd like to pay). That way, the BIN option disappears, and you may just win the item at the lower price.

- **Proxy bid:** You can decide the most you're willing to pay for an item and allow eBay's bidding program to place bids for you while you go on with your life. The proxy bidder ups the ante incrementally to beat out your competition until you're outbid or win the auction.

Feedback Stuff You Need to Know

Before you send feedback to another eBay member or read feedback eBay members have sent you, make sure you do the following:

- Before you bid on an item on eBay, **do** check the seller's feedback rating by clicking the number that appears next to the seller's User ID.

- Even if you see a large amount of positive feedback, **do** check to be sure that the seller doesn't also have a growing number of negative feedback responses — especially recently. In the eyes of other eBay members, you're only as good as your last few transactions, so beware.

- **Do** take a breather before you leave negative feedback for another eBay member. eBay won't remove feedback if you change your mind or overreact to a situation.

- The seller is **not** required to leave you feedback when you pay for the item. Feedback is based on the entire transaction, so the buyer may not post any feedback until the item arrives and you're both happy.

- If someone gives you positive feedback, **do** reciprocate by giving him or her positive feedback, too.

- If you receive negative feedback and feel your side of the transaction is worth telling, **do** be sure to give your reply in a neutral tone. You may also add a line responding to feedback you've received, to explain the situation to those who read the comment.

Wiley, the Wiley Publishing logo, For Dummies, the Dummies Man logo, the For Dummies Bestselling Book Series logo and all related trade dress are trademarks or registered trademarks of John Wiley & Sons, Inc. and /or its affiliates. All other trademarks are property of their respective owners.

Copyright © 2008 John Wiley & Sons Canada, Ltd. All rights reserved. Item 5348-2.
For more information about John Wiley & Sons Canada, Ltd., call 1-800-567-4797.

For Dummies: Bestselling Book Series for Beginners